THE DOUBLE PATRIOTS

THE
DOUBLE PATRIOTS

A STUDY OF
JAPANESE NATIONALISM

RICHARD STORRY

HOUGHTON MIFFLIN COMPANY, BOSTON
THE RIVERSIDE PRESS, CAMBRIDGE

Printed in Great Britain

FOR PENNY

Note

Following the custom in Japan the method adopted in the text is to write Japanese surnames first, personal names second—e.g. Shigeru Yoshida becomes Yoshida Shigeru.

At the risk of offending the specialist long vowel indicators have been omitted. (Okawa Shumei, for example, is pronounced Ōkawa Shūmei.) The use of these indicators, however, will mean little to the general reader; whereas the specialist will have small difficulty in recognising long vowels where they occur.

PREFACE

THE significance of the title, "The Double Patriots" (the felicitous invention of a journalist in Japan), may be explained in this way. Just as a double whisky is presumed to have twice the strength of a single tot, so a "double patriot" is credited with the possession of twice the normal inheritance of patriotic sentiment. All Japanese are—or were—patriotic. But some of them claimed to be much more patriotic than the rest. They were the extreme nationalists, and therefore appropriately labelled "the double patriots".

This work cannot pretend to be an exhaustive study of the large subject of Japanese nationalism between the two World Wars. It is concerned almost entirely with ideas, events and tendencies in the political, rather than the economic, field. And the concentration on what appear to be the most important aspects of these necessarily implies that the less important have received correspondingly little attention and, in some cases, have been omitted.

Two principal sources have been used in the preparation of this book. They are the Transcript and Exhibits of the International Military Tribunal for the Far East (the Tokyo Major War Crimes' Trial) and the Saionji-Harada Memoirs. The I.M.T.F.E. material, in quantity very voluminous, was studied at the Foreign Office Research Department, London, to whom I must acknowledge a special debt of gratitude for this and for much other help. I had access to the full Saionji-Harada Memoirs in Washington, D.C., thanks to the good offices of the Australian Embassy. At that time they had not been bound as volumes attached to the collection of I.M.T.F.E. Exhibits.

Certain individuals in Tokyo, some of them participants in the drama described in the following pages, gave me a great deal of very pertinent and useful material, verbally and in writing. I was also fortunate in being able to make use of the facilities of the Library of Congress in Washington, and of the National Diet Library in Tokyo.

PREFACE

I must express my appreciation to the Council of the Australian National University, who supported me, when I was one of their first Research Scholars, during the preparation of this work. I should mention particularly two scholars then connected with that University—Sir Keith Hancock and Professor W. R. Crocker, C.B.E. I shall not forget how much I owe to their advice, encouragement and very practical help.

To Mr. Geoffrey Hudson, Director of Far Eastern Studies at St. Antony's College, Oxford, I am indebted to an exceptional degree. He read each chapter as it was written. Through many months he never failed to give me the invaluable benefit of his profound knowledge and discriminating judgment. He was indeed, as the Japanese say, my *sensei*. Nevertheless I take sole responsibility, of course, for the views expressed in this work.

I must also express my thanks to Dr. Charles Nelson Spinks for his most generous help to me while I was in Tokyo.

Finally I must acknowledge that much is owed to Dr. Edwin Beal, Jr., of the Library of Congress; to Mr. H. Bullock and Mr. T. V. Eckersley of the Australian External Affairs Service; to Mr. H. Vere Redman, C.M.G., Counsellor of the British Embassy, Tokyo; to Mr. Ichikawa Taijiro of the National Diet Library, Tokyo; to Professor Maruyama Masao of Tokyo University, and Dr. Royama Masamichi, now President of Ochanomizu University; to Dr. S. Crawcour of Melbourne; and to former General Mazaki Jinsaburo and his family, more especially his son, Mr. Mazaki Hideki.

G. R. S.

Oxford
June, 1956

CONTENTS

CONTENTS

JAPANESE NATIONALISM

THIS work is a study of the ideas and activities of Japanese nationalist associations and groups in the ten years which began with the so-called "Manchurian Incident" of September, 1931, and ended with Japan's dramatic entry into the Second World War in December, 1941. During this time Japanese chauvinism developed ever-increasing vigour and prestige.

Its roots were popular loyalty to the Imperial Throne and the dogma of a heavenly inspired mission. Both were of comparatively recent historical origin.

Until the Meiji Restoration the peasants, forming the bulk of the population of Japan, were hardly aware of the existence of the Mikado, secluded in his capital.[1] But after 1868 the whole nation was taught to revere him as the unique Viceroy of Heaven on Earth. Confucian ethics already laid stress on the obligations due from an individual to his feudal and family superiors; they served now to authorise the creed that for Japanese the first and greatest of virtues was loyalty to the Emperor.

The term used for him was *Tenno*;[2] for which there is no very satisfactory English translation. The literal "Heavenly Ruler" or the better known "Son of Heaven" have a faintly ornate air, and for that reason perhaps are not entirely adequate.[3] "Mikado" is archaic; while "Emperor"—which non-Japanese must use—lacks that sacerdotal flavour which was the essence of the Throne's prestige. It should be noted that Japanese never accorded foreign

---

[1] Their awareness of the Shogun's existence was probably equally vague. "The idea of belonging to a nation and an empire is of recent date. Formerly all loyalty belonged to the local samurai, whose loyalty in turn went to the feudal lord." J. F. Embree, *A Japanese Village* (London, Kegan Paul, 1946), p. 59.

[2] This title was officially substituted for that of *Kotei* early in 1936. But from the seventh century A.D. the title had been both *Tenno* (for internal affairs) and *Kotei* (for external affairs). As sovereign of the Court at Kyoto the title was *Tenno*, as head of the Shogunate *Kotei*. The official change made in 1936 was in compliance with army requests.

[3] Strictly speaking "Son of Heaven" is the translation of *Tenshi*, an alternative title for the Emperor.

monarchs the title of *Tenno*. They were known as *Kotei*, a word of the highest respect but lacking the supreme force of *Tenno*. For the Emperor of Japan was unique. A Japanese writer expressed that unique position in this way: "As in the heavens the sun is not double, so on earth there exists but one *Tenno*." [1]

The Meiji Constitution declared: "The Empire of Japan shall be reigned over and governed by a line of Emperors unbroken for ages eternal" (Article I); and: "The Emperor is sacred and inviolable" (Article III). Prince Ito, in his "Commentaries on the Constitution", stated that the Throne was established when the heavens and earth were first separated, and that the Emperor was Heaven descended.

This divinity was attributed solely to the Emperor's blood relationship with the Sun Goddess, Amaterasu Omikami, and with other deities of the Shinto Olympus from whom, it was claimed, he was descended in a direct, unbroken line. While the Chinese regarded their Emperors as the representatives of Heaven there was the proviso—stressed by Mencius—that they might be overthrown if their conduct lacked virtue. The Emperor of Japan, on the other hand, always enjoyed the virtues associated with inherited divinity, irrespective of any specific qualities which he might possess.[2]

The civic duty of patriotism, common to all nations, was identified in modern Japan with the claims and obligations and ecstasies of a living religious faith. The weight of opinion was against the distinction, often drawn by Christians, between spiritual and temporal spheres of life. Fujisawa Chikao, a scholar and writer holding extreme nationalist views, remarked:

> In contradistinction to Japan, mythology and national history have been, in one way or another, severed in the West. . . . God and man have been separated and the ideal and the real, soul and flesh, the divine and the secular, never harmonise with one another.[3]

[1] Hibino Yutaka, *"Nippon Shindo Ron" or the National Ideals of the Japanese People* (Cambridge University Press, 1928), p. 92.

[2] "The Sun Goddess never said: 'Disobey the Mikado if he is bad'; and therefore whether he be good or bad no one attempts to deprive him of his authority. He is the immovable ruler who must endure to the end of time . . ." (Motoori Moringa; 1730–1801), from *Japan's Prospect* (Cambridge, Mass., Harvard University Press, 1946), Ch. VII (D. C. Haring, "Religion, Magic and Morals").

[3] Fujisawa Chikao, *Japanese and Oriental Political Philosophy* (Tokyo, Daito Bunka-Kyokai, 1935), p. 295.

The *Kokutai No Hongi*, a book published in 1937 by the Ministry of Education for the guidance of teachers in universities and schools, referred to harmony between God and man as a Japanese characteristic, and declared: "When we compare this with the relationship between 'God' and man in Western countries, we notice a great difference."[1]

The unity of government and religion was, indeed, the Japanese ideal.[2] It came near to being a reality.

Of even greater significance, as a foundation for nationalist pretensions, was the belief in a heaven-ordained mission. By no means all Japanese were convinced that it was the inevitable destiny of their country to acquire an empire overseas. Nevertheless, at least from the time of the Sino-Japanese War of 1894-5, there was a generally accepted belief that Japan was bound to follow the path of expansion abroad, by economic means if not by force of arms, and that in doing so she was obeying not only the will of the Sovereign but also a mandate imposed by Heaven. This view, needless to say, was held with unshaken conviction by the armed services. To support it they invoked the authority of the *Nihongi*.[3] Since the Emperor was unique and descended from deities who had created the whole Earth as well as Japan, it followed that the ideal world would be benevolently supervised, if not directly governed, by him. This was the distant goal of all militant nationalists.

In addition to a religious devotion to the Throne and a belief in a divine mission there was a third concept at the root of nationalist aims and activities. This was the idea that individual Japanese had a capacity for intuitive virtue unequalled by any other race. The nation was likened to a tree. Its trunk was the Imperial House and its branches the four major family groups of ancient times— the Minamoto, Taira, Fujiwara and Tachibana. From these sprouted the myriad lesser branches, twigs and leaves constituting

[1] *Kokutai No Hongi* (Cardinal Principles of the National Entity of Japan), translated by J. O. Gauntlett and edited by R. K. Hall (Cambridge, Mass., Harvard University Press, 1949), pp. 95-6.

[2] The Japanese term is *saisei ichi* (lit. "the unity of Shinto rites and politics"). *Vide* D. C. Holtom, *Modern Japan and Shinto Nationalism* (University of Chicago Press, 1947), pp. 4-7.

[3] Holtom (*ibid.*, p. 20, *et seq.*,) cites two passages—edicts issued by Jimmu *Tenno* (the first Emperor)—which were favourite texts with the army authorities. Both mentioned a future extension of the Imperial realm to embrace the universe.

the people of the land. The same sap, as it were, flowed through the one great "tree" of Japan past and present. In this sense the Emperor was head of the national family, and all its members were related to him by blood. This gave rise to such slogans as "Emperor and People are One" and "The Emperor is Japan" which so frequently recurred in the writings and speeches of nationalists up to the Surrender of 1945.

This idea of family relationship gave the Japanese some sense of participation in a special grace. They felt that they were capable of matchless virtue, provided only that they displayed what was called *chukun*—"sincerity of heart towards the Emperor". *Chukun* justified everything, including actions and words which by standards of common humanity and logic might be condemned out of hand. It was decisive in the factor of *motive*, which so greatly exercised the minds of the authorities in their reaction to the various "Incidents" engineered by extremists in the years before the Pacific War. Unselfish devotion to the Emperor enabled the individual to realise to the full his potentialities for natural goodness. He achieved *kiyoki kokoro*—"cleanliness of heart".[1] It amounted to purification, or purging, of self; and purification was perhaps the oldest, authentic Shinto rite. Japanese moral judgments, then, placed more emphasis on faith than on works. In a political trial, for example, the state of mind, the motive, of the accused was of greater interest to his judges than the action for which he was being prosecuted.

It was part of the nationalist creed that every Japanese was born with a galaxy of virtues implanted in him by the gods. Hirata Atsutane, the early nineteenth-century theologian of Shinto, wrote: "We who have been brought into existence through the creative spirits of the *kami* [deities] are, each and every one, in spontaneous possession of the Way of the Gods."[2]

It would be foolish of course to suggest that all Japanese seriously thought of themselves as children of the gods or that, even in their own estimation, they behaved with unusual virtue. But with few exceptions they were convinced that they had a birthright envied but unrivalled by other nations of the world.

---

[1] There is an interesting study of this concept in an article, "The Spirit of Japan", by Dr. Y. Haga, in *Transactions of the Japan Society, London*, Vol. XV.
[2] Holtom, *op. cit.*, p. 16.

The three elements—loyalty to the Throne, sense of mission, and belief in the possession of superlative inborn qualities—constituted the essential national character or polity of modern Japan. This national polity was known as *kokutai*. It is a concept of much importance to the study of Japanese nationalism.[1] The literal translation of *kokutai* is "the substance, or body, of the nation", "the national entity". It could be used to mean the entire social and political fabric of the nation, or, in a more restricted sense, a basic government policy framed to meet certain internal and external situations. The term could also be used in the sense of "national honour".[2] Usually, however, *kokutai* referred to the permanent and fundamental constituents of the Japanese state. Thus the defeat of Japan in 1945 did not destroy the *kokutai*. So long as the Imperial Throne remained the *kokutai* was preserved; to be enhanced, no doubt, by means different from those employed up to 1945. It will be remembered that Japanese peace feelers, before the Surrender, made the minimum demand that the *kokutai*, the national structure with the Throne as its apex, be maintained.[3]

A *kokutai* consisting of the three elements which have been mentioned above gave rise, by its very nature, to the type of chauvinism to be examined in subsequent chapters. Many other factors—economic, political and social—played a great part. Nevertheless, in the last resort, the grotesque ideology of the *kokutai* was at the source of the complex manifestations of Japanese nationalism.

[1] Cf. Chapter 7 (*infra*) in which the *kokutai meicho mondai* ("the question of the clarification of the national polity") is discussed.

[2] One of the translations given by dictionaries.

[3] *Kokutai No Hongi* (*op. cit.*), Appendix VII, quotes an interesting passage from a booklet, expounding the new post-War Constitution, published by the Japanese cabinet in November, 1946.

"The term *kokutai* can mean many things, but it is appropriate to interpret its meaning as *basic characteristics of the nation*. So interpreted, *kokutai* forms the foundation of the nation's existence, and its destiny is common with that of the State; so that if this *kokutai* were to suffer change or loss the State would at once lose its existence. We should have to conclude that even if a new State were to be established, there would no longer be anything common in the nature of the old State and the new. When we look upon *kokutai* in this way and in its relation to our country, we can say that in a word it means the immutable and solemn fact that the Japanese people look up to the Emperor as if he were the centre of their adoration, on the basis of the link that deep down in their hearts binds them to him, that the entire nation is united thereby, and that this forms the basis of Japan's existence." *Ibid.*, p. 198.

The rise of extreme patriotic, nationalist, sentiment in Japan during the nineteen-thirties coincided with that of fascism in Germany. Yet the two trends, in spite of certain similarities, differed in many important respects.[1]

Some of the numerous nationalist societies of Japan had a history going back several years before the First World War. No society, as such, succeeded in gaining anything approaching unrivalled political influence in the state. Certain organisations sought, and claimed to have enlisted, mass support. But the total membership of even the largest amounted to an extremely small percentage of the adult male population.

Again, the idea of dictatorial power in the hands of one man is unattractive to the Japanese mind. It implies self-advancement and a love of power for its own sake; above all it might tend to obscure the supreme status of the politically weak but spiritually peerless Throne.[2] The European dictatorships were, at times, among the objects of Japanese xenophobia; and it was expediency, of course, which drew them and Japan close to each other before the Pacific War. The successes of European fascism, however, had one notable effect on the course of events in Japan. They fatally undermined the resistance of those liberals and parliamentarians whose reputation had been enhanced by the long delayed but eventual victory of the Democracies in the First World War. And in this way European fascism rendered a prime disservice to the Japanese people.

Japanese nationalists formed their own passionately adored interpretation of the *kokutai*. They could not accept the sincerity of those who chose to reject it. Here we are presented with an attitude of stubborn fanaticism, impervious to the arguments of logic or of historical truth. In the opinion of these super-patriots

[1] Even the communist authors Tanin and Yohan stressed the distinction between Japanese and European fascism; for which "deviationist" opinion they were criticised by Radek (still accepted as orthodox at that time) in his Introduction to their work. C. Tanin and E. Yohan, *Militarism and Fascism in Japan* (London, Martin Lawrence, 1934).

[2] The rôle of dictator was played to some extent by Tojo early in the Pacific War, when he held the offices of War Minister and Home Minister as well as the Premiership. He showed signs of trying to ape the exhibitionist antics of Hitler and Mussolini, and for this became widely unpopular. Great power, if held by one Japanese subject, must be exercised unostentatiously—in the manner of a Yamagata—otherwise it incurs contempt as well as dislike.

the Emperor himself must necessarily share their views. But this, perhaps, is to state the argument the wrong way round. According to their *mystique* their political actions and ideas were but the unclouded expression of the Emperor's intentions. Highly placed and well-informed chauvinists—in the armed forces, for example —were well aware that the Showa *Tenno*[1] was personally unsympathetic with their expansionist plans and anti-democratic ideals. His liberal opinions, however, were attributed to the disgraceful influence of the timid (elder statesmen and Court advisers), the misguided (party politicians) and the selfish (capitalist magnates), who, by their pernicious advice to the Throne, fouled the pure essence of the *kokutai*. Even if it had been publicly demonstrated beyond all question that the Emperor was fundamentally opposed to their interpretation of his will, many extreme nationalists— those professing the greatest loyalty to the Throne—would have refused to believe the evidence of their senses. With supreme and characteristic self-deception they would have disobeyed their Sovereign while protesting unfailing obedience.

On 15th August, 1945, the Emperor's voice was heard over the radio, broadcasting the announcement of the Japanese Surrender. For the Emperor to make a broadcast was without precedent. The overwhelming weight of public feeling—enforcement by the police was hardly required—ensured that all but the incapacitated or infirm heard the broadcast. In a passage, which was no doubt directed specifically to nationalist fanatics, the Emperor said:

> We are keenly aware of the inmost feelings of all of you, our subjects. However, it is according to the dictates of time and fate that we have resolved to pave the way for a grand peace for all the generations to come, by enduring the unavoidable and suffering what is insufferable. Having been able to safeguard and maintain the structure of the imperial state we are always with you, our good and loyal subjects, relying upon your sincerity and integrity. Beware most strictly of any outbursts of emotion that may engender needless complications, of any fraternal contention and strife that may create confusion, lead you astray and cause you to lose the confidence of the world.

[1] The name "Hirohito" was unknown to many Japanese before 1945.

Despite this unmistakable expression of the Imperial will some hysterical demonstrations occurred. In certain instances they amounted to armed insurrection. They were, admittedly, few. But they took place. And the servicemen who were involved in the scattered acts of insubordination at that time were those who, by special training and indoctrination, were most fervently imbued with an active, religious faith in an Emperor whose will must be loyally obeyed.[1]

Motives of self-interest, of course, played a great part in the tangle of "Incidents" and intrigues with which both military and civilian nationalists were concerned. Personal feuds and jealousies were rife; and until the Pacific War a united front of nationalist groups or individuals was never fully achieved. For the nationalist movement embraced a great diversity of figures, from social outcasts, and terrorists, of every kind to cabinet ministers and respectable leaders of the learned professions.[2] A comparatively small number, from each of these extremes, played an outstanding part, their names recurring constantly. When they are not on the stage participating in the drama they may often be glimpsed prompting from the wings.

At the trial of General Tojo and other major war criminals the Prosecution declared:

> Militaristic cliques and ultra-nationalist secret societies resorted to rule by assassination, and thereby exercised great influence in favour of military aggression. Assassinations and threats of revolt enabled the military branch more and more to dominate the civil government and to appoint new persons favourable to them and to their policies.[3]

To what extent this somewhat melodramatic contention records the truth it is, in the final analysis, the main purpose of this study to reveal.

---

[1] For accounts of the most notable disturbances, *vide* Robert Guillain, *Le Peuple Japonais et La Guerre* (Paris, Rene Juilliard, 1947), p. 276 *et seq.*; M. Kato, *The Lost War* (New York, Alfred Knopf, 1946), p. 241 *et seq.*; T. Kase, *Journey to the Missouri* (Yale University Press, 1950), p. 258 *et seq.*

[2] Some, like Adachi Kenzo, graduated from one class to the other.

[3] Speech by J. B. Keenan, Chief Prosecutor, 4th June, 1946. International Military Tribunal for the Far East Transcript, p. 442.

THE NATIONALIST MOVEMENT
BEFORE 1931

IN his published lecture on Japanese Fascism[1] Professor
Maruyama of Tokyo University suggests that for the beginning
of what he describes as the preparatory period of fascism, lasting
up to the Manchurian Incident, we need look back no further
than 1919. "It was in 1919–20 and thereafter that we have the
rapid development of near-fascist groups. The *Genyosha* and
Kokuryukai may be regarded as exceptions." [2]

Up to about 1920, indeed, the number of extremist organisations was small by comparison with the multitude of such groups
which came into being in the years that followed. The early
societies, despite some pretended concern for the issue of "popular rights", were chiefly interested in the overseas expansion of
Japan. They were composed of samurai, mainly from Kyushu,
who had failed to adjust themselves to the revolutionary effects,
in every field, of the introduction of Western thought and tech-
niques. After the collapse of the Shogunate the more rabid patriots
discovered that the new government, while dangerously bold in
the application of disturbing innovations at home, was reluctant
to embark on an immediate campaign of expansion abroad.
Dissatisfaction led to a series of revolts, of which Saigo's in 1877
was the culmination. The energy of the irreconcilables among the
survivors of these rebellions found an outlet in the early nationalist societies, notably the *Genyosha*.

The *Genyosha* was founded in 1881 in the town of Fukuoka by
Hiraoka Kotaro, a mine-owner and former samurai who had
taken part in the Saigo Rebellion.[3] The name of the society was

---

[1] *Nippon Fasshizmu no Shiso to Undo* ("The Movement and Thought of
Japanese Fascism") in a collection called *Sonjo Shiso to Zettai shugi* ("Sonno joi'
Thought and Absolutism") (Tokyo University, Toyo Bunka Kenkyujo,
Hakujitsu Shoin, 1948). [2] *Ibid.*, p. 104.
[3] *Vide* E. H. Norman, "The Genyosha" (*Pacific Affairs*, Vol. XVII, No. 3,
September, 1944). Dr. Norman's study is based on Japanese language material,

taken from the *Genkai nada*, the "Black Sea Straits" between Kyushu and Korea. The society was an amalgamation of certain existing patriotic associations in Fukuoka and never lost a characteristic Kyushu flavour; its leaders were invariably natives of Fukuoka, which was notorious, like the Mito district north-east of Tokyo, for extremely violent nationalist feeling. Spiritually the *Genyosha* was heir to the ideas of the dead Saigo, who had pressed for an invasion of Korea and whose revolt had been an attempt to rescue the Imperial House from "unfaithful ministers".

The declared aims of the society were three: "to revere the Imperial Family"; "to respect and honour the fatherland"; "to guard strictly the rights of the people". The last suggests that the *Genyosha* was concerned with the *Minken ron* (advocacy of people's rights) which was the war-cry of such political figures as Itagaki Taisuke and Goto Shojiro in their agitation for an elected national assembly. The *Genyosha*, of course, was scarcely interested in any principle of political democracy as understood in the West. The inclusion of "people's rights", however, among its original aims was not entirely opportunist or insincere. The *Genyosha* ideal—Japanese expansion overseas—was popular; and opposition to it came from conservative realists, who appreciated that time was needed for the country to build up adequate industrial capacity before an aggressive foreign policy, with the risk of war, could be undertaken.[1] An intense national consciousness was growing fast, due largely to the introduction, in 1872, of compulsory elementary education with its rigorous inculcation of patriotic ethics. An increasingly literate public sought not only the right of suffrage but also international recognition of their country as a leading power in Asia.

The *Genyosha* was a terrorist organisation, and a school for

particularly the *Genyosha sha-shi*, the society's history published by the society in Tokyo, 1917, and the *Toa Senkaku Shishi Kiden* ("Biographical Memoirs of Pioneer Patriots in E. Asia") by Kuzuo Yoshihisa (Tokyo, Kokuryukai, 1933).

[1] "With some writers on political affairs it has become axiomatic that liberalism is inimical to a policy of expansion. Historically this is very difficult to prove, either in the case of Japan or of other nations. It will be recalled that between 1871 and 1873 great pressure was brought to bear upon the government by a group favouring a campaign against Korea. . . . It was not a liberal group which blocked this premature attempt at military adventure, but on the contrary the more conservative and cautious leader Okubo." E. H. Norman, *Japan's Emergence as a Modern State* (New York, Institute of Pacific Relations, 1940), p. 201.

spies. It made no attempt to become a political party, to be represented in due course in a national parliament. Its membership remained small, and its participation in home politics was characterised by its rôle in the General Election of 1892. The leaders of the *Genyosha* were assured by the Matsukata cabinet that the administration would pursue a strong foreign policy and greatly increase the budget for the armed forces. Accordingly the society exerted itself to terrorise anti-government candidates in the Fukuoka area. Shinagawa Yajiro, the Home Minister, had instructed the police to intervene actively on the side of the government in the Election, which was conducted with considerable bloodshed.[1] This unofficial agreement between the Home Minister and the *Genyosha* is of interest; for it was the first notable example of the close, unavowed co-operation, over a limited period and for a special purpose, between the Home Ministry and the most powerful nationalist organisations.

The first decade of the *Genyosha's* existence coincided with what the Japanese call the "Rokumeikan era". The *Rokumeikan* was a building in Tokyo in which government hospitality on a Western scale—including dances—was dispensed; and it became symbolic of the craze for Western ideas, clothes, food and customs which developed among the wealthy, especially in Tokyo. It was a time when many sophisticated Japanese appeared to reject their own culture, exchanging native art treasures for tasteless Western importations; when there was talk of abandoning the Japanese script for the alphabet, and of the permanent adoption of European dress for both men and women. The *Rokumeikan* had its place in the diplomatic strategy of the government; for it was partly an attempt to prove to foreign nations that Japan had become a civilised modern state, and therefore entitled to secure the revision of the unequal treaties—those agreements, granting foreigners extra-territorial rights, which had been forced on the Shogunate at the time of the opening of the country to Western commerce. But in the provinces there was a strong hostile reaction to the *Rokumeikan* craze; particularly as the government could show no success in negotiations for treaty revision. For its

---

[1] Twenty-five persons were killed and 388 injured in this Election. The result, none the less, was unfavourable to the government, whose successful candidates numbered 137, against 163 for the opposition parties.

part the government vehemently resisted the pressure of public opinion and at the end of 1887, by the stringent Peace Preservation Regulations, put Tokyo out of bounds to leading members of the opposition and muzzled discussion of diplomatic questions. In June, 1889, however, the outline of confidential proposals by the Foreign Minister, Okuma, in renewed treaty negotiations became known through Japanese press translation of a report in the London *Times*. It seemed that Okuma was ready to make certain concessions. There was a general outburst of public indignation, and three months later there occurred the celebrated bomb attack on Okuma in which associates of Toyama Mitsuru—by now perhaps the most notable member of the *Genyosha*—took part.[1]

However, it was outside Japan that the *Genyosha* was most active. Its leaders—Hiraoka, Toyama, Uchida Ryohei, and Shindo Kiheitai—made the society the headquarters of an intelligence service operating on the Asiatic continent. In 1882, for example, Toyama sent a hundred young men to China to gather information. Within the next five years he established intimate liaison with Japanese army intelligence agencies in that country.[2] Money for these activities was provided in the early days by Hiraoka, who was a man of substantial wealth; but by 1890 the *Genyosha* began to receive covert support from the government in the shape of payments from the Ministry of War's secret service funds.

Japan was rapidly feeling strong enough to challenge China on the issue of Korea. The heirs to the impetuous Saigo now came into their own. Through its residents abroad the *Genyosha* was able to provide the General Staff with translators, guides, maps of Korea and Manchuria, and, above all, with intimate contact with the Korean *Togaku*, or Tonghaks, whose rising in 1894 gave Japan a pretext for intervention in Korea.

The work of the *Genyosha* was under the immediate direction of Uchida Ryohei, who organised a small subsidiary group, the *Tenyukyo* ("The Society of the Celestial Salvation of the Op-

---

[1] "Although there is no direct proof that the *Genyosha* took part in all the anti-foreign disturbances and murders of the 'eighties, the whole character of its activities shows that it was one of the most important centres of samurai nationalism at this period." Tanin and Yohan, *op. cit.*, p. 33.

[2] For interesting details regarding Arao Kiyoshi, pioneer army intelligence agent in China, *vide* E. H. Norman, "The Genyosha" (cited).

pressed") to further the machinations of the Tonghaks. Its activities led to many protests to Tokyo by the Korean government; but these were unavailing, for the *Tenyukyo* was firmly supported by the Japanese army.[1]

After the Sino-Japanese War the assassination of the Queen of Korea was the work of *Genyosha* "ronins", backed by Lieutenant-General Miura, Minister in Seoul.[2]

By the turn of the century the leaders of the *Genyosha* had come to the conclusion that Japan would shortly have to fight Russia, her most formidable rival in Asia. Uchida Ryohei had already visited St. Petersburg and studied the Russian language when in February, 1901, he founded the *Kokuryukai* ("The Society of the Amur River").

To the world at large this is the best known of all Japanese nationalist associations, having been much publicised by authors and journalists as "The Black Dragon"—the literal translation of the Chinese characters for "Amur". It must be emphasised at once that the influence of this society in recent years—that is to say, since the end of the First World War—has often been greatly exaggerated. However clandestine many of its activities may have been, the existence of the society has been no secret.[3] Indeed the trend of events finally gave the *Kokuryukai* an almost entirely respectable reputation inside Japan. Nevertheless, in its early years the *Kokuryukai* was both active and influential.

Uchida Ryohei, the founder, remained head of the society until his death in 1937, when he was succeeded by Kuzuo Yoshihisa.

---

[1] Initially the *Tenyukyo* was a band of fifteen picked adventurers. The *Genyosha* understood from the Minister of War, General Kawakami, that if a fire was started in Korea the Japanese army would have to act as firemen. The *Tenyukyo* had the rôle of fire-raisers. Cf. Hugh Byas, *Government by Assassination* (London, Allen & Unwin, 1943), p. 194; also Norman, "The Genyosha" (cited).

[2] Adachi Kenzo, Home Minister in the Wakatsuki cabinet of 1931, had a hand in the arrangements for this murder. He was also implicated in the bomb attack on Okuma six years earlier.

A "ronin" was originally a kind of rogue samurai, a fighting man without a master. A certain halo of romance hovered over the name in modern times thanks to the many stories, true and fictional, surrounding the exploits of "ronins" in feudal days. In their own estimation at least the modern adventurers who bore this label felt themselves superior to the *soshi*, who were mere criminal bullies. To the outsider the distinction is small.

[3] For example, it is listed among clubs and societies in the Japan Year Books of the nineteen-thirties.

Toyama Mitsuru, so often described as head of the *Kokuryukai* by Western writers, was not even a member.[1] None the less, his name is very rightly associated with the society. If not technically a member he was its patron, protector and mentor. The truth, perhaps, is that operations were directed by Uchida, policy by Toyama.

The *Kokuryukai* was founded in the first place to repeat in Manchuria the work of the *Genyosha* in Korea; an aim well concealed beneath the generalities which comprised the official programme of the society. This referred only to five vaguely expressed ideals, which may be summarised as: harmony between the civilisations of the East and West; eradication of weakness and inefficiency in the political system; expansion overseas and the solution of problems affecting capital and labour; promotion of the martial spirit in accordance with the Imperial Rescript to the armed forces; and fundamental reform of the educational system, replacing imitation of the educational ideas of Europe and America by the establishment of schools based on the national structure (*kokutai*).

A Japanese police manual, dated January, 1936, speaks of the *Kokuryukai* as having been "active behind the scenes, particularly in the Russo-Japanese War, the North China Incident and in the frequent Chinese disturbances".[2] Certainly the activities of the *Kokuryukai*, before the Russo-Japanese War, were on a more extensive scale than those of the *Genyosha* ten years earlier. The prestige of the armed forces had risen greatly, as a result of the quick, successful struggle against China. Despite the humiliation suffered from the Three Power Intervention of 1895 the nation had gained rich rewards as a consequence of victory. It became clear that war paid dividends, and was the sure road to international recognition as a potential equal in the family of civilised states. The most powerful financial interests in Japan were prepared to back the ambitions of the army and navy; and the *Kokuryukai* received funds from such business houses as Yasuda and Okura, as well as from the army; which indeed took the

[1] For a list of over a hundred of the prominent members, *vide* Appendix I (*infra*).

[2] Shigematsu Koei, *Shiso Keisatsu Tsuron* ("Introduction to Thought Police"), Japan Police Society, 20th January, 1936; supplement, p. 5. "The N. China Incident" is probably the Tanaka government's Shantung adventure in 1928.

society under its wing as an intelligence organ. The society sent agents to Siberia as well as to Manchuria.[1] When war came Uchida organised Chinese guerrillas to harass the Russian forces, while *Kokuryukai* volunteers from Japan were attached to the army in the field as interpreters.[2]

At home, before the war, the *Kokuryukai* established a school in Tokyo for the study of Russian, and conducted a good deal of anti-Russian propaganda; but many of the society's publications, including Uchida's *Russia Going to Ruin* (1903), were suppressed. In the midst of military preparations the government was concerned to maintain a strictly "correct" attitude towards the probable enemy. Furthermore, the still considerable influence of Ito—*genro* and President of the Privy Council[3]—was on the side of an understanding with Russia.

It has been claimed that the *Genyosha* converted Ito to the belief in the necessity of war with China, and that the *Kokuryukai*, by direct pressure amounting to the threat of assassination, persuaded him to abandon his moderate attitude towards Russia.

In this connection an account should be given of a celebrated interview between Ito and Toyama.[4]

Leaders of the *Kokuryukai* had asked Toyama for his help with regard to Ito. With three of his closest associates—well versed in the art of judo—Toyama paid an uninvited call on Ito at his home. Just as they arrived Viscount Aoki was leaving the front door, where Ito was still standing. As Aoki passed Toyama he whispered: "Well, I see you have come at last. Is there going to be any beating-up?" In a voice pitched loud enough for Ito to hear,

---

[1] According to Tanin and Yohan (*op. cit.*, p. 45) these numbered hundreds; some were sent as far west as the Lake Baikal area.

[2] At least some of these were not taken very seriously by Japanese war correspondents, who called them "deaf and dumb interpreters". Byas, *op. cit.*, p. 187.

[3] The *genro* were particular elder statesmen, who had been prominent in the Meiji Restoration and in the early period of constitutional history. Altogether there have been ten *genro* since 1868, of whom Prince Saionji was the last. The institution grew out of custom; it was not formally created. *Vide* Takeuchi, *War and Diplomacy in the Japanese Empire* (London, Allen & Unwin, 1936), pp. 20–2, for a short, authoritative account of the *genro* system.

[4] This account of the Ito-Toyama interview is based on Norman, "The Genyosha" (*op. cit.*), pp. 271–2. His version refers to Aoki as being Foreign Minister at the time. This seems to be an error. Aoki was then a Privy Councillor; but he had been twice Foreign Minister in earlier years.

Toyama replied: "I don't know whether there'll be any beating-up or not." Toyama was dressed only in *yukata* (informal summer kimono), and Ito received him coldly. Toyama sat in the place of honour and launched into a harangue on the desirability of war with Russia. Ito replied that as diplomacy was a confidential matter he was not prepared to discuss the issue. Toyama: "Diplomacy, which you call secret, is something which everybody knows about. The real trouble lies in ignoring public opinion and making government a private affair. I think it right that the trend of public opinion should be given leadership. At one time Your Excellency performed many meritorious services for the state; but you have also committed many errors. In case there should be some fatal blunder in the present crisis it is not unreasonable for the people to express anxiety over such a terrible prospect." Toyama then rose and, coming close to Ito, looked him full in the face and asked: "Ito-*san*, who is the greatest man in Japan to-day?" Ito was so startled by this question that he hesitated to reply; whereupon Toyama declared: "If I may say so, that place belongs to His Majesty the Emperor." After a pause he added: "However, who is the first man among His subjects?" Ito still remained silent, and Toyama said: "You are the one." He then repeated it slowly, and went on: "If you do not hold fast at this moment we are in danger of falling into a grave predicament." Ito replied in a tone of frankness: "If that is your purpose then bear with me. Rest assured that Ito will be responsible for your wish." Toyama was satisfied with this reply and departed with a polite expression of gratitude and appreciation.

This account has been related in detail because it is an excellent example of the type of interview in which Toyama specialised. It will be noticed that his tactics were a combination of effrontery, indirect threats and flattery.

That meeting probably occurred in the summer of 1903.[1] Public opinion was almost unanimous in pressing for war against Russia. The newspapers, with the exception of the semi-government Tokyo *Nichi-Nichi*, were extremely bellicose. Although

[1] This seems a legitimate guess, judging from the fact that Toyama was in *yukata*, which is worn only between May and September. It was during the summer months of 1903 that public feeling was noticeably roused against Russia. Japan's diplomatic offensive opened in St. Petersburg in June. War started in February, 1904.

certain of the intelligentsia were involved in the anti-militarist opposition of the infant socialist movement, the great majority of educated people were caught up in this warlike fever. Leading professors of the law department of Tokyo Imperial University demanded war in the press and at public gatherings. Most significant of all, Oyama, the Chief of the Army General Staff, presented a memorial to the Emperor, early in the summer of 1903, urging a quick solution of the Manchurian question, as Japan had a strategic advantage which would be lost within a few years.[1]

The position of the *Kokuryukai* before the Russo-Japanese War was altogether stronger than that of the *Genyosha* before the war with China. In the course of twenty-five years Uchida and Toyama contrived to raise a provincial group of adventurers into an advance guard of popular nationalism.

Yet it would be untrue to suggest that pressure from Toyama and the *Kokuryukai* had a decisive influence on shaping government policy towards Russia. The Russians in the negotiations at St. Petersburg were intransigent to the point of provocation. Japanese public reaction to the Russian stand was reflected—not created—by the *Kokuryukai*. The edifice of Meiji government was still controlled very firmly by the survivors of those Clan statesmen and generals who had been its architects. The indiscipline which thirty years later was to be prevalent among the junior officers of the army did not exist at this time. If the makers of policy—the *genro*, cabinet and General Staffs—had decided against war with Russia they would still have been able to ignore pressure from any quarter, however powerful.

The point is illustrated by what happened in 1905. Impressive victories on land and sea led the public to believe that Russia was thoroughly defeated and that very substantial territorial and monetary concessions could be obtained from her, including the surrender of the Maritime Province of Siberia—in which, of course, the *Kokuryukai*, as "The Amur River Society", was particularly interested. But the responsible rulers of Japan, military no less than civilian, knew that the country was in no position to secure such terms. Military and financial opinion alike favoured an early peace; and President Roosevelt's offer to mediate—which had been sought by the Japanese Minister in Washington—was

[1] Takeuchi, *op. cit.*, pp. 136–9.

welcome news to the government.[1] The self-assurance of popular chauvinism, however, rested on the belief that Japan possessed exceptional spiritual advantages, outweighing more material factors not in her favour;[2] and Toyama organised an association, the *Konwa Mondai Rengo Doshikai*, to protest against the "weakness" shown by the Japanese delegation to the peace conference. When the treaty was signed and its terms made public this association engineered a mass meeting of protest in Tokyo. This led to mob violence on a scale which compelled the government to place the city under martial law. One of the chief objects of the agitation was to overthrow the Katsura cabinet. That this was not achieved was due to the fact that the General Staff, aware of the true condition of Japanese national strength, supported—however reluctantly—the peace settlement negotiated by the government.[3]

The critical, indeed rebellious, attitude of the *Kokuryukai* at this juncture was not to the detriment of the society's reputation. Tokyo after the Russo-Japanese War occupied in the regard of Asiatic revolutionaries the place held later by Moscow. Toyama appeared to be the opponent of all established governments in Asia, including that of his own country. Chinese, Indian and

---

[1] "Soon after the Battle of Mukden (10th March, 1905) General Kodama, chief of staff of the Manchurian expeditionary forces, made a secret return to Tokyo and told military and civilian leaders that those who started the war should know when to stop it, and urged them to seek an early opportunity of ending it." Takeuchi, *op. cit.*, p. 149.

There is evidence that at the Imperial Conference of 4th February, 1904, immediately before war broke out, it was decided that the U.S. be asked to intervene to end the war. From an extract from Prince Konoye's Diary for 1941, quoted by the Prosecution at the Tokyo Trial. I.M.T.F.E. (International Military Tribunal for the Far East) Transcript, p. 10260. Konoye was told of this by Count Kaneko. Konoye commented in his Diary: "In other words they were thinking of ending the war at the time of beginning it."

[2] This emphasis on morale is of course a familiar theme, and was much in evidence during the Pacific War. Lt.-Gen. Kawabe Masakazu, Director of Kamikaze Operations at Okinawa, told U.S. interrogators: "I wish to explain something which is a difficult thing and which you may not be able to understand. The Japanese, to the very end, believed that by spiritual means they could fight on equal terms with you, yet by any other comparison it would not appear equal. We believed our spiritual confidence in victory would balance any scientific advantages. . . ." *Mission Accomplished* (H.Q. Army Air Forces, Washington, 1946), p. 35.

[3] Its unpopularity did eventually force the cabinet to resign; but not until January, 1906.

Filippino dissidents visiting Tokyo tended to gravitate to his home in Shibuya. This of course was not a new phenomenon; but the trend was accelerated by the victory over Russia. Japan, so it seemed, was now the champion of Asiatic nationalism. This interpretation of Japan's rôle in world affairs was not necessarily that of the government at the time.[1] But it was welcomed and propagated by Toyama and his associates.

The *Kokuryukai* gave particular assistance to Chinese revolutionaries; the *Yurinkai*, reminiscent of the *Tenyukyo*, being created in 1911 to assist Sun Yat-sen. Chiang Kai-shek and Wang Ching-wei also came for a time under the influence of Toyama; who after 1937 was to claim on this score special qualifications for the tasks of negotiating peace with the one and of controlling the other.[2]

In 1908 Toyama founded a small society, the *Roninkai*. Its exact purpose was not clearly stated, but it is reasonable to suppose that it concentrated initially on strengthening Japanese influence in Mongolia. Leading members of the *Roninkai* included two prominent experts on that region, Sasaki Yasugoro and Viscount Miura, already mentioned as the Minister in Seoul who had helped to organise the murder of the Queen of Korea.[3] The *Roninkai*, with the *Genyosha* and *Kokuryukai*, formed the core of the politically active, extra-parliamentary nationalist movement up to the

---

[1] The government preferred the view that Japan was a world power—"Great Britain of the Far East"—rather than an entirely Asiatic power. A remark made many years later by Prince Saionji to his secretary, Baron Harada, illustrates the point.

"Since the time of the Meiji Restoration it has been an accepted fact not to use terms such as 'Orient' and 'Occident' in opposition to each other. In spite of the dissolution of terms contrasting East and West by the honourable intentions of the Emperor Meiji it is unpleasant to see the Right-wing elements and militarists use them." Saionji-Harada Memoirs, Part XIX, Ch. 326, (23rd May, 1939).

[2] For an excellent account of *Kokuryukai* activities in China both before and after 1911, *vide* Marius B. Jansen, *The Japanese and Sun Yat-sen* (Cambridge, Mass., Harvard University Press, 1954).

[3] In 1916 Kawashima Naniwa, who was close to Toyama and a member of the *Kokuryukai*, organised a small group known as the *Kanzan So* ("Mountain of Sweat Society") for the purpose of setting up a "Manchurian-Mongolian Empire". Kawashima's daughter, Yoshiko, got married to a guerrilla leader in Manchuria and gained some fame at the time of the Manchurian Incident (imaginative journalists called her "The Joan of Arc of Manchuria"). She was of help to the Kwantung Army when she escorted Pu Yi's wife from Tientsin. The *Roninkai* was the parent of the *Kanzan So*.

end of the First World War. There were, however, three other important nationalist organisations during this period. They were the *Zaigo Gunjinkai*, *Dai Nippon Butokukai* and *Dobunkai*. Strictly speaking they were non-political. Their founders and leaders were men of high social or official standing. Two of these societies—*Zaigo Gunjinkai* and *Butokukai*—had a national membership.

The *Zaigo Gunjinkai*, the society of ex-servicemen, was instituted in 1910 as a result of the work of Generals Terauchi and Tanaka Giichi, who reorganised for this purpose the existing *Teikoku Gunjin Gojikai* ("Imperial Association of Aid to Ex-Servicemen"). Soldiers and sailors on discharge from active service automatically joined the *Zaigo Gunjinkai*. The society was very much more than a Japanese version of the British Legion. For its organisation was based on that of the regular army. The head of the divisional district of the *Zaigo Gunjinkai* was always the major-general, second-in-command of the army division of that district. The district was divided into regimental associations, and lower down the scale were the town sections and the village, railway and factory sub-sections. These units frequently undertook some form of military training.

Zaigo Gunjin may be translated as "military men in their homes", and the society represented in the lives of many Japanese peasants an influence almost as persuasive as that of their own families.[1] This very large and socially active organisation did not take part in nationalist politics until the London Naval Treaty, of 1930, created a ferment of agitation, leading to growing political intervention by military groups in the decade before the Pacific War.

The *Butokukai* ("The Society of Military Virtues") was founded in 1895 in Kyoto, at the same time as the inauguration of the Heian Shrine. The aim of the *Butokukai* was the promotion of the samurai spirit. Its headquarters—the *Butokuden*, close to the Heian Shrine—became a centre for the practice of judo, fencing, archery and other traditional martial sports. In course of time branches were established throughout the country, and by 1912, at the end of the Meiji era, the society claimed a membership of

[1] Some typical activities of the *Zaigo Gunjinkai* in the countryside are described in J. F. Embree, *op. cit.*, pp. 124 and 146–8.

over a million and a half. Its leaders were eminent military figures. The society did not engage in political activity before the nineteen-thirties; and until that time, at least, it appears to have had no connections with the *Genyosha-Kokuryukai* groups.

In 1898 Prince Konoye Atsumaro founded the *Dobunkai* with the object of promoting the "same language" between Japanese and Chinese. The society established a college, the *Dobun Gakudo*, in Shanghai and schools in Hankow and Tientsin. The Konoye family maintained close ties with the society until the end of the Pacific War. The society on the whole represented the respectable, genuinely cultural, side of Japanese penetration in China.[1]

Until the end of the First World War, then, there were very few important nationalist associations. These, as have been seen, belonged to one or the other of two broad categories—namely the reputable, non-political type (for example, the *Zaigo Gunjinkai*), and the conspiratorial (such as the *Kokuryukai*).[2] But from about the year 1919 the number increased steadily. It was the measure of nationalist reaction to a series of events wounding to patriotic self-esteem and very damaging to the reputation of the parliamentary political parties which were in the ascendancy between 1918 and 1930.[3] These events, in popular patriotic opinion, were little less than national misfortunes.

They were: the failure, at the Versailles Conference, to secure the inclusion of the racial equality clause in the League Covenant (a clause implying the right of emigration); the termination by England of her alliance with Japan; the Nine Power Treaty (anathema to the nationalists as it put restraints on interference in Chinese affairs); the evacuation of Siberia, in 1922, with nothing to show for a four-year occupation except the retention of North Saghalin (to be surrendered three years later); the United States Congress "exclusion" legislation of 1924; the reduction of the

---

[1] Nevertheless Japanese students from *Dobun* colleges sometimes made long journeys into the interior of China, penetrating far to the West and making political and topographical investigations.

[2] Certain nationalist societies which have not been mentioned in the text appear in Appendix III (*infra*).

[3] Landmarks at the beginning and end of this ascendancy are the fall of the Terauchi cabinet in September, 1918 and the attack on Hamaguchi at Tokyo Station on 14th November, 1930.

strength of the standing army by twenty per cent (the disbanding of four divisions, in 1925, out of a total of twenty-one); the abortive military adventure in Shantung, 1927-9; the ratification of the Kellogg Pact (regarded widely as an encroachment on the prerogatives of the Emperor); and the conclusion of the London Naval Treaty of 1930.

Neither the disastrous Kanto earthquake of 1923 nor the banking crisis three years later did more than interrupt, though seriously, the general tendency towards industrial and commercial expansion. But the world depression struck Japan with alarming force. In 1930 there was a catastrophic fall in agricultural prices —quotations for rice and silk fell to the lowest figure since 1897 —and a famine in the north-east of the country.

At the same time there was the phenomenon in the years immediately following 1918 of what might be called a second *Roku-meikan* era. Western democracy, which had triumphed in the First World War, became fashionable. And Western thought, ranging from feminism to the Marxist dialectic, exercised a growing appeal, for the urban intelligentsia in particular.[1]

The Crown Prince's European tour in 1921 and Yamagata's death in 1922 were symbolic of the advent of a new world and the passing of the old. Prince Yamagata was the most powerful surviving representative of the Clan hegemony which ruled political life in Japan for half a century after the Meiji Restoration. In his old age, as the leading *genro*, he constituted a strongly conservative force, resisting change of any description, particularly in the army; which he dominated through his leadership of the Choshu Clan. The young Crown Prince—he was to be Regent in November, 1921—represented the modern generation, scientific, liberal and, it seemed, relatively democratic. His visit to England and France was a drastic break with tradition. Indeed it caused much anxiety among rabid nationalists. They were apprehensive, no doubt, not only of the physical risks of the long journey, but also of the possibility of a young mind being influenced by the very un-Japanese ideas of modern Europe.

[1] In this context it may be remarked that Tokyo had perhaps the largest student population in the world. The city contained within its boundaries at least fourteen universities, with a student population of some 43,000. To these must be added the pupils, aged from eighteen to twenty-one years, of Higher Schools.

The First World War enriched the business classes and greatly increased their numbers. Their political energies found expression in support, or manipulation, of the parties in the Diet. War profits exacerbated differences between rich and poor—wages by no means kept up with rising prices—and made possible an unprecedented public display of wealth by a section of the *narikin*, the newly enriched capitalists of the time.[1] Under the circumstances, and considering the impact of the Russian Revolution, it is not surprising that all in positions of authority should have feared the appearance of a robust socialist movement.

This anxiety gave rise to that unattractive phrase, "dangerous thoughts", in condemnation of all radical ideas. The first socialist party had been formed in 1901 but was soon suppressed. Though it reappeared in 1906 a mortal blow seemed to have been dealt the party, and the movement generally, when Kotoku Denji, a pioneer socialist, and eleven others were executed for an alleged plot against the life of the Emperor. That was in 1911. But by 1918 new vigour inspired Japanese socialism as a result of economic tensions inside the country, not to mention such events abroad as the Russian Revolution. Yet even at this stage the Left-wing movement showed a tendency to divide into a state socialist wing, nationalist in essence, and a Marxian socialist wing, some fraction of which looked to Moscow for guidance.

The prevailing mood of the time, however, could be called one of optimistic, bourgeois moderation, suspicious of military adventures abroad and radical experiments at home. The first party cabinet, under Hara, seemed to be the promise of a gradually broadening political democracy. For the time being this appeared to be a substantial advance. An American scholar has given point to the argument in these words:

> Japan entered the First World War apparently under the control of a small oligarchy, and then, as the war ended and Japan entered the post-war world, it suddenly became evident that there was no longer a small, clear-cut ruling group but instead, thousands of bureaucrats, military leaders, business men, and intellectuals, all

[1] There is a short, astringent account of some features of this war boom prosperity in A. Morgan Young, *Japan under Taisho Tenno* (London, Allen & Unwin, 1928), pp. 110–18.

contending for control of the government. There was even a growing demand that all classes be allowed to participate in politics.[1]

This clash of interests and opinions—the very life-blood of a healthy political democracy—was looked upon by believers in *Nihon Shugi* ("Japanism" [2]) as nothing but deplorable confusion. The point is important. Harmony between Emperor and people, ruler and the ruled—like the unity of religion and politics—was a deeply felt nationalist ideal. This essentially Confucian concept of the state was implicit in the opening words of the Imperial Rescript on Education (1890):

> Our Imperial Ancestors have founded Our Empire on a basis broad and everlasting and have deeply and firmly implanted virtue; Our subjects ever united in loyalty and filial piety have from generation to generation illustrated the beauty thereof. This is the glory of the fundamental character of our Empire, and herein also lies the source of Our education.

It is difficult to exaggerate the compelling power, for Japanese, of such words. To the Western mind they convey little more than the sentiments associated with legitimate national pride. To the Japanese they represent more than an idealised version of their country's history. Except to the sophisticated and critical the words carry the authority of absolute truth. They suggest to the Japanese a well-regulated social order, pervaded by a spirit of unruffled harmony, entirely excluding the possibility of bitter political dissensions; for the people have had virtue "deeply and firmly implanted" in them, and are "united in loyalty and filial piety".

By contrast, the strikes,[3] the political party and financial scandals, the "dangerous thoughts" of the nineteen-twenties were chaos and degeneracy.

Occurrences which in the West would hardly be regarded as

---

[1] Edwin O. Reischauer, *Japan Past and Present* (London, Duckworth, 1947), p. 145.

[2] The translation is ungainly but no better exists. *Nihon Shugi* implies the cultivation, to the exclusion of foreign ideas, of all the native concepts, institutions and genius of Japan.

[3] In 1919 there was even a soldiers' strike, at Matsuyama. A. Morgan Young, *op. cit.*, p. 168.

suggestive of any particular trend in national morals were interpreted by many Japanese as pointing to a general deterioration in the loyal, patriotic spirit of the country. Mention has been made of the diplomatic setbacks and economic troubles of the period. Each of these was associated to some extent—in the minds of nationalists—with the deplored tendencies of the day, the liberal and Left-wing thought prevalent in the universities, the impact of modern Western books, music and social customs. Even the great Kanto earthquake was interpreted by some as a kind of supernatural punishment for the frivolity and individualism of the times.[1]

[1] Before the Pacific War the Earthquake Commemoration Museum at Yokohama displayed posters and cartoons, etc., illustrating this point of view. According to vulgar superstition, dating from ancient times, earthquakes were caused by the motions of a giant catfish which lived beneath the surface of the land. Some of the cartoons showed this creature angrily heaving its back in irritation at the frivolity and confusion prevailing above it.

3

PRELUDE TO FASCISM

i

WHEN we look at the proliferation of nationalist groups between 1918 and 1931, against the background described in the previous chapter, we find a constantly changing pattern, with many societies coming into existence and then dying almost at once. Inaugurated with a flourish of impressive titles and ambitious aims they often collapse due to internal jealousies or lack of funds. Or they break up into splinter groups, each with claims as impressive as those of the parent society.

For this reason it is difficult to give anything like an accurate estimate of the number of nationalist societies formed during this period. By 1936 there were nearly 750 such associations in Japan.[1] But the figure includes, of course, the numerous societies established after the Manchurian Incident and a great many that were purely local in origin and membership.[2]

Of the societies indirectly associated with Toyama and Uchida the most notable in this period was, perhaps, the *Dai Nippon Kokusuikai* ("The Japan National Essence Society").[3] It was founded in October, 1919, by Tokonami Takejiro, Home Minister in the Hara cabinet, and was strongly supported by Toyama, who held the position of adviser to the society. The active membership consisted largely of builders' foremen and labour contractors, together with their gangs of workmen.

[1] Shigematsu Koei (*op. cit.*) lists a total of 741 (January, 1936).
[2] Of those listed by the police (viz. Shigematsu, *op. cit.*) about 4500 were located in the Tokyo area, 19% in Kansai (Kyoto, Osaka, Kobe region) and the remaining 36% in the rest of Japan proper.

The figures are: Tokyo area 335 societies; Kansai area 139; Rest of Japan 267 (of these Fukuoka provides 27; Kumamoto 8; the Mito area 11).

The grand total of 741 includes student groups (40), patriotic professional and trade associations (12) and a great number of small, obscure societies.
[3] *Kokusui* is sometimes translated as "fascist". This is inexact. When speaking of fascism the Japanese generally use the imported word, *fasshizmu*.

26

Many of these contractors liked to call themselves *kyokaku*, which by a literal translation means "chivalrous persons". The term requires further explanation. A *kyokaku* was considered to be the heir to the honourable tradition of the *otokodate* of Yedo— the swashbuckling coolie bosses who supplied the unskilled labour needed by the *daimyo* on their annual visits to the Shogun's capital. The *otokodate* ruled their coolie gangs with a firm but paternal authority; they were not averse to the use of force, either in controlling their subordinates or in obtaining fair treatment for them; on the whole they enjoyed a reputation among the common people of Yedo for being generous to the poor and hostile to the rich and powerful. Seen in the most favourable light the modern *kyokaku* was a rude, petty boss, used to handling men, with violence if necessary, but not without a rough sort of justice. Not unnaturally the *kyokaku* was regarded by conservative politicians and officials as peculiarly well equipped for the task of industrial mediation—just the man to bring strikers to their senses.

This office was commonly performed by the police.[1] The strikes of 1919, however, were more than the police could deal with. So Tokonami, who as Home Minister was responsible for public order throughout the country, followed the precedent set by Shinagawa in 1892, and enlisted the co-operation of Toyama in recruiting a body of patriots who would help the police to maintain industrial discipline. Such was the birth of the *Kokusuikai*.

In its statement of aims the society declared:

> By basing our actions on a spirit of benevolence we expect to put right the social order which is in peril. We expect to effect a settlement of social problems and to secure the safety of society by arranging the co-operation of capital and labour.[2]

When reading these high-sounding, vaguely expressed aspirations—they are typical of the manifestoes issued by most of these societies—it is useful to bear in mind what a Japanese is reported to have said about his own language. "We say only 60% of what we think. Other Japanese can guess 30% left

[1] Despite a thoroughly well-earned reputation for severity the police often acted as "honest brokers", genuinely eager to secure a compromise solution to a dispute.

[2] Shigematsu, *op. cit.*, supplement, p. 4.

unsaid by the way the 60% is expressed. 10% remains an unknown quality."[1] The inward meaning of the *Kokusuikai* aim quoted above is that settlement of disputes between capital and labour must be achieved according to the well-tried method of appealing to both sides to act on the basis of the *oyabun-kobun* relationship—namely that between parents (employers) and children (employees). This demanded generosity on the one side, devoted obedience on the other. On the whole the system was less unfair to the employees than would appear at first sight.[2] But it was of course inimical to the growth of an organised labour movement, and it rejected the ideas of socialism, which were condemned as unhealthy foreign importations.

The *Kokusuikai*—composed, according to the police, "of all men of chivalrous spirit throughout the nation"[3]—was a large organisation, containing perhaps as many as sixty thousand members.[4] There were branches in every prefecture. The leaders of these provincial branches were usually labour contractors; they enlisted, as members of the society, the workers dependent on

[1] Quoted by Hillis Lory, *Japan's Military Masters* (New York, Viking Press, 1943), p. 176.

[2] This is, of course, debatable ground. But the force of long-cherished tradition bound the good employer—whether head of a large factory or master craftsman employing three or four men in a home workshop—to treat his employees with a generosity beyond all standards of equity as recognised by the contract terms of the West. There was the greatest reluctance, for example, to discharge a man on the grounds of redundancy. Being one of his employer's "family" he was retained in his job in bad years as well as good. Even so critical an observer as Morgan Young noted this admirable feature of a conservatism generally condemned. "In some cases where a certain loss of business was anticipated by the employers, extremely generous treatment was accorded; for instance, the Asahi Glass Co. at Amagasaki discharged its men with handsome allowances as trade declined, the last thirty-one, all that were left when the works finally closed in November, 1921, receiving between them 34,226 *yen*. In other cases employers continued working at a loss until there was nothing left." Morgan Young, *op. cit.*, p. 232.

The above remarks refer, of course, to good employers only. That the system could be disgracefully abused goes without saying.

[3] Shigematsu, *op. cit.*, supplement, p. 4. The reference to *kyokaku* ("men of chivalrous spirit") will be noted.

[4] At one time the society claimed to have a million members. Yanaga Chitoshi, *Japan Since Perry* (New York, McGraw-Hill, 1949), p. 492. Tanin and Yohan give the membership as "about 120,000" (*op. cit.*, p. 76). We have to be very careful about accepting such claims. Sixty thousand is perhaps an underestimate; but the actual total may not have been very much higher.

them. Several Seiyukai personalities sat on the board of management in Tokyo with Tokonami, the President.[1]

With this weight of influence at the top, and with its substantial membership, the *Kokusuikai* might have been in a position to crush or deflect the proletarian Left-wing movement. However, although its members were often involved in brawls with both town and country workers—on one occasion fighting a pitched battle with the organised *Eta* of the *Suiheisha*[2]—the *Kokusuikai* failed to achieve the success expected of it. Within eighteen months of its formation it was rent by internal dissensions at the Tokyo headquarters; and this led to a split in the society. Dissenting Tokyo members moved the headquarters to Kyoto, while those remaining in Tokyo called themselves the *Kanto Kokusuikai Hombu*, "the Kanto *Kokusuikai* Headquarters".[3] It is possible that the division was related to the political rivalry of the Seiyukai and Minseito (then known as the Kenseikai), the latter becoming the backers of the *Kanto Kokusuikai*.[4]

The *Kokusuikai*—using the term to cover both wings of the society—was not much concerned either with matters of foreign policy or with important political issues at home. It represented a straightforward, militant reaction on the part of large employers and politicians to the menace of "dangerous thoughts", particularly in industry. Here was no fresh or dynamic interpretation of nationalism, but only the stale ideas of an old-fashioned paternalism, supported by the rowdy methods of the *kyokaku*. It was for this reason, perhaps, that the *Kokusuikai* lacked real prestige or power.

The same may be said of the *Dai Nippon Seigidan*, "The Japan

---

[1] They included Dr. Suzuki Kisaburo, a future President of the Seiyukai.

[2] This was near Nara, in 1922. Troops were called out to restore order. The *Suiheisha*, the organisation of the depressed *Eta* class, was thought by the authorities to be affected by anarchism. In 1924 members of the *Suiheisha* tried to kill Prince Tokugawa. Yanaga, *op. cit.*, p. 473.

[3] Kinoshita Hanji, *Nippon Kokka Shugi Undo Shi* (History of the Japanese Nationalist Movement) (Tokyo, 1940), pp. 19–20.

[4] The first president of the *Kanto Kokusuikai Hombu* was Viscount Watanabe, Minister of Justice in a later (Minseito) cabinet. There is a reference by Morgan Young (*op. cit.*, p. 252) to a noisy meeting of shareholders of the N.Y.K. shipping line at Tokyo in June, 1921, at which *Kokusuikai* members ranged themselves with Kenseikai supporters against the Seiyukai and their *soshi* (professional bullies). The *Kokusuikai* members were no doubt from the *Kanto Hombu*, which was formed on 1st January, 1921.

Corps of Political Justice", an Osaka society which came to have a national membership. It was formed in February, 1925, by Sakai Eizo, a wealthy railway magnate and building contractor. All his many employees were members of the *Seigidan*. They were admitted after taking part in a special Shinto ceremony.[1] Sakai insisted that his relationship to the members should be that of a parent to his children and that obedience to his commands, as head of the *Seigidan*, must be unquestioning. This suggests some affinity with European fascism; and indeed Sakai visited Rome in 1930. He had an interview with the Duce, and on his return to Japan he ordered the *Seigidan* to wear blackshirts.

With these fascist traits it might have been expected that the *Seigidan* would enter the arena of politics. This was debated in 1927; but it was then decided that the society should remain aloof from political parties and cliques. Being a typical *kyokaku* organisation, despite its fascist trappings, the society had perhaps neither the skill nor the inclination to enter political life through constitutional means. Furthermore, Sakai, as an old-fashioned labour boss, probably realised that the tactics of a Mussolini would not succeed in Japan. This does not exclude the possibility that, for a time at least, he cherished dreams of political power. For he was a man of exceptional energy who raised the membership of his society after 1930 to something over a hundred thousand.[2]

Activities of the *Seigidan* put an end to many industrial disputes, notably the Toyo Textiles strike of 1930, and they embraced such benevolent gestures as the dispatch of rice to famine districts in north-east Japan in 1931.[3] The membership of the *Seigidan* rose considerably between 1930 and 1934; many recruits being former members of the Left-wing *Ronoto* ("Workers and Farmers' Party"), which lost large numbers of its supporters in the wave of patriotic feeling that followed the Manchurian Incident. The *Seigidan* was very much Sakai's own private army; for he was its sole financial backer.

[1] Initiation rites were not a usual feature of Japanese nationalist societies. The *Ketsumeidan* (discussed in Chapter 5) and other "blood leagues" were exceptions.

[2] The society itself claimed 250,000 members. Tanin and Yohan speak of 180,000 and describe this figure as "exaggerated" (*op. cit.*, p. 112).

[3] *Seigidan* methods of mediation included that of taking leaders of an Osaka tram strike up to the Koyozan temples for a period of "meditation".

Other notable *kyokaku* societies were the *Yamato Minrokai* ("The Japanese People's Labour Society"), the *Kinno Remmei* ("The League of Fidelity to the Emperor"), and the *Dai Nippon Sekkaboshidan* ("Japan Anti-Bolshevik League").[1]

ii

Mention was made, in the previous chapter, of the *Roninkai*. In 1918 this society attracted a good deal of publicity, when some of its members violently assaulted in the streets of Osaka the president of the Osaka *Asahi*, a newspaper which had strongly opposed the dispatch of the Siberian Expedition. This kind of intimidation shocked liberal opinion throughout Japan, and it was very largely as a reaction to the behaviour of the *Roninkai* that Professor Yoshino Sakuzo, of the law department of Tokyo Imperial University, sponsored the formation of a society known as the *Shinjinkai* ("The Association of New Men").[2] This became a fairly influential group, comprising graduates as well as students of Tokyo Imperial University. It advocated such Left-wing ideas as the creation of a socialist state, linked with the international socialist movement, and the outlawry of war. It established

[1] The *Yamato Minrokai* was founded in 1921 by a *Kokusuikai* official, Fujishiro Tempo, and a building contractor, Kawaii Tokusaburo. It had a membership of about 20,000, mostly in the Tokyo area. It claimed the right to "transform and resurrect the life of national labour" (Shigematsu, *op. cit.*, supplement, p. 5). This meant, in practice, brawling with strikers in Tokyo.

The *Kinno Remmei* was founded in 1924 by Suzuki Isamu, a rich cattle dealer. Its membership never exceeded three thousand; but it was not dissolved until the Pacific War. A retired major-general, Baron Kikuchi Takeo, was its official president. We shall meet him again (in Chapter 7). The professed ideals of the *Kinno Remmei* were hardly different from those of the *Kokusuikai* or *Seigidan* but placed particular emphasis on imperialism.

The *Dai Nippon Sekkaboshidan*, like the *Kinno Remmei*, had a small membership, of about two thousand, many of whom were probably in the pay of the police (Tanin and Yohan, *op. cit.*, p. 77). The one noteworthy event connected with this society was the murder by its leader, Yonemura Kaichiro, of Takao Heisuke, a socialist, in 1923. Yanaga, *op. cit.*, p. 493, and Morgan Young, *op. cit.*, p. 332.

[2] Prof. Yoshino challenged the *Roninkai* to a public debate on the subject of democracy. This inconclusive and rowdy meeting was attended by over two hundred police. Morgan Young, *op. cit.*, p. 152. That was in November, 1918. The *Shinjinkai* was born soon afterwards.

connections with students in other universities and organised the *Shakai Kagaku Rengokai* ("Intercollegiate Federation for the Study of Social Science"), which met at Tokyo Imperial University in September, 1924, a date that may be regarded as being the highwater mark of Japanese academic Left-wing activity in the 'twenties. The gathering was attended by several hundred students, who declared their solidarity with the working class.[1]

But the incident most suggestive of the force of Left-wing sentiment among intellectuals occurred at Waseda University in 1923. A group of army officers visited Waseda to inaugurate a military studies society, and among them was the Vice-Minister of War. Their reception was hardly cordial; for they had the novel and humiliating experience of being shouted down by students, who had been influenced by an energetic clique of Left-wing teachers headed by Oyama Ikuo.

At this time the most pertinacious opponent of Left-wing thought in the academic world was, perhaps, Professor Uesugi Shinkichi. As early as 1913 he had formed a group to fight liberal tendencies in Tokyo Imperial University—like Yoshino he was a member of the faculty of law—and in 1919 he founded a short-lived but significant society called the *Keirin Gakumei* ("The League for the Study of Statesmanship"). His chief collaborator was a socialist writer, Takabatake Motoyuki. Takabatake had translated *Das Kapital* into Japanese with a critical commentary of his own. It would seem bizarre, at first sight, that a man like Takabatake could ever be an associate of a convinced nationalist such as Uesugi. But his socialist views were not immutable.[2] Both he and Uesugi, as students at Tokyo Imperial University, had come under the influence of Dr. Kamisugi, a scholar who propounded a theory of all-embracing nationalism. It required no great mental agility, for those of a radical turn of mind, to develop from this the idea of national socialism, to which many Left-wing Japanese were converted. The evils of capitalism would disappear if the great financial and industrial magnates surrendered their

---

[1] Yanaga, *op. cit.*, p. 471.

[2] "From about March, 1918, Takabatake Motoyuki was more frequently engaged in the national socialist movement than in the movement for socialism. . . . Takabatake was laughed at and despised by socialists at the time as being a reactionary." *Uyoku Undo no Gensei* (The Present Situation of the Right-wing Movement) (Tokyo, *Gaimusho Chosabu*, 1935), Ch. 2, p. 11.

assets to the Emperor—to the state, in other words. This would knit the Empire together into an economic as well as spiritual unity. This was the essence of state, or national, socialism as advocated by Takabatake.

Uesugi, however, was at heart little interested in such ideas. His brand of extreme nationalism was much more traditional and was closely related to the concept of an expanding, warrior Japan. There soon arose, then, a divergence of opinion between Uesugi and Takabatake. The result was the dissolution of the *Keirin Gakumei*. The disagreement between the two men exemplified a split that was to run right through the nationalist movement before the Pacific War. On the one side were those, like Uesugi, who preached *Nippon shugi* ("Japanism"), a fundamentally nostalgic, conservative *mystique*. On the other were the radical nationalists, such as Takabatake, the advocates of revolutionary reconstruction, of national socialism.

The *Keirin Gakumei*, ephemeral though it was, had some significance as the progenitor of a celebrated society, the *Kokuhonsha* ("The National Foundations Association"). When the *Keirin Gakumei* broke up Uesugi regrouped his own supporters in a body known as the *Kokoku Doshikai* ("The Imperial Fellow Thinkers' Society"). It published a periodical called *Kokuhon* ("National Roots" or "National Foundations"). The Procurator-General at that time, Hiranuma Kiichiro, was asked to be its editorial adviser. Some three years later Hiranuma, with Takeuchi Kakuji (of the Uesugi faction in the *Keirin Gakumei*), founded the *Kokuhonsha*, which at first was nothing more than the *Kokoku Doshikai* on a much expanded scale.

Shortly before founding the *Kokuhonsha* Hiranuma had been Minister of Justice; but he resigned this office in consequence of what was known as the Toranomon Incident. This was an attempt, by a man called Namba Daisuke, to assassinate the Regent in December, 1923. The affair convinced Hiranuma that the nation was being undermined by the forces of degeneracy, of which Left-wing activities were the most formidable element. As Minister of Justice he was aware of the panic—never, of course, reported in the press at the time—that had occurred in front of the Imperial Palace during the Kanto Earthquake, when a great crowd had tried to enter the Palace grounds to escape from the

33

fire.[1] These events, no doubt, had some bearing on the creation of the *Kokuhonsha*. According to one account, Hiranuma was deeply impressed by two words in an Imperial Rescript issued at the time. These were *koku* ("nation") and *hon* ("root", "foundation"). He was taking a walk, says this account, and "unconscious of himself he concentrated on the Imperial Rescript, and the *Kokuhonsha* materialised as the embodiment of his cogitations".[2]

At the outset several officials of the Ministry of Justice joined the *Kokuhonsha*; but within ten years its membership embraced a remarkable diversity of distinguished men. Among them were General Ugaki, Admiral Saito Makoto, Dr. Suzuki Kisaburo, Rear-Admiral Suetsugu, and Generals Araki and Mazaki.[3] Because of its impressive membership the society attracted the attention of foreign observers, and it was often described as a fascist organisation. However, it is nearer the truth to regard the *Kokuhonsha* as an upper-class stronghold of traditional conservatism, a kind of *Herrenklub*. At the same time, as will be evident in later chapters, the society contained an extremist element, sympathetic with terrorists. There were eventually 170 branches of the *Kokuhonsha* throughout the country; and the membership at its greatest was not far short of 200,000. Although the *Kokuhonsha* gave Hiranuma substantial prestige in the eyes of nationalists, it was regarded with suspicion by such genuinely liberal-minded statesmen as Prince Saionji; and there is little doubt that the Emperor considered Hiranuma's association with the society to be unfortunate. It is significant that the *Kokuhonsha* was dissolved in 1936, the year in which Hiranuma was appointed President of the Privy Council.

What were the ideals professed by the *Kokuhonsha*? For an answer to this question we might take a statement that Hiranuma made to the foreign press in Tokyo in April, 1932.[4] This contained four main points. The first was a reference to the unique, religious character of the Japanese nation. The second declared that any condition in Japan contrary to the moral principle on which the country was founded would have to be reformed, "and

[1] Osugi Sakae, a leading socialist, was alleged to have urged on the crowd with the words, "Remember Russia!" Morgan Young, *op. cit.*, pp. 300–1.
[2] Shigematsu, *op. cit.*, supplement, p. 2.
[3] For a fuller list, *vide* Appendix I.
[4] *Japan Advertiser*, 21st April, 1932.

the nation guided back to the right path". Hiranuma's third point was contained in a reference to Japan's special mission in Asia— he was speaking seven months after the outbreak of the Man- churian Incident. "We must use militarism", said Hiranuma, "as a means of self-defence against any force obstructing the attain- ment of our highest ideal." Finally, Hiranuma rejected the idea that there was anything in common between Japanese nationalism and European fascism.[1]

A characteristic feature of the Japanese nationalist movement was the association, from time to time, of the respectable with the disreputable. Not long after the founding of the *Kokuhonsha* Hiranuma joined Toyama Mitsuru and Ishihara Koichiro, a wealthy business magnate from the Kansai district, in launching a society known as the *Kenkokukai* ("The State Foundation Society"). This was in 1926. Its president was Professor Uesugi. Its most faithful and energetic member, however, was Akao Bin, a former anarchist.

The aims of the society were anti-parliamentary and, nomin- ally at least, anti-capitalist.[2] A member of the society was to write of it:

> The *Kenkokukai* wanted to see the abolition of the anti-nationalist political parties, and it wished to have the Emperor at the centre of political life. The society also advocated the reform of the anti- nationalist capitalist economy and claimed that all organs should be owned by the state. The *Kenkokukai* wanted socialism to be abol- ished, since socialism ignores nationalism.[3]

Well supplied with funds by Ishihara Koichiro the society was able to publish its own periodical, *Kenkoku Shimbun*, twice a

---

[1] "Fascism", said Hiranuma, "is a product of a foreign country resulting from national circumstances in that country. Our country has its independent object and its independent mission. This object and this mission are based on morality. The *Kokuhonsha* is established on this foundation and it has no relation whatever to fascism." *Ibid.*

[2] Prof. Maruyama remarks that the *Kenkokukai* was not anti-capitalist. *Nippon Fasshizmu, op. cit.*, p. 106.

Much anti-capitalist talk at this time was in reality directed against only the great *zaibatsu*, such as Mitsui and Mitsubishi. Such agitation was often encouraged from motives of business jealousy, by lesser capitalists.

[3] Tsukui Tatsui, *Nippon Kokka Shugi Undo Shiron* ("Historical Essays on the Japanese Nationalist Movement") (Tokyo, *Chuo Koron* publishing company, 1942), p. 62.

month; and Akao Bin claimed that the society's membership numbered several thousand. But Akao's principal backers soon found his personality distasteful. He had been an anarchist. He frankly advocated violence—in 1928 he was involved in a bomb attack on the Soviet Embassy in Tokyo—and he liked to take his own line on every occasion. Men such as Toyama and Ishihara and, even, Hiranuma were not averse to a discreet use of terrorist methods. But they were, of course, determined that such methods should be used only in a manner that could not affect their own standing in the eyes of the public. By this time Toyama was beginning to enjoy a certain useful, if still spurious, reputation for respectability. Hiranuma already had his eyes on such peaks as the Presidency of the Privy Council. Ishihara's business connections were international, notably with the British in Malaya. Blatant terrorism at that juncture—between 1926 and 1928— hardly served the interests of these powerful men. Accordingly they withdrew from the *Kenkokukai*; and the society almost went into liquidation. Membership dwindled so severely that it became impossible to pay the rent for the society's headquarters. Akao then set up the headquarters—if one may use this term—in Professor Uesugi's home. Uesugi was a sick man at the time, and the irruption of Akao Bin and what was left of the *Kenkokukai* may have hastened his end, for he died shortly afterwards. Akao now ran the *Kenkokukai* almost as a one-man society.

> At the time the Left-wing movement thought the *Kenkokukai* to be very strong and imagined that it was composed of several hundred members. But as a matter of fact there were only about ten members, and sometimes only three or four. But these few used to create scenes at Left-wing headquarters. Akao would boast: "I can use one spear as a hundred." Soon supporters were on the increase again, especially among the working class.[1]

Indeed, as the Manchurian Incident led to a resurgence of nationalist sentiment, the *Kenkokukai* was able to obtain, once again, backing from various sources; and, as will be seen in a later chapter, it took part in the strident anti-British agitation of 1939.

The vicissitudes of the *Kenkokukai* have been related in some detail because they epitomise the story of organised nationalism

[1] Tsukui Tatsui, *Nippon Kokka Shugi Undo Shiron*, p. 64.

in the nineteen-twenties. There is the ambitious and substantially financed beginning, followed by a cooling of enthusiasm, a falling-off of members. There are the anti-capitalist slogans coupled with attacks on manifestations of genuine Left-wing anti-capitalist activity. There is, finally, the supremely important factor of personality, decisive in the success or failure of the organisation. Akao may be regarded as a professional political agitator of minor calibre. But his persistence should be noted. It is no surprise that he should have reappeared as an active nationalist soon after the Occupation ended in 1952. But we should now turn our attention to more important figures among what might be called the inner brigade of pre-war ultra-nationalist agitators.

iii

An outstanding figure in the ultra-nationalist movement after the First World War was Kita Ikki, who has been described as "the founder of Japanese fascism".[1] The title rests on the influence exercised, on the army in particular, by the revolutionary form of nationalism advocated by Kita, notably in his book, *Nihon Kaizo Hoan Taiko* ("An Outline for the Reconstruction of Japan"), first published in 1919.[2] Both before and during the First World War Kita lived in China, where he served for a time as an intelligence agent for the army, for he had many friends among Chinese revolutionaries. In 1915, in Shanghai, he wrote "A History of the Chinese Revolution" (*Shina Kakumei Gaishi*). This work showed some affinity with the Marxist interpretation of history. But the more famous *Nihon Kaizo Hoan Taiko* "brought socialism and Japanese imperialism under one umbrella".[3] It proposed not only economic reforms—the nationalisation of banks, shipping, mines, railways, manufacturing industry, commerce and land above certain prescribed limits of value—but also an intensive armament programme for the execution of a

[1] Maruyama, *Nippon Fasshizmu, op. cit.*, p. 105.
[2] The first edition was banned. Further editions had to be so prepared as to satisfy government censors.
[3] Byas, *op. cit.*, p. 85.

bellicose foreign policy.[1] Kita claimed that Japan was fully entitled to seize the overseas territories necessary for her livelihood. These territories were to be found within the British Empire and the U.S.S.R. Japan was in the position of the proletariat, who had the right to a share in the profits of the great capitalists.

> Justice [wrote Kita] is the proper demarcation of interests. As the class struggle within a nation is waged for the readjustment of unequal distinctions, so war between nations for an honourable cause will reform the present unjust distinctions [between nations]. The British Empire is a millionaire possessing wealth all over the world; and Russia is a great landowner in occupation of the northern half of the globe. Japan with her scattered fringe of islands is one of the proletariat, and she has the right to declare war on the big monopoly powers. The socialists of the West contradict themselves when they admit the right of class struggle to the proletariat at home and at the same time condemn war, waged by a proletariat among the nations, as militarism and aggression. . . . If it is permissible for the working class to unite to overthrow unjust authority by bloodshed, then unconditional approval should be given to Japan to perfect her army and navy and make war for the rectification of unjust international frontiers. In the name of rational social democracy Japan claims possession of Australia and Eastern Siberia.[2]

In accordance with the primary aim of seizing the territories needed by Japan the internal reconstruction (or "renovation", as the term is sometimes translated) of the nation must be shaped so as to give supreme power to the armed forces.[3] This reconstruction might have to be achieved by revolutionary means, of which the most expeditious was a military *coup d'état*. The seed of this idea was to bear fruit in the insurrections of the nineteen-thirties.

[1] In the case of banks, shipping and industry generally the limit of value was 10 million *yen*. Landholding was to be limited to 100,000 *yen* at market price, and personal property to 1 million *yen* for each household. From these figures it will be seen that Kita's proposals would have affected only the great combines, the *zaibatsu*.

[2] Kita Ikki, *Nihon Kaizo Hoan Taiko* (Outline for the Reconstruction of Japan) (Tokyo, Towa Insatsu, 1924), Ch. VIII, Note 1.

[3] Particularly the army. Kita might have described Japanese soldiers, in the terms used by Coke of judges in seventeenth-century England, as "lions under the Throne".

Kita returned to Japan from Shanghai under the auspices of an energetic and fanatical intriguer, Okawa Shumei. Okawa had graduated from Tokyo Imperial University in 1911. For some years he had obtained no regular employment, but managed to scrape a living by doing translation work for the Army General Staff. During the First World War he was commissioned by a wealthy patron to write a history of the Emperors of Japan. This work confirmed him in his strongly nationalist opinions. In 1919 he found employment in the East Asia Research Institute of the South Manchurian Railway Company, and soon afterwards he obtained a position as lecturer at the Colonisation University (*Takushokudai*) in Tokyo. From this time onwards, until his arrest following the assassinations of 1932, Okawa was unceasingly active in the organisation of nationalist groups and in planning various outbreaks of violence in Japan or Manchuria.

Okawa's first essay in the organisation of nationalist societies was the *Rosokai* ("The Society of Young and Old"). This was in fact a discussion group rather than a formal organisation. Its leading figures were Okawa, Kita Ikki, Takabatake Motoyuki and Mitsukawa Kametaro. The *Rosokai*, which was short-lived, actually contained persons from the Left as well as from the Right.[1]

At this time Okawa and Kita Ikki were closely associated, first in the *Rosokai* and then, in 1920, in the formation of a small, propagandist group known as the *Yuzonsha*. The precise meaning of *yuzon*, an almost untranslatable expression, is "yet remaining".[2] The title was borrowed from a Chinese poem: "Though all the paths are ruined, there yet remain the pine trees and the chrysanthemums." Many years later Okawa declared:

> Those were the days when countless organisations, large and small, were established, some being radical organisations with democratic or anarchist principles, others advocating socialist or communist principles. At that time we believed the true reformation

---

[1] One of these was the socialist, Takao Heisuke, later murdered by the leader of the *Sekkaboshidan*.

[2] Dr. Hugh Borton, in his *Japan's Modern Century* (New York, The Ronald Press, 1955), p. 326, calls the *Yuzonsha* "the Society to Preserve the National Essence". But this title belongs rather to the *Kokusuikai*.

to be that carried out from a genuinely Japanese standpoint. Therefore we considered ourselves the pine trees and chrysanthemums of
Japan and decided on the name *Yuzonsha*.[1]

The aims of the *Yuzonsha* were the establishment of Kita's
"revolutionary Empire of Japan", the revival of the national
patriotic spirit, military preparations for the emancipation of
Asia, and research into conditions prevailing in countries adja-
cent to Japan. Together with Okawa, Kita, and Mitsukawa Kametaro, prominent members of the *Yuzonsha* included Shimizu
Gionosuke, Yasuoka Masaatsu and Iwata Fumio—all to be
associated later with other patriotic societies. Okawa and Kita,
however, came to have a difference of views. In his book Kita had
attacked the privileged position of the South Manchurian Railway; of which Okawa was an employee. Okawa, to whom chauvinism was more important than state socialism, was by no means
ready to go all the way with Kita in his opposition to the great
capitalists. Fairly soon the two quarrelled, fundamentally on the
same issue that divided, as we have seen, Uesugi and Takabatake.
The outcome was Okawa's resignation from the *Yuzonsha*, in
1923. Shortly afterwards the society broke up.

In the sphere of action the *Yuzonsha* accomplished nothing.[2]
But as a parent body it had some significance; for its leading
members fathered a number of Right-wing groups, such as the
Gyochisha and *Kinkei Gakuin*, which will be mentioned in this
chapter. In the *Yuzonsha* were gathered the advocates of the
"renovation" movement which was to become in the next decade
the agitation for a "Showa Restoration".

The immediate successor of the defunct *Yuzonsha* was the
Gyochisha ("The Activist Society"), founded by Okawa early in
1925. He was joined by several associates from the *Yuzonsha*,
notably Mitsukawa Kametaro, Shimizu Gionosuke and Yasuoka
Masaatsu. Mitsukawa led the nationalist social group in the
Gyochisha. Shimizu appears to have been primarily an adventurer,
a man of action; later he was to become a noted terrorist. Yasuoka,
a man of considerable intelligence, was chiefly concerned with the

[1] From Proceedings (12th September, 1934) of Okawa's trial before the Tokyo
Court of Appeal, cited in the I.M.T.F.E. record, Transcript, pp. 15561–89.
[2] In 1921 the *Yuzonsha* organised an attack on the house of Prince Saionji's
adopted son. But this affair was a fiasco.

promotion of "spiritual education" among intellectuals.[1] Baron Kikuchi of the *Kinno Remmei*—he was, also, a member of the *Kokuhonsha*—joined the *Gyochisha*. Other important members were Nakatani Takeo (one of Uesugi's students), Nishida Zei, Kasagi Yoshiaki and Kita Reikichi, brother of Kita Ikki.[2] The society claimed a membership of over three thousand. Branches were set up in Osaka and Kyoto.

Among the aims professed by the *Gyochisha* was one that deserves some attention here. This was the creation of a "Restoration Japan" (*Ishin Nippon*). In course of time this became the concept of the *Showa Ishin*, or "Showa Restoration". Twentieth-century Japanese looked back on the Meiji Restoration (*Meiji Ishin*) of 1868 as a period when Japan had undergone an experience of purification, shedding the dross of the antiquated Shogunate; when the feudal hierarchy, by the voluntary surrender of its privileges, had restored to the Emperor his rightful status and powers. This over-simplified and historically invalid appreciation of the events forming the Meiji Restoration gave rise to the idea—advocated, as we have seen, by Takabatake and other national socialists—that the great capitalists should surrender, or "restore", their powers to the Emperor. But not only capitalists were expected to make the surrender. The political parties in the Diet would have to show the same readiness for self-sacrifice. The Constitution, as a gift from Meiji *Tenno*, might be sacrosanct. The Minseito and Seiyukai were not. Thus it came about that when the Regent on the death of his father, Taisho *Tenno*, chose *Showa* ("Enlightened Peace") as the title for the new reign, the movement for an *Ishin Nippon*, "Restoration Japan", had as its goal the realisation of a "Showa Restoration".[3]

In 1927 there occurred the almost inevitable split in the *Gyochisha*. Okawa became involved in a dispute with Kita Ikki,

---

[1] For example under the aegis of, or in close intimacy with, the *Gyochisha* were several Right-wing student groups. Among them were the *Hi-no-kai* and *Shukokai* at Tokyo Imperial University, the *Shionokai* (Waseda), *Yuko Gakkai* (Kyoto Imperial University) and *Noroshino kai* (Hokkaido Imperial University). The *Gyochisha* also supported two private training schools, the *Daigaku Ryo* and *Shakai Kyoiku Kenkyujo*.

[2] For a fuller list, *vide* Appendix I.

[3] Another ideal cherished by the *Gyochisha* was the achievement of liberty, equality and fraternity in the spheres, respectively, of personal life, politics and economics.

with whom, of course, he had quarrelled in the days of the *Yuzonsha*. Some members of the *Gyochisha* took Kita's side in the matter. Nishida Zei withdrew from the society, and he was followed by Yasuoka, Nakatani, Mitsukawa, Shimizu and Kasagi.[1]

However, the society remained in existence under Okawa's leadership until the beginning of 1932, when it was formally dissolved, only to be revived at once under a different name, the *Jimmukai*.

A significant feature of the *Gyochisha* was the fact that it was the first society to establish a working relationship with the younger officers of the army.

The older societies, such as the *Genyosha* and *Kokuryukai*, had acted as overseas intelligence agencies for the army, but they did not enter into any close or lasting alliance with elements of the army in order to effect political reforms at home. Later on such bodies as the *Kokusuikai* and other societies of the *kyokaku* type had no special relations with any part of the armed forces, even if here and there a retired general or admiral might be found among the directors of these organisations. There were, it is true, nationalist societies such as the *Butokukai*—exalting the military arts—which had naturally close ties with the army; and there were others, such as the *Zaigo Gunjinkai*, which were under the army's control. But at least until the Manchurian Incident of 1931 these were more concerned with the general promotion of nationalist ethics than with any active participation in politics. The military societies founded before the First World War were, on the whole, conservative, and mindful of the injunction, in the Meiji Rescript to Soldiers and Sailors, against meddling in politics.[2]

However, after the First World War the Japanese army underwent a process of change, particularly with regard to the social composition of its officers, which made it less united, less assured of its high position in the state, and more sensitive to economic forces and currents of opinion. After Yamagata's death in 1922 the traditional supremacy of the Choshu Clan began to wane.

[1] The dispute between Okawa and Kita arose, this time it seems, over an issue unconnected with matters of nationalist aims or policies. The dispute appears to have been on a purely personal issue.

[2] "Neither be led astray by prevailing opinions nor meddle with politics." Imperial Rescript to Soldiers and Sailors, 1882.

The Choshu Clan had already been much criticised by officers who did not enjoy the privilege of belonging to it and who felt that Clan favouritism was blocking their promotion. Within a few years it was no longer possible to speak of the highest ranks in the army being entirely dominated by the Choshu or any other Clan. Yamagata's death left a vacuum which was filled by no single individual, but rather by a succession of rival cliques. As a result discipline throughout the army began to fall below the strict standard that had prevailed under the autocratic Yamagata and his Clan subordinates. This tendency, indeed, was perceptible even before Yamagata died. The Siberian Expedition, which tied large forces overseas for the greater part of four years, on the one hand gave young officers—such as Itagaki and Doihara—their training in political intrigue and, on the other, exposed the rank and file, in an adventure in which there was little fighting but a great deal of politics, to a variety of influences ranging from conservative democracy to bolshevism.

After the First World War there was an increase in the number of junior officers coming from the lower middle class. By 1927 it was estimated that thirty per cent of the junior officers were the sons of petty landowners and small shopkeepers, and that army officers as a whole could be divided into three strata—those in the highest ranks, conservative and still often from the Choshu Clan; the middle grade, generally with a samurai background; and the junior ranks, with a growing proportion of officers with no samurai family tradition but, for that reason, sympathetic with the problems of peasant farmers and small tradesmen.[1]

It was with the middle stratum that Okawa became intimate, especially after 1927, the year in which the *Gyochisha* suffered the defections that have been described. At that time all except the very junior ranks of the officer corps were inclined to be suspicious of Kita Ikki. Okawa became more acceptable to his army friends after his further breach with Kita. It appears that Okawa formed close relations with Major-General Koiso, of General Staff Headquarters, Colonel Okamura, of the Ministry of War, and Colonels Kawamoto and Itagaki, of the Kwantung Army General Staff at Port Arthur.[2] He now began to give

[1] Hillis Lory, *op. cit.*, p. 158.
[2] Tokyo Court of Appeal Proceedings (cited).

occasional lectures at General Staff Headquarters.[1] He was able to keep in continuous touch with Colonel Kawamoto and, later, with Colonel Itagaki, as his duties with the South Manchurian Railway Company took him to Manchuria for periods of two to six months every year.

Okawa's association with Colonel Kawamoto Daisaku poses an interesting question: Was Okawa concerned in any way with the preparations for the assassination of Chang Tso-lin, in the summer of 1928? It is now known that Colonel Kawamoto planned this affair, which was to have been the first move in a *coup d'état* designed to bring Manchuria under direct Japanese control.[2] Okawa's connection with this incident is not known. But the probability is that he was aware of the plot. He was on close terms with Kawamoto; and, as his later history was to make clear, he was an arch-intriguer, with a leaning towards terrorism. He evinced the strongest dislike of the questions asked in the Diet about Chang's death. He described them as "most reprehensible".[3]

Kawamoto's Manchurian plot in 1928 can be called the first notable indication of terrorist activity on the part of the younger officers of the modern Japanese army. But in the previous year, in

[1] Tokyo Court of Appeal Proceedings (cited).

[2] The murder of Marshal Chang Tso-lin on 4th June, 1928, was referred to at the time, by the Japanese, as "A Grave Manchurian Incident". Everybody suspected that the Japanese Kwantung Army had been implicated in the bombing attack on Chang's train near Mukden, but there was, as one authority has put it, "a notable absence of reliable news in the Japanese press" (Takeuchi, *op. cit.*, p. 257). The Premier, General Tanaka Giichi, did his best to persuade members of the Diet not to ask questions about the incident. But the Minseito, in opposition, could not neglect this chance of embarrassing the government. Many questions were asked in the Diet. None were answered. It became known that an investigation had been carried out, and a report drawn up by the Ministry of War. But it was never published.

In 1946 evidence at the Tokyo Trial confirmed that Chang Tso-lin had been killed by the Japanese, that the assassination had been planned by Colonel Kawamoto, Senior Staff Officer of the Kwantung Army, without the knowledge of his superior officers, the Chief of Staff and the Commander-in-Chief (Lt.-Gen. Muraoka). Kawamoto's plot envisaged two operations—the killing of Chang by the use of explosives, and the muster of Japanese troops in Mukden who were to open fire on Chang's bodyguard, thus precipitating hostilities with the Chinese and providing the Japanese with an excuse for an advance beyond the Railway Zone. The second operation was halted by the Chief of Staff as soon as he knew of it. I.M.T.F.E. Transcript, pp. 1818–20; 1951–3.

[3] Tokyo Court of Appeal Proceedings (cited).

Japan itself, there had been an ominous development. This was the formation of a small, clandestine group known as the *Kinkikai* ("The Society of the Imperial Flag"). Its membership did not exceed two hundred, but these included junior officers from General Staff Headquarters; and of these the most noteworthy were Lieutenants Hashimoto Kingoro and Nemoto Hiroshi.[1] This society planned a future *coup d'état*, to be called the *kinki kakumei*, or "Revolution of the Imperial Flag". However, in September, 1927, Hashimoto Kingoro—possibly because his superiors suspected him of political agitation—was posted to Turkey as military attaché. He returned to Japan in January, 1930, and was again appointed to General Staff Headquarters in Tokyo. The proposed *kinki kakumei coup d'état* was nearly carried out in October, 1931, as will be described in the next chapter.

It will be recalled that Kita Ikki quarrelled with Okawa. Thereafter Kita's devoted follower and associate was Nishida Zei. He was an army lieutenant on the reserve list, and he was the main link between Kita and junior army officers of a radical turn of mind. On this point an official Japanese source comments:

> After the dissolution of the *Yuzonsha* Kita and Nishida co-operated, and as Nishida was a reservist they had access to officers on active service and to the Reservists' Association [*Zaigo Gunjinkai*]. Gradually they influenced the Japanese army.[2]

One of the joint activities of Kita and Nishida was the organisation of a small terrorist group, about which very little is known. This was the *Hakurokai* ("The Society of the White Wolf"). Its interest lies in the fact that, like the *Kinkikai*, it included serving officers of the army among its members.[3]

These small groups had no power or prestige of their own. In the nineteen-twenties they were but obscure manifestations of an unrest that was to become, later, the constant preoccupation of

[1] The founder of the society was a civilian, Endo Tomoshiro; but the whole flavour of the *Kinkikai* was in fact military.

[2] *Uyoku Undo no Gensei* (cited), Ch. 2, p. 11.

[3] The *Hakurokai* was, in a sense, an offshoot from the *Yuzonsha*, being founded after the latter's dissolution in 1923. It continued until 1928, when it was dissolved after the arrest and imprisonment of one of its leaders, Tatsukawa Ryunosuke, for fraud. After the dissolution Nishida formed various changing cliques of terrorist plotters. Two were the *Seiko Domei* ("Starlight League"), composed of officers and reservists, and the *Shirinsha* ("Samurai Society").

Japanese governments. In 1931 Marquis Kido noted in his diary: "The plan to break down the existing political party system by means of a *coup d'état*, and to administer national affairs under dictatorship, has been made secretly ever since 1927." [1] Yet until that date, 1931, or shortly before it military participation in ultra-nationalist, terrorist activities seemed no more than a transient symptom of the discontent of a few socially dissatisfied and economically harassed junior officers. But the influence of Kita's ideas was to ferment, like yeast, unseen. Its product was the *gunji ikki*, the military insurrections, of the nineteen-thirties. [2]

iv

While these terrorist cliques were being formed there grew up a nationalist association—or, more correctly, a study circle —which, like the *Kokuhonsha*, attracted men of some importance in public life. This was the *Kinkei Gakuin* ("The Institute of the Golden Pheasant") of Yasuoka Masaatsu and Count Sakai Tadamasa.

It may be remembered that Yasuoka was a leading figure in both the *Yuzonsha* and *Gyochisha*. In the days of the *Yuzonsha* he became acquainted with Sakai, a young man of wealth and aristocratic birth who had been private secretary to the Ministers of Justice and Railways. Yasuoka had a reputation as a scholar of

[1] I.M.T.F.E. Exhibit 179—M Transcript, p. 1940. Kido, in this extract, described a discussion he had with Prince Konoye and others—in October, 1931—on the subject of army machinations. They were all disturbed at the trend of events.

[2] This may be the place to note the existence of some other terrorist societies of the nineteen-twenties, such as the *Taikosha* ("Great Deeds Association") created by Shimizu Gionosuke. It was to play a part in the still-born "March Conspiracy", to be described in the next chapter. There was, also, the *Aikokusha* ("Patriotic Society"), formed by Iwata Fumio in 1928, an organisation, composed in the main of students, which achieved brief but lurid notoriety in November, 1930. Sagoya Tomeo, the youth who attacked and inflicted mortal wounds on Premier Hamaguchi, had lodgings in the *Aikokusha* office in Tokyo. Mention, too, should be made of the *Daitosha* ("Imperial Throne Society") of Yoshida Saburo, a Fukuoka man and a great admirer of Toyama Mitsuru. Members of the *Daitosha* were bound by a "blood alliance", a sworn compact sealed with the members' blood. Yoshida established a branch of this society among Japanese residents in Dairen.

Confucian studies and he was invited to give lectures on Confucius in the *Kinkei-en,* or "Golden Pheasant garden", of Sakai's home. At first these lectures were attended chiefly by friends of the Sakai family, particularly Goto Fumio, then in charge of the Home Ministry Police Bureau, and Yuki Toyotaro, vice-president of the Yasuda Bank and a director of the Mitsui Trust Company and the Nippon Yusen shipping line.

In 1926 those attending the lectures formed themselves into the *Kinkei Gakuin.* The circle began to widen; and with Count Sakai's backing Yasuoka was able to attract a number of government officials to the *Kinkei Gakuin.* He also drew the interest, for a time at least, of some politically minded army officers. They included Nemoto Hiroshi, already mentioned in the context of the *Kinkikai,* and Shigeto Chiaki, who was to be a noted troublemaker in the army during the next decade. But the most influential military member of the *Kinkei Gakuin* was Major-General Tatekawa Yoshitsugu. At General Staff Headquarters in Tokyo he was in command of the Sections in which Nemoto and Shigeto were employed. Tatekawa, as we shall see, was to be an important figure behind the scenes in 1931, especially during the first stages of the Manchurian Incident. Yasuoka's lectures were attended, also, by Shimizu Gionosuke (of the *Taikosha*), and, at various times between 1930 and 1932, by the young naval officers, Koga Kiyoshi and Yamagishi Hiroshi, who took part in the murder of Premier Inukai on 15th May, 1932.

But such terrorist elements were hardly typical of the *Kinkei Gakuin,* which was concerned to revitalise the higher administrative machinery of the state, at the expense of the political parties, rather than to advocate such radical ideas as a "Showa Restoration". The *Kinkei Gakuin,* it might be said, provided a refresher course in advanced nationalism for ambitious civil servants. It had a lasting influence among the rising class of officials—especially in the Ministries of Home Affairs and Education—constituting the "new bureaucracy" (*shin kanryo-ha*) of the nineteen-thirties.

Yasuoka lectured on the texts and ethics of Confucius; but these were linked with a study of the Japanese "national structure" (*kokutai*). The subjects were indeed complementary. Confucian filial piety was enlarged to include the supreme moral

47

obligation of loyalty to the Imperial House. Only Japan, it was claimed, could demonstrate this larger concept of filial piety. Official approval of this doctrine was given by the Ministry of Education some years later, in the *Kokutai No Hongi*. The relevant passage deserves to be quoted.

In China, too, importance is laid on filial duty, they say that it is the source of a thousand deeds. In India, too, gratitude to parents is taught. But their filial piety is not of a kind related to or based on the nation. Filial piety is a characteristic of Oriental morals; and it is in its convergence with loyalty that we find a characteristic of our national morals, and this is a factor without parallel in the world. . . . Indeed [the concept of] loyalty and filial piety as one is the flower of our national entity [*kokutai*], and is the cardinal point of our people's morals. Hence, the *kokutai* forms not only the foundation of morality but of all branches of such things as politics, economics, and industry. Accordingly the great Way of loyalty and filial piety as one must be made manifest in all practical fields of these national activities and in the people's lives.[1]

Yasuoka's influence was felt especially in the powerful world of the higher bureaucracy and great business houses, drawing them away from the Diet political parties. In January, 1932, he helped to form the *Kokuikai* ("The Society for the Maintenance of the National Prestige"). This was a direct descendant of the *Kinkei Gakuin*. It had three directors, Prince Konoye, Viscount Okabe Nagakage, and Count Sakai. Among the members were Hirota Koki, General Araki Sadao, and Yoshida Shigeru. Indeed both the *Kinkei Gakuin* and the *Kokuikai* contained members who held, or were to hold, high positions in administrative life.[2]

[1] *Kokutai No Hongi, op. cit.*, pp. 91–2.
[2] For example, of the *Kinkei Gakuin*—Goto was to be Home Minister, 1934–6, and Minister without Portfolio, 1943–4; Yuki Toyotaro was to be Finance Minister for a time in 1937 and afterwards Governor of the Bank of Japan. Other members of the *Kinkei Gakuin* were Ikeda Kiyoshi (Governor of Osaka, 1937–9, and, later, Inspector-General of Police in Malaya), Otsuka Koreyoshi (Governor of Tochigi Prefecture and, later, in charge of civil administration in Malaya), Tsugita Daisaburo (Governor of Ibaragi Prefecture, Vice-Home Minister, 1931). All the above, except Yuki, were Home Ministry bureaucrats.

Of the *Kokuikai*—Hirota and Konoye were future Premiers. (The writer has been unable to discover whether Yoshida Shigeru was the future Premier or the less famous man with the same name, a strong nationalist, who was a Minister of State in a wartime cabinet.) Viscount Okabe became Minister of Education,

Although it is true that Yasuoka moved away from the more extreme of his former associates in the *Gyochisha*, such as Nishida Zei, he did not cut himself off entirely from ultra-nationalist terrorists and conspirators. As will be noticed later on, eminently respectable public men—Prince Konoye is one example—were not always averse to maintaining some form of contact with radical, often disreputable, nationalist adventurers. Yasuoka's position may be likened to that of a bridge connecting elements of the higher bureaucracy with the leaders of the unofficial Right-wing movement.[1]

The general high calibre of its members gave the *Kinkei Gakuin* an intellectual standing that set it apart from the general run of nationalist societies during this period. For most of them, in so far as their ideological content was of importance, were distinguished rather by the strength of their emotional convictions than by the quality of their rational thought.

It would be unprofitable, no doubt, to deal at further length with the nationalist organisations of the nineteen-twenties, the most outstanding of which have now received some mention. But if only to round out the picture a word must be said about two associations patronised in the main by retired army officers. These were Lieutenant-General Araki's *Kodogikai* and Major-General Kita Inosuke's *Kaikokai*.

The former had been founded in 1918 by a group of Seiyukai politicians headed by Noda Utaro. Some years later, however, Lieutenant-General Araki became its chief director. He was on the active list and it may be thought surprising that he was able to take a leading part in a nationalist organisation. But it could be claimed that the *Kodogikai* was non-political. It existed to propagate the concept of *Kodo* ("The Imperial Way"). This might be summed up as mystical patriotism based on extreme veneration of the Throne, rejection of foreign ideas, and preparation for the expansion of the Japanese race in Asia. Araki was to become famous for his speeches extolling *Kodo*; and

1943–4. Other members of the *Kokuikai* were Yuzawa Michio (Home Minister, 1942–3), Fujii Sadenobu (Finance Minister, 1934) and Kosaka Masayasu (Governor of Tokyo, 1932).

[1] For example, Yasuoka was associated with Toyama Mitsuru in the *Dai Nippon Junkokukai* ("Japan Sacrificial Society"), established in 1925. It claimed a membership of 10,000.

although he did not invent the word it will always be associated with his name. The *Kodogikai* flourished. It had a membership of over forty thousand, and it helped greatly to promote Araki's reputation, in the army and among the public at large, as a disinterested advocate of militant chauvinism.

The *Kaikokai* ("The Expansion Society") was founded by Major-General Kita, a retired officer, in 1924. Its aim was the propagation of nationalist thought among ex-servicemen. It had hoped, at first, to expand into a body having an influence beyond military circles, and to exercise "judicious guidance on society in general".[1] This object it failed to accomplish; and its numerical strength remained inconsiderable.[2]

V

The organisations that have been the subject of this chapter were the chief elements in the nationalist movement between 1919 and 1930.[3] But they were by no means dominant as a force in

[1] Shigematsu, *op. cit.*, supplement, p. 5.

[2] Approximately 2,500 in 1936. Apart from Kita Inosuke the leading figures in the *Kaikokai* were Gen. Oi (retired) and Gen. Shiba Goro (retired). The occasion for the establishment of the society was an address by Maj.-Gen. Kita at the Army Club, Tokyo. In the course of his speech he said: "While I see world conditions deteriorate I cannot stand idle. We, the first and second reservists and officers on the retired list, must resist the permeation of dangerous thoughts. I propose that we devote the rest of our lives to awakening public sentiment, to perfecting education, and to substantiating national defence." *Ibid.*

The Army Club was a social body, with its headquarters in Tokyo and branches at the various divisional centres throughout Japan and Korea. Both active and reserve officers belonged to it almost automatically. It was known, in Japanese, as the *Kaikosha*. This might suggest some close identity with the *Kaikokai*. But the words are, in fact, unrelated except in sound. Different ideographs are used. *Kaikosha* (Army Club) is translatable literally as "Companionship Society".

[3] One or two fairly small associations, not mentioned hitherto, deserve a footnote here. For example, there was the *Sekishinsha* ("True Hearts' Society"), created by Uchida Ryohei and centred mainly in North China, with a membership made up of Japanese residents in North China and Manchuria. Uchida made fantastic claims for its total membership, which in fact was only a few hundred. This society had a connection with an eccentric Shinto sect in Japan known as *Omotokyo* ("The Great Source Religion"). A word on this sect is in order.

Omotokyo was founded by a farmer's wife, in the Kyoto district, who believed herself to be the mouthpiece of one of the ancient national deities. As she was supposed, before 1914, to have foretold the outbreak of the First World War,

Japanese political life; for during those eleven years the influence of relatively liberal Court advisers, of large financial and business houses interested in world commerce, and of a limited but vocal parliamentary system managed to keep the nationalist societies in their place, on the periphery of real power.

Yet it cannot be denied that strong nationalist feeling had a religious sanction for the mass of the Japanese people. Accordingly, the professions of all nationalist groups—their avowals of loyalty to the Emperor, their demand for the extirpation of foreign ideas, their appeals for greater armaments and for the advance of Japanese power overseas, their attacks on party and capitalist interests—could not fail to make some impression on a technologically progressive but politically undeveloped race such as the Japanese.

Still, the Japanese are a law-abiding people. The violence advocated by some societies never attracted widespread support, however much popular sympathy there might be for individual nationalist fanatics, once they had become leading figures in a *cause célébre*.

However, from 1930 onwards economic conditions grew more severe—in 1932 there was famine in eight prefectures of Northern Japan—and the apostles of violence made more converts. The element of revolutionary feeling, always present in certain sections

---

her reputation, in her own locality at least, was considerable. After she died the cult of her memory flourished, thanks to the efforts of her son-in-law, Deguchi Wanisaburo. Indeed such veneration was paid to her memory that the police suspected the adherents of *Omotokyo* of the crime of *lèse majesté*. (Her elaborate tomb, said to resemble the Imperial Mausoleum at Momoyama, was destroyed by the police on the orders of the Home Ministry.) Deguchi was arrested and spent a period in custody. After his release he joined forces with the *Sekishinsha*, and his home near Kyoto became the society's office in Japan.

Other societies that might be mentioned were the *Nippon Kokuminto* ("Japan Nationalist Society"), *Tokai Remmei* ("East Ocean League"), and the *Kyushin Aikoku Rodosha Remmei* ("The Radical Patriotic Workers' League").

The *Nippon Kokuminto*, formed in 1929, was headed by Terade Ineshiro and Yawata Hakudo, a member of the *Kokuryukai*. Uchida and Toyama were counsellors. Nishida Zei was a member; so was Konuma Tadashi, who was to assassinate Finance Minister Inouye in February, 1932. The *Tokai Remmei* was an offshoot of the *Gyochisha*. The *Kyushin Aikoku Rodosha Remmei*, headed by Tsukui Tatsuo, was in fact made up of a coterie of the national socialist followers of Takabatake. This society was at first known as the *Taishusha* ("Mass Society") and under this name played a part in the March Incident described in the next chapter.

of the nationalist movement after 1918, became much stronger. This of course was never directed against the apex of the social order, namely the Imperial Throne.[1] None the less it threatened the existing status of the Emperor. For those who advocated a "Showa Restoration" usually had in mind a military dictatorship, in which the Emperor in fact, if not in name, would be no more than a sacred puppet, occupying a position very similar to that prepared by the Kwantung Army for the ruler of Manchukuo. So far as the Emperor was concerned such would be the very reverse of "restoration", in the sense in which the term was used for describing what happened in 1868.

Personally the Emperor was scientifically minded, and liberal in his political views. In this he was abetted by the surviving *genro*, Prince Saionji, and by those who held the key advisory positions of Lord Keeper of the Privy Seal and Grand Chamberlain. Broadly speaking, the party cabinets, especially the Minseito cabinet, supported the Emperor's leaning towards a comparatively liberal interpretation of the Constitution. They were in fact loyal to the Emperor, as he was. Most nationalists were loyal only to their idea of what he ought to be.

1930, no less than 1931, was a year of destiny for Japan. For on 1st October, 1930, after prolonged and bitter arguments in the highest circles of government the London Naval Treaty was finally approved by the Privy Council.[2] This represented a triumph for the *genro*, for the Hamaguchi cabinet, and for moderate opinion within the Navy Ministry. But it was a pyrrhic victory.

In spite of the support accorded it by such liberal newspapers as the Tokyo *Asahi* the Agreement could not be called popular. On the one hand nationalist bodies, particularly the reservists' associations, held meetings of protest against the Treaty throughout the spring and summer of 1930; on the other, no real efforts seem to have been made, by organisations interested in peace, to counteract this agitation. Indeed, as a Japanese scholar has put it, there was "an apprehension commonly felt among people that to

[1] One is not concerned here, of course, with the revolutionary activities of the communists. These were directed against the Throne as an institution and as personified by the reigning Emperor.

[2] Takeuchi, *op. cit.* Ch. XXV, discussed the Treaty very fully.

express even a doubt regarding the wisdom of the navy stand might be interpreted as 'disrupting the united opinion of the country' ".[1] The Reed-Matsudaira compromise, which involved minor concessions by Japan, was looked upon by nationalist opinion as a humiliating surrender to Anglo-American pressure. Furthermore, it was known that the Chief of the Naval General Staff was irreconcilably opposed to the Treaty, and that there had been disagreement within the naval delegation to London. Above all, there was the fact—profoundly alarming to militarist opinion —that a civilian Premier, temporarily in charge of the Navy Ministry, succeeded in obtaining the Emperor's approval of an agreement on the vital matter of defence, against the wishes of the Chief of the Naval General Staff, the traditional adviser to the Throne on the exercise of the Supreme Command at sea.

The legal aspects of the controversy scarcely concern us. But among constitutional lawyers there was sufficient support for Admiral Kato Kanji (Chief of the Naval General Staff) to make the Privy Council hesitate for over two months before recommending that the Treaty be ratified. Needless to say nationalist opinion generally was outraged.

The most formidable reaction to this success of the Hamaguchi cabinet came from the army, which regarded the defeat of the Naval Staff as an ominous precedent. As winter approached, the Army General Staff drew up the first plans for operations in Manchuria in 1931. These and other indications of future trouble are among the subjects of the next chapter. For the end of 1930 was the dividing line between an intermittent but noticeable move towards effective parliamentary government and the trend in the direction of military control of all the organs of the state. Up to that time the nationalists hardly occupied the centre of the stage. But when the curtain rose on 1931 they made a bid to act the leading part in the drama.

[1] *Ibid.*, p. 304.

4

THE MANCHURIAN INCIDENT

i

AT the end of September, 1930, a group of some twenty-five army officers in Tokyo formed a society for discussing ways and means of carrying out a programme of national reorganisation—in other words, the elimination of the parliamentary political parties, the overthrow of the Minseito cabinet and the establishment of military government in fact, if not in name. The group was headed by Hashimoto Kingoro, now a lieutenant-colonel in General Staff Headquarters, Lieutenant-Colonel Sakata Yoshiro, of the Ministry of War, and Lieutenant-Colonel Higuchi Kiichiro, of the headquarters of the Guards Division.[1] These officers did not at first call their society by any particular name, and its existence was kept secret; but by the beginning of 1931 it was known as the *Sakurakai*, or "The Society of the Cherry".

The *sakura*, the Japanese cherry, was an apt symbol. Japanese fondness for the cherry, especially when in bloom, is based on more than purely aesthetic admiration. The fact that the blossoms fall from the bough, after only a few days' glory, at the first strong gust of wind has long reminded the Japanese of the essence of the samurai code—the readiness to die at a moment's notice, if need be. This flower, then, had its place in the martial cult.[2]

---

[1] *Shukugun ni kansuru iken sho* ("Views on the Housecleaning of the Army"), p. 76. This was a pamphlet written in July, 1935, by Capt. Muranaka Koji and Lt. Isobe Senichi while under suspension for participation in the "Military Academy Incident" of November, 1934. For circulating this pamphlet both officers were dismissed the service in August, 1935. The pamphlet was preserved among War Ministry documents and was evidently accepted as reliable as to facts; for much of it was embodied in the Home Ministry Police Bureau record of the *Sakurakai* which was quoted in evidence (Exhibit 183, on 9th July, 1946) at I.M.T.F.E.

[2] There is the well-known saying: *Hana wa sakura hito wa bushi* ("As is the cherry among the flowers, so stands the warrior among men").

The membership of the *Sakurakai*—at its greatest—was just over a hundred. Those qualified to join were "army officers on the active list, of the rank of lieutenant-colonel and below, having a deep concern for national reorganisation and with no private axe to grind".[1] Twenty-nine of the members were from General Staff Headquarters; nine belonged to the Ministry of War; and about forty were instructors or students at various military academies or specialised technical military schools. The remainder belonged to *Kempei* (military police) Headquarters and to Guards and infantry regiments stationed in the Tokyo area.[2]

From the start the *Sakurakai* planned to use force of arms, if necessary, for the achievement of its aims. Nevertheless, on this score there appears to have been some disagreement. It has been explained in this way:—

> There was, first, a faction which worked for *destruction*—which thought that in order to build one must first destroy. Not a few supported these opinions, for they sounded rather virile. Then, secondly, there was a faction which thought *construction* to be the more important and paid high regard to the careful preparation of plans and theories etc, hoping to avoid destructive measures as far as possible. This faction had few supporters; for its opinions sounded rather tame. Thirdly, there was a neutral faction, made up of opportunists, with many supporters. Disputes between these three schools of thought occurred from the very beginning. The first faction was the most vigorous and apt to have the greatest influence on the members as a whole.[3]

This militant faction was led by Hashimoto, Sakata, Nemoto (now a lieutenant-colonel) and Captain Cho Isamu.[4] Behind them was Major-General Tatekawa, usually credited with the initial founding of the *Sakurakai*, although, by reason of his rank, he could not be a member.

Tatekawa was in charge of the Second Division of General Staff Headquarters. Lieutenant-Colonels Hashimoto and Nemoto

---

[1] *Shukugun ni kansuru Ikensho*. In May, 1931, there were 105 members.
[2] This is based on a list of members from War Ministry Records now in the National Diet Library, Tokyo. For the complete list, *vide* Appendix I (*infra*).
[3] *Shukugun . . . op. cit.*
[4] Cho, by an alternative reading, is sometimes called Osa; e.g. by Prof. Yanaga, *op. cit.*

were his immediate subordinates, and were in charge of the Russian and Chinese Sections respectively. We have seen that both these officers belonged to the *Kinkikai*, and that Tatekawa and Nemoto attended meetings of the *Kinkei Gakuin*.[1] The Second Division of General Staff Headquarters was possibly the most important single organ of the Japanese Army; for its function was the planning of military operations. It shared, of course, with other departments of the General Staff the privilege of the Supreme Command, which in title only belonged to the Emperor.

Every year the Second Division made an appreciation of the strategic military situation of Japan, having, of course, potential enemy nations in mind. In 1930, however, the work of the department concentrated on problems relating to Manchuria and Mongolia—on preparing, in other words, the ground for the Manchurian Incident.

At the same time these planners believed that a necessary prelude to operations in Manchuria was the drastic reorganisation of the government at home. It was realised that the Minseito cabinet —particularly with Shidehara in charge of Foreign Affairs— would be very reluctant to pursue a forward policy, risking war with China and a breach with the League of Nations, in order to secure Japanese control of Manchuria. A *coup d'état* at home would be the best means of overcoming civilian resistance to military plans abroad, of ensuring that the army, unlike the navy in 1930, was ultimately independent of cabinet control. The alternative to a *coup d'état* at home would be military action in the field, with the strongest pressure on the Tokyo government to accept the *fait accompli*.

Opinions in favour of national reorganisation gained ground. General Staff H.Q. devoted a good deal of time to this question. Participants in this extraordinary preoccupation were many members of the *Sakurakai* among the leading persons in the Second Division, such as Lieutenant-Colonel Hashimoto and Lieutenant-Colonel Nemoto. The opinions of the *Sakurakai* were partly adopted in the General Staff study of that year [1930].[2]

Although the activities of the *Sakurakai*, like those of the General Staff, were a closely guarded secret, rumours started to circulate among people in the government and outside. At the first cabinet meeting of 1931, early in January, the Home Minister, Adachi, asked the Minister of War, General Ugaki Issei, whether it was true that officers on active service were discussing politics, and whether a secret society had been formed among them.[1] Ugaki's reply is not known. But whatever it was he could hardly plead complete ignorance of these developments; for, as we shall see, he was soon to find himself in the thick of a conspiracy involving the *Sakurakai* as well as other elements in the army.

At about the same time as Adachi raised the question in the cabinet, the Chief of the Metropolitan Police Board was sufficiently worried to pay a special call on the Commandant of the Tokyo *Kempei* in order to ask this interesting question:

> Is it true that among army officers, especially those of the Central Army Headquarters, a society called the Imperial Flag Communist Party was recently formed, and that it means to bring about a revolution in the name of the Emperor?[2]

Again the answer is not known. But the question suggests a natural confusion between the *Kinkikai*, that small group which had for many months plotted a *Kinki Kakumei* ("Revolution of the Imperial Flag"), and the *Sakurakai*, which indeed had only recently been formed.

It was in January, 1931, that plans for action were first drafted and seriously discussed by the militant faction of the *Sakurakai*. A committee of eleven, including Hashimoto, Sakata, Nemoto and Cho, was formed to prepare the details of a *coup d'état*. A central figure had to be chosen to head the new military government envisaged as a result of the revolutionary *coup*. General Ugaki was selected to fill this rôle. Ugaki had let it be known that he was ready to head a government as soon as the existing cabinet resigned; which was considered to be in the near future, in view of the impending death of the Premier, Hamaguchi, who had been gravely wounded by Sagoya of the *Aikokusha* some weeks earlier.

In the middle of January Ugaki called a conference of officers, to discuss the issues of internal reorganisation and reform. Those present were Lieutenant-General Sugiyama (Vice-Minister of

[1] *Ibid.*   [2] *Ibid.*

War), Lieutenant-General Ninomiya (Vice-Chief of the General Staff), Major-General Koiso (Chief of the Military Affairs Bureau at the Ministry of War), Major-General Tatekawa, Lieutenant-Colonel Hashimoto and Lieutenant-Colonel Nemoto.[1]

It is possible that Ugaki's intention was to sound the views of known politically-minded and nationalist officers, rather than to commit himself to participation in a conspiracy. However, this conference marked the beginning of what was to be called the "March Incident".

Even to-day it is difficult to reconstruct the details of this plot; which, in the words of one authority, "has become very obscure".[2] At the time its existence was kept so secret that it was not until August—four months later—that the *genro*, Prince Saionji, was able to hear any reliable news of the affair.[3]

It seems that following the conference with Ugaki Lieutenant-General Ninomiya (Vice-Chief of the General Staff) told Hashimoto to draw up a plan for national "reconstruction". This was to be submitted to Ugaki. However, Hashimoto and his fellow conspirators were suspicious—rightly so, as it turned out—of the sincerity of Ugaki's intentions. They also lacked complete confidence in Ninomiya. They decided, therefore, to prepare two plans. One would contain details of the proposed *coup d'état*, having the final aims of the *Sakurakai* in view. The other would be a mere camouflage plan, implying that the *Sakurakai* was a relatively innocuous society, holding very restrained and moderate opinions.[4]

There is a strong probability that it was this bogus plan which was submitted to Ugaki. This would account for his apparent readiness to be associated with the conspiracy at the outset.[5]

The real plan constituted a very serious threat to existing

---

[1] *Shukugun* . . . (cited).

[2] Maruyama, *Nippon Fasshizmu, op. cit.*, p. 107.

[3] Saionji's faithful secretary, Baron Harada Kumao, through his wide contacts and indefatigable enquiries, pieced together much of the story, and reported it to his chief. Saionji's comment was: "I've heard about these things vaguely, but I did not know it was so serious. It comes as a great surprise." Saionji-Harada Memoirs, Part I, Ch. 5 (8th August, 1931).

[4] *Shukugun* . . . (cited).

[5] The precise nature of this cover plan is not known. It probably contained many recommendations for political reform along nationalist lines, but omitted all reference to the use of violent measures.

authority, even though—in the words of an officer at the time—"it was all very simple and childish".[1]

It envisaged the co-operation of civilian nationalists, headed by Okawa Shumei and Shimizu Gionosuke. The latter, it will be remembered, was then the leader of the small *Taikosha*. Tsukui's *Taishusha* was also caught up in the conspiracy. The rôle of these civilian elements was vital to the success of the plot.

The *Taishusha* was to collect a mob of some ten thousand, composed of its own members and of vagrants from the poor districts of Tokyo. This mob would assemble in two large parties in the parks at Ueno and Shiba, and would then march on the Diet —which was in session at this period. At the same time Shimizu's *Taikosha* was to provide *kesshitai* ("death-defying bands") to carry out bomb attacks on the offices of the Minseito and Seiyukai, and on the official residence of the Prime Minister.

To meet this situation the Tokyo garrison would be mobilised and a cordon of troops placed round the Diet. Martial law would be imposed; and on the pretext of restoring order a military government, headed by Ugaki, would take office. The new government would dissolve the Diet and then take steps to carry out the home and foreign policies desired by the *Sakurakai* and its civilian supporters, such as Okawa. The date chosen for the *coup* was 20th March.

Undoubtedly Hashimoto was the principal ringleader among the middle-grade officers involved in the plot.[2] He was the liaison officer between his own group and more senior officers;[3] and with Lieutenant-Colonel Shigeto he was the chief link between the military and civilian conspirators.[4]

Among the senior officers the leading figures were Major-

---

[1] Lt.-Col. Marquis Inouye Saburo (of the Ministry of War) to Harada. Inouye was on intimate terms with Lt.-Col. Suzuki Teiichi, Maj.-Gen. Koiso's right-hand man at the War Ministry Military Affairs Bureau. Suzuki told Inouye the story of the affair after it was all over. Saionji-Harada Memoirs, Part I, Ch. 5 (8th August, 1931). Inouye was one of Harada's chief friends in the army.

[2] Hashimoto (before his trial at I.M.T.F.E.) claimed to have been the sole founder of the *Sakurakai*. "The sole founder of this society is myself; the others were more or less in the capacity of assistants or as secretaries, etc."—Excerpt from the Interrogation of Hashimoto (17th January–18th February, 1946), quoted in I.M.T.F.E. Transcript, p. 15675.

[3] *Shukugun . . .* , *op. cit.*

[4] Memoirs, *op. cit.*, Pt. I, Ch. 5.

Generals Tatekawa and Koiso; to whom must be added Lieutenant-General Ninomiya.[1] The Vice-Minister of War, Lieutenant-General Sugiyama, was aware of the conspiracy and probably regarded it with favour.[2]

It is important to note that, while the driving force came from such men as Hashimoto and Shigeto, the so-called "March Incident" was in great part a senior officers' plot. This fact was to have serious repercussions later on.

Preparations continued steadily during February, meetings being held at Shigeto's house in Tokyo.[3] For his part in the conspiracy Okawa needed both money and explosives; and for this purpose Hashimoto and his group expected to be able to make use of secret service funds. However, they were unable to obtain the amount they had hoped for.[4] Okawa, therefore, had to look for extra funds elsewhere.

He was fortunate enough to acquire the sum of no less than 200,000 *yen*—about £11,000 at the contemporary rate of exchange—from a nationalist sympathiser, Marquis Tokugawa Yoshichika. This money was divided between Okawa and Shimizu. Tokugawa was told that he would be made Minister of the Imperial Household if the *coup d'état* succeeded.[5]

At the same time a number of small bombs was obtained from General Staff Headquarters for Shimizu and his followers in the *Taikosha*.[6] The bombs were to be used in the attacks on the Premier's house and on the offices of the two main political parties.

The success of the entire undertaking depended, of course, on the co-operation of the senior officers involved—particularly Ugaki, the Minister of War. At about this time, however, Ugaki seems to have considered an offer from the Seiyukai to become

[1] Memoirs, *op. cit.*, Pt. I, Ch. 5.

[2] In evidence at I.M.T.F.E. Ugaki said that Sugiyama, as well as Koiso, had recommended the conspiracy to him. I.M.T.F.E. Transcript, p. 1631.

[3] An extract from Kido's Diary even suggests that the War Minister's official residence was the place where plans were drafted. I.M.T.F.E. Exhibit 179–B. Transcript, p. 1934.

[4] *Shukugun . . . , op. cit.*

[5] Memoirs, *op. cit.*, Pt. III, Ch. 49 (30th July, 1932).

[6] These bombs do not appear to have been very formidable. They were of a type used in military manœuvres. Accounts vary as to the number handed over to Shimizu; but the figure of thirty bombs, on the evidence of both Kido's Diary and the Saionji-Harada Memoirs, may perhaps be accepted.

its president. It may be supposed that he saw himself as a soldier-premier, binding, in the manner of General Tanaka Giichi, the more conservative and nationalist of the two parties to a close association with the army and its policies. The record of Ugaki's public life—from the time when, as Minister in the Kato cabinet, he reduced the strength of the army to his tenure of the Foreign Ministry in 1938—shows little tendency on his part towards sympathy with extreme nationalists of any school. He was, in truth, an adroit politician, with some genius for the methods of negotiation and compromise. One would imagine that he would have little heart for the drastic, risky business of a *coup d'état*.

Whatever the reason may have been, some time at the end of February or the beginning of March General Ugaki firmly opposed the conspiracy. Afterwards Koiso put it abroad that Ugaki had at first supported the plot and then entirely changed his mind.[1] This may be the truth of the matter; although Ugaki's own version was that as soon as he was aware of the real nature of the plot he was against it.[2] This suggests that he was deceived by the camouflage plan put up by Hashimoto.

It is apparent, at least, that Ugaki disliked Okawa, whom he met in the middle of February, as a result of persistent entreaties on the part of Koiso.[3] According to Ugaki, Okawa at this meeting informed him of the plan to create popular disturbances on 20th March, leading to clashes with the police, and asked for an assurance that troops would not be used too rigorously in their suppression, the riots being of course no more than a device to enable the army to effect its *coup d'état*. Ugaki replied that such a request was quite outrageous, that it was the duty of the army, if called out, to deal firmly with any breaches of the peace. Okawa then spoke of the desirability of having a military government, headed by Ugaki. The latter retorted that as Minister of War it was improper for him to countenance such an idea. "At present",

---

[1] Prof. Yanaga (*op. cit.*, p. 498) accepts the theory that Ugaki changed his mind as a result of "an overture made by party leaders to back him for the premiership". Koiso was much disappointed at the "change of mind". Memoirs, Part II, Ch. 17 (10th November, 1931).

[2] *Ibid.* Also suggested by his evidence at I.M.T.F.E., Transcript, p. 1631.

[3] The meeting occurred on 11th February. Ugaki told Harada that previously he had on several occasions refused Koiso's strong plea that he should meet Okawa. Memoirs, Part II, Ch. 17 (10th November, 1931).

he said, "it is absurd for me to think of becoming Prime Minister."
Okawa went on to ask for Ugaki's help in obtaining bombs. This
request, too, was curtly refused.[1]

If such indeed was the whole truth regarding that meeting it is
strange that Ugaki should have consented to have further communication with Okawa. But in fact—as he admitted at a later
date—he met Okawa on two or three further occasions.[2]

Okawa's version—as put forward at his trial in 1934—was that
Ugaki had told him that Japan could never achieve her destiny
overseas with the sort of Diet then in session. Okawa alleged that
Ugaki had strongly attacked the political parties.[3]

At his first meeting with Okawa, on 11th February, Ugaki
may indeed have expressed some distaste for the Diet and the
parties. For on 3rd February Shidehara, Foreign Minister and
acting Premier, had declared in a committee of the House of
Representatives that the London Naval Treaty did not endanger
national defence, since it had been ratified by the Emperor. The
remark created a sensation. The Seiyukai seized on it at once as
being an effort by the government to justify the controversial
Treaty by dragging the Throne into politics. Such was the uproar
that there was a virtual cessation of Diet proceedings until
12th February, when Shidehara retracted his "slip of the tongue".
The episode served to strengthen nationalist contempt for the
Minseito government; and the confusion in the Lower House—
no less than Shidehara's indiscretion—may well have shocked
Ugaki.

On 6th March Okawa sent Ugaki a remarkable letter, begging
him to "accomplish the great work of the Showa Renovation".
He urged Ugaki not to have dealings with either of the political
parties. He went on:

> Every mouth has cursed parliamentary politics. Vital now is the
> need for a great man of ability to overcome disorder and vindicate
> righteousness. . . . The time is just ahead for a grand mission to
> descend on you. Please cherish self-respect, make up your mind to
> be the head of a group accomplishing a great work, and do not be

[1] Memoirs, Part II, Ch. 17 (10th November, 1931).
[2] Part III, Ch. 49 (30th July, 1932).
[3] Tokyo Court of Appeal Proceedings (cited). I.M.T.F.E. Transcript,
pp. 15561–89.

induced by such common people as men of the political parties to become their leader. Our comrades have been awaiting the approach of this day for thirteen years. Now, when I see that the life of the whole Empire is pending on your decision, I feel awe-inspired.[1]

Perhaps this letter alarmed Ugaki; for, if he had not done so already, he now urged Sugiyama and Koiso to cancel all plans for a *coup d'état*. In his evidence at the Tokyo Trial (I.M.T.F.E.) Ugaki said that the letter from Okawa made it clear that the conspiracy was "not a mere ordinary plot", but something more drastic.[2] According to Ugaki both Sugiyama and Koiso gave every appearance of agreeing with his opposition to the plot. "I concluded that they heartily accepted my advice—to abandon the plot—for they raised no objection. I had impressed on them that whenever they held views contrary to my own they were free to express them."[3]

Koiso seems to have undertaken the task of cancelling all the preparations that had been made. On 8th March he ordered a reluctant and disgruntled Shimizu to return the bombs. These were handed back to Hashimoto at a rendezvous in Shimbashi, Tokyo, and were returned to General Staff Headquarters in a civilian motor lorry. However, twelve bombs were found to be missing.[4]

In dealing with Okawa Koiso appears to have adopted the policy of breaking the bad news by degrees. This is suggested by Okawa's own words.

Major-General Koiso, taking charge of everything, told me that, since there would be the danger of being discovered if too many fussed about it [the conspiracy], we should pretend to have suspended it and that I should represent the civilians and he the army. However, though he went ahead with the plan Koiso later decided to suspend it. Hence it was decided to cancel it; and that was the end of the March Incident.[5]

Other officers, besides Ugaki, in sympathy with the aims of the

---

[1] I.M.T.F.E. Transcript, pp. 1610–13. The reference to Okawa's comrades "awaiting the approach of this day for thirteen years" relates, perhaps, to Okawa's debut as an active nationalist in 1919 (when he organised the *Rosokai*).
[2] I.M.T.F.E. Transcript, p. 1627.   [3] *Ibid.*
[4] Memoirs, *op. cit.*, Part III, Ch. 49 (30th July, 1932).
[5] Tokyo Court of Appeal Proceedings, *op. cit.*

plot felt that it would be unwise to put it into execution. At some date in February or March Ninomiya, Koiso and Tatekawa invited Lieutenant-Colonel Suzuki Teiichi, Koiso's subordinate in the Military Affairs Bureau of the Ministry of War, to a confidential discussion at Ugaki's official residence.[1] Ugaki himself was not present. The three senior officers, using the Minister of War's authority, told Suzuki to see Mori Kaku, an important member of the Seiyukai, and tell him, in strict secrecy, of the details of the plot. "Since the situation is such [as we have explained] and it is an order of the Minister you must go to Mori Kaku of the Seiyukai, explain the situation and arrange it so that the Diet will be thrown into confusion." [2]

In other words, the conspirators thought it prudent to have, as it were, a fifth-column inside the Diet. The immediate interest of the Seiyukai would be served by the overthrow of the Minseito government, particularly if there was any likelihood of an Ugaki cabinet, for this might include some Seiyukai members. Exactly what was meant by having the Diet "thrown into confusion" can only be guessed. The plan may have been for a representative of the army on 20th March, while disturbances raged outside, to appear on the floor of the Lower House and advise the members that, having lost the confidence of the nation, they should go into dissolution pending the establishment of a new government under a national leader such as Ugaki.[3] If such action was planned then the co-operation of the Seiyukai would be of great value.

However, Lieutenant-Colonel Suzuki refused to carry out this order. The illegality of the affair may have disturbed him. Or, more probably, he thought the risk of failure to be excessive. For if the *coup d'état* were to fall short of complete success the army's prestige might suffer irreparable harm.[4]

It must have been an acrimonious conference. Still, Suzuki carried his point, "and the incident ended there".[5] To what extent Suzuki's arguments influenced Ugaki's final decision is not known. Others supported Suzuki's stand, even though they had

[1] Memoirs, *op. cit.*, Part I, Ch. 5 (8th August, 1931).   [2] *Ibid.*
[3] Yanaga, *op. cit.*, p. 498.
[4] Marquis Kido speaks of the plan to approach Mori Kaku being given up "on the advice of Suzuki who entertained fears for the sake of the army". Kido Diary (13th July, 1931), I.M.T.F.E. Exhibit 179–B, Transcript, p. 1934.
[5] Memoirs, *op. cit.*, Part I, Ch. 5 (8th August, 1931).

at first lent encouragement to the conspiracy.[1] There was, after all, much to be said for caution, for achieving nationalist ambitions by more subtle, legal means. The hazards of a *coup d'état* would, of course, jeopardise personal careers. That this aspect of the matter was fully appreciated may be gathered from a verbal instruction by a senior officer—he is unidentified—to Hashimoto and the *Sakurakai*.

> Do not allow officers under the rank of captain to participate in this affair; because if it is unsuccessful they would have to be punished, and in such circumstances we cannot guarantee their families' livelihood. Therefore participants should be limited to those of the rank of major and above.[2]

The ringleaders among the middle-grade officers, particularly Hashimoto and Shigeto, and the civilians such as Okawa and Shimizu, were indignant when they heard that the conspiracy was to be abandoned. So far from moderating their ardour, the caution of their seniors only made the younger officers more determined to work for the overthrow of constituted authority and for "direct action" in Manchuria. Their indiscipline was aggravated. It now became increasingly difficult for such generals as Sugiyama or Koiso to restrain their juniors; and it was almost beyond their power, now, to control such organisations as the *Sakurakai*. As Marquis Kido noted at the time: "The brains of the army cannot check this kind of association, because they themselves planned such plots [as the March Incident]." [3]

Of course there could be no question of taking disciplinary action against Hashimoto and the *Sakurakai* on the score of their participation in the March Conspiracy. Indiscipline was tacitly condoned. Much blame, no doubt, was laid on the shoulders of Ugaki. Six years later deferred payment for his equivocal rôle in the plot was extracted from him, when the army declined to recommend any active service officer as War Minister in the cabinet which he was trying to form.[4]

[1] E.g. Col. Okamura Yasuji, of the War Ministry, and Col. Nagata Tetsuzan. Yanaga, *op. cit.*, p. 498.
[2] *Shukugun . . .*, *op. cit.* This instruction is said to have "greatly moved" Hashimoto. One or two exceptions to the ruling were allowed, notably Capt. Cho Isamu.
[3] Kido Diary (13th July, 1931) (cited).
[4] In his affidavit at I.M.T.F.E. Ugaki said that his refusal to co-operate with

In April Ugaki was appointed Governor-General of Korea, an office he was to hold for the next five years.[1] His successor as Minister of War was General Minami Jiro, who—if he is to be believed—only heard of the March Incident after he had taken office.[2] He was to hold the ring at home in Japan when, six months later, the Kwantung Army embarked on its Manchurian adventure. He appears to have used the March Incident, and the threat of its recurrence, as a form of blackmail against the new Premier, Wakatsuki. In August the Premier questioned him regarding the Incident. Minami countered by saying that the blame lay with the political parties. Later, at the Ministry of War, Minami told Koiso and Colonel Nagata:

> The other day the Prime Minister questioned me regarding the matter of the *coup d'état*, and I threatened him by admitting that such things happen, due to the faults of the political parties of today, and that perhaps such Incidents may occur again.[3]

It was at this juncture—between the abortive March Conspiracy and the all too successful Manchurian Incident—that those forces in Japan, including the Emperor and his highest Court advisers, who wanted to keep the nation on the road of peaceful, constitutional progress might have rallied their strength, and, by taking bold measures against military and civilian nationalists, changed the course of Japanese history. But a tragic caution, bred of the very moderation which was their striking virtue, repeatedly inhibited the action which, like that of Hamaguchi against recalcitrant naval chiefs in 1930, might have asserted the supremacy of Throne and cabinet against one powerful element in the armed services.[4]

the conspirators was one prime reason why he was unable to find a War Minister in 1937. I.M.T.F.E. Transcript, p. 1609.

[1] Ugaki's rôle in the March Conspiracy puzzled many of his contemporaries. Makino, for example, said: "It is very odd that he stopped only at the advice of Lt.-Col. Suzuki." Memoirs, Part I, Ch. 7.

[2] "I heard about it ten days after I assumed office, and I immediately asked former Minister Ugaki about it, and he answered that such was not the case. He gave a very vague answer" (Minami to Wakatsuki). Memoirs, Part I, Ch. 8 (27th August, 1931).

[3] *Ibid.*, Part I, Ch. 9 (4th September, 1931).

[4] On 10th June, 1930, the cabinet relieved of their posts the Vice-Chief of the Naval General Staff, Suetsugu, and the Vice-Minister of the Navy, Yamanashi.

Saionji, as we have seen, did not learn any details of the March Incident until the beginning of August. But he declared then that the Emperor must be put in possession of the facts. This task should be entrusted to Count Makino, the Lord Keeper of the Privy Seal. And measures would have to be taken against the ringleaders in the plot.

> You must confer with Konoye and Kido [Saionji told Harada] and after careful consideration we must have these so-called chief instigators, the Vice-Chief of the General Staff [Ninomiya], the Chief of the Military Affairs Bureau [Koiso] and Major-General Tatekawa resign when there is an opportunity. Just how should we have them resign? If these three should resign then General Ugaki would also be forced to resign from his post as Governor-General of Korea. We must do something.[1]

Yet in the end nothing was done. Harada suggested, and the *genro* agreed, that the matter should be reported to Prince Chichibu, the Emperor's brother, by Konoye. Both Harada and Kido would speak to the Lord Keeper of the Privy Seal, who would then inform the Emperor.[2]

On his return to Tokyo Harada invited Konoye and Kido to dinner.[3] He also invited Colonel Inouye, of the Ministry of War,

Immediately afterwards Admiral Kato, Chief of the Naval General Staff, resigned. Takeuchi, *op. cit.*, p. 316. Actually Yamanashi's view was much more temperate than that of Kato and Suetsugu. His removal from office was no doubt a sop to the Naval Staff faction supporting Suetsugu.

[1] Memoirs, *op. cit.*, Part I, Ch. 5 (8th August, 1931). Saionji's reference to the possibility of a forced resignation on the part of Ugaki was expressive of regret rather than hope. For both Saionji and Harada thought well of Ugaki. The problem was—how to remove people like Koiso and Tatekawa without affecting Ugaki's position as Governor-General of Korea.

[2] Prince Chichibu would have to be informed because he was, at the time, Heir Presumptive to the Throne; and he had made the army his career. Kido was at this time Chief Secretary to the Lord Keeper.

[3] In his old age Saionji resided at his villa at Okitsu, on the coast, some seventy miles by rail from Tokyo. His visits to the capital were rare and always interpreted by the public as having important political significance. For they were usually undertaken in connection with some crisis, such as a change of government, when his advice to the Throne was called for.

Harada lived in Tokyo, in order to keep in touch with affairs. He visited his chief at regular weekly intervals. In Tokyo he was the *genro's* mouthpiece, and his eyes and ears. His life appears to have been a round of interviews, lunches, dinners and telephone conversations with the most prominent men in official and business circles. Tojo at I.M.T.F.E. called him a "rumour broker". Nothing

who, as we have seen, was on close terms with Harada and had told him the story of the March Incident.

They discussed Saionji's proposals. Inouye argued that, for the time being at least, Ninomiya, Koiso and Tatekawa should not be made to resign. It might stir up trouble in the army. Although the three senior officers had certainly countenanced the activities of the *Sakurakai* Inouye believed that they now regretted having done so. Further, many officers were in favour of having the *Sakurakai* dissolved. So the wisest course—said Inouye—would be to let the army handle the problem in its own way. Wait a little, and all would be well. Inouye went on: "We should delay informing the Emperor and Princes Chichibu and Kanin for a while; we should watch the trend of the times carefully and not commit any rash acts." Harada and the others agreed.[1]

This caution was the tragedy of all temperate and liberal opinion in Japan. Give us time, said army "moderates" to civilian ministers and Court officials, and we shall have extremists under control. Give us time, said Japanese diplomats to foreign governments, and the pendulum will swing back from militant nationalism to common sense and moderation. It was a recurring theme, from 1931 almost to the eve of Pearl Harbour.

The meeting which has just been described took place on 12th August. Dark clouds were already gathering over the Manchurian horizon.[2] On 6th August the Minister of War, in a speech at a conference of divisional commanders, had openly attacked the Foreign Minister's conciliatory policy towards China. The conference had been a remarkable gathering of general officers; for in addition to the divisional commanders the Chief

could be further from the truth. Harada took pains to verify every doubtful report which reached his ears.

[1] Memoirs, *op. cit.*, Part I, Ch. 6 (17th August, 1931). Kanin was an Imperial Prince and a Field-Marshal. He became Chief of the General Staff in December, 1931.

[2] In June Capt. Nakamura, an officer on an intelligence mission, was killed by Chinese in Manchuria. This (and other incidents) was made the most of by the Kwantung Army to increase the tension between Japan and the Chinese authorities. Tani Masayuki (then Chief of the Asia Bureau of the Foreign Ministry) told Harada, in August: "The army is trying to use the killing of Capt. Nakamura, by enlarging the importance of the whole affair, as a lever for the solution of matters in Manchuria and Mongolia. It is very troublesome." Memoirs, Part I, Ch. 8 (27th August, 1931).

of the General Staff, Kanaya, the Inspector-General of Military Training, Muto, and three supreme war councillors had been present. Minami's speech caused a sensation and was, indeed, criticised next day by several newspapers. It now seemed very possible that the army would press for strong measures in Manchuria, or might take the matter into its own hands.[1]

It was not only Shidehara's "weak" diplomacy that perturbed Minami. There was also irritating pressure from the Ministry of Finance for a reduction in the army budget; and there was the unwelcome prospect of the World Disarmament Conference. This was not due to be held until February, 1932; but the government was already asking the army to choose its delegates to the Conference.

Nevertheless, preparations for the Manchurian *coup* had been made well before August. We have seen that during the winter of 1930-1 the General Staff made plans for possible operations in Manchuria. The March Conspiracy intended to organise a political revolution at home as a prelude to adventures abroad. After Ugaki had "betrayed" the cause of the Showa Restoration the ultra-nationalists in the army, more specially the *Sakurakai*, were determined to gain control of Manchuria as soon as possible.

In May the extreme nationalist clique in General Staff Headquarters—the section chiefs of the Second Division such as Hashimoto and Shigeto—held an important conference at which Okawa was present.[2] It was decided that military action should be taken against Chang Hsueh-liang, unless of course he agreed to fall in with all Japanese demands. This conference—though the details of its proceedings are not known—may well have initiated the whole series of practical measures and preparations which bore fruit in the very quick and efficient occupation of Mukden, Changchun, Kirin and other towns in Manchuria four months later.

[1] The veteran liberal member of the House of Representatives, Ozaki Yukio, and six others, belonging to "The Citizens' Disarmament League", very courageously wrote a letter to Minami, on 6th August, taking him to task for his speech. It was phrased with what seems astonishing boldness. "There is no doubt", wrote Ozaki, "that your acts are an indisputable violation of Article 103 of the Military Criminal Code. . . . Is it Your Excellency's intention to pit the divisional commanders against the politicians in a dispute over the rights and wrongs in a political argument?" I.M.T.F.E. Exhibit 184, Transcript, pp. 2193-4.
[2] Tokyo Court of Appeal Proceedings (cited).

The plans made by relatively junior section chiefs carried great weight with responsible senior officers; for the latter were susceptible to pressure, to advice on matters of policy, from their subordinates. Repeatedly, from 1931 onwards, decisions and action were taken by strictly irresponsible officers, thereby committing their seniors to approval of a sometimes unwelcome *fait accompli*.[1] On this point the following remarks, by a Japanese scholar, are of great interest.

The holders of supreme authority in Japan were actually robots of, or figureheads manipulated by, their subordinates who in turn were at the mercy of militarists serving overseas and Right-wing adventurers and hoodlums co-operating with the militarists. . . . Bodies with imposing names—for example, Imperial Conferences, Liaison Conferences between Imperial Headquarters and the government, Supreme War Council—met several times before and during the war [Pacific War] to determine the supreme national policy. But those who read the minutes of these meetings will be all the more surprised at the stupidity of their discussions. The fact of the matter is that the agenda for discussion was prepared in advance by *secretaries* of these meetings who were Chiefs of the Military and Naval Affairs Bureau of the service departments. . . . Furthermore, these "secretaries" were assisted by some members of the Military or Naval Affairs Bureau and members of the Army General Staff Headquarters who drafted essential plans. The Military and Naval Bureaux were frequently visited by fanatical Rightists and megalomaniacs . . . who indulged in big talk with field officers, in these Bureaux, who were members of officialdom on the surface but were hoodlums in their hearts.[2]

The same writer continues:

It is a well-known fact that, parallel with the march of anti-democratic and autocratic ideology centred round the military, the paradoxical phenomenon of "insubordination" or "usurpation of power" within the military groups became more and more noticeable.[3]

[1] Of course this manœuvre was not invariably successful. For example, Hashimoto was disciplined and his action repudiated after he had shelled H.M.S. *Ladybird* on the Yangtse at the end of 1937.

[2] Maruyama Masao, "A Study of the Minds of the Rulers of a Militarist Nation", *Choryu*, May, 1949. The writer is indebted to Dr. E. H. Norman for this article as translated. [3] *Ibid.*

At the end of June a conference on a higher level took place. The Minister of War invited eight directors of the South Manchurian Railway—including the newly appointed President, Count Uchida—to discuss matters with him and Kanaya, Chief of the General Staff. The Vice-Chief of Staff, Ninomiya, was also present.

Then, at a cabinet meeting early in July, Koiso—the Minister of War being away—spoke on the situation in Manchuria. But, as Harada records, "his opinions were easily demolished by Inouye Junnosuke [Minister of Finance] and by the Foreign Minister".[1]

At the beginning of August Minami delivered his address, already referred to, criticising the government's foreign policy in the presence of nearly every senior commander in the army.

All these talks and meetings were clear indications to those in touch with public affairs that some kind of military action in Manchuria was imminent. A further sign of approaching trouble was provided by the activities of Okawa.

He was now director of the South Manchurian Railway East Asia Research Institute, which by 1931 had become largely independent of the Railway Company's control.[2] The East Asia Research Institute was primarily an organisation for gathering economic intelligence. But it was a valuable auxiliary, in the field of purely military intelligence and propaganda, to the Kwantung Army, whose *Tokumu Kikan*, or "Special Service Organ", at Mukden was responsible for intelligence operations. From 18th August the *Tokumu Kikan* was under command of Colonel Doihara Kenji, an expert on Chinese affairs. One would have supposed that at this time Okawa, too, would be in Manchuria.

However, in such time as he could spare from that devoted to hatching revolutionary plots with young staff officers in Tokyo Okawa was engaged in a programme of lecture tours. In these the army did not participate openly. Okawa had begun his series

---

[1] Memoirs, *op. cit.*, Part I, Ch. 1 (13th July, 1931). "Consequently Koiso's talk at the cabinet meeting was the subject of ridicule. The object of his lecture was not realised. Koiso returned to the Ministry of War greatly disappointed." *Ibid.*

[2] The Institute was founded by Goto Shimpei, first President of the S.M.R. It became technically an independent foundation—though endowed by the S.M.R.—in 1931, with Okawa as its chief director.

of lectures as early as May, 1929, and his army friends assured him that if they co-operated with him it would be interpreted by the public as evidence of militarism and imperialism; in which case the lectures would lose much of their value.[1]

The lectures stressed the importance of Manchuria as Japan's "life line" and the need for Japanese expansion in that region. The lectures were accompanied by propaganda films. Between May, 1929, and the outbreak of hostilities at Mukden on 18th September, 1931, Okawa spoke in eighty-five different towns and villages throughout the country. After the Mukden Incident Okawa packed lectures at fifty places into a space of two months, this time with the full and open co-operation of General Staff Headquarters. Undoubtedly these lectures whipped up support for army intervention in Manchuria, and stimulated the popular belief that control of Manchuria would be the answer to Japan's economic problems.[2]

During 1931 Okawa was also busily employed in the field of nationalist party organisation. In March he and the *Gyochisha* joined the *Kokuryukai* groups and the followers of Takabatake in a loosely knit confederation with the cumbersome title of *Zen Nippon Aikokusha Kyodo Toso Kyogi Kai* ("The All Japan Patriots' Joint Struggle Society"). Its slogans were: "Imperial ownership of all property"; "abolition of the parliamentary system"; "establishment of the *Tenno* system"; "destruction of capitalism and the achievement of revolution under the Imperial Flag".[3]

This confederation was one of several attempts in 1931 and succeeding years to unify the nationalist societies, to amalgamate them in one body with a single programme. None of these attempts succeeded. There never was one all-embracing nationalist mass movement comparable with the N.S.D.A.P. in Germany.

[1] Tokyo Court of Appeal Proceedings (cited).

[2] Okawa himself declared: "Leaving aside rare instances, the lectures drew full houses everywhere." A rather fulsome statement, submitted by his lawyer on Okawa's behalf at his trial in 1934, read: "Once Okawa mounted the lecture platform the whole audience would always show their enthusiasm to brave fire and water for their motherland, being aroused by Okawa's fulminations. Thus, once the beacon was ignited at Mukden, the people united and dared the government and its hesitation, and finally accomplished the great work of establishing Manchukuo." *Ibid.*, I.M.T.F.E. Transcript, p. 15591.

[3] *Uyoku Undo No Gensei* (cited), p. 13.

But from early in 1931 there was a tendency towards unification on the part of the larger Japanese nationalist bodies; though the various efforts at amalgamation were short-lived. After the outbreak of the Manchurian Incident extreme nationalism was no longer a minority movement; for as time went by it attracted increasing favour from official authority—notably the police. Greater prestige encouraged nationalist organisations to join forces, even temporarily.[1]

The confederation of the Okawa, Toyama and Takabatake groups was known, by an abbreviation of its lengthy title, as *Nikkyo*. Its managing director was Tsukui Tatsuo, of the *Takabatake-ha*, who of course was one of those involved in the March Conspiracy—his own *Taishusha* having been allotted the task of organising the mobs of rioters who were to demonstrate against the Diet.

The fact that it was in March that *Nikkyo* was formed suggests that leading nationalists, such as Toyama, who were not directly connected with the preparations for the *coup d'état* thought it prudent to ally themselves with Okawa and Tsukui, who would hold positions of great influence if the Showa Restoration was achieved.[2]

The *Nikkyo* was not the only important attempt made before the Manchurian Incident to effect a union of nationalist societies. At the end of June the *Kokuryukai*, through its Osaka branch, established the *Dai Nippon Seisanto* ("The Japan Production Society").

This organisation will be discussed more fully later on. It is

---

[1] "The Right-wing movement, which once appeared to be a heroic movement, changed its aspect and gradually became a national movement having its main support in the public." *Ibid.*
"Scattered Right-wing groups showed a clear tendency towards becoming a more unified political force, and the fascist movement shed its negative character as a reaction to the Left." Maruyama, *Nippon Fasshizmu, op. cit.*, p. 47.

[2] There is some evidence that Hiranuma had reached, by March, a close understanding with the army conspirators. In August Hiranuma called on Saionji and talked at length about Ugaki. Saionji refused to be drawn, and pretended that he knew nothing of the March Incident. Later he said: "It seemed as if Hiranuma knew a great deal about the matter." Memoirs, *op. cit.*, Part I, Ch. 7 (21st August, 1931). Early in September Harada dined with Ninomiya and gathered that he was a frequent visitor to Hiranuma's house. "I felt", Harada records, "that this indicated a very intimate relationship between the army and the *Kokuhonsha*." *Ibid.*, Part I, Ch. 10 (14th September, 1931).

sufficient here to remark that in essence the *Seisanto* was a modernised version of the old *Kokuryukai*. Based at first in the Kansai, it moved its headquarters to Tokyo in October. It soon secured the allegiance of a number of nationalist groups, most of them in Kansai.[1]

These manœuvres by Okawa and by veteran nationalists like Toyama were preparatory to the expected hostilities in Manchuria, which, it was rightly anticipated, would create a surge of patriotic feeling throughout Japan and so sweep away the evils identified with cautious diplomacy, parliamentary interference with the armed services and all influences related to Western democratic thought.

But everything hung on the success of military action in Manchuria. That such action would soon be taken became increasingly apparent. In the words of a contemporary figure, "the Mukden Incident did not take any enlightened official in Japan by surprise".[2]

ii

The main story of the Manchurian Incident is too well known to warrant a description here. However, since the end of the Pacific War new light on some of the events has been cast by evidence at I.M.T.F.E. and by other material not available—to the Lytton Commission, for example—at the time. Accordingly, on the basis of this fuller knowledge it is possible to make a fair reconstruction of what actually happened in Mukden on the night of 18th–19th September, 1931. It reveals a tale of deceit and intrigue in which the main parties are the Kwantung Army on the one hand and the Tokyo government, with its consular representatives, on the other.

Several weeks before the first shots were fired the Foreign Ministry in Tokyo had reports from its consular officers that the

[1] Among the better known societies—of Tokyo—to be linked with the *Seisanto* was Nishida's *Kokuminto*.

[2] Affidavit by Admiral Okada Keisuke, I.M.T.F.E. Transcript, p. 1822.

Kwantung Army, or a section of it, was getting ready for war with the Chinese. The main agents in transmitting these warnings to the home government were the Consul-General at Mukden, Hayashi, and his chief assistant, Morishima. They had the task of collecting intelligence not only about the Chinese, but also about the intentions and activities of the Kwantung Army. For between army and consular service in Manchuria there existed a profound rift. The latter, with the loyalty of bureaucrats to one who had risen from their ranks, tried to follow faithfully the policy of the Foreign Minister, Shidehara; a policy regarded by all shades of army opinion as weak and ineffectual. Apart, however, from the notorious clash of views and, it may be, of personalities between consular and army officers, it was not customary for the army overseas to reveal its plans to any civilian official, however important his position might be. As Ishihara Kanji—who played a leading part in the Kwantung Army's activities at this time—explained in evidence at the Tokyo Trial:

All the consuls need to know is that in case an Incident should break out the army would be ready to meet such an eventuality; and how the army would meet it was a question of strategy which the consuls did not need to know, and which, if divulged to them, would be one of the greatest sources for the leakage of military secrets.[1]

Thus diplomats and army officers worked along separate and not always parallel tracks; the one often spied on the other.

The first specific information actually mentioning the date on which hostilities might begin seems to have reached the Foreign Ministry on 15th September. Hayashi, the Consul-General, reported that a company commander near Mukden had stated that an important Incident might "break out" on the evening of 18th September.[2]

[1] I.M.T.F.E. Transcript, p. 22179.
[2] A certain Capt. Kawakami had been entrusted with the duty—if the order were given—of capturing the Mukden airfield. This officer was stationed at Fushun, about forty miles east of Mukden. Early in September (the exact date is uncertain) he called a meeting of the local Japanese police and *Zaigo Gunjinkai* and told them to consider what action they should take if an untoward event were to occur on September 18th. I.M.T.F.E. Transcript, pp. 2006, 18933 and 22141. Ishihara described Kawakami's reference to 18th September as pure coincidence. *Ibid.*, p. 22142.

Shidehara at once protested vigorously to the Minister of War. Now only a few days previously Minami had been warned personally by the Emperor "to take extra precautions regarding the actions of the army in Manchuria and Mongolia".[1]

Under pressure from two sides—from the Emperor and from Shidehara, who represented the majority view in the cabinet—Minami decided that at least he must make some show of restraining the Kwantung Army. Without delay he addressed an urgent and confidential letter to Lieutenant-General Honjo Shigeru, the Commander-in-Chief of the Kwantung Army, instructing him to cancel any plans that might have been made for a *coup d'état*. Minami decided to send the letter by hand of a special envoy.

For this extremely important rôle Minami chose none other than Major-General Tatekawa. The latter was informed of the purport of the letter, and was told that any "Incident" must be stopped at all costs.[2]

Tatekawa failed to carry out his mission. For on the evening of 18th September—the date of his arrival in Mukden—he made no effort to hand over his letter to Honjo or anyone else, but spent his time enjoying the diversions of a *machiai* (a geisha "meeting house"). "It seems to me," wrote Harada at the time, "that it was Tatekawa's plan to have the scheme [the Mukden *coup*] carried out before the Commander-in-Chief saw the confidential letter from the Minister of War."[3]

It happened that on the afternoon of 18th September Lieutenant-General Honjo was completing a tour of inspection at Liaoyang, on the South Manchurian Railway about fifty miles south of Mukden. With him was Lieutenant-General Tamon, in command of the 2nd Division at Liaoyang. The Chief of Staff, Kwantung Army—Major-General Miyake—was at Army Headquarters in Port Arthur.

Honjo told the divisional commander that the situation was very tense, and that anything might happen; if so, each unit should

---

[1] Memoirs, *op. cit.*, Part II, Ch. 11 (23rd September, 1931). The audience with the Emperor took place on 11th September.

[2] According to Tatekawa's own story to Maj.-Gen. Tanaka Ryukichi. I.M.T.F.E. Transcript, p. 2006.

[3] Memoirs, *op. cit.*, Part II, Ch. 11 (23rd September, 1931).

take spirited action without delay. In the event of an emergency immediate action was particularly essential.[1]

While he was in Liaoyang Honjo received a signal from his Chief of Staff at Port Arthur saying that Tatekawa was due to arrive in Mukden on the 18th and asking that either Colonel Itagaki, the Senior Staff Officer, or Lieutenant-Colonel Ishihara, Staff Officer in charge of Operations, be sent up to Mukden to meet him. Honjo sent Itagaki. He then left Liaoyang for Port Arthur.

Tatekawa, travelling by rail, arrived at Mukden incognito. The Japanese Consulate had not been advised of his coming, but the Consul-General became aware of it; and the news caused him some anxiety.[2]

Tatekawa was met by Itagaki, and the two had an intimate conversation together. What actually passed between them is not known. In evidence at the Tokyo Trial Itagaki maintained that nothing was said about the purpose of Tatekawa's journey—which is hard, if not impossible, to believe. According to Itagaki Tatekawa said that he was tired after his trip, and so they confined their talk to social pleasantries. Tatekawa did mention that his superiors in Tokyo were rather worried about the conduct of some of the younger officers, whereupon Itagaki told him that there was no need for anxiety on that score and that he would have time to hear him at length on that subject next day.[3]

Some time later Tatekawa found himself in a *machiai*, having been conducted there by Major Hanaya, of the Kwantung Army Staff, who did not remain long with his guest. At midnight the geisha were alarmed by the noise of heavy artillery fire. Tatekawa consoled them by saying that they had nothing to fear, as his presence in Mukden was well known to the Kwantung Army. He slept soundly until the morning, when Major Hanaya called and told him that the Incident had already occurred.[4]

---

[1] I.M.T.F.E. Transcript, p. 22155. Ishihara, in evidence, said: "We staff officers commented on Honjo's forcefulness, as Honjo had reputedly a very moderate temperament." *Ibid.*

[2] In affidavit evidence Morishima stated that news of Tatekawa's arrival in civilian clothes "created apprehension in my mind and I so reported to the Consul". Transcript, p. 3019.

[3] I.M.T.F.E. Transcript, p. 30261.

[4] *Ibid.*, p. 2007.

When Itagaki parted from Tatekawa on the night of the 18th he went to the office of the *Tokumu Kikan*, ("The Special Service Organ"). This was both an intelligence centre and the chief communications link between the military in Mukden and Kwantung Army Headquarters in Port Arthur. For practical purposes Colonel Itagaki was the senior responsible officer in Mukden that night. Being Senior Staff Officer to the Commander-in-Chief he was in a position to give orders to the regimental commander in Mukden, Colonel Hirata, a veteran of the Russo-Japanese War.[1]

Hostilities with the Chinese began between 10.30 and 11 p.m., following the alleged explosion on the railway. Whether at that time there was indeed a bomb explosion—damaging the line—for which either Chinese or Japanese were responsible remains, even now, a mystery. It is possible that the damage to the line was caused by shellfire from the heavy guns described in the next paragraph. It is at least certain that Colonel Hirata went to the *Tokumu Kikan*, reported that firing had started between his troops and the Chinese, and proposed that he should attack and capture the Walled City—a plan which received Itagaki's prompt approval. At the same time it was agreed that a determined assault should be made, with artillery support, on the North Barracks, the Mukden airfield and other objectives.

Now this gunfire—which had so alarmed the geisha in attendance on Tatekawa—was not confined to regimental and battalion artillery.[2] Heavier ordnance was brought into play. These were two guns of unusually large calibre—24 centimetres or approximately 9 inches—which had been mounted very secretly, little more than a week previously, in the Japanese military security zone at Mukden. One gun fired on the North Barracks, the other on the airfield.[3]

[1] "It was very reasonable that Col. Itagaki, understanding the firm instructions of the Commander-in-Chief (to the divisional commander at Liaoyang) should guide Col. Hirata to take speedy and appropriate action. Col. Hirata was a very brave officer, with a courageous reputation from the Russo-Japanese War, so I believe that even if Col. Itagaki had not given him any special guidance Hirata would have taken appropriate action himself. The actions of the two practically coincided" (Evidence of Gen. Ishihara Kanji). I.M.T.F.E. Transcript, p. 22155.

[2] The Japanese infantry division had regimental gun companies and battalion gun platoons.

[3] In evidence at I.M.T.F.E. Maj.-Gen. Tanaka Ryukichi testified that he heard

During the night the Japanese Consulate tried hard to arrange a truce. Shortly before 11 p.m.—soon after fighting had begun—Morishima called at the *Tokumu Kikan* and pleaded with Itagaki to order a cease-fire. But he was told not to interfere in matters affecting the right of the Supreme Command. When Morishima insisted that everything should be settled by peaceful negotiation, that this was indeed the view of the Japanese Government, Major Hanaya unsheathed his sword and said he would kill anyone who attempted to intervene in military affairs. This piece of braggadocio silenced Morishima, who returned to the Consulate.[1] His superior, Hayashi, the Consul-General, sent desperate telegrams to Shidehara, appealing for support; and he telephoned Itagaki, urging that fighting be stopped. "All such representations", said Morishima at the Tokyo Trial, "were communicated to the military to no avail; and the occupation of Mukden continued." [2]

Meanwhile at Kwantung Army Headquarters in Port Arthur important decisions were made. For the action taken in Mukden by Itagaki would have been hamstrung had it failed to secure the backing of the Commander-in-Chief and Chief of Staff.

The first report of the Incident reached Port Arthur about 11.30 p.m. on the 18th, when the duty officer had a telegram from the Mukden *Tokumu Kikan*, stating that an explosion had occurred on the railway north of the city. Few officers were at

about the use of these heavy guns from Itagaki, who stated that their installation had been first suggested by Col. Nagata Tetsuzan of the Ministry of War. The guns were placed in position on or about 10th September. The Japanese military zone at Mukden was of course strictly guarded; but, as a cover for any preparations which might have been observed, the digging of the gun-beds was described as well-boring operations. The guns had a maximum range of some fifteen miles (the point on the railway where the alleged bomb explosion occurred was within this range). Itagaki remarked that they had a striking effect on Chinese morale, and were an example of that element of surprise so essential in war. I.M.T.F.E. Transcript, pp. 1990–2. Ishihara's evidence corroborated, in the main, this account of the use of these guns. He suggested that their installation had been decided upon as early as 1929. *Ibid.*, p. 22206 *et seq.* Harada records that Itagaki, Ishihara and Hanaya boasted that the guns were ready by 25th July. Memoirs, *op. cit.*, Part II, Ch. 13 (2nd October, 1931).

[1] I.M.T.F.E. Transcript, pp. 3020–2.

[2] I.M.T.F.E. Transcript. An urgent telegram from Hayashi to Shidehara, dated 19th September, included the request that the government "take necessary steps immediately to stop the action of the army". Hayashi also telegraphed his view that the Incident was "wholly an action planned by the army". *Ibid.*, pp. 2178–9 (Exhibit 181).

Headquarters when this message arrived. Lieutenant-General Honjo and his Chief of Staff, Miyake, had retired to their own houses for the night.[1] The duty officer passed on the news by telephone to an Operations staff officer, Captain Katakura, who was in his quarters, preparing for rest after having attended a dinner party of his Military Academy classmates at the Yamato Hotel. Katakura went at once to the Headquarters, examined the signal from Mukden and then took it to the Chief of Staff. Miyake's reaction was to summon the whole staff to his house for an immediate conference.

This was soon concluded. It was decided that, Japanese patience being exhausted, mobilisation must be put into effect at once and the Chinese rigorously punished.

The staff then moved in a body to the Headquarters, where they were soon joined by the Commander-in-Chief and his A.D.C. General Honjo was informed of the staff decision and was asked to approve it.

It is said that for a few minutes Honjo meditated, with his eyes closed. Then he gave the order: "Yes; let it be done on my own responsibility."[2]

His decision no doubt set in motion the troop movements which were carried out in the early hours of the 19th, their chief aim being to reinforce Colonel Hirata's regiment at Mukden. More probably he merely approved orders already given. For Lieutenant-General Tamon and part of the 2nd Division reached Mukden from Liaoyang, at 5 a.m. on the 19th.

A signal was sent to General Hayashi Senjuro, Commander-in-Chief of the Army of Korea, asking for one brigade to be sent into Manchuria without delay. This was in accordance with a prearranged plan whereby the Army of Korea was to have in readiness a force of this size to assist the Kwantung Army in case of urgent need.[3]

Accompanied by Lieutenant-Colonel Ishihara and the Opera-

[1] According to Katakura (in evidence at I.M.T.F.E.), the Commander-in-Chief was in his bath when the news from Mukden arrived. *Ibid.*, pp. 18890-2.
[2] "We were all silent with deep emotion and felt a great responsibility in the face of such a weighty resolution" (Gen. Ishihara, at I.M.T.F.E.). I.M.T.F.E. Transcript, p. 22119. Ishihara claimed that he was spokesman for the staff in stressing to the Commander-in-Chief the need for large-scale military action.
[3] According to Ishihara this was a long-standing agreement. *Ibid.*, p. 22237.

tions staff the Commander-in-Chief left Port Arthur by rail soon after 3 a.m. on the 19th and arrived in Mukden by noon. Major-General Miyake, the Chief of Staff, was left behind at Port Arthur, in command of rear headquarters.[1]

About six o'clock that evening the first important signals came in from Tokyo, from the Minister of War and the Chief of the General Staff. Honjo was told that the cabinet had decided that hostilities must not be aggravated or extended, that it was the wish of the Japanese Government that the Incident be settled on this basis.[2]

At this point in the story Tatekawa makes a brief reappearance. Apparently Honjo and his staff came to the conclusion, in the light of the messages from Tokyo, that it would be a good thing to hear what Tatekawa might have to say. He had, after all, come from General Staff Headquarters. It would be wise at this juncture to hear his views, and to give him those of the Kwantung Army before he returned to Japan.

Throughout the 19th Tatekawa seems to have kept well in the background; until, late in the evening, he was finally run to earth by Captain Katakura, of Honjo's staff. Katakura had trouble finding him, and it was not until midnight that he was brought to Headquarters.

Before seeing the Commander-in-Chief Tatekawa spent some time in conference with the staff. He told them that, regardless of what the Chinese might do, the Kwantung Army should on no account move into Northern Manchuria. In the early hours of the 20th he at last met General Honjo and, presumably, spoke to him to the same effect.[3] We may suppose that he now handed over the urgent letter from the Minister of War.

Within a few days, however, Japanese forces had occupied

---

[1] On the journey Honjo and his staff seem to have encountered evidence of martial feeling among Japanese civilians in the Railway Zone. Cf. Katakura's evidence at I.M.T.F.E. "A Japanese said to us: 'If you men are going to handle this matter in a slipshod and incomplete fashion, then we shall line our bodies along the railway and we want you to run over us when you return." I.M.T.F.E. Transcript, p. 18897.

It is interesting now to recall that the Lytton Commission were informed by the Japanese that the first news Honjo had of the Mukden Incident was from a press agency at about 11 a.m. on 19th September (Lytton Report, Ch. IV, p. 69).

[2] Evidence of Maj.-Gen. Katakura. I.M.T.F.E. Transcript, p. 18898.

[3] *Ibid.*, p. 18905.

Changchun and Kirin. The fact that a further advance, to Harbin, was not made at this time was due, no doubt, to tactical military considerations rather than to any desire to comply with government policy at home.[1]

It might be thought that Tatekawa's advice to the staff represented some face-saving effort to make amends for his blatant failure to carry out his mission on the previous day. But a more likely interpretation would be that he suggested, as the soundest policy from every point of view, that the Kwantung Army take one step at a time. It is improbable that he or any other officer in Mukden regarded Kirin or Changchun as being in Northern Manchuria—though these cities were more than three hundred miles to the north-east. Rather, the phrase "Northern Manchuria" would be interpreted as referring to the extensive Heilungkiang Province, across the Sungari River.

Thus the *coup* by the Japanese forces at Mukden was a complete success; and within a matter of months it was consolidated by the occupation of every important centre in Manchuria and the establishment of the state of Manchukuo.[2] All this was achieved with the disapproval, particularly in the early days, of the Emperor and of a majority in the cabinet.

In the narrative of events, that has just been given, two features warrant some further discussion. The first is what might be called the solemn farce of the Tatekawa mission. The second is the leading rôle played throughout by the staff officers of Kwantung Army Headquarters.

Harada's comment on the Tatekawa mission is worth recording.

The War Minister transmitted the wishes of His Majesty to the Commander-in-Chief, Kwantung Army, with the intention of putting a final stop to the various schemes of the army in Manchuria and Mongolia. I believe the War Minister consulted the Chief of the Military Affairs Bureau [Koiso] regarding the selection of an envoy to deliver the confidential letter to the Commander-in-Chief,

---

[1] But Katakura, at I.M.T.F.E., said that "in the light of the instructions from the central authorities the Commander-in-Chief abandoned the idea of sending troops" to Harbin. *Ibid.*, p. 18924.

[2] Jehol, the fourth province in Manchuria, was occupied in March, 1933. But traditionally it was hardly part of Manchuria. Manchukuo was inaugurated early in March, 1932.

Kwantung Army. When consulted, Koiso probably advised the War Minister that in his opinion the matter could not be settled by anyone except Major-General Tatekawa. I think he recommended Tatekawa because he and Tatekawa had a scheme. The probable arguments used by Koiso in recommending Tatekawa for the mission were that Tatekawa was one of the responsible individuals in the army plot in Manchuria and that it would be impossible for anyone but Tatekawa to restrain the young reactionary elements in Manchuria. Since Ninomiya, Koiso and Tatekawa were in complete control of the army at that time I believe that Tatekawa was recommended for the mission, on the pretext that only he could settle matters, but actually in order to accomplish their true intention of starting an incident in Manchuria.[1]

To have sent Tatekawa to Mukden at the critical time was indeed like telling a pyromaniac to forestall an attempt at arson.[2]
It is perhaps just possible that General Minami was deceived by the arguments used by Koiso in recommending Tatekawa—both Wakatsuki and Shidehara suggested, at the Tokyo Trial, that Minami had tried to check the ambitions of the Kwantung Army[3]—but it is more probable that he was well aware that Tatekawa would encourage rather than oppose the execution of the Mukden *coup*. If Minami had been genuine in his readiness to obey the Emperor's wishes, to stop any military action in Manchuria, it is strange that he should not have arranged for Tatekawa to go by air to Mukden, instead of by the relatively slow land route through Korea. The fact is that Minami seems to have tried to please everyone. While himself in sympathy with army plans for the seizure of Manchuria he made some efforts to placate the anxious Premier, Wakatsuki, and the Foreign Minister. In sending Tatekawa as special envoy he may have felt that he had at any rate outwardly complied with the wishes of the Throne. Certainly Minami had a full share of that Japanese predilection—it is a

---

[1] Memoirs, *op. cit.*, Part II, Ch. 11 (23rd September, 1931).
[2] "The truth is that there was an indication that, so far from rectifying the situation, Tatekawa agitated them still more" (Morishima to Harada). *Ibid.*, Part II, Ch. 13 (2nd October, 1931).
[3] "I am convinced Minami used his best efforts to localise the Manchurian Incident" (Shidehara). I.M.T.F.E. Transcript, p. 1338. Wakatsuki said he thought Minami was opposed to the spread of fighting in Manchuria. *Ibid.*, p. 1573.

national characteristic—for the outward proprieties which, when carried to excess, leads to self-deception and hypocrisy.

Colonel Inouye described Minami as "two-faced"—this was at the end of August—because, although at cabinet meetings he pretended to fall in with the Premier's views, on returning to the Ministry of War he would speak provocatively about Wakatsuki and other Ministers.[1]

The *genro* was very outspoken in his condemnation of Minami. It will be recalled that on 11th September the Emperor cautioned Minami regarding the actions of the army in Manchuria. Soon after this Minami called on Saionji and had to listen to some trenchant opinions on army behaviour delivered with the old man's customary directness. Saionji told him that as Manchuria was Chinese territory all diplomacy should be left to the sole discretion of the Foreign Minister. Minami replied that everything Saionji had said was right; and he went on: "The truth is that I have been admonished by the Premier many times and have even been cautioned by the Emperor. I beg a thousand pardons for this and with full responsibility I will look into the matter." [2]

Afterwards, Saionji's comment on Minami (to Harada) was: "He is useless. It is like beating the air. Such a Minister is a real problem. . . . He is exceedingly undependable." [3]

It will be apparent, from the account which has been given of the Mukden Incident, that the real initiative at Kwantung Army Headquarters belonged to such staff officers as Colonel Itagaki, Lieutenant-Colonel Ishihara and Major Hanaya. Of course the position of a headquarters staff in any army is one of considerable power. Gifted subordinates may on occasions sway the actions, even the policy, of a Generalissimo. Colonel Hoffmann at the Masurian Lakes in 1914 had the power, where the responsibility was Hindenburg's. Usually, however, the Western military commander monopolises both responsibility and power. He directs. His staff will advise; but they carry out his orders, and it is indeed their duty to respect his intentions in every branch of their work. And while a Western general may become, through negligence or ineptitude, the prisoner of his advisers, such cases are exceptional.

Undoubtedly, at Kwantung Army Headquarters in 1931,

[1] Memoirs, *op. cit.*, Part I, Ch. 9 (4th September, 1931).
[2] *Ibid.*, Part II, Ch. 11 (23rd September, 1931).   [3] *Ibid.*

neither Lieutenant-General Honjo nor his Chief of Staff exercised real power, unless it was by the consent of Itagaki and Ishihara.[1] At Port Arthur, on the critical night of 18th September, Honjo's part was to approve what had already been decided.[2] And it will be noticed that on the following night Tatekawa had a conference with the staff—discussing matters of high policy with them—before seeing Honjo.

This state of affairs was disturbing equally to civilian politicians and to the most senior military commanders. The cause of nationalism was advanced, and the objectives of an expanding Japan quickly gained, by the independent, direct action of these able younger officers; and to this extent their behaviour was condoned by their more cautious, but patriotic, seniors. Still, in Tokyo there was an entirely justified fear that insubordination in Manchuria would lead to trouble at home, to a repetition of that mysterious March Incident, of which people hardly spoke, save in whispers.

About this time—namely immediately after the Mukden *coup* —those three stormy petrels of the Kwantung Army, Itagaki, Ishihara and Hanaya, were reported as having boasted, in their cups:

> We have succeeded. Therefore when we return to the homeland this time we shall carry out a *coup d'état* and do away with the political party system of government. Then we shall establish a nation of National Socialism with the Emperor as the centre. We shall abolish capitalists like Mitsui and Mitsubishi and carry out an even distribution of wealth. We are determined to do so![3]

Such talk—the pure doctrine of Kita Ikki—was very much in the air. Well-informed persons in Tokyo were prepared for some

[1] "The condition was such that even the Commander-in-Chief Kwantung Army was in a state of restriction to quarters. Three staff officers of the Kwantung Army—Ishihara, Hanaya and Itagaki—were the centre of activities in Manchuria; and since the Chief of Staff, Miyake, was unable to control his staff he let the three do things as they pleased." Memoirs, Part II, Ch. 13 (2nd October, 1931).

[2] A staff intelligence officer who surrendered near Mandalay in 1945 described his divisional commander as being no more than an "ivory seal" (a rubber stamp).

[3] So Harada was told by Morishima; who also declared that the life of his chief, Hayashi, was in danger—the Kwantung Army considering him to be an obstacle to their plans. Memoirs, *op. cit.*, Part II, Ch. 13 (2nd October, 1931).

kind of insurrection to break out at any moment. At the end of September Harada addressed a group in the House of Peers. His remarks are of peculiar interest, for they confirm the relationship of the March Conspiracy to the Manchurian Incident, as well as containing a warning of further trouble very soon.

This Manchurian Incident [said Harada] has its prelude in the army *coup d'état*. Because the plan by an element of the army, to storm the Imperial Diet in session on 20th March, had failed, the Manchurian Incident was started to give vent to their emotions. From beginning to end the government was made a complete fool of by the army. The fact that their plot has succeeded in Manchuria will surely give a certain element of the army the confidence that they can do the same in Japan also; and there lies the real danger.[1]

And indeed in October there occurred the second serious nationalist conspiracy in Tokyo during the year—namely the dangerous though abortive *Kinki Kakumei*, or "Revolution of the Imperial Flag".

iii

The *Kinki Kakumei*—better known as the October Incident—bore a certain resemblance to the March Conspiracy. To some extent the same personalities were involved—Okawa, Hashimoto and members of the *Sakurakai*. The main objective was the same —the overthrow of the government and its replacement by a cabinet headed by a general, in this case Lieutenant-General Araki Sadao. And the ultimate aim was of course the establishment of the Showa Restoration. The October Incident, like the March Conspiracy, was also related to the question of Manchuria. The same fear, that "weak-kneed" diplomacy would check nationalist aims in Manchuria, was a motive in both conspiracies.

Nevertheless the October Incident differed from the March Conspiracy in certain important respects. Senior officers were not directly involved. The initiative, this time, was entirely in the hands of younger officers like Hashimoto. For this reason, per-

[1] Memoirs, *op. cit.*, Part II, Ch. 13 (2nd October, 1931).

haps, the plot envisaged the use of considerably more violence and bloodshed than would have been thought necessary in March. In this respect it anticipated the celebrated Mutiny of 26th February, 1936.

Although the Mukden *coup* had been so successful, and had been followed within a few days by Japanese occupation of Changchun and Kirin, nationalist opinion was not satisfied with what had been achieved. For one thing, liberal opinion, critical of events in Manchuria, was by no means silent. During September and October the Tokyo *Asahi* was lukewarm in its defence of Japanese action, advised the government to be cautious and delivered homilies on the need for close co-operation between the army and the Foreign Ministry. Early in October a writer in the Tokyo Imperial University newspaper—Professor Yokota Kisaburo—actually expressed a doubt as to whether the action by the Kwantung Army at Mukden could be entirely justified on the grounds of self-defence. The Left-wing proletarian organisations also issued statements at this time strongly opposing military action, and calling for an immediate evacuation of the occupied areas.[1]

The cabinet itself—with the exception of Minami—was plainly eager to moderate the Kwantung Army and to prevent any further advance in Manchuria, even if it was unable to undo what had already been done.

There was, then, considerable anxiety among ultra-nationalists soon after the Mukden Incident; for they were afraid that the fruits of victory were to be lost through the weakness and vacillation of the Minseito government. At his trial in 1934 Okawa declared:

> The attitude of the government was very disgusting. If they should dilly-dally, as they were doing, all would end in vain, although the lid for the solution of the Manchurian Incident had been thrown open. Its purpose would not be achieved. Hence the aim of the October Incident was, generally speaking, to crush them [the government] and to set up a political force capable of undertaking the solution of important problems. For it was obvious that they [the government]—possessing such a weak stomach as to be unable

[1] *Vide* Takeuchi, *op. cit.*, pp. 362–5.

to digest even domestic problems—could do nothing if they were also fed such big and raw stuff as Manchuria.[1]

But there was an even greater cause for disquiet among extreme nationalists—one which was never made public. This was the attitude shown by the Emperor towards the army's policy in Manchuria. Naturally criticism was directed primarily against the *genro*, the Lord Keeper of the Privy Seal, the Minister of the Imperial Household and other Court advisers.[2] Yet direct criticism of the Emperor himself was not lacking.

The Incident which was planned by Hashimoto and Okawa included a demonstration by the *Zaigo Gunjinkai*, the reservists' association. This organisation was naturally interested in what was going on in Manchuria, and was of course wholeheartedly behind any strong measures that might be taken against the Chinese. So far the *Zaigo Gunjinkai* had taken little, if any, part in nationalist political activity. The outbreak of fighting in Manchuria, however,—which the government persistently refused to regard as a patriotic war—brought the reservists into the field as vigorous nationalist agitators. Some of them, as the following remarks by Saionji suggest, were not above spreading rumours detrimental to the Emperor. At the beginning of October, weighed down with anxiety, the *genro* told his secretary that he thought there were probably communist elements in the army.

In reviewing world history, when an Imperial regime is overthrown, various measures, as a prelude to revolution, are taken; and to-day there exists a very similar situation to that. The reservists are giving publicity to a story that when one of the guards was making a tour of the Palace grounds he noticed, late at night, a light in the Emperor's room. Thinking that His Majesty, due to pressing state affairs, was working hard until late at night the guard was overwhelmed with gratitude. However, on the contrary, the Emperor was playing mahjong with the Empress. They are also saying that when the Chief of the General Staff or the Minister of War

---

[1] Tokyo Court of Appeal Proceedings, *op. cit.*

[2] "The Emperor has expressed satisfaction . . . at the government policy of trying not to extend the Manchurian Incident. However, the army is reported to be indignant that the Emperor's opinion has been so influenced by his personal attendants." Kido Diary, 22nd September, 1931. I.M.T.F.E. Transcripts, p. 1938.

report to His Majesty, the Emperor shows apparent displeasure, as though they were making these reports too frequently.[1]

This extract is quoted, because it shows that the *genro* at least was not deceived—as were so many Japanese—by the ultra-nationalists. On the contrary he perceived the essential revolutionary element informing them. There can indeed be little doubt that a successful nationalist *coup d'état* in Tokyo would either have relegated the Emperor to complete seclusion or have actually removed him from the capital—perhaps to Kyoto—and replaced him by one of the Imperial Princes.[2]

It is now time to consider the activities of the conspirators. The two main ringleaders were Hashimoto and Captain Cho Isamu. They worked closely with Okawa; but the plan for the *coup d'état* seems to have been the product of their brains alone. From the day of the Mukden *coup* these two officers practically lived in geisha houses in various parts of Tokyo.[3]

The conspirators chose Lieutenant-General Araki as their ideal military dictator. This general, because of his advocacy of *Kodo*, the doctrine of the "Imperial Way", had become the hero of army nationalists. In August he had taken up an appointment in Tokyo,[4] having previously commanded a division in the provinces. It seems that no definite approaches were made to Araki—as had been made to Ugaki in the previous February and March—and that he was chosen for the rôle of national saviour without his consent. The subsidiary figures in the new government, to be set up after the *coup*, were to be Hashimoto, as Home Minister;

---

[1] Memoirs, *op. cit.*, Part II, Ch. 14 (11th October, 1931). Earlier Konoye repeated to Harada a conversation he had had with Mori Kaku, a Seiyukai politician. Mori had declared, with indignation, that certain army officers were deploring the fact that the Emperor was "a mediocre person". "I believe", said Mori, "they say so because His Majesty does not give heed to what they say." *Ibid.*, Part I, Ch. 10 (14th September, 1931).

[2] There was a rumour that Imperial Princes were taking part in ultra-nationalist associations, including those, like the *Ketsumeidan*, which exacted a blood compact from their members. Memoirs, Part II, Ch. 14. The only Imperial Princes to whom this could refer were Prince Fushimi—soon to be Chief of the Naval General Staff—and Lt.-Gen. Prince Higashi-Kuni. And the latter, so far as can be ascertained, was the only one whose activities gave any substance to the rumour. These will be mentioned in Chapter 6 (*infra*).

[3] *The Study of the Minds of a Militarist Nation* (cited).

[4] Chief of the General Affairs Dept., in the office of the Inspector-General of Military Education.

Tatekawa, Foreign Minister; Okawa, Minister of Finance; and Cho, Chief of the Metropolitan Police.[1]

The existing cabinet was to be eliminated in a single blow, by air bombardment. The Lord Keeper and other advisers to the Throne were to be assassinated. Two regiments of the Guards Division were to be called out in aid of the revolutionaries.

Such was the outline of this grandiose plot.

On the evening of 16th October Lieutenant-General Araki went to the restaurant where Hashimoto, Cho and Nemoto were holding one of their many secret conferences. To their astonishment, he reprimanded them severely. Nothing could be achieved, he told them, by airing their opinions, "drinking saké and getting drunk". They must not do anything violent or thoughtless.

> The army officers of Japan are the so-called Kusunoki Sword, which should always be polished; but it should not be drawn indiscriminately from its scabbard. It is almost inconceivable that I should have to come here in military uniform to a place where you are drinking saké in order to admonish you on this sort of matter.[2]

The following night the three officers, with six others, were taken into custody by the *Kempei* (military police). Okawa and other civilian nationalists involved in the plot were not arrested.[3] The army officers were, of course, the real ringleaders; and the intervention by the *Kempei* effectively killed the conspiracy. However, the officers were not courtmartialled, were indeed virtually unpunished; and so the civil police were not in a position to arrest Okawa and his associates.

The only disciplinary action taken by the military authorities against the mutinous officers was to break up the group. Hashimoto was posted to a regiment in Himeji; Cho and Nemoto were transferred to the Kwantung Army. As the March Conspiracy

---

[1] Yanaga, *op. cit.*, p. 500 (footnote). Rear-Admiral Kobayashi Seizo was to have been Navy Minister.

[2] Memoirs, *op. cit.*, Part II, Ch. 16 (29th October, 1931). Kusunoki, the devoted follower of the Emperor Godaigo, was killed in battle in 1336. He became the outstanding symbol of Japanese loyalty.

[3] Associated with Okawa in the plot where Nishida Zei and Akamatsu Katsumaro, the general secretary of the Right-Wing proletarian *Shakai Minshuto* ("Social Democratic Party"). Akamatsu was already a member of Uchida's *Seisanto*.

had been overlooked it would have been embarrassing, no doubt, for the Ministry of War to prosecute the October rebels under the Army Penal Code. Too many reputations might be jeopardised were a thorough investigation—such as a courtmartial would entail—carried out.[1] Accordingly only "administrative punishment" was given.[2]

To those outside the army who were aware of the conspiracy military leaders explained this leniency by saying that really the government, by its weakness on the Manchurian question, was responsible for the trouble, and that the motives of Hashimoto and the others had been very sincere. The Prime Minister was greatly concerned at this failure to deal firmly with the conspirators; but he was powerless in the matter. The Chief of the Metropolitan Police was also worried, and equally powerless.[3]

Araki's intervention in this affair greatly advanced his prestige. Those primarily responsible for the maintenance of military discipline—namely Minami and his Vice-Minister, Sugiyama—felt unequal to the task of controlling the younger officers. So they had to ask Araki—the Bayard of ultra-nationalist, radical officers —to appease and calm the conspirators.[4]

Araki's success marked him out as the next Minister of War. For the same reason he now lost the complete support of some extreme nationalists. He became suspect in their eyes, as being allied with authority.

How did the Minister of War come to hear of the Conspiracy? It may have been through Nishida Zei. Inouye Nissho of the *Aikyojuku*—whose activities are discussed in the next chapter— believed him to have been an informer. And some members of

---

[1] According to Yanaga (*op. cit.*, p. 499), Koiso, Tatekawa and Nagata Tetsuzan supported the rebels. Certainly Tatekawa was wholeheartedly in favour of the Plot. I.M.T.F.E. Transcript, p. 1980.

[2] The phrase was Nagata's. Early in 1932 he told Konoye and Kido that action under the Army Penal Code had not been taken on account of the motives which had inspired the conspirators. The authorities had also to consider "the prestige of the national army and other factors". Maruyama, *A Study of the Minds of the Rulers of a Militarist Nation* (cited).

[3] He told Harada: "Regarding the recent Incident in the army the general intentions of the high military authorities are obscure; consequently I cannot do anything about it." Memoirs, *op. cit.*, Part II, Ch. 16 (24th October, 1931).

[4] Maruyama, *A Study of the Minds . . .* (cited). Similar tactics were attempted in February, 1936, without success; when Gen. Mazaki—the idol of the mutinous officers—was asked to persuade them to surrender.

the *Sakurakai* lost their enthusiasm for the *coup*.[1] They were headed by Nemoto; and according to Okawa it was Nemoto who betrayed the Conspiracy to the authorities.[2] Perhaps he realised that Araki, like Ugaki the previous March, was not prepared, when it came to the point, to head a new government established by violent, revolutionary means. Furthermore, the ultra-nationalists of the Kwantung Army Staff—despite their wild statements during this period—were not uniformly in favour of the projected *coup d'état*. Itagaki, and Colonel Doihara (now Mayor of Mukden), supported the Plot.[3] But Ishihara Kanji thought it inopportune.[4]

Clearly the affair was ill-considered and badly prepared. The army authorities made light of it at the time.[5] Once it had been cleared up, by the removal of Hashimoto and Cho from Tokyo, the Metropolitan Police accepted the army's version and dismissed the conspiracy as a "fake".[6]

Henceforward there were many rumours of military revolt in Tokyo—some, as we shall see, entirely justified—until there occurred the notorious Mutiny of February, 1936. The temporary success of that Mutiny shows the turn that events might have taken in October, 1931.

The October Incident had two main results. It led to the dispersal, for the time being, of several of the chief trouble-makers in the army at home. Lieutenant-Colonel Shigeto was soon posted to Manchuria. Hashimoto, as we have seen, was transferred to Himeji, and Nemoto and Cho to the Kwantung Army.[7] Further-

---

[1] I.M.T.F.E. Transcript, p. 2016.   [2] *Ibid.*, p. 1981.

[3] Tokyo Court of Appeal Proceedings (cited).

[4] Very soon after the October Incident Ishihara saw Cho in Mukden and reprimanded him for having been involved in the affair. I.M.T.F.E. Transcript, p. 2017.

[5] They described it as "a matter of slight significance". Memoirs, *op. cit.*, Part II, Ch. 16 (29th October, 1931). The day after Hashimoto and the others were taken into custody, the Procurator-General, Koyama, noticed that there was a *Kempei* guard on the house opposite his own. This was the residence of Gen. Kanaya, then Chief of the General Staff. Koyama called on Kanaya and said that he had heard that certain officers had been arrested. Kanaya, who was drinking saké (although it was in the morning), replied that it was not a serious matter. *Ibid.*, Part III, Ch. 45—C (3rd June, 1932).

[6] *Ibid.*

[7] Cho had hardly reached Manchuria when he started rumours that the Kwantung Army was thinking of declaring its independence of Japan, as the military authorities in Tokyo were not in favour of the idea—propagated by

more, by a fortunate coincidence, Tatekawa left for Europe early in the New Year. In the summer of 1931 he had been appointed a delegate to the Geneva Disarmament Conference, due to open in February, 1932.

The October Incident also paved the way for Araki's accession to office as Minister of War in December; and it was at least an indirect cause of the resignation of the Wakatsuki cabinet.[1]

Thus 1931 saw two abortive military *coups* in Tokyo.[2] So far as the younger officers were concerned the same personalities figured in both Incidents. Similarly Okawa Shumei was involved in both of them. None of the participants, it must be re-emphasised, were punished for these acts of treason. Indeed, after the October Incident, Okawa continued to journey back and forwards between Manchuria and the teahouses of Tokyo, constantly plotting—this time with persons connected with the *Aikyojuku*. This, however, belongs to the next chapter.

iv

We have spoken earlier of the *Dai Nippon Seisanto* "The Japan Production Society"), a new version of the old *Kokuryukai* and associated with several nationalist groups.[3] The *Seisanto*, formed at the end of June, 1931, was regarded as Uchida Ryohei's "last public service" (*saigo no hokoku*). For in 1932 he became ill

Itagaki and Doihara—of an "independent" Manchurian state. Cho boasted that it was in consequence of these rumours that the General Staff and Ministry of War changed their policy and accepted the idea of "Manchukuo". Cho claimed that the rumours were entirely his own invention—no-one else in the Kwantung Army had any thought of breaking with Japan. I.M.T.F.E. Transcripts, p. 2017.

[1] At the time of the October Incident Wakatsuki wanted to resign. What finally brought down the cabinet was an act of sabotage by the Home Minister, Adachi Kenzo, who was eager for a coalition with the Seiyukai. Ramsay MacDonald's "National Government" in England may have provided Adachi with an example which he sought to imitate. Wakatsuki's disapproval of his negotiations caused Adachi to refuse to attend cabinet meetings.

[2] Tanin and Yohan (*op. cit.*, p. 209) speak of *two* Incidents during the autumn of 1931—one in October, the other on 3rd November. They describe the latter as the Imperial Flag (*Kinki*) Revolution. On this point these generally well-informed authors are in error. There was in fact a single Incident, which was known either as the *Kinki Kakumei* ("Imperial Flag Revolution") or October Incident. [3] *Vide*, p. 74 (*supra*).

and remained an invalid until his death in 1937. The initial programme of this society declared that the Meiji Constitution should be respected, but that all laws and institutions incompatible with the *Kokutai* should be reformed or abolished; and there was also a demand for a state-controlled economy. Unlike most nationalist associations the *Seisanto* made an effort to secure direct representation in the Diet. It put forward its own candidates in the General Election of February, 1932. None of these were elected, and thereafter the society became increasingly involved in illegal plots, culminating in the *Shimpeitai* affair of 1933, to be described later. Even in 1931 the *Seisanto* did not remain aloof from such activities; for, as we observed, Akamatsu Katsumaro—a prominent member of the society—was implicated in the October Incident.

An interesting feature of the *Seisanto* was the large number of small patriotic labour unions—mostly from the Kansai—which it came to embrace or promote, especially after the end of 1931.[1] Including these subsidiary societies, the *Seisanto* claimed, with some justification, a membership of 150,000. But in 1931 the *Seisanto* was still relatively small.

A terrorist group formed in 1931 was the *Kakumeiso* ("The Society of the Cry of the Crane").[2] This was Pan-Asiatic and extremely anti-Russian. It had a branch in Mukden, which was frequently visited by the youthful head of the society, Suridate Hajime.[3] The *Kakumeiso* was in reality little better than an organisation of gangsters, who perpetrated in Manchuria all manner of crimes, from blackmail to kidnapping, as a form of political pressure against unco-operative Chinese. They helped to give a bad name to the Japanese authorities in Manchuria; a matter which caused many responsible Japanese, senior army officers not excepted, a good deal of genuine concern.[4]

---

[1] *Vide* Appendix I (*infra*).

[2] The title was a pun, being a homonym of *kakumei*—"revolution". The characters, of course, are different.

[3] In 1933 Suridate entered the Soviet Trade Office in Tokyo and wrecked it with a Japanese sword.

[4] The "ronin" were not the only undesirable people in Manchuria. In September, 1932, Harada was told by the Vice-Chief of the General Staff that of some 150 Japanese officials sent to "advise" the Manchukuoan government many were "loathsome characters". Memoirs, *op. cit.*, Part IV, Ch. 55 (1st October, 1932).

Also founded in 1931 were certain agrarian self-help associations. These are of some interest; but because of their relationship with the *Aikyojuku* they are among the subjects of the next chapter.

5

1932—YEAR OF ASSASSINATIONS

i

THE nationalist organisations which have been discussed so far were, on the whole, decidedly urban in character. Their main offices were usually in Tokyo, Osaka and other cities. Their members, generally speaking and with such notable exceptions as the *Zaigo Gunjin* (the reservists), were townsmen, or countrymen who had come to the towns to seek a livelihood or, as university students, to further their education.

Nevertheless, agrarian ideas occupied an important place in Japanese nationalist thought, especially during the Showa period.

Naturally those who were most practical in their patriotic dream of an ever-expanding Japanese empire appreciated the need for the strengthening of national power by central control and promotion of modern urban industrialisation. A thoroughgoing nationalist programme demanded the utmost productivity from both munitions and export industries.

Yet, at variance with this demand for greater industrial development, there existed within the nationalist movement a school of thought which preached decentralisation, local autonomy, and the importance of rural life and activities in contrast with those of the city. The doctrine was summed up in the Japanese phrase, *Nohon Shugi* ("agrarianism").

To a large extent this represented a natural reaction to the apparent materialism, modernity and ugliness of the great cities. In this respect *Nohon Shugi* contained elements evocative of the ideas of Ruskin and William Morris. But in so far as it was influenced by foreign example *Nohon Shugi* owed most to Tolstoy and Kropotkin.

Gondo Nariaki, a writer and journalist, is generally considered the representative figure of this school of thought.[1] His main

---

[1] By an alternative reading of his personal name, Gondo Nariaki was also

work—*Jichi Mimpan* ("A Popular Handbook of Self-Government")—was published, like Kita's *Nihon Kaizo Hoan Taiko*, in 1919.[1]

Gondo's ideal state was a confederation of self-governing village communities. Strong central government was anathema to him; so much so as to make his ideas appear even anti-nationalist.[2] However, at the apex of his confederation was the Emperor, the Head of the Family. This, in Gondo's view, made his ideal Japan "the Imperial House (state)" (*shashoku*) rather than a "nation" or "country" (*kuni*). The distinction is not easily explained, but is none the less real. Possibly the best interpretation would suggest that, while *shashoku* has a family or tribal significance, *kuni* implies the complete administrative structure, centralised and rigidly bureaucratic, of the modern Japanese state, which, according to Gondo and the *Nohon Shugi* school, sucked the life out of the villages for the benefit of the cities and towns.[3]

Only his acceptance of the Imperial House *mystique* saved Gondo from being, like many Japanese Left-wing writers, a thoroughgoing Kropotkin anarchist. He was of course bitterly hostile to capitalism, even the petty capitalism of small village employers and medium landowners. Perhaps if he had lived in Europe he would have joined the Socialist Co-operative

known as Gondo Seikyo. Although he had at one time been a stock-breeder, Gondo was an intellectual rather than a tiller of the soil. In his youth he had served the army as an intelligence agent in Korea, shortly before the Annexation. He was just over fifty years of age when he wrote *Jichi Mimpan*. His home was in the suburbs of Tokyo—that vast area of semi-urbanised countryside, which perhaps was the most striking example of the octopus power of great cities so strongly attacked by Gondo.

[1] The Police, who banned Kita's work, severely censored Gondo's first chapter, suppressing much of it. For he failed to subscribe to the belief that Jimmu *Tenno*, the first Emperor, was descended from the Sun Goddess. With greater historical accuracy Gondo described Jimmu *Tenno* as a tribal chief, leading his community to the acquisition of new territory. At the same time he stressed his belief that the Emperors had always enjoyed the confidence of Heaven.

[2] The point is emphasised by Prof. Maruyama, *Nippon Fasshizmu*, *op. cit.*, p. 121.

[3] Sometimes the ideographs used for Japanese concepts suggest shades of meaning which are otherwise not apparent. In the case of *shashoku*, and of *kuni*, a little—but not much—can be learned from the ideographs. The two which represent *shashoku* together have the literal meaning of "communal millet". The single ideograph for *kuni* can be interpreted from its elements to mean "spears and mouths inside a square". In other words, *kuni* has a decidedly geographical, *static* shade of meaning; whereas *shashoku* is more social, fluid and personal.

movement. This, of any organisation in the political field, would have been the most attractive to him.

How, then, does Gondo enter into the sphere of ultra-nationalism? The truth would seem to be that it was others—and causes outside himself—that dragged him into the forefront of the radical nationalist movement during 1932. He was, however, a thinker rather than a man of action; far less interested or involved in political intrigues than Okawa, Kita and that most practical leader of the *Nohon Shugi* school, whom we shall now discuss, Tachibana Kosaburo.

Tachibana was a Mito man who, when poor health compelled him to leave his high school, worked on the land and persuaded his parents—his father was a dyer in Mito—to make their family the nucleus of a communal, Tolstoyan village of five households, containing some thirty persons in all. This was established, on the outskirts of Mito, in 1920 and was known as the *Kyodai Son* ("The Fraternal Village"). Its total acreage was twelve; but it prospered, became famous in Ibaragi Prefecture and secured the patronage of people of local importance, notably a Seiyukai member of the Diet, Kazami Akira.

At the end of 1930 these patrons encouraged Tachibana to start a private patriotic academy—an old tradition in Japanese nationalist circles—and this was known as the *Aikyo Juku*, or "Land-loving School". Kazami gave financial support to the school; and he persuaded the authorities of Ibaragi Prefecture to advance some funds. Ibaragi, and the Mito district in particular, had a pronounced nationalist, patriotic tradition, rivalling that of *Fukuoka*.[1] Therefore the local authorities were inclined to support a new venture by what was already a thriving community.

The structure of the *Aikyo Juku*, on paper at least, was ambitious. The school was divided into a *shonen-bu* ("juvenile section") and a *seinen-bu* ("youth section"). The former, composed mainly of boys who had completed their Primary School education, offered a two and a half years' course. The latter was divided into two sub-sections; the first for students aged eighteen and over—there was no fixed course—and the second, also for older students, comprising a six months' course. The courses

[1] The assassins of Iii-kamon-no-Kami, shortly before the Restoration, were Mito men and were regarded, locally, as national heroes.

were a combination of practical farming and a study of Japanese patriotic ethics and history. The number of students, however, was inconsiderable. At the time of the 15th May Incident the *Aikyo Juku* contained twenty-three students.

In addition to the school Tachibana and Kazami founded a society, the *Aikyokai*, to propagate the virtues of *Nohon Shugi* nationalism. In 1932 this society had some fifteen branches in Ibaragi Prefecture, with a membership of about a thousand.

When the *Aikyo Juku* was established, in December, 1930, it advocated a variety of political and economic reforms—the programme, indeed, of the Showa Restoration with particular emphasis on the abolition of peasant indebtedness and the promotion of co-operative village communities—but it displayed no marked leaning towards revolutionary action.

But the years 1931 and 1932 saw no improvement in the acute rural distress—particularly in the *Tohoku*, or north-eastern, districts—which had been occasioned by the drastic fall in prices of rice and silk during 1930. Severe discontent rapidly developed in the countryside and threatened to make small landowners and peasants potential revolutionaries.[1]

> We can still remember [writes Professor Maruyama] the plight of the *Tohoku* peasants. Peasant poverty was the direct cause of the Fascist movement becoming revolutionary and of the Right-wing terrorism which broke out after 1931. It had a direct influence on the conversion of young army officers to revolution; as many of them came from medium and small landowner families. And as the peasantry, the *Tohoku* peasantry especially, were regarded as the core of the army the explanation of their behaviour is clear enough.[2]

It was, indeed, the army—the political radicals among the younger officers—which stirred the interests of the *Nohon Shugi* patriots towards revolutionary methods for the achievement of political and economic reforms. During 1931 both Gondo and Tachibana were invited to give lectures to army officers and cadets at military training schools in the Tokyo area.

[1] Chapters V and IX of Freda Utley's *Japan's Feet of Clay* (London, Faber & Faber, 1936) contain interesting accounts both of agrarian distress and of resulting revolutionary symptoms. Miss Utley considered social revolution to be imminent.

[2] Maruyama, *Nippon Fasshizmu, op. cit.*, p. 129.

It is probable that in this way Gondo and Tachibana were put in touch with the wider, conspiratorial nationalist circles of Nishida, Kita and Okawa. It is evident, however, that, while Tachibana moved steadily towards revolutionary terrorism, Gondo—though equally vigorous in condemning capitalism and the party cabinet system—hesitated to plunge into all the manœuvres and intrigues of an active plot. Indeed Tachibana and Gondo, though associated for a brief period, soon separated.

Gondo had his own small private academy, the *Jichi Gakkan* ("Self-government College"). In January, 1932, Gondo and his *Jichi Gakkan* joined forces with Tachibana in an organisation known as the *Nohon Remmei*, or "Agrarian League". But almost immediately this League was divided into Gondo and Tachibana factions—the former being called "the economic movement group" (*keizai undo-ha*), the latter the "political movement group" (*seiji undo-ha*). For the Tachibana faction was actively interested in preparing for a *coup d'état* in Tokyo, was in fact already in touch with Okawa, Nishida and disaffected army and navy officers and cadets. Whereas Gondo, with greater caution, declined to take a direct part in any revolutionary schemes. So the Tachibana faction broke away from the *Nohon Remmei* and, with three other small provincial farmers' unions, formed the *Jichi Nomin Kyogikai* ("the Self-governing Farmers' Co-operative Society").[1] This society established contact with Inouye Nissho's *Ketsumeidan*, or "League of Blood".

The *Ketsumeidan* grew from a small nucleus of six young nationalist fanatics, all from Ibaragi Prefecture, headed by Konuma Tadashi and Hisanuma Goro. The latter were members of the *Nippon Kokuminto*, the association formed in 1929 by Terada Ineshiro and Nishida Zei with the backing of Uchida and Toyama. In 1930, when the controversy over the London Naval Treaty was at its height, Terada summoned Konuma and Hisanuma to Tokyo. These two, with four others, founded a "death-band" (*kesshitai*).[2]

[1] This society's economic programme bore a certain resemblance to Gandhi's movement for rural self-sufficiency in India. There was a similar insistence on home spinning and weaving.

[2] The others were Kawasaki Nagamitsu, Kurosawa Taiji, Kurosawa Kanekichi and Terunuma Hatsutaro—Kinoshita Hanji, *Nippon Kokka Shugi Undo Shi*, *op. cit.*, p. 127.

It is probable that Terada and Nishida wished to create a small terrorist group—very young, simple-minded patriots would be the best material for the purpose—to carry out any drastic actions which the leaders and backers of the *Nippon Kokuminto* might consider necessary. In other words, Konuma's *Kesshitai* would be merely a tool in the hands of experienced adventurers like Nishida.

In the late summer of 1931 the *Nippon Kokuminto* was amalgamated with Uchida's *Seisanto*, and at the same time the *kesshitai* became known as the *Ketsumei Gonin Otoko* or "The Five Stalwart Blood Brothers".[1] They were bound together by an oath, sealed with their blood, to eliminate those public figures in Japan who were thought to have betrayed the country internationally, or to have enriched themselves at the expense of the farmers and peasants.

Before the end of 1931 several others joined the *Gonin Otoko*, swearing a similar oath and sealing the compact with their blood. This larger association called itself the *Ketsumeidan*.

Sensational notoriety came to the *Ketsumeidan* when it organised the murders, on 9th February and 5th March, 1932, of Inouye Junnosuke, former Minister of Finance, and Baron Dan Takuma, director of the Mitsui holding company. Members of the *Ketsumeidan* were also involved in the disturbances of 15th May, 1932, when the Seiyukai Premier, Inukai Tsuyoshi, was assassinated. However, the *Ketsumeidan Jiken* ("The Ketsumeidan Incident") is generally taken to refer to the murders of Inouye and Dan; while the murder of Inukai is known as the *Go Ju-go Jiken*, or "15th May Incident". But the two "Incidents" were really two stages of the same ambitious terrorist plot.[2]

---

[1] There were of course six members of this group. But in Japan the number 5 has a certain historical, social significance. During the Tokugawa Shogunate community life in towns and villages was based on the *goningumi*, or "five-men groups". In practice the *goningumi* exceeded five persons, being, rather, five households. For police and A.R.P. purposes the practice was revived during the Pacific War.

[2] Kinoshita (*op. cit.*, p. 133) emphasises that the *Ketsumeidan* Incident cannot be regarded as an individual terrorist outbreak. On the other hand Tsukui Tatsuo (*op. cit.*) declares that, although there was an ideological relationship between the two Incidents, there was a "spiritual difference" between them. The participants in the *Ketsumeidan Jiken*, says Tsukui, were entirely unselfish, inspired by pure idealism. This was not true to quite the same extent in the case of the 15th May. "One cannot call those who took part in *Go-Ju-Go* [15th May]

ii

The Incidents—the murders of the three public men—have often been described, and are a part of well-known Japanese history. Inouye and Dan were killed in broad daylight in Tokyo. The Prime Minister, Inukai, was shot dead in his private quarters at his official residence.

At the time the public reaction, so far as it was expressed by the leading newspapers, was one of shocked horror. But when the trials of the various accused conspirators and assassins were in progress a year later public sympathy was no longer with the victims. Indeed there was a general feeling that the prisoners in the dock should be acquitted. For in the period between the murders and the trials the nationalist thesis—that party government and selfish capitalist interests were ruining the country—seemed to have been proved. Japan had first defied and then left the League of Nations, with no serious consequences to herself except the creation of a growing anti-Japanese sentiment throughout the democratic world—a sentiment which only strengthened the cause of ultra-nationalism. Thus by 1933 the party governments and the relatively pacific diplomacy of the nineteen-twenties were discredited.

This was the express aim of those who took part in the murders. They saw themselves as the heirs of the Forty-Seven Ronin, not so much as exemplars of vengeance or even of loyalty, but as agents of the true patriotic spirit, rousing the Japanese people from their supposed civic lethargy and indifference.[1] The murders themselves—the fate of the unfortunate victims—were indeed widely regarded as of less importance than this motive which inspired the assassins.

But it is now time to go back to the preparations for these

'impure' or ambitious, but they had not quite the simplicity of those who participated in the *Ketsumeidan Jiken.*" *Ibid.* In the *Ketsumeidan* Incident the action was individual—one man against one victim. The 15th May Incident was more complicated. This, perhaps, is a Japanese way of saying that the murder of Inukai, by an armed group, was the more unsporting of the two Incidents.

[1] The celebrated eighteenth-century vendetta of the 47 Ronin, immortalised for Japanese by the drama *Chushingura*, was said to have stirred the people of Yedo out of a prevailing spirit of selfish hedonism.

murders, and the various parts played by the *Aikyojuku*, the armed services, Okawa Shumei and other elements—in addition to the *Ketsumeidan*—in these activities.

One of the most striking features of the whole conspiracy was its strongly provincial flavour. The original "Blood Brothers" were natives of Ibaragi Prefecture. The *Aikyojuku* was, as we have seen, also an Ibaragi product. And the naval element, which took the leading rôle in the murder of the Prime Minister, came from the air training centre at Tsuchiura on the Kasumigaura lake in Ibaragi Prefecture. Again, the Nichiren Buddhist priest, Inouye Nissho—who became the dominant figure in the *Ketsumeidan*—lived near Mito, in a temple on the sea coast. There were, of course, certain conspirators from other Prefectures. But Ibaragi predominated. So far as the executants of the plot were concerned the atmosphere was provincial, and confined largely to one area. Even the associations of Gondo and the *Nohon Shugi* school were primarily with the north-east of Japan.

Behind these provincial terrorists and neo-Kropotkin eccentrics, exploiting them to further the revival of nationalism, were what we might call the professional nationalists, such as Toyama and Okawa; and there was a wider circle, beyond, composed of politicians, soldiers and sailors.

Inouye Nissho, who in 1931 became the leader of the *Ketsumeidan*, had been an army spy and adventurer in China and Manchuria for many years before becoming a priest of the Nichiren sect of Buddhism.[1] Entering the priesthood, in modern Japan at any rate, in no way suggested withdrawal or retirement from secular interests and activities. The Nichiren sect, too, was especially interested in political nationalism. There was, therefore, nothing incongruous in the use Inouye made of his temple near Mito—namely as a centre of agitation against the political parties and great capitalists.

Inouye's most devoted disciple was a local school teacher named Furuuchi Eiji; and he became Inouye's chief lieutenant in the *Ketsumeidan*.

Some time during the later part of 1931 Inouye and Furuuchi began to have meetings with discontented service officers and

---

[1] Inouye's real personal name was Akira. "Nissho"—or "Sun-called"—was the name he adopted.

cadets at the Tsuchiura naval air-training station.[1] The leading spirit among the politically minded officers was Lieutenant-Commander Fujii Hitoshi. Earlier this officer had been an instructor at the Naval Academy at Etajima. There he had preached, unofficially, the gospel of the Showa Restoration to the cadets; among whom was Koga Kiyoshi, who, like his instructor, was to be stationed later at Tsuchiura. Koga, as a naval lieutenant, was a ringleader of the group which assassinated Premier Inukai.

Until the time of the London Naval Treaty controversy it was almost unknown for naval officers, below the very senior ranks, to take any part in political activities, the tradition of the navy being strongly professional and non-political. Therefore when it became known that officers at Tsuchiura were becoming interested in radical nationalist agitation the naval authorities in Tokyo prepared to take disciplinary action. But the Navy Minister, Admiral Abo, was advised by the army to be lenient in his handling of the situation. It was urged that it would be unwise to punish anyone at Tsuchiura.[2] Abo concurred with this view. But the Chief of the Naval General Staff, Admiral Taniguchi, felt that disciplinary measures ought to be taken. If his opinion had prevailed it is at least possible that the navy might have greatly strengthened its position as an effective counterbalance to the power of the army. For the rivalry between the two services was deep-rooted. Legally Taniguchi's position was correct. In this crisis, however, the spirit of nationalism triumphed, as it usually did, over the letter of the law. The outcome was the resignation of Taniguchi.[3]

[1] Inouye's brother was a regular officer in the navy—Comd. Yamaguchi, later to be involved in the *Shimpeitai* affair. This family connection no doubt helped Inouye to establish contact with the young naval officers.

[2] This was early in 1932. The source of this account is information given to Harada in June, 1932, by Koyama, the Minister of Justice. Memoirs, *op. cit.*, Part III, Ch. 45–6 (23rd June, 1932). Unfortunately, in this case, the anonymity of the term "army" is not pierced by any indication as to who made these representations to the Navy Minister. Perhaps it was Araki, Minister of War. But this can be no more than a fair guess.

[3] *Ibid.* Taniguchi was succeeded by Admiral Prince Fushimi, a Prince of the Blood and a decided nationalist. The appointment took effect on 2nd February. The army had already replaced Kanaya, as Chief of the General Staff, by Prince Kanin. "Thus, within five months of the outbreak of the Manchurian Incident the general staffs of both the army and navy were headed by imperial princes, thereby placing the imperial army and navy beyond popular criticism." Takeu-

However, as a result of the outbreak of fighting in Shanghai at the end of January, 1932, Lieutenant-Commander Fujii and other officers were posted from Tsuchiura to aircraft carriers on active service.[1] And during the Shanghai operations Fujii was killed.

This upset plans made by Inouye and Fujii for a mass killing of senior statesmen and business leaders in February. The assassinations were to have been carried out by Inouye's followers and a group of naval officers, the former using pistols already supplied by Fujii.[2]

Inouye and his *Ketsumeidan* now decided to act alone, independently of the naval group, carrying out individual assassinations.[3] A list of some twenty prospective victims was drawn up. They were prominent representatives of the three powerful groups in society most hated by revolutionary nationalists—namely party politicians, capitalist magnates and Court advisers. The list included Inukai, Tokonami and Suzuki Kisaburo from the Seiyukai, and Wakatsuki, Inouye Junnosuke and Shidehara from the Minseito. Also three from the Mitsui firm—Ikeda, Dan and Go—and two from Mitsubishi (Kimura and Kakumu) were marked down for assassination. Those on the list from the "privileged classes" and Court advisers were Prince Saionji, Count Makino, Prince Tokugawa and Count Ito Miyoji.

Two of these intended victims, Dr. Suzuki and Count Ito, were strong nationalists of the old school. Indeed the former was

chi, *op. cit.*, p. 376. But although his exalted birth had much to do with Fushimi's appointment at this particular time, the fact that he was a strong nationalist, a bitter opponent of the London Naval Treaty, must have weighed equally in his favour.

[1] In February the carriers *Kaga* and *Hosho* joined the *Natori* off Shanghai. There is no reason to question the general belief that Admiral Shiozawa started the fighting at Shanghai partly in order to win renown for the navy, which was sensitive to the greatly increased prestige enjoyed by the army as a result of the Manchurian adventure. But Shiozawa underestimated his Chinese opponents. His naval landing force was almost overwhelmed. By the middle of February Shiozawa had been relieved of his command; and to the navy's chagrin the army had to come to its rescue. The only gain to the Japanese from the unnecessary and inglorious "Shanghai Incident" was the moral example set by "The Three Human Bombs". The self-sacrifice of these three soldiers from Kyushu was given great publicity in the press and was, of course, an added stimulus to patriotic sentiment.

[2] Kinoshita, *op. cit.*, p. 127 *et seq*. Fujii obtained the pistols from the *Nichiman Shokai*, a Japanese trading company in Dairen.

[3] The principle was that one man should kill one victim (*ichinin issatsu shugi*).

regarded by Harada and his circle as a terrorist sympathiser. And Count Ito, a Privy Councillor, had been a vehement opponent of both the Pact of Paris and the London Naval Treaty. But no doubt both were regarded as "insincere" by the fanatics of the *Ketsumeidan*; for it was Suzuki's ambition to succeed Inukai as a Seiyukai Premier, and Ito had contrived to amass a great deal of money during his career.[1]

The fact that only two from the death list—Inouye Junnosuke and Baron Dan—were murdered by the *Ketsumeidan* was due to irresolution or incompetence on the part of the young men chosen to kill them.[2]

It has been suggested that Mitsui and Seiyukai interests were directly implicated in the murder of Inouye.[3] A rumour current at the time declared that the Seiyukai politician, Mori Kaku, Chief Secretary to the Inukai cabinet, had given money indirectly to Inouye Nissho and his group. Mori was on close terms with Toyama and, as we shall see, he does not escape suspicion of being privy to the conspiracy of 15th May. However, when the *genro* questioned Harada about the rumour he replied that he was unable to confirm it.[4] There is evidence, also, that early in the year Mitsui and Mitsubishi loaned very substantial sums to the army.[5] It may be that such loans were made in order to protect or advance the interests of these firms in the new, army-controlled

---

[1] "It was remarked that each war brought him [Ito] a degree of nobility and an accession of wealth, but his acquirements of wealth were even more mysterious than his elevation in rank." A. Morgan Young, *Imperial Japan* (London, Allen & Unwin, 1938), p. 57.

[2] For example, Tagura Toshiyuki was chosen to kill Wakatsuki and Makino. With two students from Kyoto Imperial University—Hoshiko Tsuyoshi and Mori Kenji—he practised firing with his pistol in a forest near Kyoto. On 11th February Wakatsuki arrived in Kyoto on an election tour. The three young men had intended to assassinate him near the railway station, but he happened to go in a direction which they had not expected. The trio shadowed the Premier for the next few days, and on 18th February Mori followed him to Matsue. "Failing, however, to kill Wakatsuki he was later assigned to kill Mitsuchi, Minister of Communications. He failed again." Public Procurator's Report, *Japan Advertiser*, 27th March, 1932.

Tanaka Kunio, a student of Tokyo Imperial University, was supposed to Inukai and Tokonami. He contrived to see Tokonami personally, but thing went wrong and he missed his chance". *Ibid.*

[3] Tanin and Yohan, *op. cit.*, p. 264.

[4] *Memoirs, op. cit.*, Part III, Ch. 38 (3rd April, 1932).

[5] *Ibid.*, Part III, Ch. 39 (8th April, 1932).

state of Manchukuo; but no doubt some of the money reached
sleeves of adventurers and terrorists both in Manchukuo
Japan. Payment of money to ultra-nationalist groups, ei
directly or through the agency of the army, was a form of in
ance attractive to many businessmen and party politicians. It
the two motives of patriotism and prudence to recommend it.

Since both the Mitsui concern and the Seiyukai had lead
representatives on the death list it would seem improbable th
they were in direct collusion with the terrorists of the *Ketsi*
meidan. It is unlikely that they would have financed, knowingly
an abattoir in which their own colleagues, as well as hated rivals,
were due to perish.

The successful assassins, Konuma and Hisanuma, were apprehended soon after the commission of their crimes. Following
Dan's murder, on 5th March, both Inouye Nissho and Hisanuma
sought refuge under the roof of Toyama Mitsuru. The latter
gave them accommodation in the quarters of the *Tenkokai* ("The
Society of Heavenly Action")—a small student group founded
and administered by Toyama's second son, Hidezo—in the adjoining house.[1] Inouye may well have believed that he and
Hisanuma would be immune from arrest while enjoying the protection of the "Grand Old Man" of nationalism.[2] However,
doubtless on the advice of Toyama, they gave themselves up to
the police within a few days.

[1] Toyama Hidezo informed the writer that it was his father's secretary, Homma
Kenichiro, who asked for Inouye to be lodged in the quarters of the *Tenkokai.*
(Homma himself was head of a similar patriotic student body, the *Shizanjuku*—
or *Shinoyamajuku*—"The Purple Mountain School"). Toyama Hidezo declared
that Homma gave no reason for his request, and that he (Toyama) was astonished
—it was aft   he had returned from Dan's funeral—to learn that Inouye had
been responsible for Dan's assassination. The whole affair, said Toyama, mysti-
fied him, because he was on friendly terms with Baron Dan, who had indeed
been a supporter of the *Tenkokai.*

Tanin and V han (*op. cit.*, p. 223) declare that Inouye Nissho sought asylum
in Gondc'   use and was not arrested until *after* the 15th May Incident. This,
of cour   an error.

[2]   elief was not ill-founded. When, in the following November, the police
r ra   a's home it created a great sensation, for no previous government
             authorise such a raid.

After Inouye had been taken into custody the naval officer, Lieutenant Koga, set to work to organise the attack on the Prime Minister. He was supplied with funds or active helpers from a variety of sources—Okawa and the *Jimmukai*, the Toyama household, Tachibana's *Aikyojuku*, the *Dai Nippon Seisanto*.

But before discussing the details of the conspiracy which erupted in the 15th May Incident it is necessary to say something about Inukai's policy as Prime Minister.

Inukai throughout his long political life had been on close terms with Toyama Mitsuru; and, according to one account, he was warned by Toyama not to take office as Prime Minister after the Wakatsuki cabinet resigned on 11th December, 1931. Toyama explained that he was no longer able to exercise complete control over his more violent and fanatical followers. But Inukai, who did not lack courage, felt that it was his duty to accept the Imperial command.[1]

If this story is true, one deduction is that Toyama, guiding —if not directing—the ferment of nationalist revolutionary unrest, knew that the next party Premier was in certain danger of assassination. Indeed the situation demanded it. Only by such terrorism could an end be put to the system of party cabinets. Toyama's personal regard for Inukai may have dictated what was both a menacing and friendly warning.[2] It is also possible that Toyama, knowing his man, feared that Inukai would feel bound to comply with the Emperor's desire for a real check to be placed on the army's policy in Manchuria. If the Emperor wanted his Prime Minister to put the clock back in Manchuria Inukai, who was loyal as well as courageous, would not hesitate to obey.

[1] Toyama Hidezo told the writer of this warning to Inukai. The story rings true. Toyama also declared that many of his father's henchmen were getting out of hand, and that (of all people!) Inouye Nissho—before he surrendered to the police—had asked to be given control of the more emotional elements.

[2] Considerations of personal friendship would not of course deflect a man like Toyama Mitsuru from carrying out what he would call a public duty.

Toyama went to Inukai's funeral. A foreigner expressed astonishment proceedings to a high official of the Metropolitan Police. The latter admitt Toyama must have known of the fate in store for Inukai but blamed the for for not understanding Japanese patriotism.

This is precisely what happened. When Saionji was summoned to the Palace to recommend a successor to Wakatsuki the Emperor declared:

> The person to lead the next cabinet must be earnestly cautioned by Prince Saionji on the matter of the mismanagement and high-handedness of the army. The army's meddling in domestic and foreign politics, trying to get its own way, is a state of affairs which, for the good of the nation, we must view with apprehension. Be mindful of my anxiety. Please convey the full import of it to Inukai. After that I will summon Inukai.[1]

The Emperor's wishes, then, were unmistakable; and he underlined them at the first audience he gave the new Premier.[2] While the first act of his cabinet was to reimpose the gold embargo, incidentally enriching certain business houses engaged in foreign trade—Mitsui in particular—and so making the Premier an immediate object of bitter enmity among popular nationalists, Inukai lost no time in trying to set at rest the Emperor's anxiety. The Premier was concurrently Foreign Minister —it was in January, 1932, that he gave the portfolio into the charge of his son-in-law, Yoshizawa Kenkichi—and he could not be accused, therefore, of stepping beyond his proper functions when, only a week after the cabinet had been installed, he made a diplomatic overture to the Chinese government. It was surrounded, however, with great secrecy.

Inukai sent a personal friend, Kayano Chochi, on a special mission to Chiang Kai-shek. Kayano was authorised to discuss with the Nanking government the fundamental causes of trouble between Japan and China; he was to inform Chiang that Inukai was prepared to negotiate a settlement in Manchuria on the basis

[1] Memoirs, op. cit., Part II, Ch. 21 (24th December, 1931).
[2] Inukai told his son, Ken (who acted as his personal secretary), that the Emperor had spoken to this effect. In evidence at I.M.T.F.E., Inukai Ken emphasised that he was sure that his father had indeed been told by the Emperor that something must be done to check the army. The Premier naturally informed Saionji of what had been said at the first audience. Later Harada told Inukai Ken that his father had been greatly impressed. "Baron Harada told me my father had spoken with great decision and that his face had shown his decision. From my own impressions, also, I am convinced that my father would have staked his life in following the Imperial wishes." I.M.T.F.E. Transcript, p. 1539.

of a mutual withdrawal of troops. Chiang was also to be asked to send an emissary to Manchuria for consultation with a special envoy from Japan.[1]

The Kayano mission was an extremely confidential, personal undertaking initiated by Inukai. The army and the Foreign Ministry were neither consulted nor informed regarding it. Elaborate preparations, indeed, were made for secret means of communication between Inukai and Kayano, who reached Nanking at the end of December, 1931.[2]

At first all seemed to be going well. Chiang Kai-shek was reported to be agreeable to Inukai's proposals, and names were suggested for the Chinese and Japanese envoys to be sent to Manchuria.[3]

Meanwhile Inukai considered ways and means of enforcing a most difficult and critical measure—namely the withdrawal of the Kwantung Army to the South Manchurian Railway Zone.

This certainly represented the Emperor's own wish. But the objections in the way were overwhelming. Araki, the new War Minister, was of course the last man to have countenanced any such move.[4] Only a few days after the appointment of the new government he had secured cabinet consent to the dispatch of reinforcements to Manchuria. The Chief of the General Staff, Kanaya, was perhaps a man of more moderate and conservative temperament. In response to pressure from the Wakatsuki

[1] I.M.T.F.E. Transcript, p. 1547. Kayano had known Sun Yat-sen in the days of the Chinese Revolution. He was on good terms with Chiang Kai-shek. There is much about Kayano in Jansen, *The Japanese and Sun Yat-sen, op. cit.*

[2] Before leaving Tokyo Kayano made arrangements to communicate with Inukai by telegraph, using a private code. *Ibid.*, p. 1547.

[3] The Chinese envoy was to have been Chou Chen, President of the Judicial Yuan. The suggested Japanese envoy was Yamamoto Jotaro, ex-president of the S.M.R. *Ibid.*, p. 1548.

[4] Araki, of course, was appointed Minister "because he stood in good stead with the young militarists and could enforce army regulations in the event of emergency" (Harada). Memoirs, *op. cit.*, Part II, Ch. 24 (12th January, 1932). At I.M.T.F.E., Inukai Ken stated that the original choice as War Minister was Gen. Abe Nobuyuki, but numbers of officers of field rank visited Seiyukai headquarters and insisted that Araki be appointed. "The reason why these young officers recommended Araki was that Gen. Abe had no sympathy with the feelings or knowledge of the atmosphere of younger officers, so that if he became War Minister he would be a mere robot; whereas Gen. Araki did know their feelings." I.M.T.F.E. Transcript, p. 1549.

cabinet he had instructed the Commander-in-Chief Kwantung Army at the end of November, 1931, to withdraw from the Chinchow region to the Railway Zone.

If the Kwantung Army was to be brought to heel, and a retirement to the Railway Zone effected, it would have to be done quickly. The tension at Geneva had relaxed, and the anti-Japanese sentiment of the world at large somewhat eased, as a result of the League Council's resolution of 10th December—it was supported by Japan—voting for the establishment of a Commission of Enquiry. This provided a breathing-space, during which the Japanese government—it was the hope of liberal opinion throughout the world—would gain control of its seemingly unruly armed services.

December, then, was a crucial month. Inukai felt that it would be necessary to have the Emperor issue a direct command, by means of an Imperial Rescript, ordering the Kwantung Army to cease further operations in Manchuria. Troops could then be withdrawn to the Railway Zone, and those contingents which had reinforced Manchuria from outside—from Japan and Korea —moved back to their original stations.[1]

It is not certain whether Inukai formally requested the Emperor to issue such a command. But the matter was, it seems, discussed between them.[2] The Emperor has been reported as having asked Inukai what he would do if the army opposed him; and Inukai is said to have replied: "Even if the entire army is against me I shall carry out this policy."[3]

However, the Rescript was, of course, never issued. Indeed it is difficult to see how such direct intervention by the Emperor at that time could have been made effective. The backing of the Privy Council might possibly have been secured. By February

---

[1] I.M.T.F.E. Transcript, p. 1540. "Premier Inukai felt that an Imperial Command was the only way to stop the fighting" (Evidence of Inukai Ken).

[2] "I am not sure whether my father asked the Emperor direct to issue an Imperial Command, or whether he made the request through the Lord Privy Seal, or whether he merely consulted Maeda" (Maeda Yonezo, Minister of Commerce and Industry; regarded as the legal expert in the cabinet). "But in any case I am convinced my father intended to ask for such an Imperial Command as soon as all preparations had been made, and that such preparations were already 90% complete" (Evidence of Inukai Ken). *Ibid.*, p. 1545.

[3] *Ibid.*

there was a decided feeling in the Council that the Emperor himself, with their support, should take measures to control the army.[1]

But there was the risk that the Emperor's command—even when couched in the solemn form of a Rescript—might be successfully defied by the real masters of the Kwantung Army, the nationalist staff officers. If this were to happen, it would be disastrous for the prestige of the Throne.[2]

This no doubt was the reason for not proceeding with what was, it must be admitted, a very hazardous policy. Action was deferred, in the hope perhaps that a more propitious opportunity would occur at a later date. But the chance, for the Emperor to intervene to reassert the authority of the civilian element in the government, had now been lost.[3]

On 23rd December, 1931, the relatively temperate Kanaya was replaced, as Chief of the Army General Staff, by Prince Kanin. At the beginning of the New Year the Kwantung Army occupied Chinchow and advanced to the Great Wall at Shanhaikwan. On

[1] After recording the fact that "members of the Privy Council are in general worried over the arbitrary, high-handed activities of the army stationed in Manchuria", and that "there is a strong opinion in the Privy Council that a State Council presided over by the Emperor should be convened and army discipline restored by all means", Harada justly comments that this was ironical. "In the past the Privy Council has been greatly instrumental in instigating and inciting the army. I feel that a great responsibility rests with the Privy Council for its past irresponsible actions." Memoirs, op. cit., Part II, Ch. 30 (16th February, 1932).

[2] At the end of 1932 Saionji, commenting on a suggestion that the Emperor caution the army regarding the Jehol operations, declared: "Even if the Emperor were to caution them now the army probably would not heed him. The Vice-Chief of the General Staff, Mazaki, and the like are used to going back and telling their staff officers such things as: 'The Emperor was very much displeased', or 'It was this way with the Emperor . . .', if the Emperor showed any distress over their reports. Then the army leaders would say: 'The Emperor is a pacifist', or 'He is too nervous' and such things, if his remarks were not to their liking. In other words they are almost saying that the Emperor's advisers and I are at fault. Therefore if the army would not heed the words even of the Emperor it would greatly impair the Emperor's prestige. So it is a very delicate matter to have the Emperor come out in such a way now." Memoirs, op. cit., Part IV, Ch. 65 (26th December, 1932).

[3] Indeed nearly fourteen years were to pass before circumstances made it possible for the Emperor to take decisive action against the military leaders who by their rashness and ineptitude had brought Japan to ruin. Even then there was a desperate attempt on the part of fanatical officers in Tokyo to seize, before it was broadcast, the recording of the Emperor's order to surrender.

8th January in Tokyo there was an unsuccessful attempt made on the Emperor's life by a Korean who threw an ineffective bomb at an Imperial procession.

Although there is no evidence to support the suspicion, it is impossible not to wonder whether ultra-nationalists—in the army for example—had anything to do with the planning of this outrage. The Emperor's views on the army's activities and ambitions, particularly in Manchuria, were no secret to the well-informed; and it can hardly be doubted that to some extremists the elimination of the Showa Emperor would not have been an occasion for unmixed regret. There was as yet no Crown Prince—the Empress had given birth to Princess Atsuko, her fourth daughter, in March, 1931—and the Heir-Presumptive, Prince Chichibu, was well liked by many nationalists.[1]

Its enemies might well have hoped that the Inukai cabinet would resign in consequence of the attempt on the Emperor's life. But when the Premier tendered his resignation the Emperor advised him to remain in office. Inukai was held officially responsible for the untoward incident by the nation at large; and his continuance in office did not enhance his prestige.

[1] Although he never gave them any encouragement. The Crown Prince, Tsugu Akihito, was born on 23rd December, 1933. It is interesting to find that Saionji some years later twice expressed anxiety to Harada about the possibility of the Emperor being removed to make way for a younger brother. In March, 1938, "with a grave and sad countenance", Saionji said: "I am probably saying this because I have aged. . . . The history of Japan includes many abominable incidents. For instance, the Emperor Suizei who succeeded the Emperor Jimmu had in reality assassinated his elder brother and usurped the Throne. Needless to say I firmly believe that this sort of thing—the wilful assassination of an elder brother by a younger for the purpose of usurping the Throne—will never happen. But, nevertheless, should persons surrounding the younger brother scheme for such an end the outcome would be unpredictable. There have been many examples of this sort in the history of both Japan and China. I would not think that any of the present members of the Imperial family would ever do such a thing. Nevertheless, lest such an incident should occur in the future precautions should be taken from the present time." Memoirs, *op. cit.*, Part XIV, Ch. 266 (27th March, 1938). Again, the following month, Saionji declared: "I do not think that Prince Chichibu or Prince Takamatsu would start anything. However, there might be someone in the Imperial Family who might be taken in by unscrupulous persons. We must be very careful to see that a situation like this does not occur. There would be no telling what would happen then. We must keep watch at all times. The matter is very important." Saionji told Harada to warn Marquis Kido and Prince Konoye regarding this matter. *Ibid.*, Part XIV, Ch. 271 (27th April, 1938).

His position was much more seriously weakened when, as was almost bound to happen, the army intercepted and decoded the messages passing between him and Kayano, his private envoy in Nanking. Inukai received a strong protest and a significant warning—that continued opposition to army wishes would endanger his life—from Mori Kaku, Chief Cabinet Secretary.[1]

Mori Kaku had strong nationalist sympathies, which overbore any loyalty he may have felt for Inukai. For there is no doubt that while holding a position of trust in the administration Mori schemed to overthrow his chief.

One instance of his activities is worth describing, as it reveals his duplicity. In the middle of January Mori put it abroad, in conversation with public men in Tokyo, that in his opinion it was time that the Emperor took a hand in the restoration of army discipline. He proposed that the Emperor should appoint a committee, quite distinct from the cabinet, with an influential man at its head, and that the committee, acting in the Emperor's name, should curb the army.

This, on the face of it, would appear to be a reasonable suggestion, entirely in the spirit of Inukai's policy of checking the army. But the true motive behind Mori's proposal was to secure official power for Baron Hiranuma. Mori wanted him—and failing Hiranuma either Dr. Suzuki Kisaburo or Count Ito Miyoji—to head the committee. This body, under such leadership, would hardly further the aims desired by the Emperor and Inukai.[2]

It seems probable that this was a scheme to manœuvre Inukai out of office, putting Hiranuma into his place. For such an unprecedented committee as Mori proposed would, by reason of its

---

[1] I.M.T.F.E. Transcript, p. 1479. Inukai Ken testified at I.M.T.F.E. that Mori had complained to him: "Your father is carrying on negotiations with General Chiang and these have been kept secret even from me. Concerning this the army is highly indignant." *Ibid.*, p. 1548. Needless to say Kayano returned to Tokyo soon afterwards.

[2] It was Tani Masayuki, Director of the Asia Bureau of the Foreign Ministry, who divined Mori's real intentions, revealing them to Harada who at once visited the Premier's house, warning Inukai Ken. This, we may suppose, effectively killed Mori's plan. Memoirs, *op. cit.*, Part II, Ch. 29 (16th February, 1932). According to Professor Yanaga (*op. cit.*, p. 562) Tani held unofficially a key rôle at this particular time as an intermediary between the Foreign Ministry and the Ministry of War.

functions, immediately rival the cabinet in importance and responsibility.

During February Mori was in close contact with Hiranuma and, by this time if not before, Araki had come to share Mori's belief that Inukai must go. Araki, too, began to favour Hiranuma as the new Premier. At the same time Araki does not seem to have stooped to the machinations employed by Mori. The two were indeed contrasting types; Mori, a politician, supple, cunning, and conspiratorial; Araki, a soldier, inflexible, single-minded and almost ingenuously outspoken.

The fighting in Shanghai exacerbated the differences between Araki and Inukai, and between Araki and Takahashi Korekiyo, the Minister of Finance, who opposed the dispatch of reinforcements to Shanghai.[1]

The disgruntled Araki spoke his mind to Prince Konoye. He said that Hiranuma ought to be made Prime Minister. Inukai had the idea that with the Emperor's help he could hold down the army. It was no wonder, then, that the army detested him. Araki went on to assure Konoye that so long as he remained Minister of War he would do his best to restrain the army; he would never allow the peace of the capital to be disturbed.[2] This assurance was, no doubt, as sincere as it was timely—there were many rumours of a *coup d'état*—for while he was certainly a voluble ultranationalist, his inflammatory speeches sharpening the fanaticism of many terrorists, Araki cannot be described, on the evidence available, as having been well-disposed towards terrorist action.

[1] Takahashi's objections were based on his estimate of Japan's economic position. He feared the possibility of military adventures in China developing into general war. "Japan", he said, "could not finance even six months' war expenditure, should perchance war be waged. The present international circumstances, from Japan's point of view, are dissimilar to those existing at the time of the Russo-Japanese War. Japan now has absolutely no righteous cause to warrant her obtaining aid from foreign nations." Memoirs, *op. cit.*, Part II, Ch. 30 (16th February, 1932). Takahashi was, of course, thinking of economic and financial aid, such as Japan received from her ally, England, during 1904–5. But now Japan was isolated diplomatically. Apart from any action that might be taken by the League there was the danger of Russian intervention; in which event Japan could expect support from no other country.

In 1937, when full-scale war was waged against China, the situation had of course changed in Japan's favour. The League had been defied with success, exposing its impotence; and Japan, by the Anti-Comintern Pact of 1936, had found herself an ally (neutralising Russia) in Germany.

[2] Memoirs, *op. cit.*, Part II, Ch. 31 (23rd February, 1932).

His decisive intervention against the October plotters has to be remembered.[1]

Konoye's opinion, as later expressed to Saionji, was that Inukai should be replaced by an Imperial Prince—Fushimi, Chief of the Naval General Staff, would be the best choice—with both Hiranuma and Makino included in the new cabinet. Konoye also proposed that Admiral Saito Makoto, who had a reputation for moderation and liberal feeling, be given an appointment in the cabinet. Konoye probably believed that Makino and Saito would form a counterbalance to the predominantly chauvinist nature of a Fushimi-Hiranuma cabinet.[2]

However, the General Election on 20th February gave the Seiyukai a notable victory; and to all appearances Inukai's position was strengthened. Needless to say the electoral result was in no sense a mandate for a conciliatory policy towards China. On the contrary, the government was expected to follow the Tanaka tradition of "strong" diplomacy. Inukai's attempt to follow the pacific line laid down by the Emperor had to be made with the utmost secrecy and circumspection—his relations with the Palace almost remind one of the double game played during the French Revolution by Mirabeau and Barnave—for his party contained politicians ripe for rebellion against their chief. Nevertheless, the victory at the polls made it more difficult for anyone to engineer Inukai's removal by constitutional means. Conversely, of course, it increased the likelihood of a resort to the method of terrorism.

On 1st March the state of Manchukuo was inaugurated, and a week later Pu Yi was installed as Chief Executive at Changchun.[3]

---

[1] It is interesting to note that in February Harada (who, surprisingly, was on intimate terms with Araki despite the profound difference of views which separated them) remarked to Saionji that Araki was being "bothered by the younger group [of officers]". *Ibid.*, Part II, Ch. 33 (29th February, 1932).

[2] In this way an uneasy compromise between political forces might be achieved. Konoye (whom Saionji described as "very worried") also suggested, to Harada, that changes be made among the Court advisers. *Ibid.*
To give Hiranuma the responsibility of a cabinet appointment would, in Konoye's view, temper his extreme opinions. Admiral Saito, according to Konoye's proposal, might be given a special office in charge of Home Affairs. *Ibid.*

[3] Indirect pressure exerted by Col. Doihara had helped Pu Yi in the previous November to make up his mind to leave Tientsin for Yingkow in Manchuria on a Japanese steamer. According to Pu Yi's evidence at I.M.T.F.E., more direct persuasion was applied by Itagaki to make him agree to becoming Chief Executive

But the cabinet did not accede to the general nationalist demand for immediate Japanese recognition of the new state. At the same time a Cease-Fire was negotiated at Shanghai.[1]

These hints of moderation were a cause of nationalist rancour, and Mori Kaku—perhaps no longer able to endure his essentially false position—asked Inukai to accept his resignation. But the Premier persuaded him to remain as Chief Secretary.[2]

Meanwhile, on 11th February, Okawa Shumei organised the *Jimmukai*, a new version of the *Gyochisha*. The *Jimmukai* took its name from Jimmu *Tenno*, supposedly the earliest mortal ancestor of the reigning Emperor. Okawa's chief associates in the society were Ishihara Koichiro, Baron Kikuchi Takeo and Colonel (retired) Kawamoto Daisaku.[3] The less prominent figures in the *Jimmukai* included many from the *Gyochisha*, notably Shimizu Gionosuke. According to Okawa's own testimony Ishihara Koichiro supplied the society with the bulk of its funds.[4]

There was no marked difference between the aims of the *Jimmukai* and those of the *Gyochisha*.[5] Despite its basic opposition to parliamentary government, the society, in close collaboration with the *Dai Nippon Seisanto*, put forward some candidates in the General Election—their principal slogan being "Down

---

of Manchukuo. Itagaki did not threaten Pu Yi himself, but told his personal advisers that the Kwantung Army would take "drastic action" if Pu Yi failed to comply with Japanese demands. I.M.T.F.E. Transcript, p. 30279. It must be remembered, however, that Pu Yi was a prisoner of the Russians when he testified at I.M.T.F.E.; he cannot, therefore, be regarded as an entirely reliable witness.

[1] Fighting continued in a desultory fashion after the Cease-Fire early in March; and the Incident was not closed until an armistice was signed at the beginning of May.

[2] Memoirs, *op. cit.*, Part III, Ch. 37 (26th March, 1932).

[3] Kawamoto, it will be remembered, was the officer who engineered the assassination of Chang Tso-lin. He was now director of the Manchuria Coal Company, Yanaga, *op. cit.*, p. 457. Ishihara was the Kansai businessman who had financed Uesugi's *Kenkokukai*. Kikuchi we have met before as a member of the *Gyochisha*, the *Kokuhonsha* and the *Kinno Remmei*.

[4] Tokyo Court of Appeal Proceedings (cited).

[5] When the *Jimmukai* was disbanded on 11th February, 1935 it issued a statement declaring that the society had worked for the Showa Restoration, the emancipation of the Asiatic races, the propagation of *Kodo* throughout the world and had opposed the political parties and Big Business (*zaibatsu*). Cf. Kinoshita, *op. cit.*, pp. 273–6.

with the Established Political Parties!"—but they obtained relatively few votes, and none were elected.

Still, the importance of the *Jimmukai* lay, not in such overt activities as participation in a General Election, but in its clandestine intrigues.

The society was alleged to have received, during February, a supply of arms from military sources.[1] These may have been obtained through the agency of Hashimoto and certain members of the *Sakurakai* who had joined the society.[2] On the other hand arms were more easily procured in Manchuria than in Japan; and Okawa, of course, had access to sources in Manchuria that could supply him with all the weapons he might require.

It was perhaps from this stock that Okawa gave five pistols and a supply of ammunition to the naval conspirator, Lieutenant Koga. The latter visited Okawa early in March, and asked for his active help in the plot to murder Inukai.

Okawa maintained, both at his initial examination following his arrest in June and at his later trial, that Koga's intentions were only vaguely known to him; that Koga, concealing the real nature of his plan, asked merely for assistance to organise a farmers' demonstration in Tokyo. The discontented countrymen of Ibaragi Prefecture were to send representatives to the capital in sufficiently large numbers to turn their demonstration—demanding agricultural relief measures from the government—into a riot. Fighting between demonstrators and police would inevitably break out—the pistols, said Koga, were for use against the police —and the expected outcome of the disturbances would be intervention by the army, the proclamation of martial law, and the establishment of a military government.[3]

The 15th May Incident was, of course, to a large extent an agrarian upheaval. The officers and cadets who murdered Inukai threw from their cars pamphlets headed "Farmers' Sympathisers". And the *Aikyojuku* provided the *nomin kesshitai*, or "death-defy-

---

[1] Memoirs, *op. cit.*, Part II, Ch. 31 (23rd February, 1932). This was a rumour which reached the ears of Konoye, who relayed it to the alert Harada.

[2] Hashimoto, according to Tanin and Yohan (*op. cit.*, p. 226), was head of the "military department" of the society.

[3] Okawa stated that he believed the Incident would develop along the lines which he had hoped would be followed in the March Conspiracy. Tokyo Court of Appeals Proceedings, *op. cit.*

ing farmers' band", which raided the power stations. Koga's description of the projected Incident as a "farmers' riot" was not entirely false. But it was certainly misleading. For the essential part of the plot was of course the assassination, by members of the armed services in uniform, of the Prime Minister in his official residence. And it is impossible to believe that Okawa was not fully conversant with every important detail of the plot. He asserted that he had no idea that the "farmers" were in fact students of the *Aikyojuku*.[1] However, the mendacity of this statement is indicated by the fact that he supplied Tachibana Kosaburo, the founder and director of the *Aikyojuku*, with money to help finance the plot.[2]

Okawa and the *Jimmukai* were, indeed, fully involved in Koga's plot. They were, to a large extent, its financial backers. It is legitimate to go further and to suggest that in fact Okawa was the most active individual behind the scenes, perhaps the ultimate co-ordinator and director of the entire conspiracy.

For with Koga and his naval group some army cadets took part in the attack on the Prime Minister. They had been in close contact with Okawa; and at one time a number of army officers had been associated with them and Okawa in preparing the details of the conspiracy. However, the army officers dropped out of the plot; and so the cadets were the only representatives of the army actively participating in the Incident.[3] Finally the party of assassins under Koga—naval officers and army cadets—numbered nine.

The part played by Tachibana's followers was relatively less serious. Their efforts to destroy the power stations were as unsuccessful as the attempt made by one of their number to blow up the Mitsubishi Bank. An attack was also made on Nishida Zei. He was seriously wounded, and was indeed lucky to recover. The attempt to kill him illustrates the jealousies and fears which

---

[1] *Ibid.*

[2] Statement to Harada by the Minister of Justice. Memoirs, *op. cit.*, Part IV, Ch. 55 (1st October, 1932).

[3] Okawa's meetings with Koga took place, in the main, at his home in Tokyo. But while in Manchuria, between 30th April and 11th May, he had plotted the 15th May outbreak with army officers and cadets. The army officers withdrew from the plot, declaring it to be "unwise". *Ibid.*, Part III, Ch. 45—C (23rd June, 1932).

divided ultra-nationalists. For, as was mentioned in the previous chapter, it was believed that Nishida—with his intimate relations with young staff officers close to the Minister of War—had been injudicious in revealing the plans for the October Incident.[1]

Tachibana's terrorist groups—*nomin kesshitai*, "the death-defying farmers"—were organised directly by Tachibana's chief lieutenant, Hayashi Seizo, a teacher at the *Aikyojuku*. The grenades and bombs which he distributed among the *kesshitai* were, it seems, supplied by Okawa—probably through Koga, acting as intermediary.[2]

Among those arrested in the months following the Incident was Toyama's secretary, Homma Kenichiro.[3] However, before he was arrested it appears that he sought the protection of Takeuchi Kakuji, one of the founders, with Hiranuma, of the Kokuhonsha and very prominent in that society.[4] Accordingly Takeuchi was detained and questioned by the police; although, unlike Homma, he was not indicted.

Hiranuma is reported to have been very angry when he learned of Takeuchi's sympathetic attitude towards Homma; and so far as Hiranuma is concerned the *Kokuhonsha* may be acquitted, perhaps, of the charge of complicity in the 15th May Incident. But there were of course elements, like Takeuchi, in the society who were ready—without, it may be, Hiranuma's knowledge or consent—to profit by the methods of terrorism and so push Hiranuma into power.

iv

Largely as a result of information extracted from Homma the police, six months after the 15th May Incident, arrested Toyama's

[1] His later participation in the 26th February Mutiny, 1936, indicated that Nishida was a supporter of Mazaki, and so in the Araki camp. He may, then, have given information, perhaps in good faith, to Araki before the October Incident.

[2] Tokyo Court of Appeal Proceedings, *op. cit.*

[3] *Vide* footnote 3, p. 107 (*supra*).

[4] Memoirs, *op. cit.*, Part IV, Ch. 55 (1st October, 1932). Takeuchi was a senior bureaucrat, most of his service having been spent in the Commerce and Industry Ministry. From 1935–6 he was Economic Adviser to the Kwantung Army. After holding various high positions in the Commerce and Industry Ministry, he became Vice-Minister of Munitions in 1944.

son, Hidezo.[1] At the same time they searched Toyama's house. It was understood afterwards that some incriminating documents were found; but no further action was taken by the authorities.

Toyama Mitsuru was now in his seventy-ninth year. The *Japan Times*, the Tokyo English language newspaper owned and edited by Japanese, published a special supplement in honour of Toyama at the end of June, 1932. No similar tribute appeared in the vernacular press at the time; and undoubtedly the *Japan Times* supplement was inspired by the wish to impress the Lytton Commission—due to return to Tokyo from Manchuria on 4th July—with the fact that Japanese nationalism was a force to be reckoned with. The supplement was financed by the *Kokuhonsha*.[2]

Among its contents was a tribute to Toyama by Inukai. The two were, as we have said, on terms of close friendship. But if Inukai was Toyama's friend, was he also his victim?

There is no direct evidence that Toyama Mitsuru aided or encouraged any of the various participants in the 15th May Incident; but his household, through his son, Hidezo, and his secretary, Homma, were of course implicated; since they provided Tachibana with funds. Furthermore, both Toyama and his son had the highest opinion of Mori Kaku—he was their choice for the office of Premier[3]—and an unsubstantiated rumour suggested that Mori was aware of the plan to murder Inukai on 15th May.[4]

The conclusion must be that Toyama Mitsuru approved of the assassination, since he did nothing to avert the tragedy. He had

---

[1] The arrest was made on 5th November, 1932. At the same time the police also raided the premises of a small youth organisation, the *Dokuritsu Seinensha* ("Independent Youth Society"), founded earlier in the year by a young nationalist, Kodama Yoshio. The raid on these premises was not occasioned by anything directly connected with the 15th May Incident. The police had received information that the *Dokuritsu Seinensha* was plotting to kill the Premier, Admiral Saito.

[2] The supplement was issued with the *Japan Times* of 26th June, 1932.

[3] In conversation with the writer Toyama Hidezo stated emphatically that both he and his father wanted Mori to be Premier in 1932. Their second choice was Hirota Koki. The latter, of course, held this office for eleven months after the February Mutiny of 1936. Mori, however, died in December, 1932.

[4] "According to rumours the assassination of Inukai was carried out with the collaboration of the Chief Cabinet Secretary." Memoirs, *op. cit.*, Part III, Ch. 44 (22nd June, 1932).

warned Inukai not to accept the Premiership. The warning had been ignored; so his old friend would have to accept his fate. What this would be must have been well known in detail to Toyama; for it is inconceivable that, with his long experience as a nationalist agitator, he should have been ignorant of his son's participation in the Koga-Tachibana plot. Considerable responsibility for the 15th May Incident attaches, therefore, to Toyama. He did not, of course, initiate the plot—its origin derived from the revolutionary unrest centred in Ibaragi Prefecture—but, like Okawa, he exploited the agitators directly concerned.[1]

It was no doubt a disappointment to all who looked forward to a nationalist revolution that the army remained quiescent on 15th May, instead of taking the opportunity of setting up a military government.

On the evening of 15th May there was a gathering of excited officers at the official residence of the Minister of War. Araki himself was absent. He happened to be in Kamakura at the time. The two most important officers present were the Vice-Chief of the General Staff, Mazaki Jinsaburo, and the Vice-Minister of War, Koiso (appointed to this office in February). An argument sprang up between these two. Koiso made a heated attack on the political parties. Mazaki, his senior, advised him to show greater caution. In this instance Mazaki followed the line advocated by his intimate friend, Araki—that in the achievement of nationalist aims army discipline must be maintained at all costs. Mazaki left the meeting, having done his best to damp down the revolutionary ardour of Koiso and other officers; but on his way out of the building he was intercepted by five young army officers. They told him that they wanted to see the Minister of War. Mazaki told them that Araki was not at home but said that he would see them on the Minister's behalf. He took them into a room, asked them to be seated and to state their business. The five officers refused

[1] None of the organisations with which Toyama was directly associated took an overt, active part in the 15th May Incident. The *Seisanto* hesitated on the brink of open participation, and then deferred action until the following year, when it organised the *Shimpeitai* affair. Tanin and Yohan (*op. cit.*, p. 256) maintain that none of the "closer adherents" of Toyama and Uchida—by which the authors mean the "Old Guard" of Fukuoka nationalists—took a direct part in the terrorist organisations of the time. "The police consider them innocent of terrorist activity." *Ibid.*

to seat themselves. They were armed with revolvers, and it looked as though they might open fire at any moment. They shouted that it was their intention to have Araki carry out a military *coup d'état* immediately. Mazaki replied that this was impossible. The officers then said that in that case Mazaki himself must take action, that if he did so a large proportion of the Japanese people would be behind him. Mazaki argued that a *coup* of this sort could not succeed. The political parties, he said, were still strong; and the Japanese people were not as simple-minded as the young officers might think. The great Saigo had tried the method of direct, "loyal" rebellion and had failed. The people would not support a violent *coup*.

The argument raged for two hours before Mazaki, on a pretext, was able to leave the room. He then had the officers arrested by the *Kempei*.[1]

The episode is interesting; for it not only illustrates the unrest and insubordination prevalent among the junior ranks of the army, but also it suggests that the five officers were ready to assassinate the Minister of War had he refused to carry out their wishes. In some respects the incident recalls what happened in the minutes immediately preceding the murder of Inukai. For when the Premier, with great calmness, asked the officers and cadets who had broken into his quarters to let him discuss their grievances, Koga apparently showed signs of being ready to talk things over, and it is conceivable that Inukai—like Mazaki, later the same day—might have played for time, and so escaped death. It was his misfortune that another group, which had entered the house by the back door, suddenly interrupted the parley. Lieutenant Yamagishi, the leader of this party, yelled the order to fire, and Inukai was instantly shot dead.[2]

The leaders of the army, then, were unwilling to seize the chance of effecting the Showa Restoration. And so there followed the arrests—some were not made until later in the year—of the immediate ringleaders in the 15th May Conspiracy. Okawa was taken into custody in June. This provoked the *Jimmukai* to plan

[1] This account is based on a report given to the writer by Gen. Mazaki. Hugh Byas (*op. cit.*, p. 27) has a reference to the incident. He makes Mazaki say: "Where the great Saigo, the most powerful militarist of his day, failed, how could Araki and Mazaki succeed?" *Ibid.*

[2] Memoirs, *op. cit.*, Part III, Ch. 44 (22nd June, 1932); also Byas, *op. cit.*, p. 25.

an act of revenge against the government. In August Dr. Imamaki Yoshio, the acting head of the society, was arrested on the charge of having plotted to assassinate the Premier, the Home Minister and the Minister of Finance.[1]

Although firm measures were taken against those directly involved in the 15th May Incident the affair put an end to party government in Japan, until after the Surrender of 1945. It accelerated the trend towards what has been called "fascism from above".[2]

The 15th May Incident had a significance for modern Japanese nationalism second only to that of the Manchurian Incident eight months earlier. After 15th May, 1932, liberalism, as a factor in official life, was a spent force. There could be no turning back from the path of overseas expansion, opened up by the seizure of Manchuria, or from the course of increasing authoritarian control at home.

The issues stirring the minds of ultra-nationalists now related to the direction and speed of overseas expansion. Where terrorist agitation was uncovered in the years between 1932 and 1936 it was found to be directed not so much against the fundamental policy of the government as against the slowness with which the policy was carried out. The direction of Japan's continental advance—whether it was to be against China, or against Russia —was a matter of considerable debate within the army. It had its place in the extremely bitter feuds dividing various cliques of senior officers—to be described later in this study.[3]

Less than a week before the 15th May Incident the *Japan Times* contained a leading article, entitled "The Challenge of Fascism". After stating that the Japanese mind rejected communism the article declared:

Fascism on the other hand safeguards the fundamental institutions of the country and at the same time puts a curb on capitalism,

---

[1] Dr. Imamaki, in a statement to the press, emphasised the dismay felt at the failure of the Saito government to live up to nationalist expectations. Tanin and Yohan, *op. cit.*, pp. 293–4.

[2] "Each tentative outbreak of revolutionary fascism—the fascist movement from below—merely served as an occasion for the further advance of fascism from above." Maruyama, *Nippon Fasshizmu* (cited), p. 160.

[3] For a discussion of the two main cliques—*Tosei-ha* and *Kodo-ha*—*vide* next chapter (6).

without eliminating private property. Hence its appeal. As for a dictatorship, the Japanese people for centuries were under the benevolent rule of a Tokugawa; and some elements might not be so averse, as some would believe, to exchanging the present economic thraldom, with its deceiving facade of freedom, for an out and out political subservience provided it was accompanied by some surcease from the grinding heel of poverty.[1]

This thesis became increasingly popular in official thought. Indeed it might be said with some justice that after the 15th May Incident the political and social atmosphere of Japan began to resemble that which prevailed under the Tokugawa Shogunate, with the modern army playing the part of the Tokugawas and their advisers.

[1] *Japan Times*, 11th May, 1932.

6

THE GROWTH OF THE ARMY FACTIONS

i

WHILE the removal of Okawa from the arena of public life in June, 1932, to some extent reduced the likelihood of further terrorist disturbances, and the recognition of Manchukuo together with preparations for Japanese withdrawal from the League mollified nationalist opinion, ultra-nationalists still had two powerful motives for resorting to terrorist action.[1]

The first was that of revenge for the arrest of Tachibana, Okawa and the others involved in the 15th May Incident. And, secondly, there was impatience at the apparently cautious policy of the government, which on the one hand seemed to be doing nothing to alleviate agrarian distress and, on the other, appeared by no means unfriendly to Big Business and the political parties.

Admiral Saito, of course, was no fascist. In securing his appointment as Premier the *genro* had accomplished a remarkable piece of political compromise. He had chosen one who, as a retired officer and an experienced administrative official, independent of party, would be acceptable to the army. And satisfaction was also given to the navy, the rival service, by the appointment. At the same time the choice of Saito met the requirements imposed by the Emperor in a remarkable document handed to Saionji by the Grand Chamberlain.

It contained seven stipulations regarding the kind of person who should be selected as the new Prime Minister.

---

[1] Okawa served only five of the fifteen years' imprisonment to which he was sentenced. But this meant that he was unable to make mischief during the few years between 1932 and the outbreak of war with China.

Japan notified Geneva of her withdrawal from the League on 27th March, 1933. Kido told Harada that he had heard that the Emperor lost about ten pounds in weight at the time of Japan's withdrawal from the League. Memoirs, *op. cit.*, Part V, Ch. 85 (23rd June, 1933).

He must be someone (said the Emperor) of high character. He must undertake a reform of existing evils in political party practice —this was a reference, no doubt, to the prevalence of corruption —and at the same time concern himself with the regeneration of discipline and morale in the army and navy.

The Emperor said that it was immaterial whether the new cabinet was a coalition or one formed by a single party. But a person sympathetic to fascism—this was the Emperor's fourth point—was absolutely unacceptable as Prime Minister.

The Constitution must be upheld at all costs, "otherwise"—said the Emperor—"I would not be able to justify myself to the Emperor Meiji".

The foreign policy of the new cabinet must be based on a concern for the preservation of international peace.

Finally, there must be a regeneration of discipline and morale in the civil service, together with a clearer distinction between the powers and functions of administrative officials and those of Parliamentary Vice-Ministers and Counsellors.[1]

The Emperor's stipulation regarding "high character"—meaning, of course, strength of purpose and complete incorruptibility —somewhat limited the choice so far as party politicians were concerned. Saionji could not well recommend anyone from the Minseito, the minority party in the Lower House. And in the Seiyukai it was difficult to find anyone of sufficient political experience, with the exception of Takahashi Korekiyo, who combined the ability and character appropriate at this critical juncture to the office of Premier.

At the same time the objection to anyone "sympathetic to fascism" ruled out such persons as Araki and Hiranuma. So under the circumstances the choice of Admiral Saito was very apt.

With Admiral Togo and Marshal Uehara, Saito was an Adviser to the *Kokuhonsha*; but his nationalist sentiments were tempered by a certain moderation and realism, born of shrewd knowledge of the world outside Japan. He may have been in sympathy with the imperial aspirations of the army, but in the progress of national

---

[1] Saionji made a note of the Emperor's wishes in the form of a short memorandum; and this, in Saionji's own handwriting, was found among the original Harada Memoirs—although Saionji had marked the paper, "to be consigned to fire". Memoirs, *op. cit.*, Part III, Ch. 45 (23rd June, 1932).

expansion he saw the need for caution and restraint. He showed no leniency towards "dangerous thoughts", but he was ready to deal firmly with all extremists—of the Right wing as well as of the Left.[1]

Saito had been Prime Minister for little more than a year when the police, on 10th July, 1933, uncovered a conspiracy which, for violent melodrama, was the equal of any so far encountered by the authorities. This was the affair of the *Shimpeitai* ("The Divine Soldiers").

There was a commercial, non-political element in the compound of personalities and motives in the plot. A touch of comedy, indeed, was provided by the manner in which Naito Hikokichi, the managing director of the Matsuya Department Store, was duped by the conspirators. At the outset Naito paid for information—the date of the projected "Incident"—on the basis of which he hoped to speculate with success on the stock market, which had already involved him in heavy losses. Later he advanced more money on the promise that he would be made Minister of Commerce and Industry in the new government to be established by *coup d'état*. He was in fact financing a revolutionary *coup* for entirely personal motives, and mainly in order to save himself from bankruptcy.

This led to a tendency on the part of some contemporary observers to make light of the affair.[2] But the authorities regarded

[1] Mr. Fleisher, editor of the *Japan Advertiser* during this period, has described how he accompanied a visiting American newspaperman to an interview with Admiral Saito in the summer of 1932. Saito was asked to comment on the opinion, held by many Americans, that conditions in Japan resembled those prevailing in Germany before the 1914–18 War. Saito replied: "Everything will be all right so long as we old men are here to put on the brakes." Wilfred Fleisher, *Volcanic Isle* (London, Jonathan Cape, 1942), p. 58.

There is a reference to what was probably the same interview in Mr. Grew's *Ten Years in Japan* (London, Hammond, 1944). An unnamed American journalist, in a written report to the U.S. Ambassador, stated: "He [Saito] said: 'I have no doubt that the little chicken often thinks back to the egg—how warm and comfortable it was; but once pecked out, there is no egg to which he can go back. We only go ahead now and hope for the best.' I asked him about the rumours of war between the U.S. and Japan. I told him both navies seemed to have the jitters but I couldn't see any prospects of war. He said: 'Don't be too sure of that. Always remember that those whose careers depend upon war always want war.' I asked him: 'Do you mean the Navy, Your Excellency?' 'Oh no, no, no,' he said. 'The Navy is all right; but the Army knows very little about the world.'" *Ibid.*, p. 97.

[2] For example Hugh Byas, who believes that the *Seisanto* organisers of the

it gravely enough at the time.[1] It was, in fact, as bloodthirsty in conception as the October Incident—the abortive *Kinki Kakumei* of 1931—and the Tokyo police came to hear of it largely by good fortune.

On 11th July, 1933, the Emperor was due to pay a visit to the Military Academy. On each occasion that the Emperor left the Palace it was customary for the Tokyo police to make special efforts to ascertain the whereabouts of known criminals and wild characters in the city; and precautionary arrests were commonly made. In fact on such occasions the Metropolitan force as a whole was put on the alert. But thanks to the 15th May Incident, and to the presence of a new and particularly vigilant Chief of Police (appointed during the autumn of 1932), the police happened to be unusually watchful during this summer. The arrival of over forty members of the *Dai Nippon Seisanto* and of other patriotic bodies at the Meiji Jingu Hall—the hostel used by pilgrims visiting the Meiji Shrine—might have been ignored by the local police had it not occurred on the eve of one of the Emperor's rather infrequent public visits. The conspirators themselves had chosen this time, because they expected that on 11th July there would be—as Harada expresses it—"a shortage of policemen due to protective measures for the Emperor's visit".[2]

The organisation most deeply involved in the conspiracy was the *Seisanto*. In 1932, partly as a result of the illness of Uchida who had exercised a unifying control over the society, the *Seisanto* had divided into two factions. The first was known as the *genro-ha*, the *genro* faction, and was composed of devoted followers of Uchida and Toyama. Its leader was Kuzuo Yoshihisa, who was to head the *Kokuryukai* after Uchida's death in 1937. The second faction, in name at least, was that of the "young men" (*seinen-ha*) and was led by Suzuki Zenichi. This faction, the more impetuous of the two, was eager for revolutionary action on a large scale.[3]

Incident had no intention of risking their lives. He describes the *Shimpeitai* as "God-sent farceurs".B yas, *op. cit.*, pp. 224–5. But his account of the Incident is instructive as well as entertaining. *Ibid.*, Ch. XV.

[1] "The Incident was no joke" (Justice Minister). Memoirs, *op. cit.*, Part V, Ch. 97 (15th September, 1933).

[2] *Ibid.*, Part V, Ch. 91 (21st July, 1933).

[3] Tsukui Tatsuo had joined the *Seisanto* in January, 1932, and he was one of

It was the *seinen-ha* which was implicated in the affair of the *Shimpeitai*. Suzuki Zenichi had been intimate with Inouye Nissho. It appears that he had promised to take an active part in the assassinations planned by Inouye. However, he did no more than provide shelter and encouragement to some of those involved in the 15th May Incident, and his inactivity was much criticised by his friends.[1]

To some extent the *Shimpeitai* conspiracy was an effort on the part of Suzuki to regain face by the rescue of Inouye Nissho, whose trial had begun on 28th June, 1933. It was planned to storm the court building and release Inouye and the other accused in the *Ketsumeidan* case. Suzuki secured the co-operation of Inouye's defending lawyer, Amano Tatsuo, of the *Aikoku Kinroto* ("The Patriotic Labour Party"),[2] and this society, with Amano and Maeda Torao as its leading figures, was committed to participation in the conspiracy.

Also in the plot was Inouye's brother, Commander Yamaguchi Saburo, a naval air officer. His rôle was to carry out a bombing attack from an aeroplane on the Premier's official residence while the cabinet was in session.

The group which gathered at the Meiji Jingu Hall on 10th July —it was their arrest which broke up the conspiracy—was the advance party of a body some hundreds strong which was to have assembled at the Shrine and marched into the city, some armed with swords, the rest with banners and propaganda leaflets.[3] This demonstration, however, was essentially a diversion to attract

the *seinen-ha*. Nevertheless he opposed Suzuki's policy of terrorism. And he was expelled from the society on the grounds of his opposition to Suzuki's methods —in spite of the fact that, after the arrest of the *Shimpeitai* ringleaders, the *Seisanto* issued a statement generally condemning the Incident. This was a characteristic example of the disunity prevalent in all but the smallest nationalist groups.

[1] Harada records that he met the Minister of Justice and the Chief of the Metropolitan Police, who gave him their views on the *Shimpeitai* Incident. "He [Suzuki] had promised to come forward at the time of the 15th May Incident. He did not, and he became a target of censure from those around him. The general story is that in the end he could not avoid starting this Incident." Memoirs, *op. cit.*, Part V, Ch. 91 (21st July, 1933).

[2] A society founded in 1930 by former students of Professor Vesugi.

[3] The majority would have been from the *Seisanto*—many of them from the Osaka region. Their banners and handbills bore the inscription "Divine Soldiers" —hence the title given to the Incident. Students from the *Aikyojuku* were also to have taken part in the demonstration.

the attention of the police.[1] For, meanwhile, others had the task of attacking the residence of Count Makino and the offices of the Minseito, Seiyukai and the Social Mass Party (*Shakai Taishuto*).[2]

There was cherished the familiar hope that the army would declare martial law and set up its own government. But now Araki—no longer a hero to all nationalists—was cast for the part of victim. He was to be assassinated, with the Premier and other members of the cabinet, by the bombs from Yamaguchi's aircraft; and his successor as Minister of War, according to Suzuki, was to be General Hayashi Senjuro. The new Premier was to be either Prince Chichibu or Prince Higashi-Kuni.[3]

It must be admitted that Prince Higashi-Kuni, no doubt unwittingly, laid himself open to a suspicion of being in collaboration with the *Shimpeitai*. Lieutenant-Colonel Yasuda Tatsunosuke (retired) played a leading part in the financial negotiations with Naito, the Department Store director.[4] While these were in progress Yasuda, for at least some of the time, was staying at Prince Higashi-Kuni's home in Tokyo. Higashi-Kuni later declared that he was in no way involved in the conspiracy. And on the whole it seems improbable that he gave active encouragement to those planning a violent *coup d'état*. None the less he appears to have had some sympathy with the extreme nationalist cause.[5]

---

[1] Memoirs, *op. cit.*, Part V, Ch. 97 (15th September, 1933).

[2] The homes of Wakatsuki and Dr. Suzuki were also on the list.

[3] Memoirs, *op. cit.*, Part V, Ch. 97 (15th September, 1933). Harada's information came from the Minister of Justice.

[4] The negotiations were carried on mostly through the agency of "go-betweens", Naito being represented by his secretary, Imamura, while Lt.-Col. Yasuda, with Fujita Isamu, acted for Suzuki Zenichi. At first Imamura was inclined to caution, mistrusting Yasuda's sincerity. But when, on their way home together from one of their meetings, he parted from Yasuda at the gate of Higashi-Kuni's house, and saw Yasuda enter the house, he was much impressed; and thereafter he trusted the conspirators. *Ibid.*, Part V, Ch. 99 (2nd December, 1933).

[5] "It was a great mistake to have let Yasuda stay at my home" (Higashi-Kuni to Harada). *Ibid.*, Part V, Ch. 105 (7th November, 1933). Harada was evidently on close enough terms with Higashi-Kuni to speak his mind to him on occasions. For example, at the end of July, 1932, Higashi-Kuni told Harada that, while he failed to understand "the present army with its young officers", he considered that the Emperor was sometimes unwise in his comments on military matters; and he went on to repeat various criticisms of the army which the Emperor was reported to have made. Harada said at once that it was very undesirable for Higashi-Kuni to relate stories reflecting adversely on the Emperor. "What Your Highness says is mainly sensational, and gossipy; and I feel this is a very casual, indiscreet attitude." Higashi-Kuni: "Well, I speak because it is [to] you,

THE DOUBLE PATRIOTS

A week after the police had unearthed the *Shimpeitai* affair a
significant meeting was held at the home of Harada's friend,
Colonel Marquis Inouye. It was a dinner party, and the guest of
honour was Prince Higashi-Kuni. The others present, in addition
to Inouye and Harada, were Prince Konoye, Marquis Kido,
Viscount Okabe, Colonel Suzuki Teiichi and Shiratori Toshio.[1]
There is little doubt that the purpose of this entirely social and
unofficial meeting was to address a tactful but unmistakable
warning to Higashi-Kuni against allowing himself to get involved
in extremist plots.

> Those of us who were gathered at that place [records Harada]
> agreed unanimously that members of the Imperial Family should
> not act thoughtlessly; also that it is undesirable for them to take a
> position as Prime Minister, or any official position.[2]

It was this unprecedented connection—however tenuous it
may have been—between a member of the Imperial Family and
a terrorist conspiracy which gave to the *Shimpeitai* affair a
peculiar gravity.[3] This may have led the authorities to treat the

Harada." Memoirs, *op. cit.*, Part III, Ch. 50 (4th September, 1932). Later in the
summer of 1932 Higashi-Kuni, while in Ibaragi Prefecture, paid a visit to the
Aikyojuku. Ibid., Part III, Ch. 51 (7th September, 1932).

[1] Shiratori was then Director of the Foreign Ministry Information Bureau
and was already showing signs of extreme nationalist sympathies disturbing to
Harada. Col. Suzuki will be remembered as the officer, from the War Ministry
Military Affairs Bureau, who refused to co-operate with Ninomiya, Koiso and
Tatekawa in the March Incident. *Vide* p. 64 (*supra*). Okabe was a director
of Yasuoka's *Kokuikai. Vide* p. 48 (*supra*). All those present were, by the standards of public life, comparatively young.

[2] Memoirs, *op. cit.*, Part V, Ch. 94 (20th August, 1933). The gathering did not
escape the notice of the military police, the *Kempei*. They thought it was part
of a plot by Konoye and the others to make Higashi-Kuni Premier in a new
cabinet. Harada had to protest to the *Kempei* Commandant and explain the true
purpose of the meeting. *Ibid*. The dinner party seems to have taken place on
18th July, 1933. *Ibid*.

[3] Three years later a mysterious case, involving the issue of *lèse majesté*, arose
in connection with the chief priest at the Iribune Kannon Temple in Tokyo.
The writer has been unable to uncover the facts of the case, which bears some
faint resemblance to the story of Rasputin. The Japanese priest, unlike the
Russian, had no direct influence over the Emperor. But it would seem that—on
account of alleged powers of prophecy—he impressed Prince Higashi-Kuni,
some of the ladies of the Court (notably Princess Shimazu) and, possibly, Prince
Kanin. And they were in the habit of visiting his temple. In the summer of 1936
the police began an investigation of the priest and his doctrines. When threatened
with arrest—the priest had forecast the Emperor's death some years later—he

Incident with particular discretion and wariness. No details of the affair were released to the press until September, 1935; and the trials of the accused did not open until November, 1937. They were treated with considerable leniency and were finally awarded short terms of imprisonment—in March, 1941,—with immediate remission of sentence. They were granted liberal bail—though before this was allowed Naito and Commander Yamaguchi died in custody—and were thus free to dabble in various intrigues, causing the authorities a great deal of anxiety.

In the final judgment, at the beginning of 1941, the President of the Supreme Court declared that he could not accept the contention of the Prosecution that Amano and the other defendants had been actuated by a desire both to overthrow the government and to change fundamentally the Constitution. The defendants, said the judge, had wanted to change the cabinet by killing its members, but it was impossible to think that they desired to carry out an illegal reform of the cabinet system and other institutions. Still, some of their acts amounted to attempts to commit arson and homicide. Nevertheless, the facts had been discovered by the police before any blood had been shed. The motives of the defendants, too, deserved sympathy. Moreover since 1933 there had been great changes in the country both internally and with regard to its international relations. Therefore it was proper to grant remission of sentence to the accused.[1]

was reported to have said: "If you prosecute me Prince Higashi-Kuni's offence against the Emperor will also be revealed." Memoirs, Part XI, Ch. 215 (24th September, 1936). This remark may possibly have had reference to Higashi-Kuni's alleged connection with the *Shimpeitai* Incident.

[1] Largely through the skilful advocacy of Amano Tatsuo the accused succeeded to getting the charge, of conspiracy to raise an insurrection (Article 78 of the Criminal Code), changed to that of having prepared to commit arson and homicide (Articles 113 and 201). The prescribed sentence for offences committed under Articles 113 and 201 was penal servitude not exceeding two years, but special provisions were attached to both Articles allowing the penalty to be remitted, according to circumstances. These provisions, for remission of sentence, were not attached to any other clauses of the Criminal Code; and the *Shimpeitai* case was, it seems, the first on record in which the provisions were applied.

The accused behaved with much independence of spirit, not to say insolence, during the trial. They refused to listen to the Procurator's final address on the grounds that they objected to his interpretation of the *Kokutai*. When the trial ended they marched in ceremonial dress from the Court Building to the plaza in front of the Imperial Palace and bowed in homage to the Throne.

The *Japan Times* described the judgment as "a triumph of law in Japan and a brilliant piece of political adjustment". 18th March, 1941.

133

Those tried and convicted of participation in the *Ketsumeidan* and 15th May Incidents were also treated, by Western standards, very leniently. But in spite of much sympathy expressed for the accused in both official and popular circles they were sentenced to periods of imprisonment, even though these were not served in full.[1]

Of course, when considering the mild treatment accorded to the *Shimpeitai* defendants, the circumstances prevailing in 1941 have to be taken into account. Japan was then heavily involved in one war and was soon to be engaged in another; and it would have been against public policy to deal sternly with those who could claim to have been true agents of the Imperial Will in the days before the country had fully "awakened" to the need for uncompromising chauvinism.

The *Shimpeitai* Incident was not the only terrorist plot to disturb the authorities during 1933. There was also the affair of the Kawagoe *Teishintai*, in November. Earlier in the autumn the police discovered that there was a plan to murder Dr. Suzuki, President of the Seiyukai, and Hatoyama Ichiro, Minister of Education, on 14th November at the town of Kawagoe, some twenty miles north-west of Tokyo. Suzuki and Hatoyama were due to address a meeting of the Seiyukai in the town on that day.

The police waited until 13th November, the eve of the projected assassinations, before making their arrests. They then took into custody over thirty persons but released all except seven by the end of November. The seven conspirators were farmers, led by one Yoshida Toyotaka. They called themselves the *Kyukoku Saitama Seinen Teishintai* ("The Saitama Young Men's Patriotic Storm Troops").[2] They proposed to raid a bank after killing Suzuki and Hatoyama, and then to go to Tokyo and assassinate the Prime Minister, Count Makino and Baron Wakatsuki, the President of the Minseito.[3] Having completed these tasks the conspirators had planned to commit *hara-kiri* on the Plaza in front of the Imperial Palace.[4] Once again there was the expect-

---

[1] By 1940 only Tachibana remained in prison.

[2] Kawagoe was in Saitama Prefecture.

[3] It was hoped to carry out the assassination of Saionji, at Okitsu, at the same time.

[4] The location of an act of *seppuku*—the formal name for *hara-kiri*—has some

ation that these disturbances would induce the army to declare martial law and assume the direct government of the country.

The whole plot, however, seems to have been badly prepared. The conspirators had only a few hundred *yen* at their disposal—hence the plan to rob the bank at Kawagoe—and a single revolver and a few swords. For a time, at least, two young army officers—Lieutenant Kurihara, of a Tokyo regiment, and Lieutenant Okura, of a Chiba tank unit—were interested in the conspiracy. However, according to the version of the affair given to Harada by the Minister of Justice, the two officers "were against the assassination plot, though they were connected with those who planned it".[1]

ii

The terrorist Incidents of 1932 and 1933, since none of them was successful, somewhat discredited the advocates of reform by *coup d'état*, although they greatly increased the expectation, now

significance, depending on whether the act is performed by way of atonement or of protest.

Where atonement is the motive the presence of appropriate witnesses is, perhaps, more important than the place where the *seppuku* is carried out—as, for example, in the case of Taki Zenzaburo described by Mitford in his *Tales of Old Japan*. Taki was condemned for having given the orders to fire on the foreign settlement at Hyogo in February, 1868. The *seppuku*, therefore, was one of atonement, and witnesses were invited from seven legations representing the countries whose nationals had been attacked.

Where *protest* is the motive the place of *seppuku* is usually as near as possible to the home or official premises of the person or organisation against whom the protest is directed. For example, in 1924 in protest against the United States exclusion policy a Japanese patriot committed *hara-kiri* in front of the Standard Oil offices in Tokyo. (He probably mistook the premises for those of the American Embassy.)

Seppuku on the Plaza in front of the Imperial Palace often combines the elements of both atonement and protest. In the case of the *Teishintai* the act would have been one of protest to the Palace—not against the Emperor but against the Imperial Household Ministry and Court advisers for having misled the Emperor—and of atonement, to the Emperor, for having broken the peace of the capital. Similarly the suicides on the Plaza after the Surrender in August, 1945, were expressions of both protest and guilt.

[1] Memoirs, *op. cit.*, Part VI, Ch. 108 (7th December, 1933). Kurihara was one of the officers who threatened Mazaki on the evening following the 15th May Incident. *Vide* pp. 122–3 (*supra*). He had then been taken into custody by the *Kempei*; but no serious proceedings were taken against him. He was to be one of the mutinous officers on 26th February, 1936.

widely held among Japanese, of revolution.[1] And each Incident, of course, strengthened and confirmed the army in its policy of gaining ultimate control of all important branches of public administration. As pressure from the younger officers—using the threat of violence as a form of blackmail—was maintained, the leaders of the army, disrupted though they were by their own contending factions, could not turn back from the course of national expansion on which they had embarked in the autumn of 1931. They apprehended, therefore, that within a few years war would ensue as the logical consequence of their policy. It was during 1933 that Araki began to speak publicly of the grave crisis which would face Japan in the years 1935 and 1936.[2] The general assumption of those who took note of these warnings was that Japanese relations with Russia and the United States would become particularly strained during those years. On the one hand Araki's eyes had always been fixed steadily on Russia, as the prime enemy of Japan.[3] And, on the other, existing naval agreements would have expired by the end of 1936. In the interim Japan would not conclude a new naval treaty except on the basis of a parity certain to be unacceptable to England and the United States.[4] And it might be expected that the Japanese would then be apprehensive of American pressure, leading perhaps to war in the Pacific.

It is now apparent that in 1933 the army—in which Araki was temporarily the dominant force—was preparing to attack Russia

[1] Tani Masayuki, who had been made Counsellor of the Japanese Embassy in Manchukuo, informed Harada while on a visit to Tokyo that "because of alarming rumours coming from Japan the sole topic of conversation [in Manchukuo] was that a revolution might arise at any time in Japan". Memoirs, Part VI, Ch. 107 (18th November, 1933).

[2] After the Grand Manœuvres in October, 1933, Araki told press correspondents that the years 1935 and 1936 would be "not only a crucial period for Japan but also for the Orient and the entire world. In order to override this national crisis we must have national unity, exalting the spirit of nationalism." *Ibid.*, Part V, Ch. 104 (1st November, 1933).

[3] At a meeting of Prefectural Governors in 1933 Araki made a characteristic speech stating that Japan would inevitably clash with the U.S.S.R., and she must establish herself in the Maritime Province and E. Siberia. I.M.T.F.E. Exhibit 3371; Transcript, p. 31836 (Evidence of Takebe Rokuzo, Director-General of General Affairs Board, Manchukuo—he was Governor of Akita Prefecture in 1933).

[4] For example the Japanese formula of the "common upper limit", presented at the London Naval Conference of 1935.

in 1935; while the navy planned to engage in war with the United States during the following year.[1]

But though such plans were made the army was by no means unanimous in support of them. Indeed Araki's pronouncements regarding "the Crisis of 1935–6" were perhaps defiant warnings to his military opponents as well as a patriotic rallying cry to the country as a whole. For there was a powerful school of thought within the army which disagreed with Araki's policy. This opinion, moreover, was gaining strength.

In August, 1933, Harada wrote:

> Relations with the United States are affected reciprocally by relations with Russia. That is to say, up to now the army has maintained that Russia must be attacked to a finish. If there is a single misstep when we attack Russia relations with the United States might become actively involved . . . The army asked the navy to take care of America. The navy agreed. . . . Within the army there are two factions; one whose members have been saying that we must attack Russia, and another which says that it would be better to be friendly with Russia and not stir up anything. In General Staff H.Q. the leader of the first group is Major-General Kobata; the second group is headed by Major-General Nagata. Nagata's contention in general has been gaining ground. To-day the general trend inclines that way.[2]

These rival factions were those which became known as the *Kodo-ha*, "the *Kodo* faction", and the *Tosei-ha*, or "Control

[1] In October, 1933, Shigemitsu Mamoru told Harada "with a very grave look" that the army seemed determined to attack Russia in 1935, that the navy intended to attack the United States in 1936. Memoirs, *op. cit.*, Part V, Ch. 101 (14th October, 1933).

At the same time Takahashi Korekiyo, speaking of the proceedings of a Five Ministers' Conference (Premier, with the War, Navy, Foreign and Finance Ministers), told Harada: "It was revealed that, according to their respective plans, the army would attack Russia and the navy would attack America, hoping meanwhile to keep the goodwill of other nations." *Ibid.*

The reason why 1935 was selected as the year for an attack on Russia was probably because it was considered that by then Japan's position *vis-à-vis* Russia would be most favourable. Early in February, 1934, the American Ambassador noted: "The opinion among the military attachés in Tokyo is that the Japanese Army will reach the zenith of combat efficiency in 1935, and that after that period time will tell in favour of Soviet Russia in point of lines of communication, organised man-power, fortification, and equipment." Grew, *op. cit.*, p. 112.

[2] Memoirs, *op. cit.*, Part V, Ch. 92 (3rd August, 1933).

faction". It has often been considered, by students of Japanese affairs, that the distinction was one between extremists and moderates.[1] But the issue, in reality, was not so simple as that, although it is true that on the whole the more radical elements—the national socialist advocates of the Showa Restoration—were to be found in the *Kodo-ha*. But although the rival faction, superficially at least, was more restrained in its political views there was no shade of temperate conservatism—let alone the faintest suggestion of liberal feeling—in its ideas. A glance at the personalities commonly associated with the *Tosei-ha* will illustrate the point.

Harada, in the passage just quoted, refers to Nagata Tetsuzan as leader of the *Tosei-ha*. Nagata, it will be remembered, at first favoured the March Conspiracy but later, like Ugaki, changed his mind. He was also closely involved in the preparation of plans for the Manchurian Incident.

Neither Koiso nor Tatekawa, could be described as having

[1] In Hillis Lory's *Japan's Military Masters* (*op. cit.*, pp. 178–9) the contrast between the *Kodo-ha* and *Tosei-ha* is expressed by the reproduction, in their original form, of comments noted for the benefit of the author by a Japanese. These are so interesting that they are worth quotation, in full, here.

"*Kodo-ha*

100% soldier. Hard-boiled sort yet warm-hearted. Ready to sacrifice rules for personal sympathy. Cause of Emperor higher than law of the land. Must make extreme sacrifices to-day to achieve 'direct rule of Emperor'. Very strongly believes in divine origin Imperial House and 'manifest destiny'. Bitter foe of communism. In private association hail-fellow-well-met; general associating with private. Battlefield commanders; no peacetime men. Death in battle highest honour that can befall a Japanese. Consider politicians no better than so many 'frogs in a well'. Believes argument useless. 'I will knock him down' type. No compromise. White or black; no grey. In organisation like steam-roller. Very restless. Unhappy in sustained peace. National socialist in their thinking but confused. Not logical. Two and two do not make four.

Tosei-ha

Law abiding. Not so 'pious'. Outward observance of national policy, but not fanatical. War Minister type rather than battlefield commanders. Capable administrators, diplomats, suave in manner. Businesslike, possessing relatively clear ideas of figures. Realistic. Watch their step. Lay stress on merit rather than personal sympathy. Respect 'status quo'. Believe in 'evolution' rather than 'revolution'. Pay due consideration to happiness of individual. Individual just as important as State. Present life as important as future. Common sense sort. Pay due consideration to private property. Believes in wisdom of co-operating with capitalists and politicians. Considers international co-operation important. Two and two make four." *Ibid.*

"moderate" opinions.[1] Itagaki, who had been promoted Major-General in 1932 and who was now (1933) attached to General Staff Headquarters, and Major-General Tojo, who was also at the General Staff Headquarters, were other members of this faction.[2]

Civilian nationalists, such as Okawa, who were disappointed at the unsympathetic attitude of Araki at the time of the October Incident and during the 15th May disturbances, have also been identified with the *Tosei-ha*.[3] Certainly Okawa, despite the March Incident, retained the highest regard for General Ugaki, who, if he cannot be described as one of the *Tosei-ha*, was undoubtedly closer to that faction than to the *Kodo-ha*.[4]

Those restless officers, Hashimoto and Nemoto, were associated with the *Tosei-ha*; and indeed the more one considers the composition of this faction, and the past history of many of its members, the less one is inclined to accept the word "Control" as an appropriate title for the group.[5] It could be said, of course, that

[1] Kido described the *Tosei-ha*—early in 1935—as being "the Koiso-Tatekawa-Nagata faction". Memoirs, *op. cit.*

[2] So were Gen. Minami (at this time a Supreme War Councillor), Lt.-Gen. Sugiyama, Chief of the Army Aviation Dept., and Maj.-Gen. Umezu, of General Staff H.Q.

[3] Cf. Yanaga, *op. cit.*, p. 510, footnote 38.

[4] Ugaki's heyday, politically, occurred, undoubtedly, during the nineteen-twenties, when he and his clique were temporary heirs to the hegemony exercised by Yamagata. In age and ideas he was almost of an older generation than the *Tosei-ha*. Nevertheless this faction contained some who were his supporters—notably Ninomiya, whom Araki removed from his post as Vice-Chief of the General Staff (to make room for Mazaki) and who, after a short period as Commander of the 5th Division, retired.

[5] After Mazaki had been removed from his position as Inspector-General of Military Training in 1935, there was some talk of Tatekawa being made Vice-Chief of the General Staff and Koiso Chief of the Air Service H.Q. Harada protested to the Premier (Admiral Okada) that such moves would be most dangerous, for they would undo all the good that had been done by the removal of Mazaki. Harada asked the Premier to convey a message to Prince Kanin, Chief of the General Staff, to the effect that although there were good points in Tatekawa there was, at the same time, "no difference between him and Mazaki in the matter of eccentricity . . . and therefore it will be useless to oust Mazaki and bring in Tatekawa". Memoirs, *op. cit.*, Part IX, Ch. 178 (14th August, 1935).

Early in 1936 Tani Masayuki told Harada that he considered both Koiso and Tatekawa to be "suspicious characters". "As a matter of fact", Harada noted in his record, "I consider Koiso is even more suspicious than Tatekawa, recalling the relations Koiso had maintained with Mori before and after the 15th May Incident, which may have been endorsed by Koiso himself." *Ibid.*, Part X, Ch. 195a (6th February, 1936).

a characteristic of the *Tosei-ha*, distinguishing it from the *Kodo-ha*, was a certain readiness for compromise, for co-operation with capitalists and with the Diet, so long as it was amenable to army wishes. Just as Okawa had broken with Kita Ikki on the issue of state socialism, so the Showa Restoration was one issue which divided the *Tosei-ha* from the more radical *Kodo-ha*. The latter, in spite of its anti-Russian policy, had ideas on economics not far removed from those of the communists.

The principal figures in the *Kodo-ha*—Araki, Mazaki, Yanagawa and Kobata[1]—were undoubtedly embarrassed sometimes by the radical agitation prevalent among their extreme juniors, the captains and lieutenants, the control of whom was the urgent problem facing all senior officers.[2] But the leaders of the *Kodo-ha* felt a genuine sympathy for the anti-capitalist views of the radicals. It must also be remembered that, to a large extent, the unrest and even insubordination among the junior officers derived from the jealousy felt by the unprivileged majority towards a fortunate élite.[3] Araki and Mazaki escaped much of this envy and dislike because they were regarded as having no ties with any political party—the view was a mistaken one—and as being inspired wholly by unselfish, patriotic motives. Furthermore it was believed that these two generals had reached their exalted positions through their own abilities, entirely unaided by any advantage accruing from Clan or family connections.[4]

[1] Lt.-Gen. Yanagawa Heisuke had been appointed Vice-Minister of War in August, 1932, in place of Koiso, who was posted to Manchukuo as Chief of Staff, Kwantung Army.

[2] The Chief of the Metropolitan Police referred to them as the "Law-breaking group of company grade officers". Memoirs, *op. cit.*, Part VIII, Ch. 158 (4th December, 1934).

[3] Another name for the *Kodo-ha*, or for part of it, was *Kogun-ha* (Imperial Forces Faction). In August, 1935, Hirota (the Foreign Minister) told Harada: "In essence the *Kogun-ha* is composed of those who have not graduated from colleges; in other words they are those who fight in the front line. There is competition between this group and the educated group—those who have completed higher schooling and who serve in the central organs such as the General Staff H.Q. or the Ministry of War. Gen. Mazaki and Gen. Araki are believed to be the leaders of the *Kogun-ha* and sympathetic to this party in this strife. In other words Mazaki and Araki are co-operating with the dissatisfied elements comprising the major portion of the army . . . this sort of thing becomes the basis for disturbances in the control of the army." Memoirs, Part IX, Ch. 179 (28th August, 1935).

[4] Both Araki and Mazaki were Staff College graduates. But Araki came from

If Okawa and his immediate followers were, in a sense, the civilian, terrorist fringe of the *Tosei-ha*, the corresponding rôle in the *Kodo-ha* was filled by Kita Ikki and Nishida Zei.

Between the two factions there existed a profound rivalry, which the army—presenting a front to outsiders—did its best to conceal from foreign observers and from the Japanese public as a whole. The struggle between the factions was at its height between 1933 and 1936. As we have seen, they disagreed on the question of Japan's future relations with Russia. Broadly speaking, the *Tosei-ha* favoured national expansion at the expense of China; whereas the *Kodo-ha* preferred to deal with Russia first.

In home affairs—where the Showa Restoration was the question at issue—the mark of the *Kodo-ha* was a certain idealism, a revolutionary fervour; while that of the *Tosei-ha* was a shrewd realism.[1]

Throughout 1933 the *Kodo-ha* maintained an ascendancy. But the position of its leading figure—General Araki—was growing weaker as the year progressed.[2] Indeed the army as a whole appears to have lost, in the eyes of the public, some of the prestige which it had acquired as a result of the Manchurian Incident. After all, there had been no striking alleviation of the country's economic difficulties. And the increase of the budgets for the armed services, together with the talk of the "1935–6 Crisis", alarmed moderate opinion.[3]

---

a lower middle-class home, with no samurai family tradition or connections. Mazaki, though of samurai stock, did not belong to the Choshu Clan which was dominant in the days when he was a junior officer. In conversation with the writer he made much of the fact that he felt handicapped and oppressed by this Choshu hegemony. Mazaki's first important staff appointment was that of Head of the Military Affairs Section at the Ministry of War (1920). "I was surrounded", he said, "by men of Choshu."

[1] "The *Kodo-ha* were idealists. They thought that they had only to restore supreme authority to the Emperor and then everything would be right. The *Tosei-ha* were more logical, and, so to speak, used the Emperor to further their own ends in imposing their own plan from above." Maruyama, *Nippon Fashizmu, op. cit.*, p. 165.

[2] Harada recorded, as early as September, 1933, a story—which seems to have been put about by Minami and Hayashi Senjuro—that Araki was "quite run down" in health and had recently been suffering from a nervous breakdown because young officers often woke him up in the middle of the night to voice their complaints. Memoirs, *op. cit.*, Part V, Ch. 97 (15th September, 1933).

[3] "The voice of resentment against the army from all circles", wrote Harada, "has become very strong. . . . We greatly fear that the military may become an

This trend of opinion was disturbing to the leaders of the army and navy—who, whatever their various internal differences might be, were determined that the temper of the nation should not be allowed to sink back in the direction of the unwarlike years of the nineteen-twenties. And so, in December, 1933, the press departments of the army and navy issued a statement to the newspapers describing criticism of the two services as being communist inspired.

> In connection with budget questions and others it appears that some people are voicing the opinion that there has been an alienation of the feelings of the people, especially of the farming community, from the army and navy. Some of them say that the crisis of 1936 is nothing but propaganda put out by the military authorities, or that those who died in past wars belonged exclusively to the lower ranks, and that no high officers died. Others are saying that the welfare of the farmers was sacrificed for the sake of the military budget. Such a movement—to separate the public mind from the military—is an attempt to disturb the harmonious unity of the public mind, the essential basis of national defence; and the military authorities cannot overlook it. The two international movements for ruining a nation's power of self-defence are the anti-war movement based on the guidance of the Third International and the movement to alienate the public mind from the military. The public is well versed regarding the first of these movements; but the second is not well known, although its effect is considerable as it is conducted by a variety of means.[1]

object of common hatred." Memoirs, Part VI, Ch. 109 (13th December, 1933). There was, for example, this characteristic exchange—at a cabinet meeting in December—between Takahashi (Minister of Finance) and Araki. "Takahashi said: 'The fact is that the Japanese army and navy claim that 1935 and 1936 will be critical years and are conducting propaganda in city and countryside as if we are on the brink of war with Russia and the United States. At present, when U.S.A. and the countries of Europe are trying to conduct affairs as peaceably as possible and trying by all possible means to avoid wars, the pro-war atmosphere of Japan is creating a very bad feeling in diplomacy; and this appears in trade relations. Therefore the military must exercise prudence in speech and action. There will be no such crisis in 1935 and 1936.' Araki, turning pale with anger, replied: 'That is not true. There will be a crisis. The military have no intention of starting a war to-day. But we must make preparations.' " *Ibid.*

[1] The statement was issued late on 9th December, 1933. Harada described it as "threatening". Memoirs, Part VI, Ch. 109.

Although this statement hinted at sinister activities on the part of communists it was, in fact, addressed to the political parties in the Diet, members of which were becoming restive at the unchecked growth of military interference in all affairs of state.[1] The army seemed to be stepping well beyond its proper field of activity; and the person who was considered to bear the responsibility for this antipathy to the army was the Minister of War.[2]

At the end of 1933 Araki was the object of intrigue and pressure from many sides, all directed to securing his resignation.[3] His ill-health at this time was a real issue. His resignation came in the New Year, on 21st January, 1934.

This was a very serious blow to the power of the *Kodo-ha*. Henceforward the *Tosei-ha* steadily improved its position at the expense of its rivals. Hayashi Senjuro, Araki's successor, was to be embroiled in an acrimonious struggle with Mazaki; and this in turn was to lead to the celebrated February Mutiny of 1936. But at the time of Hayashi's appointment as Minister of War such developments were hardly foreseen.[4]

iii

It is now appropriate, before discussing the course of the feud between the army factions, to consider briefly the nationalist movement at this period, as illustrated by the more important

[1] The *Kempei*, it appears, were concerned at the attitude of certain members of the Minseito, notably Nakajima Yadanji, and it was *Kempei* reports which prompted the issue of the statement. *Ibid.*

[2] Apparently the reaction to the statement—on the part of moderate politicians —was unfavourable. *Ibid.* A little later it was reported that Wakatsuki, and Dr. Suzuki (of the Seiyukai), threatened to embarrass the army by questions in the Diet and agreed to refrain only if Araki resigned. Grew, *op. cit.*, p. 107.

[3] In November even Mazaki joined Hayashi Senjuro in a plea to Araki to resign. However, when Araki said that he was willing to retire "somewhere in the mountains" so long as they had real confidence in their ability to keep the army under control, Mazaki and Hayashi within a few days changed their minds and asked Araki to remain in office. Memoirs, *op. cit.*, Part VI, Ch. 112 (8th January, 1934). However, Hayashi appears to have been fundamentally opposed to Araki. *Ibid.*

[4] Harada, commenting on the resignation, thought that the Araki faction was now "under a heavy shadow. It is especially worth while", he wrote, "to observe how the army will act hereafter." Memoirs, Part VI, Ch. 114 (23rd January, 1934).

societies which, like the *Jimmukai*, came into being in 1932 or were founded in the following year.

As a result of Okawa's arrest and of Dr. Imamaki's abortive plot in 1932 the *Jimmukai*, though still officially alive, was almost moribund by the end of that year. But it was not disbanded until the beginning of 1935. The *Seisanto*, too, declined as a political force after the *Shimpeitai* fiasco. It remained in existence, however, as a popular version of the *Kokuryukai*, with a considerable membership.[1]

No new civilian terrorist organisations of importance were established to play the part filled by the *Jimmukai* and *Seisanto*. Such new societies as were founded were composed—in the main —of reservists, officials, and members of Left-wing organisations converted to *Nihon Shugi* (Japanism) and state socialism.

A notable effect of the Manchurian Incident and its aftermath— Japan's dispute with the League—was the growth of strong nationalist feeling within the political associations of the Left. To some extent the change of face was due to fear of police persecution. But there was also, among many proletarian leaders, a feeling that the army—as represented by its younger officers— had some sympathy with those oppressed by capitalism. To those sceptical of the principles and abilities of the Minseito and Seiyukai cabinets the army seemed to stand for true social justice.[2] There was, finally, the element of instinctive patriotic feeling, which at a crisis overcame the attachment—less deeply felt—to the doctrines

---

[1] According to the *Japan Year Book*, 1939–40, the membership of the *Seisanto* was 150,000.

[2] Sasa Hiroo, a publicist of decided nationalist views, expressed (for the benefit of foreign readers) the patriotic aspect thus: "Patriotism means loyalty to the Emperor. That sacred loyalty extends to the other holders of authority, provided —and it is a most important proviso—that they are deemed to share the moral worth associated with that authority. . . . Public opinion could be impressed by certain sections of the Government, these sections being mainly the leaders of the combatant forces. These Service leaders are obviously authority in its moral form for the good reason that, by their office, they have shown themselves prepared for personal sacrifices and can obtain no personal gain by the exercise of authority . . . are apparently concerned only with the national welfare. Thus we find that both personally and ideologically they have an appeal to Japanese public opinion, as it is by circumstances and tradition constituted, far in excess of that of any other section of the nation. If they are disposed to exercise that appeal— i.e. to attempt to impress public opinion—such efforts are naturally very impressive indeed. For the past seven years they have been so disposed." Saso Hiroo, "Our Public Opinion", *Contemporary Japan*, Vol. V, No. 4 (March, 1937).

of international working class solidarity and the class struggle. A reversion to nationalism, in a time of crisis, is usual among the Left-wing in any country.[1]

The various splits which occurred inside the proletarian movement in Japan following the Manchurian Incident were of a complicated nature, in the sense that groups which were either "converted" as a whole or broke away as splinter parties from a parent body often underwent further divisions; and each split was marked by a change of name on the part of the group concerned.

In April, 1932, the general secretary, Akamatsu Katsumaro, of the *Shakai Minshuto* ("the Social Democratic Party"), and some thirty thousand members seceded from the party. Akamatsu and his supporters called themselves the *Nippon Kokka Shakaito* ("The Japan National Socialist Party"). This party in its turn suffered from splits and defections in the following year.[2] These were largely due to the differences between those who had a genuine faith in the efficacy of economic reform on the basis of national socialism, and those who were essentially lukewarm towards national socialism but placed the greatest emphasis on the promotion of traditional patriotic ethics. The former accused the latter of being reactionary; and the latter replied by describing the others as revived Marxists.[3] These accusations, indeed, were not without some substance. It was the same rift of opinion which had divided Kita Ikki and Okawa, *Kodo-ha* and *Tosei-ha*, and which was reflected in the internal politics of many of the large nationalist associations. In 1934 the *Kokka Shakaito*, which by

---

[1] For instance—it is only one of many such examples—at the outbreak of the 1914-18 War the German Socialists, with few exceptions, announced their patriotic support of their country's cause—the Socialist deputies in the Reichstag, at its first plenary session after 4th August, 1914, voting unanimously for war credits.

[2] Within the *Kokka Shakaito* was the *Kokka Shakai Shugi Gakumei*, "the National Socialist League", which attracted such old supporters of national socialism as Tsukui. It was headed by a retired Colonel, Ishikawa Junjuro. But this League broke up in 1933 under the stress of factional differences. In the same year Akamatsu and Tsukui broke away from the *Kokka Shakaito*—they had become converted to the traditional patriotic school of thought––to form the *Kokumin Undosha*, "Nationalist Society". For a list of leading figures in the *Kokka Shakai Shugi Gakumei*, vide Appendix I.

[3] Japanese political observers describe the two groups as (a) the *Kagakuteki kokka shakai shugi-ha*, "the scientific national socialism group", and (b) the *Junsei Nippon shugiha*, "the orthodox (or pure) Japanism group".

this time had lost many leading members, renamed itself the *Aikoku Seiji Domei*, or "Patriotic Government League".[1]

After the secession of the Akamatsu group the *Shakai Minshuto*, under Katayama Tetsu, rallied under the principles of anti-communism, anti-fascism and anti-capitalism.[2] And to gain strength the party effected a merger with the *Zenkoku Ronoto Taishuto* ("The National Labour-Farmer Mass Party"), the strongest legal Left-wing proletarian party. The two parties, having merged, called themselves the *Shakai Taishuto*, or "Social Mass Party". This remained the most powerful tolerated political expression of genuine working class activity.[3] By comparison with the Right-wing and radical national socialist societies the *Shakai Taishuto* cannot be described as a nationalist party in the true sense of the word. Indeed it deserves to be called less nationalist than either the Seiyukai or Minseito. However, like the other political parties, it found it only prudent to pay lip service to chauvinist ideas and it expelled members who were believed to retain "dangerous thoughts".[4] Some of its members established close connections with the army; and it is not far-fetched to claim that within two or three years of the outbreak of the Manchurian

[1] Chairman of the *Aikoku Seiji Domei* was Koike Shiro. For the names of prominent members, *vide* Appendix I. The society organised a youth group—the *Ishin Seinen Tai*, "Restoration Youth Unit"—under Sasaki Takeo as an "advance guard", *zenei-tai*. This was confined to young men under the age of thirty and was organised on a semi-military basis of squads (*han*) and detachments (*shitai*)—the squad, the smallest unit, consisting of seven men—and was thus evocative of the S.A. units in Germany. The *Ishin Seinen Tai* was, in fact, a potential terrorist body; for the main principle advocated by its leaders was the idea that in death, self-sacrifice, lay the greatest achievement of the patriot. However, it did not take part in any noteworthy conspiracies.

Mitsukawa Kametaro—one of the original members of both the *Yuzonsha* and *Gyochisha* (*vide* pp. 39 and 40 *supra*) and, of course, one of the "old guard" of national socialists—did not join forces with Akamatsu, but, with Shimonaka Yasaburo, formed the *Shin Nippon Kokumin Domei* ("the New Japan National League") in 1932. Amano Tatsuo and the *Aikoku Kinroto* joined this League.

[2] These were summed up in the concise Japanese phrase, *San Han Shugi*; for which a clumsy English translation would be "the three anti-isms principle".

[3] The *Taishuto* controlled two powerful associations of trade unions—the *Nippon Rodo Kumiai Kaigi* ("Congress of Japanese Trade Unions") and the *Zenkoku Rodo Kumiai Domei* ("National Trade Union League").

[4] For example Kawakami Hajime and Hososeko Kanemitsu, who were shortly afterwards arrested as communist sympathisers. Oyama Ikuo, a member of the Left-wing intelligentsia who had been President of the *Ronoto* (the "Labour-Farmer Party"—the kernel of the *Zenkoku Rono Taishuto*), resigned his position with the party and went abroad.

Incident the *Shakai Taishuto* had become strongly influenced by fascist ideas.[1]

Throughout 1932 and 1933 various efforts were made by leading nationalist societies to form a united front. Such unity as was achieved, however, was neither firm nor permanent. There were several of these temporary amalgamations, culminating in the *Aikoku Undo Ichi Kyogikai* ("The Patriotic Movement United Consultative Society"), formed in December, 1933.[2] But this confederation of societies, despite an ambitious programme calling for the establishment of nationalist assemblies in every town and village in the country, was no more robust than the *Nikkyo*, of 1931, to which reference was made in a previous chapter.[3] But there was one feature of the *Aikoku Undo Ichi Kyogikai* which was of future significance, and therefore of some interest. At its inaugural meeting the association in framing its programme used the phrase *Tenno yokusan* ("assistance to the Emperor"). The programme included a declaration that according to the principles of the *Kokutai* "the rendering of assistance to the Emperor" was a national duty. It appears that this was the first time the phrase was used. It was to receive Imperial sanction seven years later, when, in October, 1940, Konoye's *Taisei Yokusankai* was founded. This was the celebrated "Imperial Rule Assistance Association".[4]

---

[1] "Kamei Kanichiro and others showed a tendency to link up with the military. The waves of the fascist movement gradually permeated the ranks of the proletarian movement." Maruyama, *Nippon Fashizmu, op. cit.*, p. 110. "The tide of Fascism began to permeate the proletarian fighting lines"—*Japan Year Book*, 1939–40, p. 129.

[2] Two of the most noted were the *Kokunan Dakai Rengo Kyogikai*, "The Joint Consultative Society for Solving the National Crisis" (June, 1932), and the *Kokutai Yogo Rengokai*, "United National Polity Defence Society" (December, 1933). The former, often known by the title of *Kokkyo*, included under its wing the *Seisanto*, *Jimmukai*, Akamatsu's *Kokka Shakaito* and Mitsukawa's *Shin Nippon Kokumin Domei* (of which Amano's *Aikoku Kinroto* formed part). The *Kokkyo* organised a confederation, the *Daido Kurabu* (United Club), of youth societies from the *Seisanto*, *Jimmukai*, etc. The *Kokutai Yogo Rengokai* was an amalgamation of eighty patriotic bodies—most of them small and of little influence. The *Aikoku Undo Ichi Kyogikai* was a federation of the societies already amalgamated in the *Kokkyo* and *Kokutai Yogo Rengokai*.

[3] *Vide*, pp. 72–3 (*supra*).

[4] The Preparatory Commission for the New Political Structure—the body which recommended the setting up of the I.R.A.A.—had a predominantly Right-wing, nationalist complexion. Yanaga, *op. cit.*, p. 546. In their deliberations they may well have had in mind the ideas first propounded by the *Aikoku Undo*

In May, 1933, a society composed principally of reservists came into being and rivalled the *Kokuhonsha* as an influential nationalist organisation among senior officials, particularly those connected in any way with the Ministry of War. This was the *Meirinkai* ("The Society of Enlightened Ethics"), under the presidency of a retired general, Tanaka Kunishige.[1] On the board of directors with him were three retired service officers of high rank and Ishihara Koichiro, the Kansai businessman who financed the *Jimmukai*.[2]

The chief aim of the *Meirinkai* was to stimulate nationalist political activity on the part of retired officers, to urge them to attack the political parties and to support any administrative reforms put forward by the army. But it was not a particularly extreme or radical organisation; and its aims made no mention of the Showa Restoration. Within a year or two of its foundation the society obtained the complete understanding and support of the Ministry of War. Officers on the active list became members, and, in 1936, the police regarded the *Meirinkai* as being to some extent the tool of the Ministry of War.[3] Thus the society belonged to the camp of the *Tosei-ha*. Like the *Kinkei Gakuin* and the *Kokuhonsha* it promoted Japanese nationalism, of a strong and irrational, but not revolutionary, character, among leading men in official life.[4]

The *Dai Ajia Kyokai*, or "Great Asia Association", was of a similar character, but its basis was broader than that of the *Meirinkai*, since it included a number of statesmen among its members, as well as retired officers. The *Dai Ajia Kyokai* was

Ichi Kyogikai. It was part of the ultra-nationalist thesis that the Diet had always failed to render truly disinterested and loyal assistance to the Emperor. The assemblies in towns and villages, suggested in the programme of the *Aikoku Undo Ichi Kyogikai*, were to be the elements in a great national movement to replace the Diet as the main organ for reflecting public opinion.

[1] Tanaka began to organise the *Meirinkai* in May, 1932 (before the 15th May Incident). But formal inauguration did not take place until a year later.

[2] The three officers on the board of directors were Lt.-Gen. Okudaira (or Okuhira) Shunzo, Lt.-Gen. Yamada Torao and Rear-Admiral Gondo Denji.

[3] Shigematsu, *op. cit.* Supplement, p. 7.

[4] Although hostile to the political parties the *Meirinkai* recognised the parliamentary system, and it favoured political action through constitutional means. However, its only success in any General Election was in February, 1936, when one of its candidates (out of six who stood for election) was returned for Kofu City. The society published a monthly paper, *Meirin Shimpo*.

founded at the beginning of March, 1933. Its leaders were drawn from a diversity of fields. They included Nakatani Takeo—of the old *Gyochisha* and *Aikoku Kinroto*—and Shimonaka Yasaburo, of the *Nohon shugi-ha*, or "agrarian school".[1] With them were the retired generals, Kikuchi Takeo, of the *Kokuhonsha*, and Matsui Iwane.[2] Hirota Koki, Prince Konoye, Admiral Suetsugu Nobumasa and Tokutomi Iichiro were other prominent members.[3]

The ideal pursued by the *Dai Ajia Kyokai* was that of a league of Asiatic countries under the leadership of Japan. Many Japanese were beginning to think that the world would shortly be divided into three great power groups, the Asiatic, the Anglo-Saxon and the Soviet, and that international peace would be best secured on that basis—the Third Reich was in its infancy, an unknown quantity, at this period. An Asiatic bloc—in which China, the Netherlands East Indies and Siam would be associated with Japan—would of course provide Japan with markets and an assured source of raw materials, and at the same time would compensate for the loss of international goodwill suffered as a result of secession from the League of Nations.

The ideal was of course incorporated into the *Kokutai* and appeared to have been successfully achieved in the *Dai Toa Kyoeiken* ("The Greater East Asia Co-Prosperity Sphere"), of the Pacific War period. But of greater interest than the aims of the *Dai Ajia Kyokai*—they were shared, naturally, by all aggressive patriots—is the fact that this society illustrates, in the composition of its leading members, the way in which respectable

[1] He was one of the leaders, close to Tachibana, of the *Nohon Remmei*, *vide* p. 100 (*supra*). He was a member, too, of the *Kokka Shakai Shugi Gakumei*.

[2] Matsui Iwane was a very active supporter of the school of thought which advocated expansion at the expense of China. He was in fact associated with the *Tosei-ha*. He was regarded as having a peculiar understanding of Chinese problems, and in 1937 (after two years as president of the *Zaigo Gunjinkai*) was recalled to active service and appointed Commander-in-Chief of the Japanese forces in the Yangtse area. "Japan", he told press correspondents (shortly before the Nanking Massacre), "has no intention whatever of invading China territorially or economically" (*Japan Weekly Chronicle*, 2nd December, 1937). He was sentenced to death as a convicted war criminal by I.M.T.F.E.

[3] Hirota was to be appointed Foreign Minister in September, 1933. Konoye succeeded Prince Tokugawa as President of the House of Peers in June, 1933. Admiral Suetsugu, a determined opponent of the London Naval Treaty, was still on the active list and was to become Commander-in-Chief, Combined Fleet in November, 1933. Tokutomi Iichiro ("Soho") was an extremely well-known publisher and journalist and a member of the House of Peers.

public men of the highest standing—such as Konoye—came, in the nineteen-thirties, to be associated with what might be called "professional nationalists", such as Nakatani, who themselves were associated with terrorists and men on the borderline of the criminal underworld. This was not, of course, an entirely new phenomenon—modern precedents had been set by Hiranuma's *Kokuhonsha* and Yasuoka's *Kinkei Gakuin*—but it became a more generally recognised practice in the years following the Manchurian Incident.[1]

Closely linked with the *Dai Ajia Kyokai* was the *Dai Toa Remmei*, or "Greater East Asia League", which had similar aims and whose leading figures were Matsui Iwane, Nakano Seigo (a member of the Diet) and Colonel Ishihara Kanji, who as one of the Kwantung Army Staff had helped to engineer the Manchurian Incident.[2] The *Dai Toa Remmei* favoured the *Tosei-ha*, and strongly backed General Hayashi as successor to Araki.[3]

It will be recalled that during 1933, while the *Koda-ha* under General Araki was the dominant faction in the army, military attention was fixed on the controversial issue of a future war with Russia, planned for 1935, while the navy appears to have consented to be ready to engage in war with the United States by 1936.

Undoubtedly the navy, usually more moderate in its plans and ambitions than the army, was much influenced at this time by its Chief of Staff, Prince Fushimi. He was a pronounced nationalist and of sufficient strength of character to force his policy—readiness for war with America within three years—on the cautious and temperate Navy Minister, Admiral Okada.[4] Nevertheless the latter continued to resist various attempts on the part of younger

---

[1] People like Saionji—those genuinely imbued with Western liberal ideas—always regarded Hiranuma's connections with the *Kokuhonsha* as one reason why he was unfitted for the highest office, e.g. that of the Presidency of the Privy Council. But their views became increasingly outmoded after 1931.

[2] Nakano had formed his own nationalist party, the *Tohokai* ("Eastern Society"). In October, 1943, he committed *hara-kiri* in his home, following a dispute with General Tojo. (He favoured a Japanese attack on Russia, in order to help Germany.) His funeral was the occasion of what was probably the last public appearance of Toyama Mitsuru.

[3] Memoirs, *op. cit.*, Part VI, Ch. 112 (8th January, 1934).

[4] *Ibid.*, Part V, Ch. 104 (1st November, 1933). Saionji (in November) once remarked: "I would like to remove His Highness [Fushimi] from his responsible position by some means or other." *Ibid.*

officers in the army to secure naval support for the Showa Restoration movement.[1]

The resignation of Araki was a setback, no doubt, to extreme nationalist officers in the navy, as in the army. And during 1934 there was a decline in their influence within the navy as a whole. However, in June, 1934, Rear-Admiral Sakano was abruptly relieved of his duties as Chief of the Naval Information Bureau for having issued a statement to the press emphasising the navy's traditional policy of abstention from all political activities.[2] The statement had been made at a time when it was apparent that the Saito cabinet—due to the Teikoku Rayon scandal—could not long continue in office. Ugaki was a possible candidate for the post of Premier; but the Minister of War was against his appointment and favoured Hiranuma. The latter, however, pushed the candidature of Admiral Kato Kanji, a strong nationalist whose fight against the London Naval Treaty in 1930 allied him closely with Fushimi. But in backing Kato Hiranuma expected to be given the post of Home Minister in the new cabinet and he intended, as Prince Saionji remarked at the time, "in essence to do the work of the Prime Minister".[3] Kato, then, was to be no more than a figurehead. Whether he knew this or not he must have relied on political support from the navy during the negotiations which would precede the formation of a new cabinet. Rear-Admiral Sakano's statement to the press was, therefore, a veiled warning to Kato that the navy—or the moderate elements in the navy—would not give him political support. Kato's reaction was strong enough—it must have been shared by Fushimi—to force Sakano's removal from the Information Bureau.[4]

These manœuvres show how far the navy, unsettled by the London Treaty, had moved away from its traditional neutrality in the field of politics. Whereas nationalism as a political force was stronger in the army than in the navy—which never exercised the

---

[1] Admiral Okada (to Harada): "I wish to have this kept a secret. We are annoyed by the young army officers who are trying to entice the navy. But we are taking the utmost precautions against the army." *Ibid.*, Part VI, Ch. 107 (18th November, 1933).

[2] The statement was issued on 4th June, 1934. Memoirs, Part VII, Ch. 134 (9th June, 1934).

[3] *Ibid.*, Part VII, Ch. 137 (29th June, 1934).

[4] *Ibid.*, Part VII, Ch. 134.

general political influence held by the army—the navy, nevertheless, was faced with internal feuds, with the problem of radical-minded young officers, with those issues, in fact, which in the army produced the factions of *Kodo-ha* and *Tosei-ha*. As in the army, so in the navy it was the latter faction which prevailed.

7

THE FACTION FIGHT

i

EARLY in 1934 the American Ambassador noted that it was generally felt that Araki's retirement was "a victory for the Liberals and the political parties". But he added the proviso, "if there is any real improvement in the political situation it probably represents the calm before the storm".[1]

It was the *Tosei-ha* which profited by the resignation of Araki; and there was to be no revival of liberal and parliamentary forces to challenge successfully the political power of the army. Nevertheless, during 1934, there were some important signs that moderate elements, represented by the Palace and the *genro*, were by no means powerless. They were still capable of at least a spirited rearguard action. The voluble Araki was out of office, and firm measures were taken to prevent any nationalists considered to have extreme opinions from gaining possession of the highest official positions in the state. Thus the year was one of remarkable outward calm, considering the ferment at home and abroad created by the Manchurian Incident in the two preceding years. And although the Amau Statement was to come as a temporary shock to the world, it seemed, on a short view perhaps, that Japan was about to settle down and for some years digest in peace her substantial territorial gains in Manchuria.[2] The Foreign Minister, Hirota, resumed negotiations—suspended in the previous October—with the Russian government on the sale to Japan of the Chinese Eastern Railway; and in the autumn of 1934 there was talk of a *rapprochement* with Great Britain.[3] At home no

---

[1] Grew, *op. cit.*, p. 108.

[2] Amau Eiji, Foreign Ministry spokesman, issued a statement on 17th April, 1934, declaring that Japan and China alone had the responsibility for maintaining peace in East Asia. Foreign powers were informed that Japan would oppose any attempt on their part to lend assistance, even technical or financial, to China.

[3] Grew (*ibid.*, p. 131) recorded that the Soviet Ambassador even referred to the possibility of an Anglo-Japanese alliance. Harada described the plans for a

unseemly "Incidents" disturbed the peace of the capital; and when the Saito cabinet resigned during the summer it was succeeded by the moderate Okada cabinet, in the cast of its ideas, and to some extent in the composition of its leading members, a replica of its predecessor.

The calm—as Mr. Grew implied—was deceptive. The next three years were to witness renewed violence, first at home and then on the continent in the form of the general attack on China.

However, in 1934 the forces of nationalism were, to some extent, held in check. Of this there were two indications of significance.

The first related to the Presidency of the Privy Council. This august body of twenty-six members, including the President, was established in 1888 to discuss, under Ito, the drafts of the Constitution and the Imperial Household Law. It remained as a permanent organ of the state, with its own regulations governing the extent of its jurisdiction. Article VIII of these read: "Though the Privy Council is the Emperor's highest resort of counsel it shall not interfere with the executive." [1] The Privy Council was in fact primarily an advisory body. And it was regarded as the authoritative interpreter of doubtful points relating to the law and practice of the Constitution. Although the Emperor's treaty-making power was legally unhampered by any organ of the state it was the usual—though not invariable—practice for important international treaties and agreements to be referred to the Council for scrutiny before ratification. It was considered proper, also, for the cabinet to submit the drafts of imperial ordinances to the Council for advice.

Law rather than policy was the true field of the Privy Council. But as time went by—and particularly during the Showa period —the Council showed a growing interest in questions of high policy, and, despite the regulation which has been quoted above, exercised a strong influence, amounting at times to interference, on the executive power. And as the prestige of the Diet fell after 1931 so that of the Privy Council rose. Its influence—as the prolonged debate on the London Naval Treaty showed—was

rapprochement as "very secret"—Hirota informed him of them—and not even discussed in the cabinet. The Ambassador in London (Matsudaira) was instructed to make a tentative approach to the British government. Memoirs, Ch. 155 (14th November, 1934).   [1] Takeuchi, *op. cit.*, p. 38.

decidedly nationalist, reflecting the views of two of its out-standing members, Hiranuma, who became Vice-President in 1926, and Count Ito Miyoji.

The Presidency of the Council was an office of great import-ance; for its holder would become, in a strictly unofficial sense, an "elder statesman". Prince Saionji, due to his advanced age, could not be expected to perform his duties very much longer. It seemed clear that his functions—particularly that of advising the Throne on the choice of a new Premier—would be inherited by senior Court advisers and statesmen, of whom the President of the Privy Council must be one.[1]

In April, 1934, the President of the Privy Council, Baron Kuratomi, resigned due to age and ill-health. It seemed a fore-gone conclusion that Hiranuma, the Vice-President, would be his successor. For Hiranuma had been Vice-President for eight years and was the dominant personality in the Council—Kuratomi had been described as his "puppet".[2] The Prime Minister thought the appointment of Hiranuma to be inevitable.[3]

The genro, however, was determined to keep Hiranuma out of this high office. "If Hiranuma should become President," he de-clared, "some of the militarists may be happy; but only evil will come of it, and there will be no benefits." [4]

His own choice was Baron Ikki, an expert on the Constitution and former Minister of the Imperial Household, a man of liberal feeling.[5] Ikki, however, was reluctant to accept the position. Saionji had to make a special journey to Tokyo to persuade him to accept—it was no easy task. But in the end the genro had his way. No word of Kuratomi's resignation was allowed to appear in the press until, a fortnight after the resignation, Ikki's accept-ance was assured.[6]

---

[1] At the next change of cabinet in July, 1934, Saionji attended a meeting in the Palace of ex-Premiers at which the President of the Privy Council and Lord Keeper of the Privy Seal were also present. This gathering of elder statesmen became customary at later changes of government.

[2] By Saionji. Memoirs, op. cit., Part VI, Ch. 128 (3rd May, 1934).

[3] Ibid., Part VI, Ch. 127 (27th April, 1934).

[4] Ibid., Part VI, Ch. 128.

[5] By an alternative reading of his name Ikki is often referred to as Ichiki.

[6] Ikki's appointment, wrote Harada, "dispersed the atmosphere of fear; it made the public very happy, and from faint pieces of evidence I gathered that the Emperor was very well pleased". Memoirs, op. cit., Part VI, Ch. 129 (7th May, 1934).

If this was a blow to Hiranuma and to nationalist opinion as a whole an even greater setback was in store for them two months later.

As soon as the Teikoku Rayon scandal became known—in which members of the government were alleged to have been involved—it was evident that the Saito cabinet could not continue in office much longer.[1] Strong nationalist opinion hoped and worked for the appointment of Hiranuma—or of someone like Admiral Kato Kanji, as figurehead, with Hiranuma holding the real power behind him—to succeed Saito. As a wise manœuvre Hiranuma strove to gain the goodwill of Count Makino, Lord Keeper of the Privy Seal; for the latter, as the most intimate political adviser to the Throne, possessed great influence when it came to the choice of a new Premier. And it seems that Makino was at least mildly inclined to regard Hiranuma with favour.[2]

Saionji was much disturbed at the possibility of Makino being won over by Hiranuma. But he avoided a direct approach to Makino on the subject. Instead, he instructed Harada to pass on an urgent warning, against Hiranuma, to Makino through the latter's Secretary, Marquis Kido. For just as Saionji trusted the judgment of his faithful lieutenant and adviser, Harada, so Makino relied on the counsel of Kido.

Accordingly the two Secretaries met; and Harada, knowing the *genro's* mind, was very positive in his remarks to Kido. These two, Harada and Kido, were to drift apart as events moved, from the outbreak of the China Incident in 1937 to the Pacific War, steadily away from the course of moderation enjoined by Saionji. But at this time they were still close to one another. Even so, Kido was probably already much more prepared than Harada to accept what he must have regarded as the inevitability of a militant nationalist Japan, very different in both its internal and external aspects to the nation of the nineteen-twenties. It was

[1] Kuroda Hideo, Vice-Minister of Finance, was charged with corruption, in connection with the affairs of the Teikoku Rayon Company, on 19th May. Later two cabinet ministers, Nakajima (Minister of Commerce and Industry) and Mitsuchi (Minister of Railways) were alleged to be involved. In December, 1937, all were acquitted; and it was revealed that the police had used questionable methods to extort confessions. *Japan Weekly Chronicle*, 23rd December, 1937.

[2] Saionji (to Harada): "I don't know whether it is because they are both from the Satsuma Clan, but the Lord Keeper of the Privy Seal seems to feel an attachment for Hiranuma." Memoirs, Part VII, Ch. 131 (22nd May, 1934).

for this reason, perhaps, that in talking to Kido Harada refrained from making any very spirited criticism of Hiranuma, but referred to the danger that might be expected to come from "men behind Hiranuma"—although Hiranuma himself was of sufficient calibre and strength of character, as Harada must have known, to plot his own course of action in any circumstances. None the less Harada declared that if Hiranuma were made Premier he would exercise a harmful influence on the Palace.

You must give a serious warning to the Lord Keeper of the Privy Seal [Harada told Kido]. I say this because, although it is all right for Hiranuma himself to become Prime Minister, the men behind Hiranuma and those who will later be behind him will utilise his position as Premier to create various difficult situations. It is a fact that to present them with such an opportunity might be the basis of some unforeseen injury to the country. It is clear that if Hiranuma becomes Premier he will certainly extend his hands into the affairs of the Imperial Palace. He will not only damage relations between the Palace and the administration, but he may also create a gulf between the two; and things will then go badly for the Palace. There should be a return to normal conditions if possible; and the way to bring this about is to calm down everybody. The basis for this has first to be formed, and then—when the times demand it— an appropriate administration should be formed. The *genro* has to bear in mind that it calls for the utmost caution to prevent the creation of an unfavourable atmosphere, which might upset the fundamental basis. That is what I believe.[1]

Here, again, we see the expression of that vain hope, cherished by the forces of moderation, that given time the country might be guided out of the rapids of violent nationalism into which it had been swept in 1931.

In this instance, however, Saionji was entirely successful. Kido was reported as being in full agreement with Harada.[2] And although the Minister of War supported Hiranuma, Makino evidently came to accept Saionji's views.[3]

[1] *Ibid.*   [2] *Ibid.*
[3] Hayashi's view was that either the Saito cabinet should continue in office, or Hiranuma should be made Premier as "the most appropriate man". Memoirs, Part VII, Ch. 133 (4th June, 1934).

Thus, when Saito resigned on 3rd July the appointment of Admiral Okada as his successor—it had been agreed upon by Saito, the Court and the *genro* at the end of May—was made with little preliminary debate among those who advised the Throne on the matter.[1] The Emperor himself was much relieved at the decision. "If it is to be Okada," he told the *genro*, "it will ease my mind a great deal." [2]

In the appointments of Ikki and Okada Saionji achieved a notable triumph at the expense of the nationalists. But the fact that even such a stalwart liberal as Makino seemed inclined to regard Hiranuma with favour was symptomatic of the whole trend of feeling at that time, affecting nearly every shade of political belief in Japan. Both Kido and Konoye were moving closer to the army and the nationalists. Indeed in the habit of the Japanese, who have a genius for compromise, statesmen were trimming their sails to the prevailing wind. To control extreme forces—the argument went—one had at least to make a convincing pretence of being to some extent on their side.

Thus, in September, Konoye—who, it will be recalled, was on the governing board of the *Dai Ajia Kyokai*—suggested to Harada that it might be prudent to make at least one change among those, such as the Lord Keeper of the Privy Seal and the Grand Chamberlain, who were close to the Emperor. For these Court advisers, said Konoye, were being accused by the public of being too fond of Western ideas and ways. Would it not be wise, asked Konoye, to have at least one official Court adviser who could not be regarded in this light? In this way public criticism might be appeased. Saionji's reaction, when Konoye's

---

[1] At the meeting between the *genro* and the ex-Premiers, the President of the Privy Council and Lord Keeper of the Privy Seal at the Palace to discuss the question of the new Premier, both Wakatsuki and Kiyoura at first seemed to favour General Ugaki; but the proposal was dropped—probably because it was considered hazardous in view of Ugaki's unpopularity with the *Kodo-ha*. *Ibid.*, Part VII, Ch. 138 (6th July, 1934). Towards the end of May, Saito told Harada that he felt the cabinet would soon have to resign and that Admiral Okada was the most suitable successor as Premier. Harada mentioned this to Kido, who agreed with the choice. Kido then pressed the claims of Okada on the Lord Keeper of the Privy Seal, the Grand Chamberlain and the Minister of the Imperial Household, and obtained their support for Okada. *Ibid.*, Part VII, Ch. 132 (28th May, 1934).

[2] *Ibid.*, Part VII, Ch. 138 (6th July, 1934).

proposal was reported to him, was characteristic. He said to Harada:

> Right-wing people are what you call fanatics. I am absolutely opposed to having them in the Emperor's Court or in the Ministry of the Imperial Household. It is very difficult to tell a sensible man to act in such a way as to be acceptable to the Right wing. I have not much longer to live, and I hope that people like Konoye, Kido and you will prevent these fanatics from getting into the Imperial Court.[1]

In November there occurred an Incident of which the public knew nothing until after the end of the Pacific War. This was yet another plot to assassinate the Premier, Lord Keeper of the Privy Seal and other high officers of state. This time the plot was an exclusively military affair, although Kita Ikki and Nishida Zei were probably to some extent aware of it. The leaders were officers of the rank of captain and lieutenant attending a course at the Tokyo War College. Their supporters were a group of cadets at the Military Academy.

The Ministry of War came to hear of the plot and, largely due to immediate action by Nagata Tetsuzan, arrested the ringleaders, Captain Muranaka, Lieutenant Isobe and Lieutenant Kataoka. These officers were suspended, but not courtmartialled. There was a considerable sensation among higher officers of the army. For it was believed that Mazaki, the Inspector-General of Military Training, was actively sympathetic with Muranaka and the other two officers—even if he had not been behind them.

The whole affair, in fact, became part of the factional struggle between *Tosei-ha* and *Kodo-ha*; the latter claiming that the conspiracy was the invention of the *Tosei-ha*, fabricated in order to discredit Mazaki—whose appointment made him responsible for all army education and training—and so force him from his office as Inspector-General. The *Tosei-ha*, on the other hand, maintained that Nagata and the War Ministry had nipped in the bud a revolutionary plot, arising from radicalism and indiscipline condoned, if not encouraged, by Mazaki and his clique. There can be little doubt that this view—that of the *Tosei-ha* —should be accepted in this instance, rather than the version put about by Mazaki and the *Kodo-ha*.

[1] *Ibid.*, Part VIII, Ch. 150 (27th September, 1934).

Mazaki went so far as to accuse his enemies—particularly Nagata—of having transferred an officer from General Staff Headquarters to the command of a cadet company at the Military Academy with the sole idea of using him as an *agent provocateur*, to incite the cadets to plot a revolutionary conspiracy and to put them in touch with Muranaka at the Army College—Muranaka having been known to have made some careless remarks about the desirability of a military *coup d'état*.[1] Certainly Mazaki was most vehement in protesting his complete innocence in this affair, and he succeeded at least in impressing the Chief of the Metropolitan Police with his sincerity.[2] The fact that the ringleaders of the plot were not courtmartialled was cited by the *Kodo-ha* as evidence that the case against them rested on a trumped-up charge.[3]

The truth of the matter, undoubtedly, was that as those concerned in previous military conspiracies were not courtmartialled the authorities were reluctant to take drastic measures against Muranaka and his associates.[4] In the existing state of public opinion, moreover, a courtmartial would be bound to lower popular regard for the army. For although news of the trial might be banned from publication in the newspapers, rumours of its existence would inevitably reach the public. Above all, Muranaka

[1] The officer in question was Capt. Tsuji Masanobu, who reported the existence of the conspiracy to the Ministry of War. Mazaki, in a statement to the writer, claimed that his enemies arranged to have Muranaka implicated in the plot because "they knew that he respected me. Thus their aim was to make it seem as though there was a seditious plan at the Military Academy, question the responsibility of the Inspector-General of Education, who was the most responsible person—and I was the Inspector-General—and so have me removed from my position."

[2] "Gen. Mazaki told the Chief of the Metropolitan Police that it was not a good thing for regular soldiers to have political connections, and that if there was ever a situation where a *coup d'état* was imminent he would lead any number of regiments to fight against it. Mazaki seemed to be very much in earnest, and as a result the Chief of Police trusted him. But I thought it was dangerous to trust Mazaki." (Harada) Memoirs, *op. cit.*, Part VIII, Ch. 158 (4th December, 1934).

[3] Mazaki told the writer: "I demanded a thorough investigation at a courtmartial. The Ministry of War was astonished at my attitude. The officers at the Ministry feared the exposure of their secret plot—the use of Tsuji as *agent provocateur*—if a thorough investigation at a courtmartial were to be made. So they then took a conciliatory attitude."

[4] It should be noted, nevertheless, that the Prime Minister told Harada that Nagata and others expected to settle the matter by courtmartial. Memoirs, Part VIII, Ch. 161 (30th December, 1934).

knew too much about the details of the March and October Incidents of 1931. This was to be proved eight months later when, in collaboration with Lieutenant Isobe, he wrote and circulated in secret the pamphlet, *Shukugun ni Kansuru Iken Sho*, which revealed the seditious activities in 1931 of such figures in the *Tosei-ha* as Koiso and Nagata.[1] If Muranaka were put on trial he might insist on exposing the past history of those who now claimed to be the champions of control and discipline in the army.[2]

But this, of course, in no way establishes the innocence of Muranaka and the others involved in the "Military Academy Incident", as it was called. And Mazaki's own interpretation of the machinations of the *Tosei-ha* on this occasion seems a little ingenious.

They would light a fire [he said, speaking of Nagata and his clique], then they would put it out themselves, and say that someone else had started the fire. Skilfully manipulating the political situation created by the incident they would use it to increase their own influence.[3]

It is certainly true that the effect of the Military Academy Incident was to enhance the position of the *Tosei-ha*. But unless the point of view of the *Kodo-ha* is accepted in its entirety—and this would include the preposterous theory that the Mutiny of February, 1936, was deliberately engineered by the *Tosei-ha* to discredit its opponents still further—the conclusion must be that the army was faced, in November, 1934, with a genuinely dangerous threat of a *coup d'état*.

If the Minister of War was not already considering ways and means of removing Mazaki from his position as Inspector-General this Incident probably made him decide that such action would have to be taken. Henceforth he was entirely ready to support Nagata in any measures taken to strengthen the *Tosei-ha* at the expense of the rival faction.

[1] For writing the pamphlet, in July, 1935, Muranaka and Isobe were dismissed from the army. *Vide* p. 54 (*supra*).
[2] This interpretation is endorsed by Prof. Yanaga (*op. cit.*, p. 512).
[3] A statement made to the writer, in October, 1949.

Early in 1935 the government was compelled to deal with a resurgence of radical nationalist activity on the part of Deguchi Wanisaburo and his religious sect, *Omotokyo*, to which reference was made in a previous chapter.[1] Deguchi—supported by Toyama, Uchida and the *Seisanto*—asked his followers to sign a petition, addressed to the Throne, praying for the institution of the Showa Restoration under a cabinet headed by an Imperial Prince.[2] Nearly four hundred thousand signatures were obtained before the police were instructed to take firm measures against those who had organised the petition. For ordinary subjects to petition the Throne had always been regarded as improper; and in former days it was an offence punishable with the greatest severity. The matter of the *Omotokyo* petition was aggravated by reports that Deguchi was contemplating some kind of insurrection on the occasion of the presentation of the petition.[3] The police avoided taking any action against Toyama and Uchida, but they arrested Deguchi; and later in the year *Omotokyo* was suppressed.[4]

No faction in the army was connected with the affair of the *Omotokyo* petition, although its aims were very similar to those of the *Kodo-ha*.[5]

Meanwhile Mazaki, conscious that his position was endangered as a result of the military conspiracy of the previous November, had reached an understanding with a member of the Seiyukai, Kuhara Fusanosuke, who had his own following in the party and was at odds with Dr. Suzuki Kisaburo, the official head of the Seiyukai. At the same time Mazaki maintained his close alliance

[1] *Vide* pp. 50-1, footnote 3 (*supra*).

[2] Unfortunately the writer has been unable to discover whether any particular Prince of the Blood was mentioned.

[3] Memoirs, *op. cit.*, Part VIII, Ch. 162(a) (16th January, 1935).

[4] "It was an event unprecedented in Japan for such a numerous religious body to be suppressed. . . . Perhaps *Omotokyo* had by that time lost all its glamour as a religion and was being maintained only by dint of Deguchi's personal influence." Sugiyama Heisuke, "Religious Racketeering", *Contemporary Japan*, Vol. V, No. 4, March, 1937.

[5] The Chief of the Metropolitan Police stated positively that the army, with the possible exception of a few individual officers, was not involved in the affair. Memoirs, *op. cit.*, Part VIII, Ch. 162(a) (16th January, 1935).

with Araki. Both generals were intimate with Hiranuma; so that in 1935 it was possible to speak of "the Mazaki-Araki-Hiranuma faction".[1]

Throughout the first half of 1935 there was a keen struggle between this faction and the government. Mazaki, working through Kuhara, seems to have tried to bring a charge of corruption against the Minister of War and other members of the cabinet. However, this manœuvre, aiming to overthrow the government, came to nothing.[2]

A more serious threat to the government was the agitation, which greatly stirred Japanese life in the spring of 1935, concerning the *Kokutai Meicho Mondai*, or "the Question of the Clarification of the National Polity". The question arose in February as a result of a speech in the House of Peers by Baron Kikuchi Takeo. Kikuchi declared that the works of Professor Minobe Tatsukichi of Tokyo Imperial University, a fellow-member of the House of Peers and the leading authority on constitutional law in Japan, were disloyal, in that they spoke of the Emperor, in the exercise of his sovereign powers, as being the highest organ of the state.

At first sight there would appear to be nothing unreasonable or improper in this interpretation of the position occupied by the Throne. Nevertheless it gave real offence to the majority of Japanese. For in their view—and it was based on the tradition of centuries—the exalted status enjoyed by the Emperor was not susceptible to exact, legal definition. For, as was pointed out in the introductory chapter to this study, that status rested upon an inherited divinity. And, for the ordinary Japanese, discussion of the Emperor and of his proper functions in relation to the Constitution was a matter of great delicacy, as it involved the risk of blasphemy. There had never been in Japan any political theory or tradition of a "social contract", of the ruler having been entrusted with sovereign powers by the people and of exercising those powers subject to certain conditions.

---

[1] *Ibid.*, Part VIII, Ch. 165 (25th February, 1935).
[2] It is not easy to decide how serious was the threat to the government implicit in these activities. Mazaki has denied all knowledge of any intrigues, to which he was a party, against members of the government. But at the time it was reported to the *genro* that "it appeared as though Kuhara and Mazaki were going to launch a corruption scandal against the Ministers of Finance, War and Railways". *Ibid.*, Part VIII, Ch. 164 (15th February, 1935).

To speak, then, of the Emperor, in the exercise of his sovereign powers, as "the highest organ in the state" seemed—to those who were genuinely shocked by the phrase—to place him in a category differing only in degree, not in kind, from such organs of the state as the Privy Council or the cabinet.

This of course was to introduce a rationality, a theory of sovereignty comparable to those applicable to other nations, unwelcome to Japanese self-esteem. It was naturally rejected more especially by those whose emotions were stronger than their intelligence.

However, the book from which Baron Kikuchi extracted the offending phrase had been published twenty-seven years previously.[1] Yet, although within the academic world such nationalists as Uesugi had fought a running fight with Minobe over his interpretation of the Constitution, no government had been so influenced by nationalist prejudice as to victimise the scholar who was accepted, even by his enemies, as an outstanding expert in the field of constitutional law.

The fact was that Minobe's books were read by few except specialists; and until 1935 the public as a whole had never heard of Minobe's *kikan setsu*, or "organ theory".

Kikuchi's speech in the House of Peers, attacking Minobe, was echoed vigorously by nationalist bodies throughout the country. They had no difficulty in exciting public opinion on the issue. The *Kokutai Yogo Rengokai*, *Meirinkai* and *Zaigo Gunjinkai* were particularly active in stirring up popular agitation against Minobe.[2]

In face of this outcry the government felt unprepared to protect him, even though the Prime Minister regarded the accusations of disloyalty as baseless.[3] A retired officer, Major-General Eto, brought a charge of *lèse majesté* against Minobe, who was then questioned by the police. However, he was not arrested. But the

[1] *Kempo oyobi Kempo Shi Kenkyu* ("Studies in Constitutional Law and History"), published in 1908.
[2] Early in March the *Kokutai Yogo Rengokai* published a pamphlet, in connection with the Minobe issue, called "Clearing out Evil Thoughts and The Protection of the Nation's Foundations" (*Kyogyaku Shiso no Soto to Kokuhon no Bogyo*). The society held a typical rally in Tokyo in May, at which Baron Kikuchi was prominent. Members of the *Zaigo Gunjin*, at a meeting in the Officers' Club in Tokyo in April, carried out a ceremonial burning of Minobe's books.
[3] Memoirs, *op. cit.*, Part IX Ch. 173 (31st May, 1935).

charge was investigated for some months before the procurators decided that it could not be sustained.

The Prime Minister, reporting the matter to the Emperor, said:

> Up to now, so far as the publishing laws are concerned, the works of scholars have been handled magnanimously. But when their contents are circulated in society, and public opinion becomes severe, naturally even a professional book will be read. Therefore the above action had to be taken out of necessity.[1]

Thus, as this statement so plainly reveals, intelligence was forced to bow to prejudice. Minobe felt compelled to resign from both the House of Peers and Tokyo Imperial University.

Even the Emperor's own favour did not save Minobe from being driven out of public and academic life. For the Emperor, like many intelligent Japanese of his own generation, had a regard for Minobe's scholarship and disapproved of the agitation raised against him. In conversation with the Grand Chamberlain the Emperor declared:

> It is understandable to argue as to whether sovereign power is vested in the Emperor or in the State; but it is a very silly business to argue as to whether the Emperor-Organ theory is good or bad. My own personal view is that sovereignty of the State is better than sovereignty of the Emperor, but in the case of Japan—where the State and the Emperor are the same—either would be excellent. If a great scholar comes out with a theory of the sovereignty of the Emperor that is compatible with a monarchical organ this tends to act as a check on despotism. Much is being said about Minobe; but I believe he is not disloyal. Just how many men of Minobe's calibre are there in Japan to-day? It is a pity to consign such a scholar to oblivion.[2]

---

[1] *Ibid.*, Part VIII, Ch. 168 (11th April, 1935).

[2] Memoirs, Part VIII, Ch. 170 (3rd May, 1935). The Emperor went on: "In Article III of the Imperial Constitution there are words to the effect that the Emperor is the sovereign of the nation. This shows that he is nothing but an organ." *Ibid.* It must be admitted that Ito and the other architects of the Constitution would hardly have read the Article in that light. What traditionalists were most scared of was any concept, applied to Japan, of the sovereignty of the *state* (as opposed to that of the Emperor). For this might lead in turn to the theory of the sovereignty of the people.

It is possible that the Emperor's favour saved Minobe from arrest. But there was another factor in the case which spared him the ordeal of imprisonment and indictment.

Though the public were entirely unaware of this, Minobe, in the eyes of his nationalist detractors led by Kikuchi, was no more than a scapegoat. The unacknowledged but real objects of enmity and attack were Baron Ikki, the new President of the Privy Council, the *genro*, the Lord Keeper of the Privy Seal and the Okada cabinet. The condemnation of Minobe—together with the demand that the government should "clarify the *Kokutai*"—was in reality a skilful counter-attack by nationalist forces, associated with Hiranuma and the *Kodo-ha*, in response to the setbacks they had suffered in the previous year, when Hiranuma had been kept out of the high offices of President of the Privy Council and Premier. And the Chief of the Metropolitan Police, who was not in sympathy with the ambitions of Hiranuma, fully appreciated the true nature of the agitation against Minobe.[1]

The "organ theory" was an issue most advantageous to those who wished to discredit public men such as Ikki and Makino who were known to cherish liberal opinions. As a means of bringing ultra-nationalist pressure to bear on the Palace it only just fell short of direct criticism of the Emperor himself. It was also a more subtle and intelligent method of attack than that of a *coup d'état*—which, in any case, had always been ridiculously unsuccessful up to now.

The agitation put the liberal advisers to the Throne on the defensive; and the whisper of "dangerous thoughts" in high places greatly advanced the position of Hiranuma, with his reputation for rigid, irrational nationalism. It is natural to wonder whether Kikuchi, who was a director of the *Kokuhonsha*, planned his speech in the House of Peers in collaboration with Hiranuma. Although this remains a matter of speculation the possibility of some such intrigue cannot be dismissed.

In April Baron Ikki, pleading ill-health, wanted to resign; and he recommended Hiranuma as the new President of the Privy

[1] "The Chief of Police fully recognised the fact that the purpose of raising the Minobe issue was to denounce Ikki." Memoirs, Part VIII, Ch. 166 (3rd April, 1935). Undoubtedly this accounted, in large part, for the fact that Minobe was not arrested. A year later Minobe was lucky to escape death at the hands of a fanatic.

Council. The Lord Keeper of the Privy Seal and the Grand Chamberlain agreed that the safest course would be to promote Hiranuma. So it seemed that the manœuvres of Hiranuma and Mazaki were going to achieve an almost immediate success. But the proposal, that Hiranuma should succeed Ikki, naturally distressed the *genro*, who, in spite of his great age, was not prepared to abandon the struggle without a further fight. At all costs Ikki must be persuaded to remain in office. The possibility of his resignation at this time was very alarming. "If Ikki should resign", remarked Admiral Saito, "the Hiranuma faction will sing in triumph." If the worst came to the worst, and Ikki insisted on leaving his post, then Count Kiyoura or Saito must be appointed as his successor.[1]

The *genro's* secretary called on Ikki and pressed him to change his mind. The argument lasted for hours, Ikki being adamant. But at last he consented to remain as President for the time being.[2]

As the summer advanced there were signs that the *Zaigo Gunjinkai*, the mass organisation of reservists, would make the "organ-theory" and the "clarification of the *Kokutai*"—meaning the repudiation of the constitutional theory of the state—the central issues at its annual congress during the autumn.

In exploiting the agitation among the reservists Baron Kikuchi was particularly active. Among his many nationalist affiliations was the *Sanroku Kurabu*, the "36 Club", of which he was a director. This was a small society, part of the civilian wing of the *Kodo-ha*, and its declared aim was to rouse the nation to awareness of the great crisis—of which Araki had spoken so often—expected in 1936. It published a monthly magazine, *Ichi Kyu San Roku* ("1936"), and a newsheet every ten days—*Sanroku Joho* ("36 Bulletin"). These of course called for the establishment of the Showa Restoration and the total rejection of constitutional ideas, which were alleged to have been borrowed from the West. Kikuchi was also head of a group known as the *Nippon Seishin Kyokai* (The "Japanese Spirit League"). Among its advisers were Araki, Mazaki, Admiral Kato Kanji, Vice-Admiral Suetsugu, Hiranuma and Matsuoka Yosuke. This society, too,

[1] *Ibid.*, Part VIII, Ch. 169 (19th April, 1935). Makino and Konoye were also mentioned by the *genro* as suitable candidates.　　　[2] *Ibid.*

had its own monthly publications—*Nippon Seishin* and *Nippon Seishin Panfuretto* ("Japanese Spirit Pamphlet"). But it was the *Sanroku Kurabu* which was the more intimately associated with the activities of the reservists, the *Meirinkai* and *Zaigo Gunjinkai*, with regard to the issue of the "organ-theory".

The *Sanroku Kurabu* appears to have invited parties of reservists, throughout the summer and autumn of 1935, to Tokyo where the society—which paid their travelling expenses—accommodated them, at its own expense, at the *Gunjin Kaikan*, the national headquarters and central hostel of the *Zaigo Gunjinkai*. Here these parties of reservists were liberally entertained and at the same time indoctrinated with ultra-nationalist propaganda.[1] It was not surprising, then, that the *Zaigo Gunjinkai*, as a body, was in a ferment of almost revolutionary excitement, over "treachery in high places", by the end of the year.[2]

Both Ikki and the Lord Keeper of the Privy Seal, Makino, became in consequence objects of popular enmity; for the opinion of reservists carried great weight, particularly in farming areas.

In September Harada noted that the agitation was "a plot by the Right wing to expel the *genro*, the senior statesmen and others close to the Emperor by means of the Emperor-Organ theory in order to seize power for itself under the leadership of Hiranuma".[3] In such circumstances—and they constituted a threat both to the cabinet and to the Constitution as a whole—Harada was naturally puzzled at the failure of the government to take action against the ultra-nationalists, especially in view of the fact that Mazaki had been forced to resign—a development which will be discussed below. He asked the Prime Minister why he did not make "a quick counter-attack". The latter, exhibiting the caution which so fatally handicapped all moderate forces in Japan, replied: "We cannot afford to make a mistake. There is no alternative but to assume a passive attitude."[4]

Thus it became apparent that Ikki's resignation could not be long delayed, and that Makino's resignation was also probable. Ikki finally resigned in March, 1936. Only six months previously Saionji had declared: "I am absolutely against the promotion of

---

[1] Memoirs, Part IX, Ch. 185 (15th October, 1935).
[2] *Ibid.*, Part IX, Ch. 187.   [3] *Ibid.*, Part IX, Ch. 184
[4] *Ibid.*

Hiranuma. In any case we must make that sort of man powerless as soon as possible for the good of the world." [1]

This time, however, the *genro* was unable to have his way, and Hiranuma at last became President of the Privy Council. He then resigned from the presidency of the *Kokuhonsha*; and in June, 1936, the society was formally disbanded.

Makino resigned as Lord Keeper of the Privy Seal in December, 1935. Like Ikki he gave ill-health as the reason for his retirement. But, as the *genro* commented at the time, the general view was that Makino had resigned in consequence of the attack on Minobe.[2] He was succeeded by the moderate, liberal ex-Premier, Admiral Saito.

Apart from the "organ-theory" agitation ultra-nationalist opinion was exacerbated by the removal of General Mazaki from his position as Inspector-General of Military Training. This occurred in the middle of July.

The action had been planned some months earlier. In April it was reported that the Minister of War intended to make Mazaki resign during the summer.[3] Every August the Japanese army underwent a series of promotions and transfers; and the *Tosei-ha* decided to make full use of the coming August as an occasion for postings and appointments unfavourable to the *Kodo-ha*. It was appreciated that Mazaki would oppose such action, and therefore it was essential to secure his resignation before the August transfers were made. Furthermore these could be used as a bargaining counter to induce his resignation.[4]

---

[1] *Ibid.*

[2] Saionji, whose own vitality remained remarkably undimmed by his great age, was unsympathetic towards Makino's plea of failing health. He remarked that the function of the Lord Keeper of the Privy Seal was "constant aid to His Majesty", and that this was a mental responsibility, not involving physical strain. *Ibid.*, Part IX, Ch. 190 (13th December, 1935).

[3] Gen. Terauchi Hisaichi, who may be classed as one of the *Tosei-ha*, passed on this information to Harada. He also said that Hayashi intended to liquidate the Mazaki faction. Memoirs, Part VIII, Ch. 169 (19th April, 1935). Terauchi was then Commander-in-Chief, Formosa.

[4] According to a memorandum by Lt.-Gen. Matsuura Toyoichi (in the writer's possession) the Minister of War on 15th July told Mazaki that if he consented to resign he could have his say in the August promotions and changes. Mazaki refused the offer. (Matsuura, one of Mazaki's devoted admirers, had been in the Personnel Bureau of the Ministry but in March, 1935, was appointed Commandant of the Infantry School, Chiba.)

In the past Hayashi had been on close terms with Mazaki, and even when he aligned himself unmistakably with the *Tosei-ha* Hayashi was considered by Mazaki to be the victim of bad advice, the catspaw of Nagata, rather than the originator of what the *Kodo-ha* considered to be drastic and unfair measures. For Nagata was regarded as the villain of the piece; and there was some justification for this view. Undoubtedly Nagata had worked hard to influence the Minister of War against Mazaki.

However, the Minister's opinion alone would never have sufficed to force Mazaki's resignation. For the Inspector-General was one of the so-called "Big Three" in the army. The other two were the Minister of War and the Chief of the General Staff. And it was the rule that important personnel appointments—those affecting general officers—should be made by the Minister of War only after consultation with the other two members of the "Big Three". Therefore, in order to carry his view Hayashi needed the agreement of the Chief of the General Staff, Prince Kanin. Unfortunately for Mazaki Kanin was, if anything, more determined than Hayashi to appoint a new Inspector-General. For some time he had been receiving unfavourable reports, on Mazaki's general attitude and influence in the army, from Nagata, Minami (now Commander-in-Chief of the Kwantung Army), Sugiyama (Vice-Chief of the General Staff) and from his own military aide, Lieutenant-General Inagaki. The *Tosei-ha*, in fact, succeeded in securing Kanin's wholehearted support. Indeed he wanted to have Mazaki removed from the active list.[1]

It was expected that Mazaki would put up a stiff fight, that he would refuse to resign. He would have to be dismissed. But the consequences might be alarming.

Prince Kanin's resolve to support Hayashi was a trump card in the hands of the *Tosei-ha*. It meant that Mazaki was in a minority at meetings of the "Big Three". Furthermore it would be difficult for him to resist the express wishes of a Chief of the General Staff who was also a member of the Imperial Family.

---

[1] According to Matsuura's Memorandum (cited). Matsuura was so intimate with Mazaki (who accepts the Memorandum as reporting the true facts) that he was unlikely to have included a statement—Kanin's wish to have Mazaki removed from the active list—so unfavourable to his friend unless it were true.

"Prince Kanin is most determined," remarked Inagaki, on the eve of Mazaki's dismissal. "So everything will be all right." [1]

Up to the last, however, Nagata was afraid that Hayashi might waver. "It must be done," said Nagata, "with bold, resolute decision this time; but the Minister of War is so influenced by others that he may hesitate in his decision. That is the only thing I am worried about." [2]

The Prime Minister, too, felt it necessary to stiffen Hayashi's resolution, by telling him not to worry about the fate of the cabinet. Even if there was an upheaval in the army causing the cabinet to resign Hayashi was to "go ahead boldly". "The main objective", the Premier told him, "is to remove Mazaki, who is at the root of all this mess. So I want you to do it now." [3]

It was on 10th July that Hayashi, having invited Mazaki to come and discuss the August transfers, informed him that it was proposed to move him from the position of Inspector-General of Military Training to that of Supreme War Councillor. At the same time the Minister disclosed the fact that Prince Kanin had been in favour of more drastic measures.[4] Mazaki entirely rejected the Minister's proposals; nevertheless he asked to be given a few days in which to think the matter over. He also asked that a meeting of the "Big Three", which had been arranged for 12th July, should be postponed. Both the Minister and the Chief of the General Staff declined this request, and the conference was held as originally planned.

The meeting on the 12th was inconclusive. Mazaki refused to express an opinion on the various personnel changes and appointments put forward by Hayashi. Again the Minister, supported by Prince Kanin, told him that he would have to resign. The conference was adjourned until 15th July.

During the next two days Mazaki's friends rallied to his support. In particular Generals Araki and Hishikari made great efforts to induce the Minister and the Chief of the General Staff

[1] Memoirs, *op. cit.*, Part IX, Ch. 177 (22nd July, 1946).   [2] *Ibid.*
[3] Premier (by telephone) to Hayashi, 15th July. *Ibid.*
[4] "Although His Imperial Highness intends to have you removed from active service I have reported to His Highness that this cannot be done." (Hayashi to Mazaki) Matsuura Memorandum.

to change their minds.[1] At first neither Hayashi nor Kanin showed any sign of weakening. But eventually Araki and Hishikari persuaded Hayashi to agree to reconsider the matter if Kanin's views could be modified in any way. Thereupon Araki and Hishikari again visited Kanin and urged him to alter his decision. Kanin, however, remained firm. It was evident that the strength marshalled against the Inspector-General was overwhelming.

On the 14th Mazaki visited Hayashi and made a strong plea to be retained in his position. To change the Inspector-General at this time, said Mazaki, would undoubtedly provoke controversy in the army; this would lead to criticism of the Chief of the General Staff, and so harm the prestige of the Imperial Family. Mazaki was careful to disclaim any personal motives in the matter. His case was that his resignation at this particular time would be an unfortunate precedent, unless the Minister of War also resigned his office. Hayashi replied that his decision had been virtually forced on him by the Vice-Chief of the General Staff (Sugiyama), the Vice-Minister (Furusho) and Nagata.

At the meeting of the "Big Three" on 15th July Mazaki appears to have made a bitter attack on the *Tosei-ha*. He brought up the question of the 1931 Incidents and referred particularly to the activities, during the March Incident, of Nagata. His point— and it certainly did not lack piquancy—was that it was entirely illogical for people like Nagata to talk about discipline and "control" when they themselves had been in the thick of a conspiracy, involving bloodshed, only four years earlier. Hayashi is said to have ignored the point. Both he and Kanin reaffirmed their wish to have Mazaki resign. On this note the meeting closed.

Hayashi and Kanin then visited the Emperor—who was at the Hayama Villa on the seacoast near Tokyo—and secured immediate Imperial sanction for the appointment of a new Inspector-General.

Mazaki had at first intended to present a memorial to the

---

[1] Araki and Hishikari were both members of the Supreme War Council. The latter had been Commander-in-Chief, Kwantung Army, and Ambassador to Manchukuo in 1934. In December of that year he was replaced by Minami—a clear victory for the *Tosei-ha*.

Throne protesting against the views of the Minister and Chief of
the General Staff. His plan was to seek an audience after the conference of the "Big Three". He would thus have presented his
case on the same day as Hayashi and Kanin saw the Emperor.
However he understood that it would be a vain move. Certainly
he realised that the Court was surrounded by his enemies.

Mazaki's resignation was announced on 16th July. The general
press reaction was favourable to Hayashi. The Emperor himself,
according to the Minister, was very pleased.[1] So was Prince
Chichibu.[2] The navy, too, seemed to reflect some satisfaction at
the outcome.[3]

At the same time a number of rumours circulated in Tokyo.
The more sensational of these said that elements of the *Kodo-ha*
would carry out a violent *coup d'état*, which would be worse
than the "15th May Incident", and that Araki in his mortification
and distress had committed *hara-kiri*.[4]

Araki, however, was present at a stormy session of the Supreme
War Council which was held on 18th July, two days after the
resignation of Mazaki and the appointment of General Watanabe
Jotaro as Inspector-General in his place. Mazaki, who had been
appointed Supreme War Councillor on 16th July, attended the
meeting.

Araki made an emotional attack on the Minister of War for
having forced Mazaki to resign. His point of view was, of course,
that the Minister could not demand the resignation of the Inspector-General, who in theory was immediately under the
Emperor, with direct access to the Throne and responsible to the
Emperor alone. Watanabe, the new Inspector-General, came to
Hayashi's rescue by pointing out that in the case of a disagreement among the "Big Three" matters could be decided by a
majority vote. Mazaki agreed that this was so, but claimed that
a majority vote was only valid if the Minister also assumed responsibility for it—in other words if he resigned. Hayashi seems
to have remained silent on this particular point. The truth was, of
course, that he was unready at that time to risk causing a cabinet

---

[1] So Hayashi told the Premier. Memoirs, *op. cit.*, Part IX, Ch. 177 (22nd July,
1935).　　　　[2] *Ibid.*　　　　[3] *Ibid.*
[4] *Ibid.* Strict press laws made the capital peculiarly susceptible to all kinds of
rumours.

crisis by his own resignation.[1] But he countered Araki's attack by complaining of the prevalence of factions in the army—mentioning, in particular, the Saga faction. This was a reference to the support enjoyed by Mazaki and Araki in the Saga district of Kyushu, and to the fact that several officers of the *Kodo-ha* stationed in Tokyo came from that district.[2] Araki replied by saying that he could name other factions equally powerful.[3] He then went on to expose the details of the March and October Incidents, the support given to these conspiracies by Nagata, Koiso, Tatekawa and others. This, as he had intended it should, created a sensation at the meeting, some of the generals present professing never to have heard of such allegations.[4] The Minister of War, however, defended Nagata, saying that the latter was a reformed character and that he was now entirely trustworthy and impartial.

Araki and Mazaki were in a minority at the meeting. They failed to gain support even from quarters where they might have expected it. General Hishikari, for example, seemed faint-hearted in the assistance he gave to Araki at the conference. Thus at the Supreme War Council the *Kodo-ha* could only register a protest. It was not possible to reverse Hayashi's decision, which in any case had by then received Imperial sanction.[5]

There is little doubt that a large section of the more irrational and simple-minded ultra-nationalist officers, particularly of middle and junior rank, regarded the resignation of Mazaki as having

[1] Matsuura (in the Memorandum already cited) claimed that in conversation with another officer at the beginning of August Hayashi stated that he could not resign during the Mazaki crisis because he had to think of his position as a cabinet minister.

[2] Araki and Mazaki were sometimes known as leaders of "the Saga group". Two notable members of this group, by birth, were Colonels Shichida Ichiro of the Inspector-General's Office and Mutaguchi Renya of General Staff Headquarters. Both were to become Lieutenant-Generals during the Pacific War.

[3] On the whole the affiliations of the *Tosei-ha* were with Central and North-Eastern Japan. Araki, while implying that factions hardly existed in the army, said that if there were any factions they were those associated with Nagata and his friends.

[4] For example, Matsui Iwane, who was said to have shown astonishment at Araki's revelations.

[5] This account of the Supreme War Council session of 18th July is based on the report given in Matsuura's Memorandum. Every allowance has been made for any bias in favour of Mazaki evident in the report.

been engineered by his personal enemies, both in the army and outside, in order to defend Minobe's "organ-theory". Mazaki, in the view of these uncomplicated and emotional patriots, was a straightforward, courageously honest and unselfish warrior who was convinced that the true genius of Japan had been thwarted by the malice and folly of civil and military leaders long influenced by ideas borrowed from abroad. If Minobe represented all that was anathema to extreme Japanese nationalism, Mazaki in the eyes of the *Kodo-ha* was the symbol of pure *Nihon Shugi*, "Japanism".

Passions were so stirred by the affair of Mazaki's resignation that it was hardly surprising that within a few weeks an explosion occurred. This was the murder on 12th August, in the Ministry of War, of Major-General Nagata, who, as we have seen, was regarded as the *eminence grise* behind Hayashi and Prince Kanin. The assassin, Lieutenant-Colonel Aizawa Saburo, entered Nagata's room and without warning drew his sword and cut down his victim. It was a bloody scene; for Aizawa's first stroke failed to dispatch Nagata, and a Colonel Shimmi, who happened to be in the room, tried to protect Nagata and was severely wounded. In the mêlée Aizawa succeeded in killing Nagata with further cuts of his sword. "But", as he told the judge at his trial, "I was ashamed that I had failed to kill Nagata with one stroke of my sword." [1]

Aizawa had travelled up to Tokyo from his station at Fukuyama, on the Inland Sea. He was one of many ultra-nationalist officers affected by the changes and promotions announced on 1st August, and he had been posted to a regiment in Formosa. This may well have been due to the fact that on 16th July, having heard of Mazaki's resignation, he had visited Nagata at the Ministry of War and remonstrated with him. Indeed Aizawa on that occasion had contemplated killing Nagata. However, he had changed his mind. He only demanded that Nagata resign.

There is some evidence that between that date and 12th August Aizawa saw Mazaki and had his prejudice against Nagata fanned by inflammatory words.[2] Nevertheless no convincing testimony

[1] For a vivid account of the murder—one which could hardly be bettered—*vide* Byas, *op. cit.*, pp. 95–8.

[2] Prince Higashi-Kuni knew Aizawa, and he told Harada that it appeared that "Mazaki had spoken fiercely to Aizawa".

was produced at his trial to show that Aizawa had been directly instigated by anyone else to commit his crime. The view of the police, after an examination of the case, was that Aizawa had acted of his own accord. The Director of the Home Ministry Police Bureau remarked: "In the final analysis it seems that there was nothing planned behind the scenes." [1]

Aizawa was confined in the quarters of the 1st Division, and there his courtmartial was held; circumstances which had a direct bearing on the February Mutiny of the following year.

This, the most sensational of all "Incidents" inside modern Japan, will be discussed in the next chapter; which is also the place for a brief account of the activities of Mazaki and the *Kodo-ha* during the last months of 1935. For these were the prelude to the February Mutiny; just as the dismissal of Mazaki created the particular atmosphere in which that Mutiny was possible.

[1] Memoirs, Part IX, Ch. 179 (28th August, 1935). Mazaki, talking to the writer, strongly denied that he had prompted Aizawa to attack Nagata.

8

THE FEBRUARY MUTINY

i

HAYASHI resigned some three weeks after Nagata's murder. It was in accord with tradition that he should accept responsibility for the outrage. Okada tried to persuade him to remain in office; but Hayashi felt that further trouble might be expected unless he gave way to another Minister of War.[1] He was succeeded by General Kawashima.

On taking office the new Minister of War was told by the Premier that once the government's foreign policy had been decided upon—and this would be settled after consultation with the two armed services, the Foreign Ministry and the Ministry of Finance—"there must be no incidents arising out of military officers acting contrary to that policy".[2]

The significance of these words lay in the fact that the Kwantung Army was about to embark on an ambitious political manœuvre in North China. Whatever knowledge the military authorities at home may have had of Kwantung Army plans was not shared, of course, by the cabinet.[3] Nevertheless, the Foreign Ministry, through its Consuls in China, was able to forecast broadly what were the intentions of the Japanese Army on the continent. Thus at the beginning of October, 1935, the Embassy in Peking reported to Hirota, the Foreign Minister, that a political move by the army was imminent. Wakasugi, an Embassy official, cabled Hirota:

> My observations of the recent situation lead me to believe that the army, for the sake of national defence, is intending to organise a

---

[1] Affidavit by Admiral Okada, I.M.T.F.E. Transcript, p. 1831.
[2] Memoirs, *op. cit.*, Part IX, Ch. 182 (14th September, 1935).
[3] "The government of Japan had no way of learning what the plans and activities of the Kwantung Army were in those years." Affidavit by Admiral Okada, I.M.T.F.E. Transcript, p. 1825.

combined autonomy (practically an independent state), out of the five provinces of North China, free from the domination of the Nanking government.[1]

The fact that the Foreign Minister had to learn of army plans from diplomatic and consular missions abroad is a striking commentary on the independence of the Supreme Command.[2] And it was, of course, the hope of the Prime Minister that by discussion with the army at home some unified control might be achieved by the government and the military authorities over the forces abroad. This hope was entirely vain.

As winter approached, the Japanese Army, working mainly through the agency of Major-General Doihara, extended its influence in North China by the establishment of the East Hopei Autonomous Council and the Hopei-Chahar Political Council. Although these régimes were only the partial fulfilment of a grandiose plan to detach the five Northern provinces from all allegiance to Nanking, they represented, none the less, the acquisition by Japan of substantial territorial spheres of influence.

The initiative in these moves lay, of course, with the Kwantung Army and, to a lesser extent, with the Japanese garrison in North China.[3] These two military forces were separate entities, and some rivalry and jealousy existed between them. While Doihara was in North China—he was there from September, 1935, until

---

[1] Cable from Wakasugi to Hirota, 2nd October, 1935. I.M.T.F.E. Exhibit No. 197. Transcript, p. 2283.

[2] It was not only in Manchukuo and North China that the army was undertaking independent political activity at this time. It was during the summer of 1935 that the Germans began conversations with Oshima, Japanese Military Attaché in Berlin, with a view to negotiating a German-Japanese treaty of alliance. From these overtures there developed the Anti-Comintern Pact. In December, 1935, matters had progressed far enough for the Army General Staff in Tokyo to send one of its specialists on German affairs—Lt.-Col. Wakamatsu —to Berlin to join Oshima in the talks with Ribbentrop and Blomberg. When interrogated by S.C.A.P., Oshima emphasised that no communications were sent to the Japanese Foreign Ministry with regard to these matters, which, said Oshima, were purely military. Oshima declared: "I wish to point out that Japanese military and naval attachés are not under the jurisdiction of the Ambassador but are directly responsible to their respective staff headquarters in Tokyo." They were within their rights, he said, if they entered into negotiations with the military of another nation, provided such negotiations related only to military matters. I.M.T.F.E. Transcript, p. 5917.

[3] Japanese forces were stationed in Peking and other places between that city and the sea by virtue of the Boxer Protocol of 1901.

March of the following year—his activities were resented by Lieutenant-General Tada Shun, commanding Japanese forces in that area. For Doihara was acting under the order of the Commander-in-Chief, Kwantung Army, General Minami.[1] The foundations on which Doihara was able to build had been laid by the Umezu-Ho agreement of June, 1935. This understanding between Tada's predecessor and the local Chinese commander opened the way for Doihara's arrival in North China, as it stipulated that General Sung Che-yuan, commanding Chinese troops in the Peking-Tientsin region, should employ the services of a Japanese military adviser. It was with mixed feelings that Colonel Sakai Takashi, Chief of Staff successively to Umezu and Tada, accepted Doihara in that capacity; for Sakai was the North China garrison's expert on the manipulation of "autonomous" movements. The two régimes inaugurated at the beginning of December, 1935, reflected the rivalry between the Kwantung Army and the North China garrison. The former controlled the East Hopei Autonomous Council, the latter was in charge of the Hopei-Chahar Political Council.[2]

The General Staff in Tokyo seem to have been little more than complacent observers of these events. Such, at least, was the Premier's opinion at the time.[3]

As for Hirota, he was as powerless as Shidehara had been four years earlier. The army, he remarked, appeared to think that anything was permissible in North China.[4]

The comment of the aged but alert Saionji was curt and contemptuous. The Japanese Army, he said, was interfering in North China affairs "for the sole purpose of enhancing its ego".[5]

The ulterior policy—presaging the general war against China less than two years later—was clearly implied in a letter from the

---

[1] Evidence of Maj.-Gen. Tanaka Ryukichi, I.M.T.F.E. Transcript, p. 2036. Tanaka at the time was on the staff of the Kwantung Army and actively involved in negotiations with Mongol leaders in Chahar. He maintained that Tada was so vehement in his annoyance that eventually Doihara was placed under his command. *Ibid.*

[2] However, in March, 1936, both régimes came under the aegis of the North China garrison.

[3] "It appears that the General Staff is being more or less led around by the Kwantung Army." (Premier to Harada.) Memoirs, *op. cit.*, Part IX, Ch. 188 (28th November, 1935).

[4] *Ibid.*   [5] *Ibid.*, Part IX, Ch. 190 (13th December, 1935).

Chief of Staff of the Kwantung Army, Major-General Nishio, to the Vice-Minister of War, Lieutenant-General Furusho. The letter dealt with propaganda matters relating to military activities in North China. Propaganda, said the letter, must be directed to convincing the whole world of the righteousness of Japan's cause "as soon as the advance of the Kwantung Army into China Proper takes place". The letter continued: "It must be made clear that when we do send our military forces to China some time in the future we do it for the purpose of punishing the Chinese military clique and not the Chinese people at large." [1]

These marks of expansion in North China—the curtain-raiser of later full-scale aggression—were, it should be noted, related to the consolidation of the power of the *Tosei-ha*; which was, as we have seen, the "China faction". Had Araki and Mazaki been able to maintain a dominant position in the army there is little doubt that the direction of military activity would have been turned not towards China, but against Siberia. The decline of the *Kodo-ha* enabled the army to turn south. [2]

ii

Before Japanese expansion South of the Great Wall was fairly under way the *Kodo-ha* made a supreme effort to upset by violence the hegemony of the *Tosei-ha*.

At the end of December, 1935, some thirty army officers of junior rank met at a restaurant in the Shinjuku district of Tokyo to protest against the appointment of Admiral Saito, the ex-Premier, to succeed Makino as Lord Keeper of the Privy Seal.

[1] Letter dated 9th December, 1935. I.M.T.F.E. Exhibit 195, Transcript, p. 2277.

[2] Professor Yanaga (*op. cit.*, p. 569) expresses the view that the removal of Mazaki from his post as Inspector-General "was in effect the triumph of the Kwantung Army and the Control faction of the army and was designed to remove those who were in favour of limiting and localising the Manchurian Incident". As such it was a necessary preliminary to the unhampered activities of the military in North China. The phrase "limiting and localising the Manchurian Incident" is perhaps misleading, for it suggests that the *Kodo-ha* had a leaning towards moderation. Whereas, in fact, Araki and Mazaki wished to limit military activities *vis-à-vis* China only, as a prelude to preparations for war with Russia.

But the gathering was more than a mere gesture of protest. Kita Ikki and Nishida Zei were there; and plans for an armed insurrection were discussed. The nature of these can only be guessed. No doubt they included the decision to assassinate Saito. The meeting, which was of course confidential, was of sufficient menace to make the Minister of War uneasy when he heard of it. He appears to have made up his mind to order disciplinary action against the officers concerned.[1]

Yet nothing was done. The War Minister's passivity was to cost Japan dear. For the gathering at Shinjuku must have discussed some of the plans to be put into execution two months later, during the February Mutiny.

At the New Year there were other portents of a threatening nature. The 1st Division, stationed in Tokyo, was under orders to proceed to Manchuria some weeks later. Reports reached the police that a group of young officers in the Division had plotted to assassinate General Watanabe, Mazaki's successor as Inspector-General of Military Training. The police took into custody the alleged ringleader of the plot and subjected him to an interrogation. This officer—his name was Deguchi—was found to be on friendly terms with Mazaki. Although Deguchi stubbornly refused to give any information—beyond the repeated assertion that the conspiracy had been plotted by himself and others, acting purely on their own behalf—the police believed that Mazaki had instigated the whole affair.[2]

Again no measures were taken to deal with what were obviously explosive elements in the 1st Division. Meanwhile the courtmartial of Aizawa for the murder of Nagata was proceeding within the 1st Division's barracks and was being accorded

[1] Memoirs, *op. cit.*, Part X, Ch. 193 (17th January, 1936).

[2] Deguchi, like Mazaki, was a native of Saga Prefecture in Kyushu. Memoirs, Part X, Ch. 195 (6th February, 1936). In his statement to the writer, Mazaki emphatically denied that he had ever plotted violence, or encouraged the use of violence by junior officers at any time. It must be confessed that Mazaki impressed the writer as a man of considerable frankness and sincerity.

Some time in January, 1936, Yoshida Shigeru met Mazaki. The latter said that he was convinced that senior officers close to Ugaki would "start a revolution to stamp out the movement for national socialism, or at least to eliminate it from the army". (The "national socialist movement" referred, of course, to the advocates—e.g. Kita and Nishida—of the Showa Restoration.) Yoshida was favourably impressed with Mazaki's sincerity. He described him, to Harada, as being "quite gentle". But Harada warned Yoshida to be on his guard. *Ibid.*

considerable publicity in the press. Much sympathy was aroused for the defendant; who, while admitting the facts of the charge against him, occupied the attention of the court, and of a wider audience outside, with a passionate dissertation on his motives. These reflected in full the fanaticism of the *Kodo-ha*, the accusations of treachery and weakness against the cabinet, *genro*, senior advisers to the Throne and the great capitalist combines. The Aizawa trial, in fact, became a sounding board for the views of the *Kodo-ha*. Important officials were called or listed as witnesses; and thus the offence which had brought Aizawa into court—the murder of Nagata in the Ministry of War—became of minor interest compared with that attached to the question of the political and economic factors which had motivated the accused.[1]

A general election was impending. No doubt it was the hope of ultra-nationalists that public interest in the issues raised by the Aizawa trial—they included the old controversy over the London Naval Treaty—would find some echo in the election results. At least the Minseito, long the object of nationalist abuse, might be expected to suffer an overwhelming defeat at the polls. The election was due to take place on 20th February.

However, with their contempt for party politics it is questionable whether those who were plotting an armed rising in Tokyo attached much significance to the outcome of this election. None the less it must have come as an unwelcome surprise to them. For the Minseito won seventy-eight seats, making it the largest party in the Lower House in place of the Seiyukai, which lost sixty-eight seats. The striking gains made by the *Shakai Taishuto* ("The Social Mass Party") were less disturbing to nationalists of the *Kodo-ha* school than were the electoral victories of the Minseito. The *Shakai Taishuto*, which increased its representation from three to eighteen members, favoured national socialism and expressed the discontent of farmers and soldiers alike. On the other hand the Minseito was the party that had provided such Premiers as Hamaguchi and Wakatsuki. In so far as any political party could be said to have filled the rôle, the Minseito represented liberal, as well as business, interests in Japan.

---

[1] Hayashi and Mazaki were called as witnesses. But the latter refused to say anything about his resignation during the previous summer. Saito was due to be called later.

That the Mutiny occurred six days after this general election may have been more than a coincidence. But the 1st Division's imminent departure overseas had a greater bearing on the date selected for the rising. If the conspirators had been allowed more time for preparation the Mutiny would have been, no doubt, on a larger and even more dangerous scale.[1]

The rebel troops were headed by no officer above the rank of captain. But as in previous conspiracies there were two categories of principals involved. There were those directly in command of operations—those who carried out the assassinations and the seizure of buildings in the centre of Tokyo. The main figures here were Captains Nonaka and Ando, and Lieutenant Kurihara.[2] Behind these men were others, who directly or indirectly instigated them to violence, with promises—not always explicit—of powerful support as soon as the "Incident" had succeeded.

This category included those senior officers—the leaders of the *Kodo-ha*—such as Mazaki, Yanagawa and Kobata, who expected to benefit from the abrupt overthrow of the cabinet resulting from a military rising. Yet it is unlikely that Mazaki took the initiative in stirring the discontented officers of the 1st Division to armed revolt. The embers of insurrection were already fully alight. The most active incendiaries were Kita Ikki, Nishida Zei and the two cashiered officers, Muranaka and Isobe, whose part in the "Military Academy Incident" and authorship of a clandestine pamphlet, exposing the conspiracies of 1931, were described in the previous chapter.[3] It seems possible that Muranaka and Isobe formed the channel of communication between Mazaki and the rebel officers; and it was through them that certain funds reached Nonaka and Ando.[4]

Considerable financial support was provided by Ishihara

[1] According to Tsukui Tatsuo (*op. cit.*, p. 106): "The 26th February Incident began earlier than was planned; this was because the 1st Division was under orders to leave for Manchukuo. Kita and Nishida, leaders of the Incident, admitted it was premature."

[2] Kurihara, it will be remembered, was one of the officers who had threatened Mazaki after the 15th May Incident; and he had been connected, to some extent, with members of the Kawagoe *Teishintai* in 1933. p. 135 (*supra*).

[3] *Vide* pp. 159–61 (*supra*).

[4] Isobe, for example, collected money from various civilian sympathisers. Memoirs, *op. cit.*, Part X, Ch. 210 (19th July, 1936).

Koichiro.[1] Another backer was the politician and shipping magnate, Kuhara Fusanosuke. Some of the funds reaching the conspirators represented the proceeds of virtual blackmail. It appears, for example, that Ikeda Seihin, of the Mitsui firm, gave money under duress.[2]

The retired general, Tanaka Kunishige, of the *Meirinkai* and Marquis Tokugawa Yoshichika, who had been involved in the March Incident of 1931, were evidently in league with the conspirators. According to the Commandant of the Tokyo *Kempei*, Tanaka and Tokugawa "planned to visit the Emperor and report on future events when the insurgent group succeeded".[3] In other words they were expected to fill the rôle of such senior Palace officials as the Grand Chamberlain and Lord Keeper of the Privy Seal, who of course would have been killed by the rebels.[4]

There were, too, several senior army officers, aware of the impending revolt and not unsympathetic towards it, who waited to see what would happen, hesitating to commit themselves. Later, General Terauchi, Minister of War in the Hirota cabinet, declared:

In connection with this Incident there are those not directly involved but who knew that such plans were afoot. Yet they kept quiet. Some directly incited the men to action; others kept quiet. A really disgraceful group of men were gathered together. And yet if all who were thus involved resigned it would be difficult to find men to take their places.[5]

Although the Mutiny was primarily associated with the *Kodo-ha* it was not entirely confined to that faction. Officers such as Tatekawa and Hashimoto, belonging to the *Tosei-ha*, who had an instinct for fishing in troubled waters gave passive support to the conspirators.[6]

[1] The Chief of the Tokyo *Kempei* told Harada that Ishihara had given a million *yen* to the conspirators. Memoirs, *op. cit.*, Part X, Ch. 210 (19th July, 1936).
[2] (Terauchi to Harada.) *Ibid.*, Part X, Ch. 199 (28th March, 1936).
[3] (*Kempei* Comdt. to Harada). *Ibid.*, Part X, Ch. 210 (19th July, 1936).
[4] It will be recalled that before the March Incident Tokugawa had been promised, by Okawa, the post of Imperial Household Minister, provided the *coup* succeeded.
[5] Memoirs, *op. cit.*, Part X, Ch. 209 (8th July, 1936).
[6] Harada learned that both these officers were privy to the conspiracy. *Ibid.*

The fact was that until the Mutiny was clearly demonstrated to have failed there were many who were ready to seek an accommodation with those who might become overnight the new rulers of Japan.

iii

The events that occurred in Tokyo on the morning of 26th February, 1936, have often been described; but a brief recapitulation here may not be amiss.

Some time before 5 a.m. that day rather more than fourteen hundred troops of the 1st and 3rd Infantry Regiments of the 1st Division left their barracks. Their leader was Captain Nonaka Shiro, a company commander in the 3rd Infantry Regiment.[1]

They took possession of a group of important buildings in Nagatacho, immediately to the west of the Imperial Palace. These included the Imperial Diet, the Ministry of War and the head-quarters of the Metropolitan Police. Simultaneously parties of mutineers went to the official residence of the Prime Minister and to the homes of the Lord Keeper of the Privy Seal, the Grand Chamberlain, the Minister of Finance and the Inspector-General of Military Training. Two parties made their way out of Tokyo; one to the *genro's* villa at Okitsu, the other to Yugawara, where Count Makino happened to be staying.

Four of these seven distinguished victims had remarkable escapes from death. Okada's brother-in-law was shot dead by rebels who mistook him for the Premier. Admiral Suzuki, the Grand Chamberlain, was seriously wounded; but he was to re-cover and live to be Premier during the last stages of the Pacific War. Saionji had prior warning of attack and made an escape from Okitsu to Shizuoka. Makino by a narrow margin gained

---

[1] The total number of rebel soldiers was at least 1,480. They included fifty sympathisers from the Imperial Guards Division. They amounted to about ten per cent of the infantry strength of the Tokyo garrison, which consisted of six infantry regiments. Of these the 1st Division provided two—two other regiments of this division were stationed outside the city—and the Imperial Guards Division four.

Nonaka's regimental commander, who tried in vain to order the men back to barracks, committed suicide.

safety in the hills behind Yugawara.[1] Admiral Saito, Takahashi and General Watanabe were killed in their homes.

An attack was also made on the offices of the Tokyo *Asahi*, and its presses were wrecked.

These dramatic events took place while the city lay under a blanket of snow—a feature of the February Mutiny that gave it a peculiar historic significance in the eyes of fanatical nationalists. For a scene cherished in the hearts of the Japanese and portrayed in paintings and on the stage—the revenge of the Forty-Seven Ronin—was set against the backcloth of winter in Yedo, with snow on the ground.

By eight o'clock that morning these acts of violence had been accomplished, and Nonaka with the rebel officers had set up their headquarters in the Sanno Hotel. They hoped and expected that senior officers, such as Mazaki, who were sympathetic with their cause would take over the government immediately. For this reason, no doubt, they refrained from putting a cordon round the extensive grounds of the Imperial Palace. They were reluctant also, it may be supposed, to secure the person of the Emperor, whom they held in religious veneration. If they contemplated such drastic measures they may have dismissed them as unnecessary. For the attacks on Saito and Suzuki—the latter had been left for dead—had removed the most influential of the evil counsellors in constant attendance on the Throne. The way was now clear for a direct approach to the Emperor by the leading figures of the ultra-nationalist cause, who would advise His Majesty to establish the Showa Restoration.

The rebel officers issued a manifesto, which in vague terms stated their aims. After saying that the economic difficulties of the time had been caused by the selfishness of those who had "amassed wealth", the document went on to make the familiar accusations against "Elder Statesmen, financial magnates, government officials and political parties". The London Naval Treaty was cited as an instance of their treachery. The manifesto then referred to the attack on Hamaguchi, the *Ketsumeidan* and 15th May Incidents,

---

[1] In Fleisher, *Volcanic Isle* (*op. cit.*, pp. 63–8), there is an interesting account, by Admiral Okada's private secretary, of the Premier's escape.

Mazaki informed the writer that Tsukumo Kunitoshi, a member of the Diet, gave Saionji warning of the revolt. There is no mention of this in the Memoirs.

and the assassination of Nagata. "Those Incidents, however, have failed to remind men of their responsibilities." Finally the manifesto declared:

The recent strained relations between Japan and other powers are due to our statesmen's failure to take appropriate measures. Japan now confronts a crisis. Therefore it is our duty to take proper steps to safeguard our fatherland by killing those responsible. On the eve of our departure to Manchuria we have risen to attain our aims by direct action. We think it is our duty as subjects of His Majesty the Emperor. May Heaven bless us and help us in our endeavour to save our fatherland from the worst.[1]

The document was delivered to the principal newspaper offices by rebel soldiers. They announced that during the afternoon a "new law of State" would be promulgated.[2]

It was at this juncture that the resolution shown by the Emperor proved to be decisive. The absence of Saito and Suzuki meant that action, in the early stages at least, depended largely on the Emperor's own initiative.[3]

The surviving members of the cabinet made the Imperial Palace their rendezvous. The members of the Imperial Family—including the Chiefs of the Army and Navy General Staffs—also gathered at the Palace. Here, too, went those, such as Hiranuma and Mazaki, who represented the cause of extreme nationalism. The chiefs of the army made the *Kaikosha*, the Army Club, their meeting place. But at this crisis they looked to the Palace for action. All depended on what attitude was taken by the Emperor.

This was expressed immediately, in clear terms. The Emperor at once referred to the disturbance as a mutiny. "I will give you

---

[1] Quoted by Byas, *op. cit.*, pp. 123–4. The document was signed by Nonaka and Ando.

[2] Grew, *op. cit.*, p. 153. Iwabuchi Tatsuo, in "The Genealogy of the *Gumbatsu*", *Chuo Koron*, July, 1946, declares that the rebel officers did not go into action in order to establish any particular cabinet or any particular system of government—such as Kita's Revolutionary Empire of Japan. "Only restore imperial power and let the light of the nation shine forth. Then politics will be put right automatically. Such is 'Restoration' " (Iwabuchi). He maintains, in fact, that the young officers were pure idealists. However, Iwabuchi is perhaps biased in favour of Mazaki and the *Kodo-ha*.

[3] "All action was taken on His Majesty's own decision." Memoirs, *op. cit.*, Part X, Ch. 196 (14th March, 1936).

one hour," he said to the Minister of War, "in which to suppress the rebels." [1] He refused to accept the resignation of the remaining cabinet ministers. He told Goto, the Home Minister, that he would not consider the question of a new cabinet until the rebels had been put down. His comment on Nonaka and the other mutinous officers was direct and uncompromising. "Any soldier who moves Imperial troops without my orders is not my soldier, no matter what excuse he may have." [2]

There is evidence that Mazaki, together with Admiral Kato Kanji, asked Prince Fushimi, Chief of the Naval General Staff, to recommend Hiranuma to the Emperor as the new Premier with Mazaki as Minister of War. At the same time a message was sent by Mazaki, through an intimate friend, to Hiranuma urging him to agree to be Prime Minister. [3]

The Emperor's firm stand, however, prevented such recommendations being accepted. [4] And even if some generals wanted to conciliate the rebels the Navy Minister, Admiral Osumi, assured the Emperor from the first that the loyal support of the navy could be relied upon in any action taken to deal with the mutiny. [5]

Thus, while the mutineers remained in possession of Nagatacho, troops of the Imperial Guards Division were placed round the Palace, the First Fleet was ordered to concentrate in Tokyo Bay, and naval ratings from Yokosuka were brought to the port area of the capital.

The following day limited martial law was proclaimed in the city, and a martial law headquarters set up, under Lieutenant-General Kashii. By the early hours of that morning, 27th February, troop reinforcements had arrived in Tokyo. It was now apparent that the rebels would have to surrender or be suppressed by force of arms.

The Emperor was impatient for the matter to be settled with-

---

[1] Memoirs, *op. cit.*, Part X, Ch. 196 (14th March, 1936).

[2] *Ibid.*

[3] Memoirs, Part X, Ch. 200. It must be said here that Gen. Ninomiya, who gave this information to Harada, was not a first-hand witness; and he had an aversion to Mazaki.

[4] According to Ninomiya, Fushimi refused to make these recommendations to the Emperor. *Ibid.*

[5] Osumi went to the Palace with an armed naval escort.

out further delay, if necessary by an immediate attack on the buildings occupied by the rebels.[1] But the military chiefs opposed hasty action. They thought it was possible to induce Nonaka and his colleagues to surrender with a good grace. Not unnaturally Araki and Mazaki—who, as Supreme War Councillors, had a say in the anxious discussions at the Army Club—took this view.

February 27th, then, was a day of parley with the rebels. Meetings were held between three senior officers—Mazaki, Abe and Nishi—and rebel leaders at the official residence of the Minister of War.

Mazaki tried to persuade the rebels to surrender. Later Mazaki cited these efforts on his part as proof that he had never countenanced the rebellion. For the mutineers, he said, would have killed him during these negotiations had he in fact originally encouraged them to rise in arms. "If I had instigated them earlier and then admonished them on the grounds that their direct action was outrageous they would have shot me instantly." [2]

Certainly General Nishi, after witnessing the scene, appears to have been convinced that Mazaki could have had nothing to do with the mutiny; and he said as much to General Abe. The latter, however, seems to have been unimpressed. He merely commented that Mazaki was a clever man, able at persuasion.[3]

No settlement having been reached on the 27th or on the following day Martial Law Headquarters issued a statement, early on the morning of the 29th, declaring that, although the rebels had been "sincerely admonished time and again to return to their original posts", they had "failed to listen". Accordingly it had been decided to secure "a settlement by military force".[4]

The same morning a special order was addressed to the rank and file of the rebels by Lieutenant-General Kashii. This was expressed in dignified language, telling the soldiers that, although

[1] Kido told Harada that the Emperor kept asking members of the Supreme War Council: "Why are the rebels not suppressed by now?" Memoirs, *op. cit.*, Part X, Ch. 196 (14th March, 1936).

[2] Statement to the writer by Mazaki. He remarked that the atmosphere during these parleys was extremely tense, and that the lives of himself and the other two generals "were really in danger".

[3] Mazaki stated (to the writer) that Nishi countered Abe's remark by saying that Mazaki was not clever, but "talked with honesty and sincerity".

[4] Martial Law, H.Q. Bulletin No. 4.

they might have acted "from unalloyed motives in absolute obedience to superiors", they had now been ordered by the Emperor to return to their barracks. If they were to keep up their resistance they would make themselves traitors. They would be spared punishment if they returned to their quarters without delay. But this language was not easily intelligible to soldiers raw from the country. So a very simple paraphrase of the order was roneographed, and copies were dropped on the rebels from aircraft. This simplified version read:

1. It is not too late yet, return at once, therefore, to your original units.
2. Those who resist will all be shot, as they are rebels.
3. Your fathers, mothers, brothers and sisters are all weeping because you will become traitors.

The plain emotional appeal was effective. By noon on the 29th large numbers of rebel soldiers had surrendered. The complete surrender was effected by 3 p.m. that day. Nonaka killed himself in the Sanno Hotel; but Ando and the other officers surrendered.

If all the rebel officers had followed Nonaka's example the February Mutiny might have acquired a glamour which, however spurious, would have accorded its leaders lasting fame, like that attaching to the memory of the Forty-Seven Ronin. But Ando persuaded the others to surrender with him in the expectation that there would be a prolonged trial, with opportunities of advocating the ideas of the Showa Restoration in a blaze of publicity.

Such calculations, however, were wide of the mark. During the afternoon of the 29th the Minister of War, General Kawashima, gave a statement to the press. He spoke of the rebellion as "an unprecedented insurrection within the Japanese Army, violating military discipline and causing anxiety to His Majesty the Emperor". He said it had "gravely soiled the honourable history of the Empire" and had thereby "left a blot on the divine reign of Showa".

These were exceptionally strong words for a Japanese general to use in public regarding what was generally recognised as having been a shameful and humiliating episode. The statement reflected the disgust felt by the Emperor.

The whole affair brought discredit on the movement for the Showa Restoration. Indeed Japanese nationalism for the moment appeared to have suffered a setback—although, as events showed, this was only temporary.[1] Mazaki's reputation sustained a severe blow. The general whisper in Tokyo was that he had been responsible for the outbreak of the mutiny. Within a few weeks he was under interrogation by the *Kempei*.[2]

The rebel officers were tried and convicted in secret. Thirteen of them were condemned to death, and executed on 12th July. Kita, Nishida, Muranaka and Isobe were also condemned to death, but were not executed until September of the following year. Nagata's murderer, Lieutenant-Colonel Aizawa—who in other circumstances might have escaped with a sentence of imprisonment—was convicted, and executed on 7th July, 1936.

The February Mutiny—or "26th February Incident" as it was called[3]—was the climax of revolutionary nationalism in Japan. Thereafter the position of the *Tosei-ha* seemed virtually unassailable.

[1] "Everybody expected that the Incident would give a fillip to the Japanese nationalist movement; but the result was just the opposite." Tsukui Tatsuo, *op. cit.*, p. 106.

[2] Mazaki told the writer that his enemies in the *Tosei-ha* deliberately put about rumours that he had been behind the revolt. Indeed he claimed that it had been engineered indirectly by the *Tosei-ha* in order to ruin him.

[3] "*Ni Ni Roku*" ("2, 26", viz. 2nd month, 26th day)—it is by this term that the Incident is commonly described in colloquial Japanese.

9

AFTERMATH OF THE MUTINY

i

THE *Tosei-ha* exploited the February Mutiny, using the fear of its recurrence as a means of enforcing the political demands of military leaders on the government. Thus, when the new cabinet under Hirota was being formed, Terauchi—who had been appointed Minister of War—declared that the army would not allow persons with liberal leanings to enter the administration.[1]

The conclusions of a Japanese authority, who has been quoted earlier in this study, are of particular interest.

There is a continuity in the young officers' revolutionary movement from the so-called Military Academy Incident of November, 1934, through the Lieutenant-Colonel Aizawa Incident, to the 26th February Incident; but with each outbreak, regardless of the intentions of the participants, the only result was always the further extension of the political territory of the upper military class. The 26th February Incident marks an important turning point. It was the culmination of a "putsch" which had been germinating for several years. After the 26th February Incident the fascist movement from below, centring on the young officers and the popular revolutionary Right wing, faded into the background; and with the development of military ascendancy the *Tosei-ha* smashed the *Kodo-ha*. Instead of Araki, Mazaki, Yanagawa and Kobata such generals as Umezu, Tojo, Sugiyama and Koiso were to have the dominant power. They used the threat of revolutionary fascism outside the army as a lever for securing, stage by stage, the acceptance of the army's political demands.[2]

[1] Hirota wanted Yoshida Shigeru to be Foreign Minister. But Yoshida was reputed to be a liberal, and was Makino's son-in-law. Terauchi successfully opposed the appointment. He also vetoed the appointment of Dr. Mikami Sanji, a liberal professor of Tokyo Imperial University, as Minister of Education.
[2] Maruyama, *Nippon Fasshizmu* (cited), p. 161.

The price of peace at home was, of course, armed expansion abroad. Its direction had been suggested by the political advances made by the army in North China during the second half of 1935. The forthcoming offensive would be against China. With regard to Russia preparations would be defensive in nature. Thus Japanese penetration in Chahar and Inner Mongolia was rather a move to protect Manchukuo from a possible Russian attack through Outer Mongolia than an attempt to secure a spring-board from which to launch an offensive towards Lake Baikal, although of course Inner Mongolia might serve this purpose very well at a later date. Early in 1936 Russia and Outer Mongolia concluded a pact of mutual assistance. This had the effect of sharpening Japan's interest in a pact with Germany, directed against Russia; and in April, 1936, the Foreign Ministry entered the negotiations begun by Oshima, the Military Attaché, in Berlin.

The celebrated Anti-Comintern Pact of November, 1936, was, from Japan's point of view, a measure of defence against Russia; a move to protect the Empire's north-western flank while an advance into China was in progress. For the secret annexe to the Pact—its existence was of course denied by Japanese government spokesmen at the time—provided that in case Russia attacked, or threatened to attack, either of the signatory powers, measures for the protection of their mutual interests would be discussed immediately.[1] And during the final deliberations of the Privy Council on the Anti-Comintern agreement it was pointed out, on behalf of the Foreign Ministry, that "the fact that the conclusion of the Pact will further strengthen Japan's position ought to prove quite effective in making China decide her attitude".[2]

If the February Mutiny had been successful and the *Kodo-ha* had seized power, no doubt every effort would have been made to negotiate an offensive alliance with Germany against Russia. Even without it an attack on Russia might well have been launched.

A few weeks before the Mutiny occurred there was a

[1] Record of the proceedings of the Investigation Committee of the Privy Council, which recommended that the Council approve the German-Japanese Pact against the Communist Internationale and the secret attached Pact against the Soviet Union, 20th November, 1936. I.M.T.F.E. Exhibit 484. Transcript, pp. 5958–66.   [2] *Ibid.*, p. 5963.

disturbing affair on the Manchukuo-Russian frontier. Some time in January, 1936, a Japanese detachment, numbering about a hundred in all, crossed the border into Siberia. The Foreign Minister, Hirota, referred to the incident as an "escape" by Japanese officers and men to Russian territory.[1] Yet there appears to have been some fighting, as four officers were killed.[2] News of the affair was rigorously censored; and even to-day the episode remains obscure. It is possible that the action of these troops amounted to desertion from the Kwantung Army.[3] But a more likely interpretation of this strange affair is that it was a suicidal foray designed to provoke the Soviet forces to retaliatory action and so cause a general war between Japan and Russia.[4]

However, even the *Kodo-ha*—though action against Russia would have been preferred—accepted, to some extent, Japan's growing military commitments in North China. For example, Araki—that inveterate advocate of war with Russia—confessed during the summer of 1936 that, however much he disliked the situation in North China, it was unrealistic to suppose that Japan could halt her expansion in that area. "It is like telling a man", he said, "not to get involved with a certain woman when she is already pregnant by him." [5]

In November, 1936, war with China—the inevitable consequence of the policy pursued by the *Tosei-ha*—was brought nearer by the Suiyuan Incident. This episode, like the affair on the Manchukuo-Russian border ten months earlier, hardly redounded to the credit of Japanese arms. Inner Mongolian forces—the

[1] (Hirota to Harada) Memoirs, *op. cit.*, Part X, Ch. 195 (6th February, 1936). Hirota admitted that he did not have full knowledge of the affair, as the army was keeping it secret.   [2] *Ibid.*

[3] Yuasa Kurahei (Saito's successor as Lord Keeper of the Privy Seal) said that he had heard that young officers "rather than be sent home to Japan to be punished had invaded Russian territory and got themselves killed". *Ibid.*, Part X, Ch. 201 (22nd April, 1936). The frontier incident took place, as we have seen, before the outbreak of the February Mutiny. There was, then, hardly a connection between the two events. But the Kwantung Army officers may have faced punishment for insubordination, or revolutionary nationalist activities.

[4] The reported strength of the Japanese force—"about a hundred"—suggests that it may have been an infantry company which would have had a company commander and three, or (at the most) four, other officers. It looks as though the company commander and his platoon officers were fanatics, whereas the men in the ranks allowed themselves to be disarmed and captured.

[5] Memoirs, *op. cit.*, Part X, Ch. 208 (1st July, 1936).

nucleus of which was a Kwantung Army unit commanded by Colonel Tanaka Ryukichi—attacked Chinese troops in East Suiyuan. The latter resisted with determination, and succeeded in routing their opponents.[1]

The Foreign Ministry in Tokyo was, naturally, embarrassed. Arita Hachiro, the Foreign Minister, remarked, in private: "The Kwantung Army does not submit to central control, and that creates a very dangerous situation indeed." [2] No such admission, of course, could be made in public. To save Japan's face the Foreign Ministry issued a statement categorically denying that Japanese forces had been involved in the fighting.[3]

But among the forces in the field there was the natural desire for revenge; and when, in the following summer, the news of the clash at Lukouchiao, near Peking, reached Tokyo the Minister of War, General Sugiyama, was said to have believed that it had been instigated by those who smarted from the reverse in Suiyuan.[4]

ii

Meanwhile, at home, the Hirota cabinet was little more than a façade concealing the essentially military government of Japan. The position of Prime Minister immediately following the Mutiny was, of course, more than usually difficult. It was indeed an unenviable honour—one that Konoye, the *genro's* first choice,

---

[1] According to Yanaga (*op. cit.*, p. 571) Lt.-Gen. Tojo, then Chief of Staff of the Kwantung Army, had planned the abortive attack. Both Tojo and Tanaka had worked hard for Mongolian "autonomy" under Prince Teh.

[2] Memoirs, Part XI, Ch. 222 (4th December, 1936).

[3] The statement, dated 21st November, 1936, read: "Japan is always concerned over the conditions prevailing in the adjoining districts of Manchukuo territory, but she has had nothing to do with the clash that took place between the Suiyuan troops and the Inner Mongolian forces. It hardly requires mentioning that the Japanese Army, not to say the Japanese Government, is not assisting the Mongols in any way." *Japan Year Book*, 1939–40, p. 196.

[4] "When the incident first occurred the thought which came to us was that the Minister of War had seemed very worried recently. The reason for it was the question whether or not the young officers overseas might start something before the August promotions and transfers; especially whether a certain staff officer, Tanaka Ryukichi, who failed at Suiyan, might start something." Memoirs, *op. cit.*, Part XII, Ch. 244 (14th July, 1937).

felt unready to accept.[1] Terauchi, the new Minister of War, seems to have dictated not only the composition of the cabinet but also its basic policies, in education and finance as well as national defence and diplomacy. So that when, in August, 1936, the government announced a seven-point programme of guiding principles these represented what might be called the charter of the *Tosei-ha*. They included, first and foremost, the provision of "adequate national defence"; in other words greatly accelerated rearmament, a prospective war with China as its primary aim. There was also a declaration to the effect that the "living of the people" would be improved by economic and health measures. This was a sop to the advocates of the Showa Restoration. It envisaged increasing government interference in the field of capitalist economics. Another basic principle was the "renovation" of education. This was to find expression in the *Kokutai no Hongi*, published in 1937 by the Ministry of Education—a book of profound influence, especially in the primary and middle grade schools. Reference was made to this work in the introductory chapter to this study.[2] Further guiding principles related to the exploitation of Manchukuo, the encouragement of emigration and the expansion of trade and industry. The entire programme was directed towards achieving efficiency in war. Indeed, during the latter half of 1936 the Minister of Finance frequently spoke of Japan as being engaged in constructing "a quasi-wartime economic system".[3]

The restoration, in May, of the requirement that the Minister of War should always be a general, or lieutenant-general, on the active list merely underlined the formidable character of the power attained by the army.[4] The reversion to the active service

---

[1] Konoye was actually recommended to the Throne by the *genro*. However Konoye asked that the recommendation be withdrawn, pleading that his health was not sufficiently robust for him to take on the duties of Premier. Much embarrassed, Saionji had to return to the Palace and, this time, put forward Hirota's name. "Never before," said Saionji (to Kido and Harada), "have I been placed in such an awkward position as this." *Ibid.*, Part X, Ch. 196 (14th March, 1936).

[2] p. 3 (*supra*). Saionji was sent a copy by the Ministry of Education. He thought little of it. "Looking through it", he said, "I find that it deals not only with religion but with history, psychology and everything else. The whole thing is a conglomeration that cannot be understood." *Ibid.*, Part XII, Ch. 237(a) (8th May, 1937).   [3] *Japan Year Book*, 1939–40, p. 137.

[4] Prof. Yanaga (*op. cit.*, p. 525) describes the restoration of the active service

requirement—instituted by Yamagata in 1903—was justified by Terauchi and military leaders on the grounds that it was necessary for the maintenance of army discipline. This argument, needless to say, was used repeatedly in support of the army's political demands.[1]

There is no doubt that Terauchi was sincerely resolved to ensure that there should never be another mutiny. His aim, he said, was "the total reform of the army".[2] And he appears to have been determined to secure Mazaki's conviction.

The latter, after interrogations by the *Kempei* over a period of three months, was committed to a military prison in July, 1936, to await courtmartial. Yet, if his own story is to be believed, Mazaki would have been released at the end of the year had it not been for Terauchi's refusal to accept the opinion of the military prosecuting staff—that there was no valid case against the prisoner.[3] Araki, of course, stood by his friend, even going so far as to tell the Chief of the Tokyo *Kempei* that if Mazaki were released he, Araki, would undertake to become a Buddhist priest, that Mazaki would follow suit, and that the two of them would become mendicants. For the world seemed hopeless to Araki so long as Mazaki was in custody. In his depression, so he told the *Kempei* Commandant, he felt that he and Mazaki should retire altogether from the secular world. "I cannot bear to live", he said, "in such a disagreeable society." [4]

However, Mazaki was held in prison despite the pleas made on his behalf. Terauchi's position—and that of his successor, Sugiyama—was fortified by an Imperial Rescript given to the Minister of War by the Emperor immediately after the February Mutiny. The Rescript was phrased in unusually strong language,

requirement as "without question the most important single step that put the military on the road to supremacy". But this is, perhaps, somewhat of an overstatement. For while it had been possible from 1913 to 1936 for generals and lieutenant-generals on the reserve to take office as Minister, in fact all the Ministers of War during those twenty-three years were on the active list.

[1] "Whenever a War Minister opposed a proposed measure or demanded the adoption of a measure at a cabinet meeting or Imperial Conference he would say: 'Under the circumstances it would be impossible to maintain order in military circles', or 'then we cannot guarantee our ability to control military personnel'." Maruyama, *A Study of the Minds of the Rulers of a Militarist Nation* (cited).

[2] Memoirs, *op. cit.*, Part X, Ch. 199 (28th March, 1936).

[3] Statement to the writer by Mazaki.

[4] Memoirs, *op. cit.*, Part XI, Ch. 212 (13th August, 1936).

condemning the Mutiny. "The occurrence", it said, "of such an affair as that of the 26th February violates the Emperor Meiji's Rescript to Soldiers and Sailors. In addition it debases the history of our country, Japan." [1]

An Imperial Rescript is of course intended for publication. But in this instance Terauchi kept the document to himself, probably because he felt that it was dangerously outspoken. When he resigned, in January, 1937, he did not give the Rescript directly to his successor, but left it in a drawer at the Ministry of War so that Sugiyama should find it.[2] The latter—he was, of course, also a member of the *Tosei-ha*—was thus strengthened in his resolve to secure, if possible, the punishment of Mazaki.

Events, however, worked in Mazaki's favour. Prince Konoye had from the first opposed the prosecution of Mazaki. Soon after Mazaki's arrest Konoye's views created anxiety in the mind of the *genro*.

> Somehow [remarked Saionji] Konoye seems to defend Mazaki and Araki. On hearing his opinions I cannot tell whether they are his own, or whether he is being forced to say such things. I don't know whether he is saying such things out of fear, or whether he thinks that he will be in a better position, in view of the present situation, if he expresses such opinions. It is indeed regrettable for a man of such noble birth and character.[3]

Konoye at this time was President of the House of Peers. He was only forty-five years of age and clearly eligible as a future Premier. Like Kido he was one of Saionji's protégés. Nevertheless, although he respected the *genro*, he did not share the old man's pronounced liberal views. Indeed Konoye seems to have become decidedly nationalist during the early nineteen-thirties. We have seen that in 1933 he was one of the leading members of the *Dai Ajia Kyokai* ("The Great Asia Association").[4] Still more indicative, perhaps, of the trend of his mind is the fact that

---

[1] Memoirs, Part XIII, Ch. 253 (25th October, 1937).

[2] *Ibid.* Actually Terauchi's immediate successor was Lt.-Gen. Nakamura Kotaro, who held the post for eight days only and then resigned because of "ill-health". His brief term of office was a face-saving device for the benefit of Sugiyama. The latter had refused to enter Ugaki's cabinet and therefore (to save Ugaki's face) he could not well enter the Hayashi cabinet immediately afterwards. The week's delay preserved the outward courtesies.

[3] Memoirs, Part XI, Ch. 212 (13th August, 1936). [4] *Vide* pp. 148–50 (*supra*).

in 1935 Konoye was reported to have said that Saionji was really too old for his job, that Saionji's ideas—and those of other senior statesmen—were very much out of date and constituted an obstacle to the progress of the country.[1]

As soon as he became Premier in June, 1937, Konoye began to press for Mazaki's release. He told the Minister of War that as Mazaki's case had been under examination for twelve months and nothing had come of it, the presumption was that the man was innocent.[2]

Konoye's repeated efforts on behalf of Mazaki almost suggested that he was in close sympathy with the *Kodo-ha*; and it may be noted, in parenthesis, that he cherished socialist leanings in his youth. As will be seen in the next chapter, the power of the *Tosei-ha* during the China Incident was regarded by Konoye as excessive, and he seems to have considered ways and means of reviving the *Kodo-ha* as a counterbalance. But the truth was that on taking office Konoye wished, if possible, to satisfy everyone. He was genuinely scared of the possibility of another armed outbreak in Tokyo if Mazaki were convicted by courtmartial. In this connection it must be remembered that Konoye's highly nervous, sensitive disposition was not allied to great strength of character.[3] His aim on becoming Premier was, in his own words, "to reduce internal friction".[4] He was eager not only to secure Mazaki's release but also to obtain an Imperial pardon for all participants in earlier nationalist "Incidents".

Sugiyama, the Minister of War, firmly opposed Konoye's views on the Mazaki case. Yet, although the *Kodo-ha* had been defeated by its rivals, there was still a body of support for Mazaki among military leaders—those not positively identified with any faction. Their opinion was strengthened by the affair of the stillborn Ugaki cabinet.

[1] Memoirs, Part XI, Ch. 212 (13th August, 1936).
[2] *Ibid.*, Part XII, Ch. 243 (5th July, 1936).
[3] This is not to say that Konoye lacked moral, as well as physical, courage of a high order. Mr. Grew, for example, paid a remarkable tribute to Konoye only a fortnight before Pearl Harbour. "He [Konoye] alone tried to reverse the engine, and tried hard and courageously, even risking his life and having a very close call as it was. . . . It is difficult for anyone not living in Japan and understanding the forces and stresses loose in this misguided country to appreciate what Konoye was up against." Grew, *op. cit.*, p. 416.
[4] Memoirs, *op. cit.*, Part XII, Ch. 243 (5th July, 1937).

General Ugaki was unable to form an administration at the beginning of 1937—the matter is discussed in detail in the next chapter—but he had been granted the high honour of an invitation, by the Emperor, to become Prime Minister. Now it was known, of course, that he had seriously considered heading a *coup d'état* in March, 1931. If Mazaki had encouraged "direct action" on the part of junior officers, so had Ugaki. Thus General Minami—early in July, 1937—said to Konoye:

> The distressing view in the army is as follows: "If Mazaki is found guilty then Ugaki and Mazaki are from some points of view equally guilty. To issue an Imperial decree to Ugaki and then to condemn Mazaki, against whom no concrete evidence regarding the 26th February Incident can be found, is indeed outrageous." [1]

A political settlement of the Mazaki case could hardly have been avoided; especially after the outbreak of hostilities with China during the summer of 1937. It was, in fact, in October of that year that Mazaki was acquitted by courtmartial and released.[2]

iii

In July, 1936, after the publication of the sentences awarded to the ringleaders of the February Mutiny, the Chief of the Tokyo *Kempei* remarked that, while the financial world and general public were expecting further evidence of the Minister of War's disciplinary purge of the army, the extreme Right wing was dissatisfied. The latter, he said, regarded the punishment meted out to Nonaka and the others as too severe; it was thought that the leaders of the army must have curried favour with Saionji and his circle. There was, accordingly, a desire to register a protest by means of "direct action", the aim of the ultra-nationalists being—in the words of the *Kempei* Commandant—"to make the spirits of the executed men live on".[3]

[1] Memoirs, Part XII, Ch. 143 (5th July, 1937).
[2] "This is very bad", commented Saionji, when he heard the news. *Ibid.,* Part XIII, Ch. 251 (13th October, 1937).
[3] Memoirs, Part X, Ch. 210 (19th July, 1936).

Nevertheless, in spite of their resentment and threats of revenge, the extreme nationalists appear to have been disheartened by the failure of the Mutiny and by the generally unfavourable reaction of the public towards those involved.

Soon after the Mutiny there was one of those attempts at unification which from time to time rallied the hopes and energies of nationalist agitators. Tsukui Tatsuo, Akamatsu Katsumaro, Suzuki Zenichi, Matsunobu Shigeru, Shimonaka Yasaburo, Koike Shiro and Nakano Seigo—representing their various groups—collaborated in March, 1936, to form the *Nigatsukai*, or "February Society".[1]

Afterwards Tsukui wrote:

> The *Nigatsukai* did not prosper. A sense of melancholy oppressed its leaders and killed their enthusiasm. The Army Staff thought domestic reform the concern of the Hirota cabinet rather than that of the Japanese nationalist movement.[2]

The comment is significant. It indicates that the army, being now in control of the government, had for the moment no further use for those agitating for such domestic aims as state socialism or the reform of the Constitution. In other words military leaders—and here is meant not only responsible senior officers but also the section chiefs at the General Staff Headquarters and Ministry of War—no longer required the services of civilian terrorists and adventurers in the field of high politics. The army was now in power, and was determined if possible to control or divert the energies of its own revolutionary elements. For the time being, at least, its auxiliaries—the civilian agitators —might, if they wished, attempt to win seats in the Diet, forming a reliable *claque*, but no further "Incidents" were desirable.

Without support from important elements of the army the Japanese nationalists were ineffective. Thus the *Nigatsukai*—a "direct action" group in spite of its professed readiness to enter

---

[1] Tsukui and Akamatsu represented the *Kokumin Undosha*. Suzuki Zenichi, of *Shimpeitai* fame, was out on bail. Matsunobu, a state socialist, had been prominent in the *Kokka Shakai Shugi Gakumei*. Shimonaka (an "agrarian" nationalist) was one of the leaders of the *Dai Ajia Kyokai*. Koike headed the *Aikoku Seiji Domei*. Nakano the *Tohokai*.

[2] Tsukui Tatsuo, *op. cit.*, p. 106.

politics by capturing seats at a general election—died almost as soon as it was born.[1]

For a time there appears to have been an amalgamation of forces between Nakano Seigo, Ishihara Koichiro and Colonel Hashimoto Kingoro. Hashimoto was reported to have threatened to organise an armed rising in August, 1936, one of its aims being to assassinate the *genro* and Court advisers. For Hashimoto claimed that they must have prevented the Emperor from granting a pardon or reduction of sentence to the ringleaders of the February Mutiny.[2]

It was probably for this reason that Hashimoto was retired from active service at the August transfers. Then, in his own words, he "entered the front line of the renovation movement".[3] In October he formed the *Dai Nippon Seinento*, ("The Japan Young Men's Party"), a society with such fascist appurtenances as a special uniform for its members.[4]

Membership was small, but the *Dai Nippon Seinento* had sufficient funds at the outset to publish, three times a month, its own magazine, *Taiyo Dai Nippon*.[5] It was in this periodical that Hashimoto offered a disingenuous justification of that active participation in politics by army officers which, because it flatly ignored the injunction laid down by the Rescript to Soldiers and Sailors, was resented by all save extreme nationalist politicians and which military leaders themselves professed to condemn. The article was written in March, 1937, during a session of the Diet in which certain members were bold enough to criticise the army.

[1] Though this is not stated by Tsukui it appears very probable that what happened was this. Having formed their society the leaders of the *Nigatsukai* went to the General Staff and Ministry of War and solicited financial and moral support. But the army's interest was lukewarm, if not positively hostile. This reaction was probably enough to kill the *Nigatsukai* immediately.

[2] (Tokyo *Kempei* Commandant to Harada.) Memoirs, *op. cit.*, Part XI, Ch. 212 (13th August, 1936).

[3] From an article by Hashimoto in *Taiyo Dai Nippon*, 17th December, 1936. I.M.T.F.E. Exhibit 2185.

[4] A blue uniform with the insignia of a white ball on a red background on each side of the collarband. The insignia, Hashimoto's invention, was the exact reverse of the *Hi no Maru*, the national flag. It was hung on a flag at his headquarters, and strangely enough was not regarded as in any way a desecration of the *Hi no Maru*. *Vide* Fleisher, *op. cit.*, pp. 79–80. In some respects the society is reminiscent of Sakai's *Seigidan*. Cf. p. 30 (*supra*).

[5] Membership subscription was only 1 *yen* a year. But no doubt businessmen such as Ishihara Koichiro gave Hashimoto financial backing.

In the present 70th Session of the Diet [wrote Hashimoto] Liberals, who stand for the maintenance of the *status quo*, are busily denouncing the military for mixing in politics. This is a subtle trick on their part to spread anti-military thought among the people through the Diet, thereby separating the people from the military and obstructing the military's movement for political renovation. Liberals cry aloud against mixing in politics by the military, quoting the Imperial Rescript wherein it is graciously commanded: "Do not be misled by public opinion and do not meddle in politics, but devote yourselves solely to the performance of loyal service." But we interpret the Imperial words to mean "not to be a stickler for politics". Needless to say, not only soldiers but also other persons, such as physicians and merchants, have their own duties according to their occupation. However, is there any reason why, because of this, soldiers, physicians and merchants should not mix in politics? There is no reason why politics should be taboo and entrusted only to professional politicians.[1]

In such manner could the express commands of an Emperor be twisted, to suit a purpose quite contrary to their intent, by one who claimed to be the ardent champion of direct Imperial rule.

Among ultra-nationalists, then, there prevailed after the Mutiny a sense of discouragement and frustration. These feelings might have led to the occurrence of further revolutionary explosions at home if the war with China had not broken out in July, 1937. For it is questionable whether the *Tosei-ha* could have kept control of the restive elements in the army if Japan had called a halt to her expansion on the continent.

The suppression of the February Mutiny was the last triumph of the *Tosei-ha*. The war with China and the Pacific War were, in the final analysis, desperate and, as it turned out, disastrous attempts to consolidate that triumph.

[1] *Taiyo Dai Nippon*, 17th March, 1937. I.M.T.F.E. Exhibit 2185. (The article was entitled: "From the point of view of national defence it is the duty of the Military to mix in politics.")

10

WAR WITH CHINA

i

IN January, 1937, the Minister of War was involved in an angry scene in the Diet with a member of the Seiyukai, Hamada Kunimatsu. Hamada had made an outspoken attack on the army for its usurpation of political power. Terauchi, indignant at such criticism from a party politician, accused Hamada of having insulted the army and demanded an apology. An excited battle of words ensued.[1]

The episode brought to a head ill-feeling which had been brewing between the army and the political parties during the previous weeks. For both the Minseito and Seiyukai had shown themselves openly hostile to the Hirota government; and attacks on the government were in effect attacks on the army—for example, criticism in the Diet of the Foreign Minister for having concluded the Anti-Comintern Pact was in reality directed against the army, which had of course undertaken the initial negotiations with Germany.

Perhaps the new Diet Building—it was officially opened by the Emperor in November, 1936—put fresh heart into the political parties. For they displayed a certain vigorous independence of spirit, as though determined to make a final bid for the recovery of lost prestige; a development that naturally disturbed the army.[2]

The Hamada incident led Terauchi to press Hirota for an

---

[1] Hamada said that his apology would take the form of *hara-kiri* if it was established that he had in fact insulted the army. But he challenged Terauchi to commit *hara-kiri* if the accusation could not be substantiated. Both men seem to have lost their tempers, but the loss of face was Terauchi's. He could hardly take Hamada's challenge seriously. He had been made to look a fool by a civilian.

[2] Gen. Piggott, H.M. Military Attaché in 1936, relates a story of Terauchi pointing to the new Diet Building and asking, rhetorically, whether it had been worth the money spent on it. "Would not two new divisions be better?" asked Terauchi. Maj.-Gen. F. S. G. Piggott, *Broken Thead* (Aldershot, Gale & Polden, 1950), p. 265.

immediate dissolution of the House of Representatives. But Hirota was not prepared to ask the Throne for a dissolution. Accordingly Terauchi resigned, bringing the cabinet down with him.

It was at this juncture that General Ugaki received the Imperial command to form a government. This was the first occasion on which the recommendation of a new Premier was not left primarily to the initiative of the *genro*. On grounds of old age Saionji felt unable to carry out the duties of travelling up to Tokyo, conferring with various leading figures in public life, and finally visiting the Palace to offer his choice of a new Prime Minister. Indeed the old man would have welcomed complete retirement; but this, as his secretary remarked, "existing conditions would not allow".[1]

After Hirota's resignation the Lord Keeper of the Privy Seal, Yuasa, was consulted by the Emperor. Yuasa then visited Saionji. It may be accepted that both Yuasa and the *genro* favoured Ugaki as Hirota's successor. But the initiative now lay with Yuasa; and although Saionji's views still carried considerable weight they could probably no longer decide the issue. For after Ugaki's failure to form a cabinet Yuasa approached Hiranuma—who begged to be excused the task of becoming Premier—and then General Hayashi. Saionji cannot have approved the invitation to Hiranuma. Neither can he have regarded the appointment of Hayashi with favour. Speaking of Hayashi, at this time, he declared:

> A military man cannot really understand such things as the welfare of a nation or the welfare of a people. They [military leaders] advocate national unity, but their national unity is not unity at all. It just means submission to them.[2]

It appears probable that immediately after Hayashi's appointment Saionji—feeling, perhaps, that his opinions were now of little account—decided to ask the Throne for permission to retire altogether from his rôle as *genro*. But Yuasa, still new to the duties of Lord Keeper of the Privy Seal, was against any idea of Saionji retiring; a view undoubtedly shared by the Emperor,

---

[1] Memoirs, *op. cit.*, Part XII, Ch. 237(a) (8th May, 1937).
[2] *Ibid.*, Part XI, Ch. 231 (19th February, 1937).

whose position was becoming increasingly lonely and difficult as time went by. Yuasa told Harada:

> Of course the faith of the Emperor in the Lord Keeper of the Privy Seal is implicit, but it is very clear that it does not come up to his faith in the Prince [Saionji]. . . . Because there seem to be movements to ruin the advisers [Court officials] the mere presence of the Prince will give them strength. Should the resignation [of Saionji] become positive there would be real danger. . . . Furthermore the Grand Chamberlain [Admiral Hyakutake] is inexperienced, and if it becomes clear that the Prince is going to decline, the advisers will not be able to carry on.[1]

The *genro* could hardly refuse such a plea. It was equivalent to a message from the Emperor himself. And so Saionji, despite his great age, gave up the idea of complete withdrawal from public life and, to the irritation of the nationalists, remained in his position of *genro* until his death.

General Ugaki, of course, ought to have been Hirota's successor. He had accepted the Imperial command, and the appointment was welcomed by the political parties, big business and the public at large.[2] The determined opposition of the army, which effectively prevented Ugaki from finding a Minister of War for his cabinet, was generally interpreted at the time as having been due to memories of his reduction of the army's strength by four divisions in 1925, when he was Minister of War in the Kato cabinet. However, this was not the real reason why, some twelve years later, he found himself faced with such uncompromising antipathy from the leaders of his own service. The real objections to Ugaki's appointment were two.

The first was his long-standing association with the political parties. He had been connected especially with the Minseito; but, as we saw in an earlier chapter, there had been a time, early in 1931, when he might perhaps have become President of the Seiyukai.[3] It was unfortunate for Ugaki that the occasion for the

[1] Memoirs, Part XI, Ch. 231 (19th February, 1937). Kido, too, wanted Saionji to carry on. "Please have the Prince endure a little longer," he told Harada.

[2] "Ugaki was supported by almost the entire press and majority of people, who sent him thousands of letters and telegrams of encouragement to fight against the adverse situation in which he was quite unexpectedly put." *Japan Year Book*, 1939–40, p. 141.   [3] *Vide* p. 60 (*supra*).

fall of the Hirota cabinet should have been the Hamada incident in the Diet. For Terauchi now cherished peculiarly bitter feelings towards the parties. As outgoing Minister of War his opinions carried most weight at the conference of the "Big Three" held to select a Minister for the new cabinet. At this moment Terauchi would probably have opposed appointing a Minister of War to a cabinet headed by anyone associated with the Minseito or Seiyukai.

Furthermore, those, like Terauchi, who wanted to keep the army under effective disciplinary control and, at the same time, to pacify restless elements by firm measures against China and the gradual introduction of a war-time economy at home, felt that their work would be undone if Ugaki were to head a government. He would be bound to come to some understanding with one or other of the political parties. The result would be to compromise the basic programme laid down by the army and accepted by the Hirota cabinet. Ugaki was in fact generally suspect from a nationalist point of view.

The second and more serious objection to Ugaki related to his part in the March Conspiracy of 1931. At first—it will be remembered—he had appeared to be in favour of that projected *coup d'état* but later strongly opposed it. He had been accused of changing his mind; and much resentment was felt against him on that score.

Also, as was mentioned in the previous chapter, many senior officers, belonging to no particular faction, considered that it was improper for one who had been involved in the first of the series of military conspiracies to head a new government at this moment, with the Mazaki issue unsettled and the Minister of War committed to a policy of restoring unity and discipline in the army.[1]

Nevertheless among some high officers—among retired generals in particular—there was pronounced sympathy with Ugaki. There was the feeling that it was the plain duty of the army to supply a Minister of War to a Premier officially appointed by the Throne. The "Big Three"—the retiring Minister, the Chief of the General Staff and the Inspector-General of Military Training—did indeed formally canvas the post of Minister of War among various generals. But this was a mere pretence. For,

---

[1] *Vide* p. 200 (*supra*).

on the day that the Imperial command was given to Ugaki, Sugiyama (Inspector-General), Nishio (Vice-Chief of the General Staff) and Umezu (Vice-Minister of War)—the main elements of what was known as the "Little Cabinet" [1]—held a meeting and decided that a Ugaki government was unacceptable. This view was conveyed to Ugaki before he arrived at the Palace for his first audience.[2]

However, General Abe, now on the retired list, made strong representations, on behalf of Ugaki, to the Chief of the General Staff, Prince Kanin. He pointed out that the refusal to provide a Minister of War amounted to an infringement of the Imperial prerogative.[3]

This argument seems to have impressed Kanin, who tried to persuade his subordinates at General Staff Headquarters to accept it. But his plea was ineffective.

The officer at General Staff Headquarters who appears to have been the real arbiter in the matter was Ishihara Kanji, now a Major-General, whom we have met before as Itagaki's colleague in Manchuria at the time of the Mukden *coup*.[4] The day after Kanin's vain attempt to secure some moderation of the hostile attitude towards Ugaki, Ishihara visited Abe and told him, in carefully phrased language, to mind his own business.

> It is desirable [said Ishihara] for you not to cause anything at this time. We are not absolutely opposed to having Ugaki serve the nation. However, the Mazaki case is not yet settled. In particular, since there is the March Incident, with many other matters, to consider we think that it is a very inopportune moment now. We do not have any objection to General Ugaki himself.[5]

Abe asked Ishihara whether the March Incident was "the only issue confronting Ugaki". Ishihara replied that it was.[6]

[1] Others included the Vice-Inspector-General of Military Training, the Commandant of the *Kempei* and the Director of the Military Affairs Bureau. Hillis Lory, *op. cit.*, p. 124.
[2] When the Emperor's command reached him Ugaki was out of Tokyo, and it was late at night when his car approached the Palace. It was stopped in the Plaza by Lt.-Gen. Nakajima, Commandant of the *Kempei*, who opened the door and informed Ugaki that the army's "advice" was that he should decline to become Prime Minister. Byas, *op. cit.*, p. 139.
[3] Memoirs, *op. cit.*, Part XII, Ch. 241 (18th June, 1937).
[4] *Vide* Ch. 4(ii) (*supra*).
[5] Memoirs, *op. cit.*, Part XII, Ch. 241 (18th June, 1937).   [6] *Ibid.*

The frustration of Ugaki's ambition—he had always wanted to head a cabinet[1]—contradicted the wishes of the Emperor and of the public generally. It was indeed a spectacular proof of the almost dictatorial power enjoyed by the *Tosei-ha*.

This faction now exerted itself to secure the appointment of its own nominee, General Hayashi, as Prime Minister. Ishihara was particularly eager to see Hayashi appointed, for he believed the latter to be under his influence. Two or three years previously Ishihara had persuaded Hayashi to accept a tentative five year plan for rearmament, with special emphasis on the expansion of the army and navy air services. The cabinet which was to put the plan into operation was to have Itagaki as its Minister of War and Suetsugu as Navy Minister. Ishihara calculated that he would be able to manipulate the relatively simple Hayashi from behind the scenes. He expected to be in a position to exercise the same influence over Itagaki, when the latter became Minister of War. In other words the Hayashi cabinet, as planned by Ishihara, would be in large measure an Ishihara cabinet.[2]

When Ugaki abandoned his efforts to form a government Yuasa, as we have seen, sounded Hiranuma on his readiness to become Premier. But Hiranuma did not respond to the invitation. "If in future", he told Yuasa, "there should be a conflict between the Right and the Left I believe it would be most appropriate for me to serve the Throne in my present position." [3]

Hiranuma had been closer to Araki and the *Kodo-ha* than to the military faction now in power. It was to his interest, then, to wait a little longer in his new post as President of the Privy Council. And it may be that he had heard a rumour that Saionji might retire at last; in which event he might expect to step into the *genro's* shoes.

The Imperial command was now given to General Hayashi.

---

[1] It was said that Ugaki had once been told by a fortune-teller that he would be Prime Minister of Japan one day. The prophecy was fulfilled in the ironic circumstances which have been described. Technically Ugaki was Prime Minister for five days, even though he failed to form a government.

[2] Ikeda Seishin was to be Minister of Finance, Tsuda Shingo Minister of Commerce and Industry. "Gen. Hayashi swallowed the plan whole. Ishihara and others thought that if Hayashi were to come out they could do as they wished, therefore they vigorously advocated Hayashi." Memoirs, *op. cit.*, Part XI, Ch. 230 (10th February, 1937).

[3] *Ibid.*, Part XI, Ch. 229 (31st January, 1937).

The cabinet which was formed turned out to be different from that envisaged by Ishihara. Much to his chagrin it contained neither Itagaki nor Suetsugu. Hayashi wanted Itagaki to be his Minister of War, but the "Big Three" declined to nominate him. Terauchi never favoured Itagaki for that position.[1] Ishihara, for his part, was too cunning to approach Terauchi directly on the issue. The suggestion that Itagaki be made Minister came from Hayashi. Terauchi and Sugiyama, the Inspector-General, were men of some strength of character, not of the calibre susceptible to obvious pressure. They had their own neat plan. They exchanged places, Sugiyama becoming Minister of War and Terauchi Inspector-General.

Ishihara, however, did not give up hope of being able, at some later date, to manœuvre his friend, Itagaki, into the cabinet as Minister of War. Harada noted that Ishihara was very clever in his dealings with Terauchi and Sugiyama, never discussing with them matters outside the bounds of his military duties. Thus Terauchi, in conversation with Harada, described Ishihara as entirely correct and mild in his attitude. Harada noted that Ishihara seemed to be playing a double game. "Perhaps he keeps in step with younger men under him by saying: 'Itagaki must be made the War Minister', at the same time saying to his superior, General Terauchi: 'I do not even dream of making Itagaki a Minister.'"[2]

It was Harada who appears to have made Terauchi suspicious of Ishihara. By May Terauchi's opinion of Ishihara had hardened into watchful dislike. He remarked (to Harada):

> Just because Ishihara can use him as he pleases he is urging that Itagaki be made the War Minister with the purpose of using him as a robot. We think that is absolutely no good. And because Ishihara can't use me freely he evidently is expressing dissatisfaction. Great care should be taken with regard to Ishihara.[3]

It is possible that Terauchi might have worked to secure the retirement from active service of both Ishihara and Itagaki, who

[1] Later Terauchi, speaking of the office of Minister of War, remarked to Harada: "Itagaki is out of the question. He isn't that sort of person." Memoirs, *op. cit.*, Part XII, Ch. 238 (20th May, 1937). One cannot be sure what was meant by this comment. Probably Terauchi considered that Itagaki lacked the independence of view necessary for a Minister.

[2] Memoirs, Part XI, Ch. 232 (12th March, 1937).

[3] *Ibid.*, Part XII, Ch. 238 (20th May, 1937).

was now commanding the 5th Division at Hiroshima, had the war with China not broken out in the summer.[1]

Only the *Tosei-ha* regarded the Hayashi government with any warmth, and in the *Tosei-ha* there were those like Ishihara who were disappointed at the choice of War and Navy Ministers—the latter being the somewhat liberal and temperate Vice-Admiral Yonai.

Hayashi encountered obstacles from the very beginning. It was difficult for a man with the mentality of a drill-sergeant to show the resilience and ability for compromise required in the task of organising a cabinet. He had little use for the Diet and its two main parties. He refused to appoint their members to his cabinet unless they agreed to renounce party allegiance; and he decided to govern without the assistance of parliamentary vice-ministers and counsellors.

The outcome was a cabinet of eight members, including the Premier, instead of the usual thirteen. Hayashi himself took charge of the portfolios of Foreign Affairs and Education in addition to the Premiership.[2] Yuki, Minister of Finance, was concurrently Overseas Minister. Yamazaki, the only party politician in the government, was saddled with the Ministry of Communications and the Ministry of Agriculture and Forestry; while Godo, a retired Vice-Admiral turned businessman, was Minister not only of Railways but of Commerce and Industry as well.

The only measure for which this abbreviated and short-lived cabinet is remembered was its abrupt dissolution of the House of Representatives on 31st March, 1937.

The army budget—the largest in Japanese history up to that date—had been passed. That important business concluded—the one function of the Diet for which the army had real respect—the Premier made up his mind to dissolve the Lower House, explaining his action in a statement characteristic of the Japanese military mind. It accused the House of having discussed government legislation in a manner "extremely lacking in earnestness" and announced that the Throne had been petitioned for the dissolution "in expectation of sound political awakening on the part of the people".[3]

---

[1] Terauchi hinted that he would like to see both officers "discharged". *Ibid.*
[2] At the beginning of March Hayashi gave the Foreign Affairs portfolio to Sato Naotake.   [3] *Japan Year Book*, 1939–40, p. 142.

It appears that during March Ishihara Kanji exerted a good deal of pressure in the background to secure this dissolution of the Lower House. No doubt he advised Hayashi to ask for the dissolution. He certainly uttered threats that if the House were not dissolved very drastic trouble might be expected.[1] This hint of yet another bloody "Incident" in Tokyo must have caused the police some anxiety; for among those who urged the Premier to dismiss the House was the Chief of the Home Ministry Police Bureau.[2]

The results of the general election which followed the dissolution hardly suggested that "sound political awakening" desired by Hayashi and the *Tosei-ha*. The Minseito and Seiyukai, both hostile to the government, retained together their absolute majority in the House. The *Shakai Taishuto*, which was even more opposed to the government, maintained that increase of its strength which had been such a striking feature of the election held in the previous year. The party almost doubled its representation.[3] The only groups of any size in the Lower House which supported the government were the *Showakai* and *Kokumin Domei*; but their joint strength, by comparison with the opposition parties, was negligible. And it was not improved by the election. Indeed the *Showakai* now returned eighteen members instead of twenty-four; while the *Kokumin Domei* returned eleven members, as before.

If Hayashi had been able to rely on the support of a mass nationalist party, putting up candidates in each constituency and assisted by friendly co-operation from the police, he might perhaps have turned the election to his advantage. But the various nationalist bodies, as we have noticed, did not collaborate for long and had little interest in the franchise as a method of securing their aims.[4]

---

[1] So Yuasa told Harada. Memoirs, *op. cit.*, Part XII, Ch. 237(b), (8th May, 1937).

[2] This official, it must be said, assured Harada that he had not recommended dissolution to Hayashi in response to any pressure from Right-wing groups or individuals. *Ibid.*, Part XII, Ch. 236 (20th April, 1937). But the denial does not ring true. Threats uttered by an officer such as Ishihara could not be ignored by those responsible for peace and order in the capital.

[3] From nineteen members to thirty-six.

[4] "The pattern of Japanese fascism is not that of one big movement, but of loyalty to the leader of one's little group. Many groups—among them some of

Hayashi, for all his Cromwellian contempt for the elected legislature, perceived the value of parliamentary support. When it was too late he tried to persuade Konoye to organise and lead a new political party on a national basis which could be depended upon to support the government. But Konoye refused to undertake the task.[1]

Konoye was already being mentioned as Hayashi's successor. For after the election it was apparent that the cabinet could not survive much longer. The *Tosei-ha*, to maintain its supremacy, needed a popular Prime Minister. Konoye was the ideal choice. On this there was general agreement, though Hayashi would have preferred Sugiyama.[2]

It was extremely difficult to get Konoye to promise in advance that he would accept the Premiership if the Imperial command was given to him.[3] Saionji did his best, through the mediation of Harada, to overcome Konoye's reluctance. In the end it was Kido who persuaded him to accept office.[4]

Again Yuasa had the chief responsibility, following the cabinet's resignation on 31st May, of recommending a new Premier to the Throne. This time of course there was complete agreement between Yuasa and the *genro* on the choice to be made.

Yet it is doubtful whether Saionji would have been so wholeheartedly in favour of Konoye if he had realised how far the latter, through a mixture of weakness and genuine sympathy with nationalist feeling, was prepared to co-operate with the army.

It is true that Saionji rejected the idea of overt opposition to the army, a policy which he considered to be fatal to the liberal

the violent ones—were based on 'small masters'. The actual location for plotting, etc., of Right-wing revolutionary groups was usually a *machiai* or restaurant. The whole atmosphere is feudal." Maruyama, *Nippon Fasshizmu, op. cit.*, p. 178.

[1] It was not until the last days of the cabinet that Hayashi approached Konoye on the subject of a new party. "Konoye declined because he attached much importance to his position as President of the House of Peers; since, in view of Saionji's age, the President of the House of Peers was likely to assume the rôle of *genro*." Baba Tsunego, *Konoye Naikaku Shiron* (Historical Essay on the Konoye Cabinets) (Tokyo, Takayama Shoin, 1946), p. 116.

[2] Memoirs, *op. cit.*, Part XII, Ch. 239 (3rd June, 1937).

[3] Harada, referring to Konoye's reluctance, noted that poor health was always pleaded as the excuse. *Ibid.*, Part XII, Ch. 238 (20th May, 1937). Konoye was indeed something of a hypochondriac.

[4] *Ibid.*, Part XII, Ch. 239 (3rd June, 1937).

cause. An open, declared struggle between the moderate camp and the nationalists could only end in the decisive defeat of the former. It was now too late to put the clock back to 1930. But with patience and skill, intelligently used, it might be possible to redress the balance of forces. "If there should be a fight", remarked Saionji, "the Constitution will be thrown out of the window. Even now it is half abandoned, so no matter what the criticism there is no other way but to handle things gradually." [1]

For the Constitution safeguarded the Emperor's position. Whereas the nationalist ideal of direct Imperial rule—in practice, of course, dictatorship by the army—weakened it to the point of danger.

> The so-called "Imperial Absolutism" which has become popular recently is an extremely risky phrase. It is like having the Emperor sitting on top of a fishing pole. Should anything go wrong he must assume responsibility and abdicate, and somebody else must replace the Emperor. Generally speaking the principle of the Japanese Constitution is like Mount Fuji; that is, the foundation is solid and the Emperor sits on the peak.[2]

But Konoye was to disappoint Saionji by appearing unnecessarily eager to appease the various elements of the nationalist cause. After the China hostilities had broadened into a general war, with campaigns south of Peking and along the Yangtse valley, the Emperor told Yuasa: "Konoye is just watching the military do as they please." [3] Still, he appreciated the difficulties of the Premier's position and felt sorry for him.[4] However, Saionji's judgment was less charitable. When Konoye supported the idea of an amnesty for all those convicted of having participated in the various nationalist disturbances from the *Ketsumeidan* Incident onwards, the *genro's* comments were bitter. "It would be better if he resigned if he is going to do such illogical things. There is no absolute need to retain Konoye as Prime Minister." [5]

[1] Memoirs, *op. cit.*, Part XI, Ch. 215 (24th September, 1936). The "fight" of course referred to an open struggle between moderates and extremists.
[2] *Ibid.*, Part XII, Ch. 239 (3rd June, 1937) (Saionji to Harada).
[3] *Ibid.*, Part XIII, Ch. 255 (18th November, 1937).
[4] *Ibid.*
[5] *Ibid.*, Part XIII, Ch. 250(a) (9th October, 1937). Harada noted that Saionji spoke "very harshly".

Again, later: "Konoye's future will become very dark and considering his position it will be very regrettable to have him end up as the puppet of the Right. Konoye must grow a great deal more and so become the head of an enlightened government." [1]

This development had been foreseen by Harada soon after the new government was organised; and he made a special plea to the Chief Secretary of the Cabinet. "I have known Prince Konoye for a long time," said Harada. "As he is of weak character it is well known that he is easily influenced. So please see that he does not meet certain groups or hear certain propaganda." [2]

Harada's friendship with Konoye enabled him to act as the Prime Minister's unofficial adviser. Konoye's position, indeed, was lonely, for he was on close terms with none of the members of his cabinet, until he invited Kido in October to succeed Yasui as Minister of Education.[3]

But if the influence of Harada, who so faithfully served the ideals of the *genro*, was ever dominant, it was immeasurably weakened by the chain of developments that followed the outbreak of fighting in North China on 7th July.

ii

The Japanese were often accused of hypocrisy for referring to their war with China which began in the summer of 1937 as the "China Incident". The title was, it is true, of convenience to the Foreign Ministry in a world in which wars, thanks to the Pact of Paris, had become unfashionable. And of course in Japan, as elsewhere, a polite name may serve as a lacquer screen to hide at least part of a reality both ugly and embarrassing.

But it was not entirely a matter of humbug. In 1894 and again

[1] *Ibid.*, Part XIII, Ch. 252 (30th October, 1937).

[2] *Ibid.*, Part XII, Ch. 243 (5th July, 1937). "Certain groups" and "certain propaganda"—we cannot be sure precisely what was in Harada's mind when he addressed this warning. But ultra-nationalists, such as Hashimoto, or Amano Tatsuo and Suzuki Zenichi (both still out on bail), were of course implied.

[3] *Ibid.*, Part XIII, Ch. 246 (24th July, 1937). Harada noted that it was a "cause of great dissatisfaction" to Konoye that there was nobody in the cabinet whom he could call a true friend. Harada suggested that he consider offering Kido a portfolio; Kido, of course, being intimate with both Harada and Konoye.

in 1904 there had been substantial, if not unanimous, agreement among the rulers of Japan, both military and civil, on the necessity for war. In 1937, however, the first stages of the fighting in North China, like those in Manchuria in 1931, occurred without the prior consent or knowledge of the government as a whole. They were essentially military conspiracies—independent action in the field planned and carried out by a section of the army—and were thus not inappropriately labelled "Incidents". The name, suitable enough as a description of the initial skirmishes outside Peking in July, 1937, was not abandoned when fighting spread to Shanghai in August and developed into full-scale war.[1]

There was a lack of unanimity among responsible leaders in Tokyo as to how the hostilities should be regarded. There was not indeed the same pronounced, though largely concealed, clash of opinions between the civil and military elements of the government as had occurred within the Wakatsuki administration after the Mukden *coup*. By 1937 there were few if any liberals in public life, with the exception of Saionji, of sufficient influence or strength of conviction to maintain an effective opposition to the army. Nevertheless Konoye himself, the Court advisers, the Foreign Ministry and the leaders of the navy were not only from the outset in favour of seeking a settlement with the Chinese government, but were also eager to find some way of putting a stop to the fighting long after it had developed into war on a continental scale. The Emperor, needless to say, regarded the struggle with the same dislike as he had evinced towards the Manchurian Incident. To him, and to those like Konoye who wanted to gratify the wishes of the Throne as well as the aspirations of the army, the use of the word "Incident"—or "Emergency"—had the advantage of leaving the door open for a settlement. For it is easier to wind up an "Incident" than to terminate a "War".

---

[1] It is important to note that the Japanese used the word *jihen* for the Manchurian and China Incidents, and the word *jiken* for such occurrences as the February Mutiny and the 15th May Incident. The Japanese compounds are different from each other, and have different meanings. The fact that both have been translated as "Incident" does not do justice to the niceties of the Japanese language. For whereas *jiken* means an "event"—and is therefore adequately translated as "Incident"—*jihen* means an "emergency", something a great deal more extensive and serious than *jiken*.

The first shots, like those that heralded the Mukden *coup*, occurred in the hours of darkness. There remains, then, a confusion of evidence, making it difficult to say which army started the fighting in the area of Lukouchiao, near Peking, on the night of the 7/8th July, 1937. Initially an infantry company, part of the Japanese garrison in the Legation Quarter at Peking, appears to have been involved. It was carrying out night manœuvres, apparently directed against the railway bridge crossing the Hun River, about ten miles west of Peking. This bridge and the famous Marco Polo Bridge cross the river in the vicinity of the small walled town of Wanping; which at the time was garrisoned by troops of the Chinese 29th Army.

Japanese manœuvres, with their shrill yells of command and sudden charges of soldiers with fixed bayonets, were always realistic affairs; and in the darkness, late at night, Chinese soldiers at Wanping may well have thought this activity to be both provocative and alarming. Whoever fired the first shots, it appears that serious fighting did not begin until the Chinese refused to open the gates of Wanping to a Japanese officer. The latter demanded entry to enable his troops to search for Chinese who were alleged to have fired on them.

The morning of the 8th found the Chinese barricaded behind the town walls and the Japanese in position behind the railway embankment leading to the Hun River Bridge; they had brought up battalion artillery and were shelling the town. In a field between the railway embankment and the walls of Wanping lay the body of a dead Japanese officer.[1]

The failure of the Japanese to capture Wanping within the first few days had, perhaps, much to do with the extension of hostilities to a wide area round Peking and Tientsin. For reasons of *amour-propre* the local Japanese command insisted that the little town surrender. The demand was resolutely refused; and a very determined resistance was put up by the Chinese forces defending the town.

---

[1] This account has been taken from John Goette, *Japan Fights for Asia* (London, Macdonald), Ch. 1. The author, an American correspondent, was with the Japanese forces during much of the fighting in North China. He and the U.S. Assistant Military Attaché visited Wanping on the morning of 8th July. There is also a brief account in *Japan's New Order in East Asia* by F. C. Jones (Oxford University Press, 1954), pp. 31–3.

The Chinese 29th Army, of which the Wanping garrison formed a part, was commanded by General Sung Che-yuan, Chairman of the Hopei-Chahar Political Council, the régime established by the Japanese Army in North China at the end of 1935. His position was very similar to that of the "Young Marshal", Chang Hsueh-liang, between 1928 and the outbreak of the Manchurian Incident. That is to say, Sung was subjected to continuous Japanese pressure, and had at his elbow a Japanese military adviser, but was able to exercise a great deal of independent authority. Encouraged by the stand made at Wanping and, no doubt, by the knowledge that, thanks to the Sian Incident, Chiang Kai-shek would firmly support Chinese resistance in the north, Sung Che-yuan opposed a Japanese demand that he withdraw all his forces from the Peking area. This led to a brief action on the southern outskirts of Peking, in which the Japanese were entirely successful, followed by the retreat of Sung Che-yuan's main force to the south. The city of Peking was then occupied by the Japanese.

Meanwhile the spirited behaviour of the Chinese at Wanping, and the show of resistance put up by Sung Che-yuan at Peking itself, encouraged a similar display of independence on the part of the East Hopei régime. Of this the most striking evidence was the savage action taken by the militia at Tungchow, on 29th July, who killed their Japanese officers and then massacred some two hundred and thirty Japanese and Korean civilians, including a very large number of women and children.

By early August the Japanese were in complete military control of both the Peking and Tientsin areas, and undoubtedly expected to effect a local settlement; in other words, a cease-fire agreement with the Chinese commanders on the spot, followed by the establishment of a securely dominated puppet rule for the region centred on Peking and Tientsin, and the consolidation of Japanese power in that area pending the next move forward.

A local settlement, at any stage, of the North China hostilities would have been extremely difficult to achieve, short of an extraordinary and unprecedented display of moderation on the part of the Japanese Army. The new temper of the government in Nanking encouraged a spirit of obstinate enmity to any Japanese proposals that might involve concessions on the part of the

Chinese. The Japanese, on their side, had to regain face after the setback at Wanping; and if there was ever any chance of their pursuing a conciliatory policy it was dashed by the Tungchow massacre.

Morishima Morindo, at that time Director of the East Asia Bureau of the Foreign Ministry, has claimed that, while attempts were made to settle the Incident locally, the government did not support these efforts but sent more troops from Japan "for aggressive purposes".[1]

Indeed, during the whole of July the attitude of the Konoye government wavered. When the news of the fighting near Peking reached Tokyo the Minister of War, Sugiyama, lost no time in proposing to the cabinet that three divisions be sent to North China immediately. This was successfully opposed by Konoye, with the backing of the Navy, Foreign and Home Ministers. Within a few days, however, Sugiyama again asked that reinforcements be authorised by the cabinet. This time Konoye gave way. Sugiyama probably blackmailed Konoye with the threat of resignation if his demand was not accepted. Certainly Konoye told Yuasa that, if the army's wishes were thwarted, the Minister of War would be forced to resign; and this would mean the fall of the cabinet.[2] "Therefore," Konoye continued, "as there may be no-one who can possibly check the army, there is no other way for me to assume the responsibility." [3]

Professor Maruyama, in a very interesting comparison of the mentalities of Japanese and Nazi leaders, refers to the brazen lust for power, the consistency between thoughts and deeds, which characterised the latter; whereas

> in the case of Japan it is like a severe nervous breakdown, and the action is always underlined by an inferiority complex. . . . The ruling political power itself had oversensitive and weak nerves behind the fine front that was maintained. . . . Konoye's name will immediately occur to anyone who thinks of an example of a leader with such a "weak mind".[4]

[1] Nobutake Ike, "Japanese Memoirs—Reflections of the Recent Past", a review article in *Pacific Affairs*, Vol. XXIV, No. 2, June, 1951, p. 188. The work reviewed is Morishima's *Imbo, Ansatsu, Gunto* (Conspiracy, Assassination, Sword) (1950). Morishima was Consul at Mukden in 1931; *vide* Ch. 4(ii) (*supra*).
[2] Memoirs, *op. cit.*, Part XII, Ch. 244 (14th July, 1937).　　　　[3] *Ibid.*
[4] Maruyama, *A Study of the Minds of the Rulers of a Militarist Nation* (cited).

Perhaps Konoye's well-meaning submission to the power of the *Tosei-ha* was a sign rather of over-confidence in his ability to restrain the army than of "weakness of mind". At all events, however, Konoye, in the words of Harada, "made a pathetic decision".[1]

While the dispatch of reinforcements naturally aggravated the situation from the point of view of the Chinese government, it is possible that a truce might have been arranged had serious negotiations been conducted between a Japanese plenipotentiary, enjoying the support of the army, and the leaders of the Kuomintang in Nanking. But the army, both in Tokyo and in North China, was on the whole stubbornly opposed to anything other than a local settlement. It was considered that Nanking's jurisdiction did not extend to Hopei and Chahar.

Yet it appears that Ishihara Kanji urged Konoye to send Hirota, the Foreign Minister, by air to Nanking. Although, in view of his close attachment to Hayashi, we have associated him with the *Tosei-ha*, Ishihara seems to have been one of those who favoured a war with Russia rather than China; and he had been eager to avoid any clash of arms in North China.[2]

Ishihara Kanji, as we have seen, was an extremely influential figure in the General Staff, sufficiently so to have a say in such matters as the formation of a new cabinet. Yet, while he could manipulate, to some extent, the action of certain superiors, such as Prince Kanin or General Hayashi, he was not able to dictate to his own subordinates. They rejected the idea of any approach to Nanking. "We hear in Tokyo", commented Harada, "that those abroad are very powerful and cannot be controlled, but it is the young officers of the General Staff Headquarters or of the War Ministry who are to be criticised." [3]

Thus Ishihara, who in the Kwantung Army, six years earlier, had been one such "young officer"—in point of rank and political influence—was now in turn susceptible to the irresponsible power of his own subordinates.

They were headed by Colonel Kagesa Sadaaki, a leading China expert at General Staff Headquarters. He resented any suggestion of interference by the Foreign Ministry in the army's handling of Chinese affairs. His reaction to the proposed mission to Nanking

[1] Memoirs, Part XII, Ch. 244 (14th July, 1937).   [2] *Ibid.*   [3] *Ibid.*

must have been vitriolic. For he was to utter drastic threats against Hirota's life when the latter, towards the end of the year, tried to negotiate peace through the mediation of the German Ambassador in China.[1]

In the second half of July Hirota, finding that he was making no headway in direct talks with the army, enlisted the help of the navy.[2] Admiral Yonai, the Navy Minister, had always favoured restraint in China; and Hirota hoped that he and other senior naval officers in Tokyo might be able to bring a moderating influence to bear on the *Tosei-ha*. It was now that Hirota learned a strange story from the Vice-Minister of the Navy, Yamamoto.

He was told that a staff officer of the North China Garrison Headquarters, Wachi by name, had been recalled to Japan immediately after the fighting had started. Yamamoto went on:

> The reason why Wachi was recalled to Japan was because if he were left over there he would cause trouble for us. We figured it would take him several days to return to Japan and that in the meantime we would be able to settle the Incident there. Although we took advantage of his absence and tried in every way to settle the Incident he flew back to Japan and our objective could not be accomplished. Moreover it would have been unfavourable if he started causing trouble while he was in Japan, so we decided to send him back.[3]

Hirota's comment was that it was unforgivable for the army "to mislead Japan for the purposes of one General Staff officer", but that this merely revealed "the pitiful condition of the lack of control within the army".[4]

The story itself and Hirota's comment are both interesting and significant.

The staff officer in question was Colonel Wachi Takazo. It is noteworthy that in 1931 he and Kagesa, as majors, were attached to the Toyama Army School and were at the same time members of the *Sakurakai*. Furthermore, the regimental commander in charge of operations against Wanping—Mutaguchi Renya—was a fellow-member of that society.[5]

This suggests, without stretching presumption too far, that

---

[1] *Ibid.*, Part XIII, Ch. 257 (10th December, 1937).
[2] *Ibid.*, Part XIII, Ch. 246 (27th July, 1937).   [3] *Ibid.*
[4] *Ibid.*   [5] Cf. Appendix I (*infra*).

Wachi and Kagesa—through past association—were on fairly close terms, and may indeed have collaborated at this crisis. For if, as Yamamoto inferred, there was some possibility of Wachi "causing trouble" while he was back in Japan, his most natural confederate in such an event would be Kagesa, the officer at General Staff Headquarters who was particularly anxious to see strong action taken in North China. Mutaguchi's past connection with these two, as a member of the *Sakurakai*, should not perhaps be accorded too much importance—although it suggests, again, some long established collaboration. But when to these indications we add the fact that, during the earlier part of the summer, the Minister of War had seemed worried at the prospect of officers in North China starting some "Incident" before the August transfers and promotions,[1] then indeed we seem to have stumbled on evidence of a planned conspiracy as having been responsible for the outbreak of fighting near Peking; and the whole affair near the Marco Polo Bridge looks less like a spontaneous explosion, due to confusion and excitement on both sides.

In comparing this Incident with the Mukden *coup* it will be noted that Wachi travelled to Tokyo by air, when it had been expected that he would come by ship and train; whereas, in 1931, Tatekawa—whose mission was urgent—neglected to fly to Mukden, but took the longer sea and land route instead.

It has been said that the Japanese were genuinely reluctant to become involved in fighting with the Chinese at Shanghai.[2] While this may well have been true in so far as the army was concerned, the pretext for hostilities at Shanghai suggests the existence of a plot on the part of the local Japanese naval authorities. A junior officer and a sailor, Oyama and Saito, from the Naval Landing Party Headquarters sought to enter, at night, the airfield at Hungjao. It is not impossible that they were ordered to "capture" it.[3] They were both killed by a Chinese sentry; which

[1] *Vide* p. 195, footnote 4 (*supra*).

[2] For example, Fleisher (*op. cit.*, p. 106): "Having watched most closely the day-to-day developments through the month of July, 1937 which led up to the outbreak of the Sino-Japanese War, I believe that the Japanese never wanted to become involved at Shanghai."

[3] This view is supported by M. Young, *Imperial Japan* (cited), p. 296. The idea seems less fantastic when one remembers that on many occasions during the Pacific War parties as small as six men were ordered to attack and capture strongly held Allied positions—these being, of course, always surprise attacks.

implies that their behaviour was suspicious, if not provocative. This was the spark that set off the explosion at Shanghai. If the navy on this occasion expected to retrieve the loss of face sustained in 1932, it was, in the event, disappointed. As earlier, the army had to come to its rescue. Then, having captured the city only after bitter fighting, the army decided to advance up the Yangtse towards Nanking.

iii

While the war progressed, with increasing ferocity, in Japan's favour, there was a pronounced tightening of nationalist pressure on every quarter from the Palace downwards, and a corresponding depression of spirits in the dwindling camp of liberals.

As early as mid-July Saionji had declared, gloomily: "There are people of other countries besides China who have seen through the intentions of Japan. Therefore extreme caution is necessary. If Japan does not watch her step she will be made a fool of by the other nations." [1]

Now, as summer gave way to autumn, he became acutely anxious. "The Incident will somehow have to be concluded rapidly, or we shall be in trouble." [2] And again (referring to the army): "What is going to happen? What are they planning to do?" [3]

For, bred in the old school of economics, he felt that, apart from the danger of complications with other countries such as England and America, the army's policy could only lead to national bankruptcy, with all the social upheaval associated with a devastating financial panic.

At home Saionji's worries were aggravated early in December by the news that the Emperor's personal life was being subjected to interference by the army.

At the half-yearly transfers and promotions in the previous March Colonel Machijiri, of the War Ministry Military Affairs

[1] Memoirs, Part XIII, Ch. 246 (27th July, 1937).
[2] Ibid., Part XIII, Ch. 251 (13th October, 1937).
[3] Ibid., Part XIII, Ch. 252 (30th October, 1937).

Bureau, was appointed a resident military A.D.C. at the Palace. When the appointment was made there were whispers that its purpose was to prepare the way for the time when an overt military government would be set up. Machijiri, according to this rumour, was greatly trusted by military ultra-nationalists. He would constitute, therefore, a kind of Fifth Column on their behalf within the Palace.[1]

It may be doubted, perhaps, whether Sugiyama, the Minister of War at the time, would have sanctioned the appointment if he had regarded it in that light. For Sugiyama of course was almost as eager as Terauchi to restore some semblance of order and discipline in the army. However, he may have considered Machijiri a reliable watch dog; one who could be relied upon to report on the way in which Yuasa and Admiral Hyakutake, the Grand Chamberlain, were carrying out their duties, and, also, on the nature of the advice which they were giving to the Emperor. For, it will be remembered, both Yuasa and Hyakutake were new to their jobs.

Saionji was clearly ill at ease regarding Machijiri's appointment; and in August he sent a message to Yuasa telling him to warn the Emperor about Machijiri's character.[2]

At the beginning of December Yuasa reported that Machijiri was exerting his influence to discourage the Emperor from visiting his laboratory—the Emperor's hobby was the study of marine biology—and indeed was permitting, if not endorsing, remarks by officers, attached to the Palace, to the effect that it was "extremely outrageous for the Emperor to be studying biology in this Emergency (Incident)".[3] Yuasa felt that he could hardly recommend the Emperor to ignore the views of his military aides; for then His Majesty would be between two factions—namely Yuasa's and Machijiri's. At the same time the latter's point of view was supported by the Vice-Chamberlain, Hirohata, who suggested that instead of visiting his laboratory the Emperor might care to call in a teacher of the Confucian Analects or of Chinese composition.[4]

The issue was settled, in this instance, by the mediation of the

[1] Memoirs, Part XI, Ch. 232 (12th March, 1937).
[2] Ibid., Part XIII, Ch. 249 (20th August, 1937).
[3] Ibid., Part XIII, Ch. 257 (10th December, 1937).   [4] Ibid.

Navy Minister. Approached by Harada Admiral Yonai agreed to speak to Sugiyama. The latter said that he would try to induce Machijiri to be more reasonable.[1]

However, the question arose again at the beginning of the next year. This time the Grand Chamberlain expressed his firm disapproval of the Emperor's biological studies. Once again Saionji, through his secretary, intervened to remove an unnecessary restriction on the Emperor's freedom.[2]

These relatively minor incidents at the Palace have been noted, because they were symbolic of the irrational nationalist attitude of mind characteristic of the army, and of a growing body of opinion outside, during the years of the war with China. The anti-scientific bias implicit in the objections raised to the Emperor's hobby is equally characteristic. For with his scientific mind there was associated the Emperor's liberal humanism, which so disturbed the ultra-nationalists in high places.

Thus, at last, nationalism reached its finger into the Palace— the one development Saionji feared above all else. Had he known that his own protégé, Kido, would be the one to cause more damage, through nationalist influence, than Machijiri was capable of, then indeed the *genro* might have despaired of the future of his country.

iv

At the end of 1937 moderate opinion in Japan sustained a double shock. Early in December Admiral Suetsugu was appointed Home Minister in place of Dr. Baba Eichi. Suetsugu, friend and ally of Hiranuma, was a notorious ultra-nationalist and was much disliked by the Emperor and the Court. When the Lord Keeper of the Privy Seal, Yuasa, was informed of the appointment he was greatly distressed, and he prophesied, correctly, that the power of the Right wing would now be enhanced.[3] That Konoye should have made this appointment was disturbing enough, but what was more shocking—in the eyes of the *genro*

[1] *Ibid.*   [2] *Ibid.*, Part XIV, Ch. 263 (11th February, 1937).
[3] *Ibid., op. cit.*, Part XIII, Ch. 258 (18th December, 1937).

and his secretary—was the discovery that Kido had actually encouraged Konoye to choose Suetsugu.

Harada at once protested strongly to Kido. "You know very well what sort of person Suetsugu is. His relationship with the Emperor hitherto has been very bad, and I think you know well what his relationship with Hiranuma is. Why did you approve of this?"[1]

Kido's reply was that the alternative might have been the Premier's resignation—Konoye had been making one of his periodical efforts to retire—and that if Suetsugu were given a position of responsibility he "would not be able to do anything serious".[2]

However, within a few days of his appointment Suetsugu promoted Tomita, Chief of the Peace Preservation Section of the Home Ministry, to be head of the Ministry's Police Bureau. Tomita was described by Harada as the "person with the most extreme fascist tendencies in the whole of the Home Ministry", as a man who was on very friendly terms with Maeda Torao of the *Shimpeitai* and as one who "tenaciously urged the destruction of the status quo". "He had now become the Police Bureau Chief, responsible not only for peace and order in the Imperial Capital but for all Japan. People who knew the facts were very astonished."[3]

The Emperor sent for Suetsugu and asked him to explain why he had promoted Tomita. The Emperor also declared that he had heard Tomita was a fascist. He asked whether this was so.

Suetsugu's answer is not known. But he was, of course, much embarrassed; and it appears that he did not hide the fact from others. So there was comment to the effect that the Emperor ought not to have tried to interfere in the matter, Konoye himself remarking that he thought it was rather severe of His Majesty to have mentioned Tomita by name. Some ultra-nationalist supporters of Suetsugu went so far as to spread rumours that the Lord Keeper of the Privy Seal had intentionally slandered Tomita; and there were renewed demands that the Court "be cleared of corruption".[4]

In spite of the Emperor's antipathy Tomita remained Chief of

---

[1] Memoirs, *op. cit.*, Part XIII, Ch. 258 (18th December, 1937).   [2] *Ibid.*
[3] *Ibid.*, Part XIV, Ch. 259 (27th December, 1937).   [4] *Ibid.*

the Police Bureau for six months, until he was succeeded by the less extreme Homma Sei, Governor of Akita Prefecture, in June, 1938. A few weeks later Tomita visited Konoye and, in the manner of Toyama, warned him that he might be assassinated. "There may be circumstances", said Tomita, "in which you might become the victim. We do not want to make you the victim, but depending on circumstances it might be unavoidable." [1]

The other blow to moderate opinion came from outside Japan and was coincidental with the appointment of Suetsugu as Home Minister. This was an attempt, on the part of impetuous officers of the army and navy, to force the country into hostilities with Great Britain and the United States. In quick succession there occurred on the Yangtse the shelling of H.M.S. *Ladybird* and the bombing attack on the U.S.S. *Panay*. The first was directed by Hashimoto Kingoro, now commanding an artillery regiment on the Central Front. The second was the work of naval air officers —the air service, from the days of the unrest at Tsuchiura in 1932, was the most insubordinate, chauvinist wing of the navy.

Extremely prompt action was taken in Tokyo, by the naval authorities in particular, to condemn these outrages and to offer apologies and full compensation to the British and American governments. The officer in command of the naval air service in Central China, Rear-Admiral Matsunami, was recalled immediately, together with the fliers involved in the bombing attack. Both Yonai and the Navy Vice-Minister, Yamamoto, hoped that the army would follow suit and take disciplinary measures against Hashimoto.[2] But action was delayed until the following year, when—partly no doubt as a result of continual demands by the

[1] *Ibid.*, Part XIV, Ch. 288 (28th August, 1938). The occasion for the threat is not known. It may have been related to the Ugaki-Craigie conversations then proceeding, to which nationalists objected very strongly. It will be noted that Tomita used the first person plural in his threat to Konoye. It is probable that his closest associates, as prospective terrorists, were Maeda Torao and Amano Tatsuo—the *Shimpeitai* conspirators (out on bail).

[2] Yamamoto said to Harada: "We have done all that we can. Japan can do no more. The reason we changed the officer in charge was in the hope that the army might transfer Regimental Commander Hashimoto or make him resign. But just what is the army going to do with him? We want the army to do the proper thing, just like the navy, towards England so that international courtesy can be maintained. The army is really outrageous. I have been thinking Hashimoto might get hit by a bullet (die at the front) but he doesn't get hit!" *Ibid.*, Part XIII Ch. 258 (18th December, 1937).

British Ambassador—Hashimoto was recalled to Japan and, for the second time, retired from the active list.[1]

Within a week of the attacks on the British and American warships General Matsui's forces captured Nanking; and there was the widespread expectation in Japan that this would mean the end of the war. Konoye himself predicted that the fall of Nanking would lead to the collapse of Chiang Kai-shek's government.[2] Meanwhile peace offers were being made to China through the mediation of the Germans.

But the new year, 1938, opened with peace no nearer and with the forces of nationalism excited by military victories and at the same time enraged by the obstinate resistance of the Chinese. All the instinctive, irrational elements of national pride seem to have been exasperated by China's refusal to admit defeat. For the traditional veneration of the *bushi* (warrior) ideal, combined with the cumulative effects of six years' propaganda by military and civilian nationalists, led to a general belief—to which perhaps the intelligentsia alone were immune—that war as waged by the Japanese was fundamentally different from that fought by any other country. To oppose Japanese arms was not only stupid. It was also—especially in the case of Asiatic nations—sinful. Thus it could be claimed by native propagandists, in all seriousness, that the army of Japan represented "the divine sword that slays not".[3]

While the Minister of War, Sugiyama, was eager to fight Chiang Kai-shek to a finish, Ishihara Kanji, at General Staff Headquarters, wanted hostilities in China to cease, so that preparations could be made for war with Russia. Ishihara, as we saw earlier, favoured an immediate negotiated settlement of the China

---

[1] In his book, *Behind the Japanese Mask* (London, Hutchinson, 1946), pp. 52–3, Sir Robert Craigie records that to the embarrassment of the Japanese government he repeatedly insisted that Hashimoto be withdrawn and "severely reprimanded".

After his return to Japan in 1938 Hashimoto dissolved the *Seinento* (*vide* p. 202, *supra*) and set up in its place the *Dai Nippon Sekiseikai*, "The Japan Patriotic Society".

[2] Memoirs, *op. cit.*, Part XIII, Ch. 258 (18th December, 1938).

[3] Kawai Tatsuo, "The Goal of Japanese Expansion" (*Hatten Nippon no Mokuhyo*) (Tokyo, Hokuseido, 1938). In October, 1934, the army had published a celebrated pamphlet, expounding this idea, beginning with the sentence: "War is the father of creativeness and the mother of culture."

Incident, as soon as the first shots had been fired near Peking; but he had been unable to secure the agreement of other officers at General Staff Headquarters. Now, at the beginning of 1938, his view so far prevailed as to give Konoye the impression that the General Staff—in contrast to the Ministry of War—favoured the idea of peace with China as the necessary prelude to war with Russia.[1]

This, of course, was the ideal of the *Kodo-ha*. But this faction was now virtually powerless, its leading members scattered or in retirement. Yet, as the struggle with China continued—each day adding to the Premier's anxious wish to be relieved of his thankless responsibility—Konoye appears to have toyed with the idea of gradually reviving the power of the *Kodo-ha* as a counter balance to the *Tosei-ha*, which of course was in control not only of the fighting in China but also—it might be said—of the government in Japan.[2] Viewed in this light the reconstruction of the Konoye cabinet, which took place in May, 1938, had particular significance.

During the previous fifty years there had been only one ministerial reorganisation on a large scale not involving the resignation of the cabinet. That was a cabinet reconstruction carried out by General Katsura during the Russo-Japanese War. It was regarded as an exceptional case in Japan's constitutional history.[3]

Between 26th May and 3rd June, 1938, the War, Foreign, Finance, and Commerce and Industry Ministers resigned and were replaced. Sugiyama was succeeded by Itagaki, fresh from his military defeat at Taierchwang, Hirota by Ugaki, while the portfolios of Kaya and Yoshino Shinji were given to Ikeda Seihin. Araki replaced Kido as Education Minister, although the latter remained in the government as Minister of Welfare.

Konoye was probably very pleased to see Sugiyama leave the cabinet. Their views on the China Incident had differed

---

[1] Memoirs, *op. cit.*, Part XIV, Ch. 260 (19th January, 1938).

[2] Konoye, speaking of the army, remarked (early in April): "We are indeed likened to marionettes, and it is a very dangerous situation." *Ibid.*, Part XIV, Ch. 267 (9th April, 1938).

[3] Royama Masamichi, "New National Government", *Contemporary Japan*, Vol. VII, No. 2, September, 1938. Dr. Royama's article is most cautiously phrased—as was inevitable at that time. But he refers, guardedly, to "discords among the constitutionally established organisations within the Military structure".

profoundly. As the leading figure of the *Tosei-ha* Sugiyama, in Konoye's opinion, was altogether too powerful. It is possible that Konoye tacitly supported, if he did not actively encourage, Ishihara Kanji and officers at General Staff Headquarters who schemed to have Sugiyama removed from the Ministry of War. Finally they won Prince Kanin to their point of view; and Sugiyama was appointed to the command of the forces in North China. At the same time the Vice-Minister, Umezu, resigned and was succeeded by Tojo, Chief of Staff of the Kwantung Army.

Before he left his post at the Ministry of War Sugiyama, speaking for Umezu as well as for himself, protested to Prince Kanin:

> If you do what General Staff Headquarters wants the army will revert again to a situation where subordinates order their superiors. It will be a sad state of affairs. It is very regrettable that we cannot have your understanding of our efforts to restore military discipline. Umezu and I have wholeheartedly devoted ourselves to the restoration of military discipline. For that reason we have been very unpopular.[1]

However, Kanin—in Sugiyama's own words—"turned a deaf ear".[2] It must be granted that, while eager to prosecute the China war to the utmost, Sugiyama, supported by Umezu, endeavoured to carry on Terauchi's efforts at restoring discipline in the army. For example, after the massacres perpetrated at Nanking, Sugiyama recalled General Matsui Iwane and two divisional commanders, one of them an Imperial Prince, to Japan and he took steps to replace many thousands of reservists who had been called to the colours during the summer of 1937 and had been largely involved in the Nanking atrocities.[3] Umezu—as Konoye frankly admitted[4]—would have no truck with unruly subordinates and in consequence was much disliked by them. So much so that Machijiri—who in March, 1938, was transferred from the Palace to a staff appointment in China—told Konoye, before leaving Tokyo, that feeling against Umezu was so high that he wondered whether a second Nagata Incident might occur.[5] Umezu, like

[1] Memoirs, *op cit.*, Part XV, Ch. 275 (26th May, 1938).   [2] *Ibid.*

[3] The Imperial Prince was Lt.-Gen. Prince Asaka. Konoye stated that 50,000 reservists would be recalled home. *Ibid.*, Part XIV, Ch. 263 (11th February, 1938).

[4] *Ibid.*, Part XIV, Ch. 270 (22nd April, 1938).   [5] *Ibid.*

Sugiyama, was indignant at having to leave his post. He was bitterly critical of Konoye, and accused him of having no insight into his "laborious efforts to bring back military discipline".[1]

It will be remembered that only a year earlier Ishihara had tried hard to secure Itagaki's appointment as Minister of War, under Hayashi, thinking that he would be able to control Itagaki from behind the scenes. Now, however, his regard for Itagaki had cooled. The latter appears to have become suspicious of Ishihara and the two were no longer close to one another. Ishihara's choice was Lieutenant-General Tada Shun. Nevertheless, he must have preferred Itagaki to many other possible candidates. Furthermore Itagaki was supported by Okawa Shumei—now out of prison— who was on friendly terms with both Ishihara and Tada.[2] Konoye was very eager to have Itagaki as his Minister of War. He was comparatively young, and Konoye felt that he was a receptive person—one who would be ready to listen to the views of others. Above all, it was Konoye's belief that Itagaki was not, like Sugiyama, immutably committed to any faction in the army.

Tojo, on the other hand, appears to have been Umezu's own choice as his successor; and it was hoped that he would act as the representative in Tokyo of Sugiyama, as well as Umezu, during their absence. In other words Tojo was regarded as a staunch member of the *Tosei-ha*.[3] Yet Konoye, perhaps because he was unaware of these considerations, does not seem to have been opposed to the selection of Tojo to succeed Umezu. Indeed he thought the combination of Itagaki and Tojo would work well. At the beginning of May he told Harada that, partly in order to prevent Ishihara from being too powerful, it might be a good thing "to put together a Saigo Takamori type like Itagaki, and Tojo, who has a head for details".[4]

According to Mazaki, Konoye wanted to have him restored to the active list. The best way to put a stop to the China Incident might be the reinstatement of the *Kodo-ha*. As described in the previous chapter, Konoye always felt some sympathy with

---

[1] *Ibid.*, Part XV, Ch. 275 (26th May, 1938).
[2] Mazaki's statement to the writer.　　　　　　　　　　[3] *Ibid.*
[4] Memoirs, *op. cit.*, Part XIV, Ch. 272 (4th May, 1938). The meaning here is that Itagaki, like Saigo, was a bluff, open-hearted man responsive to ideas and emotions; while Tojo, a contrasting type, was calculating, precise, and un-emotional. Itagaki and Tojo—the heart and the head.

Mazaki and exerted himself—against opposition from such different quarters as Saionji and Sugiyama—to secure Mazaki's release from custody. The appointment of Itagaki as Minister of War would, Konoye hoped, open the way for the return of Mazaki to the active list. The choice of Araki as Minister of Education was also a step in this direction. But Konoye's plans—and they may have been only very tentative—seem to have been frustrated mainly through the influence of Tojo, who was resolutely against the resuscitation of the *Kodo-ha*. Itagaki relied a great deal on Tojo's advice. The latter indeed occupied the position which at one time seemed to be within the grasp of Ishihara—namely that of guide, and controlling counsellor to the Minister of War.[1]

Konoye's fundamental aim, of course, was to play off one army faction against another, so that ultimately he would be in a position to hold the balance between them. His tight-rope manœuvres, it must be admitted, were conducted with considerable delicacy and skill. They make the somewhat enigmatic Konoye perhaps the most interesting political figure in recent Japanese history.

v

In July the desires of those, such as Ishihara, who looked forward to a war with Russia seemed to be nearly accomplished. For after the Russians had occupied a hill feature, Changkufeng, on the Manchukuo-Soviet Border close to the north-east boundary of Korea, the local Japanese forces made a determined effort to eject them.

Once again there was impetuous, unauthorised action in the field by officers keen to see Japan embroiled with a foreign power.

---

[1] This estimate of Konoye's plans to revive the influence of the *Kodo-ha* is based largely on statements made by Mazaki to the writer, as well as on what is implied in the Saionji-Harada Memoirs. This view is also that of Iwabuchi Tatsuo, a journalist and specialist in the modern political intrigues of the Japanese Army. It is interesting to find that Prof. Yanaga (*op. cit.*, p. 575) speaks of Konoye "in desperation" trying to restore the *Kodo-ha* "as a counterbalance to the Control faction, which was now unopposed and unchecked and was getting out of hand". *Ibid.*

The chief ringleaders in the affair seem to have been Tanaka Ryukichi—whom we have met earlier as having been involved in the Suiyuan Incident—and Cho Isamu, who was posted abroad following the October Incident of 1931. The attack on the Russian position appears to have been carried out largely as a result of their independent action.[1]

The attack might well have been fully supported by the army authorities in Tokyo—we have seen that the General Staff, inspired by Ishihara, was pressing for war with Russia—had not the Emperor intervened.

Kanin and Itagaki sought an audience with the Emperor to secure his approval of the use of strong military measures against the Russians. The Emperor, however, sent them a message through his Chief A.D.C. to say that on no account would Imperial consent be given to the use of force.

Nevertheless, Kanin and Itagaki insisted on having an audience. On arrival at the Palace they committed what must have been a calculated act of discourtesy. They made the Emperor wait an hour before going in to see him.[2]

The Emperor was aware that the Foreign and Navy Ministers had agreed to certain troop distributions being made as a precautionary measure, but had absolutely opposed the idea of any aggressive steps being taken against the Russian forces at Changkufeng. When the Emperor received Kanin and Itagaki he asked them whether they had been in consultation with the Foreign and Navy Ministers. They replied that both Ugaki and Yonai had agreed to the use of force. The Emperor naturally felt that he had been deceived. He said, angrily:

> The actions of the army in the past have been abominable. Speaking of the Liutiaokou case in the Manchurian Incident and the actions at the Marco Polo Bridge at the beginning of this Incident, there was absolutely no obedience to central orders. There are instances when the methods used have been arbitrary and underhand, which is altogether improper in my army. I feel it is abominable in various ways. Nothing like that must happen this time.[3]

The Emperor then spoke sternly to Itagaki. "Hereafter you may not move one soldier without my command."[4]

[1] Memoirs, *op. cit.*, Part XV, Ch. 286 (13th August, 1938).
[2] *Ibid.*, Part XV, Ch. 283 (28th July, 1938).   [3] *Ibid.*   [4] *Ibid.*

The repercussions were considerable. Itagaki felt much humili-
ated, and said that he could never look into the Emperor's face
again. He felt he must resign at once. Prince Kanin, also, wanted
to resign. They would probably have done so, had not the
Emperor asked Konoye to urge Kanin and Itagaki to remain in
office.

Afterwards Harada reported to the *genro* that the officers at
General Staff Headquarters were furious, and bitterly critical of
the Emperor on the grounds that he lacked confidence in the
army.

Saionji's comment was, as usual, very apt. "Just whose General
Staff Headquarters and army is it?" [1]

Although both Tanaka Ryukichi and Cho Isamu tried to pro-
long the fighting—with the result that some sections in the navy
considered a plot to have them removed—there can be no doubt
that it was the Emperor's explicit command to the Chief of the
General Staff and Minister of War which prevented the army, in
particular General Staff Headquarters, from enlarging the Changkufeng Incident into the occasion for wider hostilities against the
Soviet Far Eastern forces.

The reader may feel inclined, at this point, to ask why, if the
Emperor could put a stop to the Changkufeng affair, he did not
intervene with equal decision at other times to check the army's
adventures on the Continent. The answer lies in the nature of the
Emperor's position under the constitutional practice of the day.
Although Article XI of the Meiji Constitution stated, without any
qualification, that the Emperor had the supreme command of the
army and navy, it had become almost axiomatic that in reality he
exercised this command on the advice of the Chiefs of the General
Staff, just as he exercised "the legislative power with the consent
of the Imperial Diet" (Article V). Thus his action in the matter of
Changkufeng, like his behaviour at the crisis of the February
Mutiny, was hardly in accord with what had become constitutional practice, although in theory his stand was perfectly legal.

In other words his action was the reflection of an exceptional
personality. Whether his grandfather, Meiji *Tenno*, also played
from time to time a decisive part in political and military affairs is
unknown. He was certainly a man of character. If the materials

[1] Memoirs, *op. cit.*, Part XV, Ch. 283 (28th July, 1938).

for a definitive biography are ever released the result should be of great interest to the historian.

What is surprising is that the present Emperor, Showa *Tenno*, should have been able to make his opinions count in matters of policy on one or two important occasions—the last, of course, being his casting vote in favour of accepting the Potsdam Declaration in 1945.

Itagaki's collapse in face of the Emperor's displeasure may certainly be regarded as a curious phenomenon. It is true that he was young for a Minister of War; but the Emperor was the younger man. Possibly it was the unexpected force of the Emperor's reaction that shocked Itagaki, suddenly destroying his self-confidence, if only temporarily. He may even have felt uneasy, at heart, at having kept the Emperor waiting.

Much of the rancour felt by nationalists at such intervention by the Emperor was directed, of course, against Yuasa, the Lord Keeper of the Privy Seal, who as the closest day to day adviser to the Throne was rightly presumed to exert a good deal of influence on the Emperor's attitude and behaviour.[1]

Konoye was on indifferent terms with Yuasa; but this might have been expected, for Konoye was becoming increasingly impatient with those who refused to compromise with the forces of nationalism. However, Kido—whom the *genro* had hoped would act as a steadying influence on Konoye—was plainly becoming an apologist for the extreme nationalist cause.

During September, in conversation with Harada, Kido criticised Yuasa for being too "legalistic" in his view of nationalist agitators. He accused Yuasa of failing to understand the trend of the day.

There are some existing regulations [said Kido] which are not in keeping with the present age, and government cannot be carried out just by the application of laws. . . . It is an excessive demand to say all matters must be settled according to the application of the law. I believe this is where the Prime Minister and he [Yuasa] do not

---

[1] Kido's Diary makes it clear that it was the Emperor's practice to seek the advice of the Lord Keeper of the Privy Seal on all political matters, and on the line to be taken during important interviews—at which, in any case, it was customary for the Lord Keeper to be present.

agree. The Right wing is also quite advanced and cannot be dealt with in this manner.[1]

Harada expressed his decided disagreement with this point of view. He said that he still believed it was necessary to maintain order in strict accordance with the law. "I believe this is true", he told Kido, "of any age or in any society." [2]

A few days later Kido said to Harada: "The Emperor has too much of the scientist in him and has no sympathy for the ideas of the Right wing. It is very troubling that he should be too orthodox." [3]

Harada on this occasion does not appear to have remonstrated with Kido, but contented himself with noting, for the benefit of the *genro*, what Kido had said, adding at the same time the interesting comment:

> In reality the Right has no substance. All that exists are anti-foreign feelings, such as reverence for the Emperor and expulsion of foreigners [*sonno joi*], loyalty and patriotism. They have no regular employment and no special knowledge. They are only thinking of driving others out by feelings alone.[4]

Saionji's reaction was to observe, sadly, that Japan was being "greatly swayed by the Right wing", that it was too late—he had no longer the strength—for him to say anything, to try to alter the political current of the day.

> There is nothing to do [he remarked] but remain silent and observe matters. The atmosphere may change in ten or twenty years, and a more advanced form of government may appear; but at the present time there is nothing to do but to endure this.[5]

In the same month of September, Ugaki—the last notable survivor in active politics of the comparatively liberal nineteen-twenties—resigned. At the time the generally accepted reason for his resignation was his objection to army insistence on the control of all relations with China. But it now appears that, according to

[1] Memoirs, *op. cit.*, Part XVI, Ch. 291 (16th September, 1938).
[2] *Ibid.*
[3] *Ibid.*, Part XVI, Ch. 292 (21st September, 1938).
[4] *Ibid.*
[5] *Ibid.*

Yonai, Ugaki "resigned first of all, because of personal danger".[1]

Meanwhile, during the summer, Ribbentrop—now the German Foreign Minister—had made the first suggestions to the Japanese Embassy in Berlin that the Anti-Comintern Pact should be transformed into a full military alliance.[2] Oshima who was still military attaché—he was to become Ambassador in October—sent his assistant, Kasahara, by air to Japan in July to report on the matter to the General Staff. Tokyo wanted the proposed alliance to be directed chiefly against Russia—the Changkufeng affair had revealed the power of the Soviet Far Eastern Army—and authorised the opening of discussions in Berlin with that end in view.

With the autumn the China Incident spread to the south, to Canton; and once again Konoye showed signs of wanting to resign. Indeed it was now probable that the cabinet would not continue in office many months longer.[3] The stage was being set for a change of government and a further move towards alliance with foreign fascism.

[1] The Ugaki-Cragie conversations—which were supposed to be confidential—exacerbated nationalist feeling against the Foreign Minister. During a visit to Hokkaido during the summer Ugaki was the object of an unrealised assassination conspiracy.

[2] When the Anti-Comintern Pact was concluded it was signed, on the German side, by Ribbentrop, Ambassador in London and Minister-at-Large, not by von Neurath, the Foreign Minister. The negotiations leading up to the conclusion of the Pact had been in the hands of Ribbentrop and Blomberg. However, after the war, von Neurath declared that he refused to sign the Pact, because it was "dangerous business". Cf. G. M. Gilbert, *Nuremberg Diary*, (London, Eyre & Spottiswoode, 1948), p. 135.

[3] In September Konoye made the pathetic plea: "After about a year of this I could be excused." Memoirs, Part XVI, Ch. 291 (16th September, 1938).

THE ATTRACTION OF THE AXIS

i

DURING the autumn of 1938 there were suggestions that Konoye, on giving up the Premiership, should be appointed Lord Keeper of the Privy Seal in place of Yuasa. To introduce Konoye into the Palace—perhaps the last stronghold of liberalism in Japan—would have been very gratifying to nationalist opinion. The proposal was strongly resisted by the *genro*, who declared:

> It must have been very trying for Konoye to have to continue in office and I sympathise with him there. However, it was only due to the support of the army that he was able to do so. Therefore if he were to become Lord Keeper of the Privy Seal the army's influence would extend to the Palace, and that is a vexing matter. Although the army has influence in all administrative affairs we hope to keep army influence out of the Palace.[1]

It is doubtful whether Saionji at this stage could have prevented Konoye being given this Court post if there had been a united demand by the Ministry of War and the General Staff that such an appointment be made. However, although Yuasa was disliked by the army, he was not subjected to the intimidating pressure that had been applied to Makino three years earlier; and it was not until June, 1940, that he resigned, to be succeeded by Kido. It is possible that the army considered that the tide of nationalism was now too strong for it to be checked in any way by the Palace, although the Emperor's attitude regarding the Changkufeng crisis must have been remembered with acrimony.

For the autumn of 1938 saw not only Germany's diplomatic triumph at Munich—clearly perceived as such by public opinion in Japan[2]—but also the Japanese capture of Canton and Hankow.

[1] Memoirs, *op. cit.*, Part XVI, Ch. 299.
[2] Though not by Saionji. "The public", he remarked, "seem to think that

Following these victories Konoye made a peace offer to China in the hope of winding up the hostilities before the end of the year. The offer—in the form of a statement made on *Meiji Setsu* (The Emperor Meiji's birthday), 3rd November—is memorable to-day only because it included, for the first time in an official pronouncement, the celebrated phrase, "a new Order in East Asia"; meaning an anti-Communist bloc of Japan, Manchukuo and China, controlled by Japan. The statement of 3rd November, though it demanded the acceptance of Japan's right to station troops at certain points in China and the grant of economic concessions, did not ask for the payment of an indemnity—a demand made by the Japanese government at the beginning of the year, when Hirota had been Foreign Minister.[1]

It is probable that the army—which naturally had played its part in drafting the Konoye statement—dropped the indemnity demand as a necessary concession to Wang Ching-wei; who, until Subhas Chandra Bose appeared on the scene during the Pacific War, was to be, on grounds of prestige and political standing, the most impressive of the quislings manipulated by Japan. After the fall of Hankow the General Staff in Tokyo, in the person of Colonel Kagesa, established secret contact with Wang Ching-wei.[2] Kagesa may have hoped to inherit in future the mantle of Doihara, especially as the latter had failed during the late summer to persuade two prominent Chinese, T'ang Shao-yi and Wu Pei-fu, to serve as leaders of a new political régime in Japanese-occupied China.[3]

Much of the credit for obtaining first the interest, and then the co-operation, of Wang Ching-wei must go to Kagesa—assisted, during negotiations in China, by Inukai Ken—although he

England has yielded to Germany, but England holds the upper hand. The attitude of Chamberlain has really commanded my admiration. England is still England." *Ibid.*, Part XVI, Ch. 294 (4th October, 1938).

[1] On 22nd January, 1938, in a speech by Hirota in the House of Representatives.

[2] It will be remembered that Kagesa was a leading expert on China among the medium rank officers of the General Staff. p. 220 (*supra*).

[3] T'ang Shao-yi was assassinated while the Doihara negotiations were in progress. Wu Pei-fu, with obstinate courage, refused to re-enter political life. In a statement made during an interrogation in Tokyo (on dates in January and February, 1946) Doihara claimed that his approaches to these two Chinese had been made with a view to getting their help as intermediaries between the Japanese government and Chiang Kai-shek. I.M.T.F.E. Exhibit 2190-A, Transcript, pp. 15713 *et seq.*

worked under the general supervision of Doihara, who maintained a clandestine organisation, the Doihara *Kikan* (the Doihara "Organ" or "Agency"), at Shanghai for the purpose of directing all relations with prospective Chinese puppets.[1] At the beginning of December Kagesa went to Shanghai, accompanied by Inukai Ken.[2] On 21st December Konoye reported to Harada that Kagesa's mission had been successful. Wang Ching-wei had made his escape from Chungking to Hanoi.[3]

The defection from Chiang's government of a man of Wang Ching-wei's reputation seemed to offer a reasonable hope that the end of the China Incident was now in sight. Yet there was no sign that the Japanese army was prepared to consolidate its gains in China, calling a halt to the policy of overseas expansion. On the contrary, the prospect of a settlement in China merely gave the army greater freedom to plan other adventures, against the Soviet Far East, or to the south at the expense of the British, Dutch and French colonies.

The diplomatic successes of Germany and Italy, the evident weakness of Great Britain and France, and the supposed isolationism of the United States, all encouraged the army in the belief that an advance to the south—rather than to the north-west—was the course to be pursued.

To this end a full alliance with Germany and Italy was clearly desirable. War in Europe now seemed not only inevitable but very near. It might provide—so the *Tosei-ha* believed—an admirable occasion for Japanese military action against Hong-Kong, Malaya and French Indo-China. Political pressure alone would, in such circumstances, probably force the Dutch to comply with any demands Japan might make regarding the Netherlands East Indies. Russia, of course, was a danger; but to some extent she might be regarded as neutralised by the existing Anti-Comintern Pact. Furthermore, England's difficulties in a war

[1] Doihara was on special duty in China, in charge of his *Kikan*, between August, 1938, and June, 1939. A Five Ministers' Conference (Premier, War, Navy, Foreign and Finance Ministers) on 8th July, 1938, had decided to effect the downfall of the Chiang Kai-shek régime by recruiting prominent Chinese to serve as leaders of a unified puppet government. I.M.T.F E. Exhibit 3457, Transcript, p. 37356.

[2] There they met emissaries of Wang Ching-wei (who, of course, was in Chungking).

[3] Memoirs, *op. cit.*, Part XVII, Ch. 308 (30th December, 1938).

against Germany and Japan might tempt Russia to move in the direction of India and the Persian Gulf. There remained the question of the attitude of the United States.

Here, it need hardly be said, was a problem which Japanese nationalism never seriously faced. Perhaps only the navy fully appreciated the formidable dangers of a possible war with America. The army either grossly underestimated American power or thought that in some way its application would be thwarted by superior Japanese fighting morale. It was the classic miscalculation of the *Tosei-ha.*

By the beginning of 1939, then, the Japanese Ministry of War and Army General Staff were ready to conclude a new and closer alliance with Germany and Italy, aimed, of course, primarily against England and France.

If Japan had been either a fascist state, on the German or Italian model, or an autocracy, like that of Kemalist Turkey, or a thoroughgoing military dictatorship, like that of Primo de Rivera's Spain, she would scarcely have hesitated—circumstances being what they were—over her course of action. She would have signed the Axis Pact early in 1939.

But it has been said that "the multiple character of political power was destined to be the basic evil of modern Japan'.[1] Under a monarchy—especially, perhaps, when the sovereign is invested with an aura of divinity—real political unity is possible only if one of three conditions prevails. Either the sovereign must possess autocratic powers and have the character and ability to use them; or government must be in the hands of officials, appointed by the sovereign and responsible to him, and they must be men of outstanding qualities of mind; or, thirdly, there must be real parliamentary control of policy.[2]

In Japan, during the years in question, none of the conditions was fulfilled; although the second certainly prevailed during the Meiji Era. But by comparison with the political leadership of those days that of the years immediately preceding the Pacific War was clumsy and unstable, at times almost nerveless. For the divisions within the oligarchy were profound. The army—more especially

---

[1] Maruyama, *A Study of the Minds of the Rulers of a Militarist Nation* (cited).
[2] The three conditions mentioned form part of Prof. Maruyama's thesis (*A Study of the Minds,* etc.). The writer accepts them as valid.

the *Tosei-ha*—had the major share of power in its grasp; the residue—in 1939 still considerable—was divided among the navy, the Court, the civil bureaucracy and certain cabinet ministers, depending on their strength of character and gifts for intrigue.

This state of affairs is well illustrated by the struggle that proceeded, almost entirely unknown to the public, within governing circles in Tokyo over the question of adherence to an unrestricted pact with Germany and Italy.

The issue became acute after Konoye resigned at the beginning of January, 1939, to be succeeded by Baron Hiranuma. Superficially, at least, the new cabinet was, if anything, less nationalist in character than its predecessor. For Suetsugu was not among its members. On the other hand—no doubt to balance the loss of Suetsugu—Hiranuma excluded Ikeda Seihin from his cabinet. The War and Navy Ministers were unchanged. And Arita was invited to remain as Foreign Minister.

Arita had succeeded Ugaki, when the latter resigned in the previous autumn. At that time there was a nationalist element in the Foreign Ministry eager to see Shiratori as the new Minister; and after Ugaki's resignation it had petitioned Konoye to that effect.[1] However, Shiratori was promoted—probably as a consolation prize—to the Embassy in Rome. There he was to act as the faithful second to Oshima in the fight for a full alliance with Germany and Italy.

When Hiranuma asked Arita to stay in office as Foreign Minister he obtained his consent only on condition that the army's proposals for strengthening the Anti-Comintern Pact were not adopted. On this score Hiranuma gave him an explicit pledge. He told Arita:

> I am of the same opinion as yourself. I am opposed to the strengthening of the Anti-Comintern Pact to the extent of waging war against England and France. Should the army coerce us I shall resign together with you.[2]

There is little doubt that Hiranuma regarded the question of an alliance with Germany as one of pure expediency. So far from

---

[1] Memoirs, *op. cit.*, Part XVI, Ch. 295 (7th October, 1938). Significantly, the supporters of the petition were all young men.

[2] *Ibid.*, Part XVII, Ch. 310 (5th January, 1939).

cherishing any ideological sympathy with European fascism he regarded the phenomenon with suspicion. Here was a Right-wing movement alien to truly Japanese ideas. The fact that some Japanese appeared to be mesmerised by the success of Hitler made German fascism, in Hiranuma's view, all the more dangerous. But while he looked at European fascism with some distaste Hiranuma, with his profound hatred of communism, regarded Soviet Russia as Japan's prime enemy. As will be seen, he was prepared to go a long way with the army—further, certainly, than his pledge to Arita implied. Hiranuma's military affiliations had been with the *Kodo-ha* rather than with any other faction of the army. He was therefore inclined to be lukewarm towards proposals for an advance to the south, if these envisaged toleration of growing Russian power in Asia.

When Hiranuma became Premier Harada felt that he must try to establish some sort of understanding with this veteran nationalist, who had been so consistently opposed by the *genro*. He visited Hiranuma at the beginning of February, and in the course of his remarks declared:

> When an explanation is made in terms of the Emperor's desire to conduct a constitutional government it is said that Saionji, Makino, the Lord Keeper of the Privy Seal or other close officials, who do what they please by using the Emperor's name, are behind it. As a result the spirit of the constitution is ignored and matters are conducted in such a way that the Emperor's wish cannot be conveyed to the people. Considering your past record and social position I feel you are best fitted as the Premier to convey his ideas as well as his high virtues directly to the people. I thought I would say this to you after we became better acquainted, but I feel there is no sense in not coming to the point; therefore I express my feelings and desires openly.[1]

Harada records that the Premier—whose reticence was famous[2]—nodded and said that he understood. However, it will

---

[1] *Ibid.*, Part XVIII, Ch. 313 (7th February, 1939).

[2] By general repute Hiranuma was as uncommunicative as Calvin Coolidge. It was said that when he went to report his assumption of the Premiership to the Grand Shrine he remained in silent meditation throughout the long train journey from Tokyo to Ise, not even talking to his private secretary. Takahashi Yusai, "Hiranuma the Silent", *Contemporary Japan*, Vol. VIII, No. 1, March, 1939.

be seen shortly that Hiranuma was prepared to defy the Emperor's wishes.

Pressure by the Ministry of War and the General Staff, encouraged by urgent messages from Oshima in Berlin, was soon applied to the new cabinet. In the middle of January Yuasa expressed his indignation at the methods used by the army in their agitation for the conclusion of an Axis alliance. "Men of the rank of colonel make their own decisions at will and strengthen the anti-Comintern programme of Japan, Germany and Italy. Moreover they are threatening members of the cabinet." [1]

The Emperor himself, at this period, made the following remarkable comment on the army: "I am perplexed with the present army. They will never understand unless Japan is forced by other nations to return Korea and Manchukuo to their original status." [2]

It was probably at the Emperor's suggestion that Prince Chichibu, in the same month of January, addressed junior officers at General Staff Headquarters and pointed out the risks involved should Japan ally herself with Germany in a struggle against England. In particular Chichibu emphasised that there was no possibility of separating Great Britain from the United States. But his hearers, as he reported later, could not appreciate his argument. [3]

Perhaps the strongest support for the Emperor's view came from the Navy Minister, Yonai, and his Vice-Minister, Yamamoto. Together with Arita they maintained a firm opposition to the proposed alliance. At meetings of the Five Ministers' Conference —the inner cabinet—Arita and Yonai were ranged on one side, with the Minister of War, Itagaki, and the Minister of Finance, Ishiwata, on the other. Between them, seeking a compromise agreeable to both parties, was Hiranuma.

In the preparation of the draft for the new treaty the initiative at first lay with Oshima in Berlin. Few, if any, ambassadors, in their relations with the government of the country to which they were accredited, can have been on terms as close as those that existed between Oshima and the Nazi leaders. From the tone of his communications to the Foreign Ministry it was difficult, so Arita declared, to know whether Oshima was a Japanese or a

---

[1] Memoirs, *op. cit.*, Part XVII, Ch. 312 (25th January, 1939).
[2] *Ibid.*   [3] *Ibid.*

German diplomat.[1] Similarly Shiratori appeared to be devoted to the aims of Italian fascism. So that the partnership of Oshima and Shiratori became as notorious as that of Araki and Mazaki some years earlier.

The draft of the proposed treaty of alliance was composed by Ribbentrop, Oshima and Count Ciano, in direct consultation.[2] It provided for full military assistance in the event of one of the signatory powers being attacked; and it was to have a duration of ten years.

However, the compromise achieved by Hiranuma, as the result of debates in the Five Ministers' Conference, emphasised that the alliance should be directed primarily against Russia. Oshima and Shiratori seem to have anticipated that some such counter-proposal would be made; and even before it arrived from Tokyo Shiratori advised Ciano to reject it.[3]

To explain its views the Japanese government sent in February a special mission to Rome and Berlin. It comprised a Foreign Ministry official, Ito Nobufumi, a colonel of the army and a naval captain.[4] While stressing the desirability of having the alliance directed against Russia, the mission informed the Ambassadors that the Japanese government agreed to let the provisions regarding military assistance apply *vis-à-vis* Great Britain and other countries, should they become communist.[5] Oshima and Shiratori not unnaturally interpreted the stipulation regarding communism as a disingenuous formula contrived by Arita to rob the alliance of all its force so far as Great Britain and France were concerned. Oshima cabled Tokyo, firmly rejecting the view conveyed by the Ito mission.

Early in March the Japanese government sent fresh instructions to Oshima and Shiratori. This time the stipulation regarding communism was dropped. But the proposal that the pact be directed principally against Russia was reiterated. If Germany and

---

[1] *Ibid.*, Part XIX, Ch. 318 (23rd March, 1939).

[2] Telegram, Ribbentrop to Ott (German Ambassador, Tokyo), 26th April, 1939. I.M.T.F.E. Exhibit 502. Transcript, p. 609.

[3] Ciano's Diary, 6th February, 1939. I.M.T.F.E. Exhibit 500. Transcript, p. 6096.

[4] Col. Tatsumi, of the Army General Staff; Capt. Abe of the Naval General Staff.

[5] Interrogation of Oshima. I.M.T.F.E. Transcript, pp. 6064–5.

Italy were to be attacked by countries other than Russia—by Great Britain and France, for example—Japanese military aid should be limited to advice only; though economic help, according to circumstances, might be given to the power attacked. Oshima and Shiratori revealed these proposals confidentially to Ribbentrop and Ciano, at the same time refusing to convey them officially to the German and Italian governments. The two Ambassadors protested to Tokyo and threatened to resign unless revised instructions, more in keeping with their own wishes, were sent to them.

With some reason Ciano noted in his diary that he now doubted the possibility of "an effective collaboration of Fascist and Nazi dynamism with the phlegmatic slowness of the Japanese".[1]

Meanwhile, in Tokyo, there had been rumours of an impending military revolt on a scale more ambitious than that of the February Mutiny. These probably originated from the wild talk of young officers in the Ministry of War and General Staff. But Konoye especially seems to have been worried. He disclosed his fears to Yonai, who made little of them. Nevertheless, the navy appears to have made preparations to land a large contingent of bluejackets in the port of Tokyo.[2]

Pressure by the army was revived as soon as Oshima's latest protest became known. The army's impatience made the Emperor sufficiently anxious to deliver a strictly confidential order to his Chief A.D.C., Lieutenant-General Usami.

He told Usami that if the army tried to force the views of Oshima and Shiratori on the government the cabinet might fall, since both Hiranuma and Arita would remain obdurate. Accordingly Usami was to go to the Ministry of War and General Staff Headquarters and obtain a fundamental review of the whole question. Usami was to regard the Imperial order as very secret, for his ears alone.[3]

With what sincerity Usami carried out this order may be

---

[1] I.M.T.F.E. Exhibit 500 (cited), 8th March, 1939. Transcript, p. 6096. M. Guillain (*op. cit.*, p. 20) touches on the same point when he speaks of the "clumsy heaviness" (*lourdeur*) of Japan and the cynicism of Germany.

[2] According to the Navy Vice-Minister. Memoirs, *op. cit.*, Part XVIII, Ch. 316 (2nd March, 1939).

[3] Reported to Harada by the Lord Keeper of the Privy Seal. *Ibid.*, Part XIX, Ch. 318 (23rd March, 1939).

guessed from the fact that he failed to observe the Emperor's wish for secrecy. For the day after the Emperor had spoken to Usami, Machijiri—who had returned from China to become Chief of the Military Affairs Bureau at the Ministry of War—called on Yuasa and protested that there must be, surely, some way of concluding the new alliance without causing the fall of the cabinet.[1]

Machijiri seems to have headed the group in the Ministry of War most intimately associated with Oshima and his views. The General Staff group was led by Colonels Kagesa and Iwakuro. Ishihara Kanji was less eager for the alliance to be concluded—unless its force were to be concentrated against Russia. Kagesa was particularly annoyed with Arita's stand. He told Harada: All the paper work [for the proposed treaty] is completed, but it is very regrettable that only the Foreign Minister will not compromise. It seems he is influenced by high officials close to the Emperor.[2]

Nevertheless, in spite of the agitation by the army—particularly by the younger elements of the *Tosei-ha*—the fresh proposals, sent to Berlin and Rome at the beginning of April, reaffirmed the view that the alliance should be directed mainly against Russia. But there was greater readiness to offer Germany and Italy all help short of war in the event of hostilities between these nations and a country other than Russia. However, the Japanese government asked that express approval be given for Arita—following the signature and publication of the treaty—to assure the British, American and French Ambassadors in Tokyo that the alliance was not directed against their countries.[3]

Oshima and Shiratori immediately informed Tokyo that these proposals, like the last, were unacceptable; and they advised Ribbentrop and Ciano of their action. Ribbentrop told the Ambassadors—Shiratori was in Berlin in April for the celebrations

---

[1] *Ibid.* Yuasa and Machijiri (whose attitude was said to have been "very impertinent") exchanged angry words; but Yuasa, according to his own story, had the best of the argument. In what was clearly a reference to Usami's breach of confidence, Yuasa commented (to Harada): "There have been many instances where knowledge which His Majesty ordered not to be disclosed has been brought to the attention of the person concerned." *Ibid.*

[2] *Ibid.*, Part XIX, Ch. 319 (27th March, 1939). Harada, of course, denied that Arita had been influenced in any way by the *genro*.

[3] Telegram, Ribbentrop to Ott, 26th April, 1939 (cited), I.M.T.F.E. Exhibit 502.

of Hitler's birthday—that a firm decision, accepting or rejecting the unrestricted alliance desired by Germany, must reach Berlin before the end of the month.[1]

A deadlock seems to have been reached at the end of April between the contending forces in Tokyo. To break it Hiranuma made some concessions to the army. This, of course, was against the spirit of the pledge he had given to Arita in January. No doubt Arita's view, and that of the Navy Minister, was that the limit of concessions had been reached and that the time had come to abandon further negotiations.

But Hiranuma was determined to reach some agreement with Germany; and he told Konoye: "I might do something entirely opposed to the will of the Emperor, but I cannot help that. I shall be fully responsible for my action."[2]

These words were astonishingly frank for a Japanese, even in confidential talk. They reflected, however, an honesty of mind uncommon among sincere nationalists.

On 4th May Arita, with a bad grace, handed the German Ambassador a message for Hitler from Hiranuma. The following phrases were included in the text:

> Japan is firmly resolved to stand at the side of Germany and Italy even if one of those two powers is attacked by one or several powers without the participation of the Soviet Union. . . . Japan, in view of the situation in which it now finds itself, is neither presently nor in the near future able to extend to them in a practical manner any effective military aid. However . . . Japan would gladly grant this support if it should become possible through change of circumstances. I should especially like to receive Germany's and Italy's express consent to the foregoing point. . . . I may add that the planned agreement rests upon the foundation of mutual confidence and that to doubt the sincerity of my country in the slightest would be tantamount to destroying the real basis of the agreement and would make its execution impossible. The thoughts which I have just portrayed arise from reflections of a moral and spiritual nature and cannot be influenced by reasons of expediency.[3]

[1] Telegram, Ribbentrop to Ott, 26th April, 1939 (cited). I.M.T.F.E. Exhibit 502.   [2] Memoirs, *op. cit.*, Part XIX, Ch. 323 (5th May, 1939).
[3] Telegram, Ott to Ribbentrop, 4th May, 1939. I.M.T.F.E. Exhibit 503. Ott noted that Arita was "visibly in a bad mood". *Ibid.*

The German Ambassador lost no time in obtaining, from his friends in the Japanese Army, clarification of some of the points in this message. He was assured that the treaty would bind Japan unmistakably to the Axis. He was told that the army had wanted to lay down clearly the "change of circumstance" which might make full military aid possible; that it had been the army's hope that the message from Hiranuma would declare categorically that Japan would certainly not be neutral in any war in which Germany and Italy were involved. Reporting these conversations to Berlin, Ott remarked: "The Japanese attitude must astonish the Axis, which is accustomed to unequivocal decisions, but it arises necessarily from lack of unified leadership." [1]

There had been, in fact, considerable debate, before the Premier's message was sent, as to whether Berlin and Rome should be given an assurance that Japan would not remain neutral in the event of those countries going to war. Hiranuma was strongly in favour of such an assurance—thus demonstrating his readiness to "do something entirely opposed to the will of the Emperor"—but, needless to say, Arita and Yonai firmly opposed him. Hiranuma maintained that the words, "not neutral", carried no implication of military support. Arita and the Foreign Ministry condemned the phrase as ambiguous. [2]

The outcome of this debate was the choice of the sentence—at the beginning of the extract quoted from the Premier's message—that "Japan is firmly resolved to stand by Germany and Italy even if one of those two powers is attacked by one or several powers without the participation of the Soviet Union."

But Arita now wanted to resign. He said that he could no longer stay in office as the Premier's opinions had drawn closer to those of the Minister of War. [3] Evidently Hiranuma had been won over, in some degree, to the army's point of view. [4]

In this crisis the Emperor's word was of some effect. The Chief of the Army General Staff, Prince Kanin, tried to obtain the Emperor's consent to the unrestricted alliance. With Hiranuma in his present mood Kanin's approach to the Throne, had

[1] Telegram, Ott to Weiszacker, 6th May, 1939. I.M.T.F.E. Exhibit 504.
[2] Memoirs, *op. cit.*, Part XIX, Ch. 323 (5th May, 1939).
[3] *Ibid.*, Part XIX, Ch. 324 (9th May, 1939).
[4] Yuasa remarked that Hiranuma "because of his selfishness had united with the army". *Ibid.*, Part XIX, Ch. 325 (16th May, 1939).

it been successful, would have turned the front of Arita and the navy. However, the Emperor refused to listen to Kanin's arguments, and indeed severely reprimanded him.[1]

It was for this reason that the army agreed, for the time being, to postpone Japanese commitment to a full military alliance, pending a "change of circumstances". Yet, later in May, Yonai reported that in spite of the Emperor's firmness with Prince Kanin the Prime Minister still supported the army and the Ambassadors in Berlin and Rome, "who take action contrary to the will of the Emperor".[2]

In these circumstances it is surprising that Arita allowed himself to be persuaded, by Hiranuma, from his intention to resign.[3] But perhaps he felt it was his duty to remain in office to support, with Yonai, the Emperor's determination to keep Japan from closer association with the Axis.

On 22nd May Germany and Italy formally signed a treaty of military alliance. In a cable to General Ott on 15th May, advising him of the forthcoming signature of the bilateral pact, Ribbentrop declared:

> Mussolini the other day gave expression to anxiety as to whether ... the Japanese government would in the end not find strength for a positive decision. .... The Fuhrer declared in the last few days repeatedly, in talking to me, that the Japanese attitude was becoming less and less comprehensible.[4]

The conclusion of the bilateral Axis Pact eased, for the time being, the contentious atmosphere in Tokyo; for it would have been undignified for Japan to rush in with her adherence, in the wake of Italy. The Japanese government showed no sign of resenting the impatience displayed by Germany and Italy when they signed their military alliance without waiting for Japan's final decision. But the idea of a military pact with the Axis against any country other than Russia was now in abeyance.

[1] Memoirs, Part XIX, Ch. 325 (16th May, 1939).
[2] Ibid., Part XIX, Ch. 326 (23rd May, 1939).
[3] Ibid., Part XIX, Ch. 325 (16th May, 1939).
[4] I.M.T.F.E. Exhibit 486-K.

ii

It was during this crisis that Kido was seen in his true colours
—as one who was prepared, for reasons of expediency, to co-
operate with extreme nationalists. Indeed, ever since he had given
up his appointment as Secretary to the Lord Keeper of the Privy
Seal in October, 1937, in order to enter the Konoye cabinet, he
had been moving away from the liberal influence of the Court
—and of the *genro*—that had shaped his early political ideas.[1]

We have seen that before sending Hitler his personal message
of 4th May Hiranuma had come to share, to a considerable extent,
the army's readiness for a full military alliance with Germany and
Italy. He was well aware, of course, that such an alliance was most
distasteful to the Emperor; but he hoped that the latter might be
persuaded to modify his opposition.

To this end Yuasa would have to be converted, in part, at least,
to Hiranuma's own views. Feeling perhaps that a direct approach
stood little chance of success, Hiranuma asked Kido to act as
intermediary between himself and the Lord Keeper of the Privy
Seal. This was during the latter half of April. The manœuvre
failed, as the Palace continued to support the stand taken by the
Navy and Foreign Ministers.

When Harada learned that his friend Kido was letting himself
be used in this way by Hiranuma, he was greatly upset. He saw
Kido at once, and expostulated with him. Kido replied that it was
necessary to appear to have some understanding of the army's
point of view. One must pretend to follow, to be led by, the
army if there was to be any hope of secretly controlling this restless force. Furthermore, remarked Kido, the Emperor was a
scientist, a lover of peace, and very much of a liberal. Unless the
Emperor's views were changed there would be a gulf between
His Majesty on the one hand and the army and the Right-wing
groups on the other.

Kido's attitude shocked and disgusted Harada, who declared

---

[1] James T. C. Liu, in an interesting article on "Tokyo Trial Source Materials"
(*Far Eastern Survey*, American I.P.R., 28th July, 1948, Vol. XVII, No. 14),
speaks of Kido during the late nineteen-thirties as "trying to shake loose from the
genro's influence".

angrily that Kido knew very well that the Right-wing groups were "cheap and unpresentable". He said that it was Kido's duty to do what he could to persuade the army and the civilian ultra-nationalists to comply with the Emperor's will. Harada concluded by saying that he had thought of "killing five or six of these men who will become obstacles in the future".[1]

An open breach between Kido and Harada might have been expected following this expression of disagreement. However, the two remained outwardly on friendly terms; but in their political opinions they were now sharply divided.

There is little doubt that it was Kido's ultimate intention, in any official position that he held, to support the prestige of the Throne and to restrain the extravagances of the nationalists, both in the armed services and outside. But he shrank from the prospect of a clash between the Court and the extreme nationalists. He was prepared to go to almost any lengths in dissimulation, paying lip-service to chauvinism, in order to avert an internal struggle that might prove fatal to the position of the Emperor.

Kido was now Home Minister; and his readiness to compromise with extreme nationalism made him one of the weakest holders of this office in modern Japanese history.

The stormy issue of the unrestricted alliance with the Axis had barely subsided when the army provoked a quarrel with Great Britain, over the question of the asylum granted to alleged Chinese gunmen by the British Concession in Tientsin.[2]

The particular problems giving rise to the Tientsin dispute hardly concern us here. But the controversy led to the phenomenon of widespread anti-British demonstrations in Japan and in Japanese occupied China. These took the form of mass meetings attended by members of the leading nationalist bodies. Among these the *Kenkokukai* was particularly active. In Tokyo there were processions of demonstrators in front of the British Embassy; in occupied China the demonstrators converged on British Consulates, shouting slogans and, occasionally, throwing stones. In retrospect the entire agitation, which was at its height during

---

[1] Memoirs, *op. cit.*, Part XIX, Ch. 322 (24th April, 1939).

[2] A further issue in dispute was a deposit of bullion, amounting to nearly a million pounds sterling, placed by the Chinese National Government in a bank in the British Concession. This was claimed, on behalf of the North China puppet régime, by the Japanese government.

July and August, is seen to have been surprisingly lacking in spontaneity, sometimes noisy but scarcely menacing; and British subjects, in Japan at least, suffered no personal molestation.[1]

Yet the anti-British agitation worried the Japanese authorities; although in its early stages it had been tolerated—by the Home Minister for example—as a useful safety-valve for the feelings of extremists who had been frustrated on the issue of the Axis alliance.

On 27th May, the anniversary of Admiral Togo's victory in 1905 at Tsushima, there was, it appears, a plot, by Fukuoka supporters of Toyama Mitsuru, to assassinate Yuasa, Matsudaira Tsuneo (the Minister of the Imperial Household), Admirals Yonai and Yamamoto, Ikeda Seihin, the ex-Premier Okada, and others. This conspiracy came to nothing; but its interest lies in the attitude reported to have been taken by the Tokyo *Kempei*. The latter declared that they would of course assist the civil police in the duty of protecting the lives of the prospective victims; but if "anything should happen they [the *Kempei*] alone would assassinate the officials".[2]

In other words, if there had been any sign on Navy Day (27th May) that a portion of the Tokyo garrison actively sympathised with the nationalist demonstrations that occurred—the processions to the Yasukuni Shrine and the Palace Plaza—to the extent of leaving their barracks, in the manner of the February Mutineers, to attempt a *coup d'état*, then the Tokyo *Kempei* would have been on their side.

When the anti-British demonstrations began a few weeks later they were organised directly by the *Kempei* and financed by the army—that is to say, by the Ministry of War.[3] On the Tientsin question the Ministry of War adopted a more drastic line than that of General Staff Headquarters. On the whole the General Staff supported Lieutenant-General Homma, the Japanese commander at Tientsin, who, while maintaining strong pressure

---

[1] Nevertheless a bomb attack was planned against the British Ambassador and the Imperial Household Minister in July. The intending assassin was arrested outside the Embassy. Craigie, *op. cit.*, p. 77.

[2] Memoirs, *op. cit.*, Part XIX, Ch. 327 (31st May, 1939). Not unnaturally Harada commented: "It cannot be ascertained whether they [*Kempei*] are the protectors of the officials or the agents of the Right wing." *Ibid.*

[3] *Ibid.*, Part XX, Ch. 333 (18th July, 1939).

against the British Concession, was reluctant to push matters so far as to risk hostilities with the British garrison. On the other hand Homma's Chief of Staff, Major-General Yamashita, was in favour of armed action if necessary and was with difficulty held in check by Homma. The Ministry of War supported Yamashita.[1]

It must be borne in mind that a breach with Great Britain would have provided the "changed circumstances"—referred to in Hiranuma's message to Hitler at the beginning of May—in which full military co-operation with Germany might become feasible. It is possible to speak of a plot by the Ministry of War during the summer of 1939 to embroil Japan in a bitter struggle with Great Britain, for it was believed that in any case an Anglo-German war was imminent. Itagaki, the Minister of War, was wholeheartedly behind the extreme anti-British stand both at Tientsin and elsewhere. And the *Kempei* were directly controlled by the Ministry.

This accounts for the anxiety felt by the Emperor with regard to the Tientsin crisis and the demonstrations that accompanied it. He asked Hiranuma, in July, whether the anti-British agitation could not be controlled. The Premier replied that the matter was one of great difficulty. The Emperor also spoke sternly to the Minister of War, and indeed appears to have lost his temper with him, saying that there was nobody so foolish as Itagaki.[2] The latter, dumbfounded at this attack, felt that he must resign, and was only prevented from doing so by the Chief A.D.C., who, on the Emperor's orders, assured him that he still retained His Majesty's confidence.[3]

Kido, as Home Minister, had of course a prime responsibility so far as the anti-British agitation in Japan was concerned. But when criticised for not checking it he said:

> Home Ministers heretofore have haphazardly suppressed things, so there are many instances where they have backfired and trouble has ensued. I am planning to let things take their course and then to suppress them boldly.[4]

This may have been a sincere reflection of his views at this

---

[1] Memoirs, Part XX, Ch. 330 (24th June, 1939).
[2] *Ibid.*, Part XX, Ch. 332 (11th July, 1939).   [3] *Ibid.*
[4] *Ibid.*, Part XX, Ch. 333 (18th July, 1939).

juncture. Yet it is significant that the *genro* should have referred to Kido at this time as having "a tendency, by nature, to lean towards the Right".[1] No doubt the truth of the matter was that Kido at first favoured the anti-British agitation as a form of encouragement to the Japanese negotiators at the Tokyo Conference, which opened in July to seek a settlement of the Tientsin dispute.[2]

Early in August the Emperor spoke to Kido on the matter, and told him that the occurrence of the anti-British demonstrations was shameful. Kido answered that although he wished to suppress them there was the risk that if he did so "public peace and order would be harmed".[3]

The dread of a repetition of a 15th May Incident or of a Mutiny, like that of 1936, was sufficient to cow the spirits of all save the most courageous. If, as Yonai alleged, a man of the calibre of Ugaki allowed fears for his personal safety to influence his course of action it is, perhaps, unfair to judge Kido too harshly. Lacking the unusual courage of a Hamaguchi or Inukai and the solid conviction of a Saionji, Kido was moreover half attracted, like Konoye, to the dynamic force—fanatical nationalism—that threatened him.[4]

Events saved Kido from facing the consequences of his leniency towards the army-inspired anti-British movement. As soon as Ribbentrop concluded the German-Soviet Pact there was a revulsion of feeling in Japan against Germany; and correspondingly there was an immediate easing of Anglo-Japanese tension. The Hiranuma cabinet, which had been made to look foolish, resigned. Temporarily, at any rate, pro-Axis nationalism had suffered a setback.

Yet Kido's term of office as Home Minister was an unfortunate

[1] Memoirs, Part XX, Ch. 335 (5th August, 1939).
[2] The agitation was of course intended to put pressure on the British Ambassador and others at the Tokyo Conference. An example of the liaison between the military authorities at Tientsin and the civil authorities in Tokyo was provided by a convivial meeting, on the eve of the Conference, between Maj.-Gen. Muto Akira—Deputy Chief of Staff, Tientsin, and a delegate to the Conference—and the Chief of the Metropolitan Police, together with the Chief of the Home Ministry Police Bureau. *Ibid.*, Part XX, Ch. 333 (18th July, 1939).
[3] *Ibid.*, Part XX, Ch. 336 (14th August, 1939).
[4] The irrepressible Okawa appears to have exerted some influence on Home Ministry officials at this time. *Ibid.*

augury for his career, later, as Lord Keeper of the Privy Seal; for his weakness had been clearly revealed.

iii

When the Hiranuma cabinet resigned, the *genro* remarked, bitterly:

> The next cabinet is beyond me. If there was anyone I thought would be better than another I would speak up. . . . Our foreign policy is our biggest failure since the beginning of our history. It is distressing to have the power of the army as it is to-day. . . . Japan should combine with Great Britain, the United States and France.[1]

A few days later he said that nobody was qualified to become Prime Minister unless he "had tasted the bitter suffering of drinking three *to* [about eleven gallons] of vinegar through his nose".[2]

The Lord Keeper of the Privy Seal, together with Kido and Konoye, thought that Hirota was the best choice as the new Premier. The army, on the other hand, favoured the retired general, Abe Nobuyuki. But Yuasa felt that Abe lacked experience and was therefore unsuitable; a view that was shared by Hiranuma.[3]

However, when Hirota was approached by Yuasa he refused to be considered for the Premiership.[4] Accordingly Yuasa bowed to the army's wishes and, after visiting Saionji to get his formal approval, submitted General Abe's name to the Emperor.

Abe's appointment as Premier took the public by surprise, for he was practically unknown outside the army. And in the army his career—as a Japanese writer put it—had been one of "watchful obscurity".[5] He was identified with neither *Tosei-ha* nor *Kodo-ha*. His closest affiliations had been with Ugaki. When the latter in the nineteen-twenties had carried out his reduction of the army's strength, Abe, as Chief of the Military Affairs Bureau, had drafted the disarmament plan.[6] He maintained his friendship with

[1] Memoirs, Part XXI, Ch. 338 (1st September, 1939).
[2] *Ibid.*, Part XXI, Ch. 339 (11th September, 1939).
[3] *Ibid.*, Part XXI, Ch. 338 (1st September, 1939).   [4] *Ibid.*
[5] Iwabuchi Tatsuo, "Japan's New Premier, General Abe", *Contemporary Japan*, Vol. VII, No. 8, October, 1939.   [6] *Ibid.*

Ugaki during the years that followed; and in 1937, as was mentioned in the previous chapter, he tried to persuade the General Staff, through Prince Kanin, to abandon its stubborn opposition to the formation of an Ugaki cabinet.

General Abe, in fact, was a man of moderate views and one unlikely, in the normal course of events, to enjoy the confidence of military nationalists. But they had been thrown into temporary confusion by the shock of Germany's sudden diplomatic *volteface*. At this particular moment Abe was generally acceptable to the army as a person who could be relied upon to offend nobody, and to pursue a steady, cautious policy until the trend of events in Europe was clarified by the progress of the Anglo-German struggle that was now imminent.

When the new cabinet was being formed the Emperor, whose reluctance to enter into closer association with the Axis now appeared to be justified, adopted a strong line on the question of Itagaki's successor at the Ministry of War. He told the Lord Keeper of the Privy Seal that he was most indignant at the faults committed by the army, and that military discipline would have to be enforced. He made it clear that he would accept only Umezu or Hata Shunroku—who had succeeded Usami as Chief A.D.C. at the end of May—as the new Minister of War. "Even if the Big Three decide on someone else and submit his name to me, I have no intention of allowing that choice." [1]

Umezu, as we saw, had been greatly disliked by his subordinates at the Ministry of War because as Vice-Minister he had faithfully carried out the policy, begun by Terauchi and continued by Sugiyama, of restoring some semblance of discipline in the army.[2] Hata, during his three months at the Palace, had won the Emperor's trust—whereas his predecessor, Usami, was reported to have had neither a will of his own nor an understanding of the wishes of the Emperor.[3]

[1] Memoirs, *op. cit.*, Part XXI, Ch. 338 (1st September, 1939).
[2] The Emperor may have had particular confidence in Umezu, as one who would obey, as well as enforce, any Imperial command. On 2nd September, 1945, Umezu, as Chief of the General Staff, was chosen as one of the delegation to the Surrender ceremony on board the U.S.S. *Missouri*. Earlier he had said that if this odious mission were to be forced on him he would commit *hara-kiri*. However, the Emperor's personal persuasion made him carry out the task. T. Kase, *Journey to the Missouri, op. cit.*, pp. 5–6.
[3] Memoirs, Part XIX, Ch. 327 (31st May, 1939).

In accordance with the Emperor's will on this occasion, Lieutenant-General Hata was appointed Minister of War. It was noted by Harada, at the time: "General Hata, having been Chief A.D.C. and close to the Emperor for a while, knew well the points that were worrying the Emperor. He was also quite well aware of the outrageous features of the army." [1]

Indeed between the Emperor and his new Minister of War there existed an unusual sympathy. The Premier, for his part, was said to be "determined to obey the Emperor's wishes to every extent".[2] It now seemed possible that a start might be made to that "return of normal conditions" long desired by the *genro* and his dwindling body of supporters.[3]

The settlement of the Nomonhan Incident in the middle of September seemed to confirm this possibility. For over two months Japanese and Russians—together with satellite forces of Manchukuoan and Outer Mongolian troops—had been engaged in sporadic, though bitter, fighting in the region of Lake Nomonhan on the north-west frontier of Manchukuo. The fact that the German-Soviet *rapprochement* should have occurred at a time when Japanese soldiers were fighting the Russians—and suffering considerable casualties in the process—aggravated the resentment felt in Tokyo at Germany's violation of the Anti-Comintern Agreement.[4] In a position of renewed diplomatic isolation Japan had no choice but to wind up what had been a singularly inglorious adventure on the part of the Kwantung Army.[5]

[1] Memoirs, Part XXI, Ch. 339 (11th September, 1939).

[2] *Ibid.* Referring to Abe the *genro* remarked: "It seems that he is sensible and his reputation is quite good." *Ibid.*

[3] *Vide* p. 157 (*supra*)—(Harada (in May, 1934) presenting to Kido the arguments against having Hiranuma as Premier).

[4] It would have been possible—under the terms of the secret annexe (*vide* p. 193, *supra*)—for Japan to ask Germany to consider the Nomonhan Incident as amounting to a Russian attack on one of the signatories of the Anti-Comintern Pact.

[5] The Japanese press published much exaggerated claims of air victories during the fighting. But these glowing reports did not camouflage from the public the fact—it was the general whisper throughout the country—that the Kwantung Army had sustained heavy losses in encounters with Soviet mechanised forces. The Chief of Staff of the Kwantung Army, Lt.-Gen. Isogai, resigned a few weeks after the Cease-Fire. As Yuasa's Chief Secretary remarked to Harada: "He lost the battle so it is natural that he should submit his resignation." Memoirs, *op. cit.*, Part XXI, Ch. 343 (6th November, 1939).

This was not Isogai's first military defeat. He had been involved with Itagaki

Admiral Nomura Kichisaburo, on becoming Foreign Minister shortly after the Cease-Fire at Nomonhan, declared: "I believe that the path which Japan must take is the middle course." [1]

This, indeed, represented the mood of the country during the autumn of 1939 and the succeeding winter. Much—perhaps everything—depended on the progress of the European War.

Japanese nationalists, though upset by the German-Soviet Pact, were impressed by the blitzkrieg in Poland; and those who had always felt drawn towards Germany were inclined to listen with favour to Berlin's suggestion of a German-Japanese-Russian understanding that would leave Japan free for action at Great Britain's expense in South-East Asia. For example, Oshima, early in September, heartily agreed with Ribbentrop when the latter put this point to him. [2]

At the same time sentiment towards the United States had hardened as a result of their abrogation of the Treaty of Commerce of 1911. [3] And in the New Year a surge of spontaneous popular indignation—a much more profound emotion than any

in the serious reverse at Taierchwang, in 1938. Still, he was to regain face at the end of 1941, with the capture of Hong-Kong.

It is of interest to note that, when an exchange of prisoners was arranged in the spring of 1940, Russia returned 111 Japanese prisoners of war, whereas Japan had only two Russian prisoners for repatriation. *Ibid.*, Part XXIII, Ch. 361 (2nd May, 1940) (The Foreign Minister, Arita, to Harada). This was an unusually high figure for Japanese prisoners of war (though it was exceeded at Taierchwang).

[1] *Ibid.*, Part XXI, Ch. 340 (30th September, 1939). Before accepting office as Foreign Minister, Nomura obtained an assurance from the Premier that the Kwantung Army would be brought under control.

[2] Telegram, Ribbentrop to Ott, 9th September, 1939. I.M.T.F.E. Exhibit 507. Transcript, pp. 6127-9. The Japanese government on 25th August sent a Note to Germany protesting against the German-Soviet Pact. But Oshima did not hand the Note to the German Foreign Office until 18th September—after the end of the Polish campaign—though he deceived his own government by informing them, at the end of August, that he had delivered the Note promptly. Telegram, Weizsaecker to Ott, 18th September, 1939. I.M.T.F.E. Exhibit 506. Transcript, pp. 6124-5.

When Saionji heard that Oshima had agreed to Ribbentrop's suggestion of a Russian-Japanese pact he remarked: "His attitude is disloyal to his own Emperor." Memoirs, *op. cit.*, Part XXI, Ch. 340 (30th September, 1939).

Oshima was recalled to Japan in October, 1939, being succeeded in Berlin by Kurusu Saburo (Shiratori was similarly recalled from Rome).

[3] Grew's outspoken speech to the America-Japan Society, Tokyo, on 19th October seems to have impressed responsible men of moderate views—such as Admiral Nomura—but, thanks to unfavourable and sensational publicity in the newspapers, it no doubt exacerbated popular anti-American feeling.

stirred up by the fabricated anti-British agitation on the Tientsin issue—swept the country as a result of the interception and search of the *Asama Maru*, Japan's largest liner, by a British cruiser.[1]

Even so, the Yonai government—the Abe cabinet resigned in January[2]—might have been able to set Japan firmly on the "middle course" had not the spectacular German victories of May and June, 1940, powerfully revived sentiment in favour of close alliance with the Axis. Towards the end of February, 1940, Heinrich Stahmer, who had arrived in Tokyo in January as Hitler's personal envoy, reported to his home government that Japan was trying to keep clear of European entanglements, and that no important decisions could be expected pending military operations in Europe. But he went on: "The influence of the army, greatly weakened since last summer, is already growing again. A further increase is to be expected." [3]

The Yonai government in spite of growing pro-German, nationalist pressure, maintained the "middle course" more consistently and for longer than might have been anticipated. Certain aggressive moves and government statements were designed to placate nationalist feeling and to keep the cabinet in office. Immediately after the capitulation of France the Japanese government sought from Germany a declaration of her indifference to the fate of French Indo-China; and on 19th June Tani Masayuki, Vice-Minister of Foreign Affairs, demanded that the French government allow the dispatch of Japanese inspectors to North Indo-China for the purpose of investigating shipments of arms from the colony to China. At the same time naval units manœuvred off Haiphong, and a division was moved to the Kwangsi–Indo-

---

[1] H.M.S. *Liverpool* stopped the *Asama Maru* and removed German technicians on board at a point some thirty-five miles from the China coast. "The news of the incident had an electrifying effect on the whole country. Never in my experience have I known such a violent and universal outburst of vituperation." Craigie, *op. cit.*, p. 82.

[2] The Abe government was generally criticised for having failed to check rising prices. At the same time it had angered the Foreign Ministry by a proposal to set up a Ministry of Trade, the functions of which would have interfered, to some extent, with those of the Foreign Ministry. The proposal had to be dropped; and the whole affair was damaging to the cabinet's prestige. Finally 250 members of the Lower House, of all parties, passed a resolution of non-confidence in the government. The Yonai cabinet was completed on 16th January, 1940.

[3] Telegram, Stahmer to Weizsaecker, 23rd February, 1940. I.M.T.F.E. Exhibit 511. Transcript, pp. 6141–2.

China border. Yet, as the German Ambassador in Tokyo reported to Berlin, Arita's policy was based on a determination to keep the cabinet from otherwise inevitable collapse.

> There is undoubtedly a danger [reported Ott] that the Foreign Minister might make tactical use of a free hand, given to Japan by Germany with regard to French Indo-China, in his attempt to bring about a compromise with America. The attitude of the Foreign Minister is at bottom unchanged.[1]

Similarly, Arita's pronouncements on Japan's interest in the Dutch East Indies were made primarily in order to take the wind out of the sails of the nationalists—a manœuvre perceived and much resented by many of them.[2]

However, in the end—as was almost inevitable—the army forced the resignation of the cabinet.

On 5th July the police nipped in the bud a terrorist conspiracy organised by supporters of Maeda Torao, of the *Shimpeitai*.[3] Forty-seven of these adventurers—the number is significant[4]— had plotted to assassinate the Premier (Yonai), Admiral Okada, Yuasa, Makino, Harada, Ikeda Seihin and Matsudaira Tsuneo, the Minister of the Imperial Household. Baron Ikki—who had been Hiranuma's predecessor as President of the Privy Council— Arita, the Foreign Minister, and Machida Chuji, leader of the Minseito, were also marked down for assassination. A collection of weapons—pistols, hand grenades, swords and "Molotov cocktails" (beer bottles filled with petrol)—was seized by the police, who made the arrests a few hours before the acts of terrorism were timed to begin.[5]

When reporting the affair to the Emperor, Kido—now Lord Keeper of the Privy Seal—showed a characteristic tendency to excuse, if not to justify, the conspirators. Kido noted in his Diary: "I stated to His Majesty that their actions were to blame

[1] Telegram, German Ambassador to Foreign Ministry, Berlin, 19th June, 1940. I.M.T.F.E. Exhibit 520. Transcript, pp. 6162–5.

[2] *Ibid.*, 3rd July, 1940. Exhibit 531. Transcript, 6239–40.

[3] *Vide* p. 130 (*supra*).

[4] Suggesting that the conspirators saw themselves as twentieth-century heirs to the Forty-Seven Ronin.

[5] Memoirs, *op. cit.*, Part XXIII, Ch. 369 (10th July, 1940). Harada refers to the plot as the "Imperial Friends' Riot Incident". And Kido's Diary, 5th July, 1940. I.M.T.F.E. Exhibit 532. Transcript, pp. 6241–2.

but, as to their motives, the administrators must reflect seriously upon them." [1]

Here again we see, as typically Japanese, interest concentrating on the motive, behind an act of violence, rather than on the act itself.

The possession of pistols and hand grenades—although in fact there were only two grenades—by the conspirators suggests that they had received practical help from either the army or navy. Nevertheless, any such support must have been indirect and unofficial. For Harada, referring to the affair, noted: "Although it is said to be something like the 26th February Incident the army did not go into action." [2]

No doubt military ultra-nationalists were confident that they would be able to overthrow the Yonai administration by peaceful means.[3]

Kido's appointment as Lord Keeper of the Privy Seal at the end of May was of inestimable advantage to the army, and indeed to nationalists as a whole. It will be noticed that his name was not included among the list of victims chosen by the terrorists for assassination on 5th July. Yet he was hardly regarded by either the Emperor or Yuasa, the retiring Lord Keeper of the Privy

---

[1] Kido's Diary, 5th July, 1940.

[2] Memoirs, Part XXIII, Ch. 369 (10th July, 1940).

[3] Army officers had, in fact, been involved in a terrorist plot at the beginning of the year. A Major Ito, of the Signals Department of the Ministry of War, was arrested by the *Kempei* in Kobe on 4th January. He had been intercepting and studying Foreign Ministry cables and was much shocked at what he considered to be manifestations of Japan's "weak diplomacy". With about a dozen other officers he planned to blow up the British and American Embassies, and to kill Yuasa, Ugaki, Matsudaira Tsuneo (Minister of the Imperial Household) and others regarded as pro-British. Major Ito visited Kobe in order to consult a senior officer (not identified). The latter, alarmed, informed the *Kempei. Ibid.*, Part XXII, Ch. 350 (10th January, 1940).

Some time earlier a group of officers—among them Major Ito—visited Konoye, and although nothing was said about an impending "Incident" their manner of farewell, at the end of the interview, made Konoye sense that the officers did not expect to see him again. It was as though they were departing to their deaths. *Ibid.*

All diplomatic communications from Tokyo, from foreign embassies as well as from the Foreign Ministry, appear to have been subject to interception by the armed services. Thus, in May, 1939, Arita (Foreign Minister) said to Harada: "I cannot tell the ambassadors of other nations not to send cables because the Japanese army and navy will intercept them. I don't know what to do." *Ibid.*, Part XIX, Ch. 325 (16th May, 1939).

Seal, as an agent of the nationalists. For they both considered him as the best choice for the office of Lord Keeper; and the Prime Minister, Yonai, shared this view. Only the wise Saionji seems to have had doubts regarding the wisdom of the appointment. But he refused to commit himself officially. Privately, however, he suggested that either Baron Ikki or Admiral Okada should succeed Yuasa.[1]

Undoubtedly Kido's appointment enabled the army to feel secure in possession of the Emperor—and in no purely metaphorical sense.

On this point a conversation, earlier in the year, between the Prime Minister and Ikeda Seihin is of much interest. Speaking about the army, and its excesses, Ikeda said:

> The army feel that their big blunder at the time of the 26th February Incident was that they didn't win the Emperor over to their side. This time there is said to be a plan of first winning the Emperor to their side and then starting a disturbance. Does the navy have ideas on methods of protecting the Emperor, either by getting him aboard a warship or by other means, in such an instance?[2]

Yonai replied that adequate preparations had been made for such an eventuality, and that Ikeda need feel no anxiety on this score.[3]

From the army's point of view the promotion of Kido to succeed Yuasa repaired the "blunder" at the time of the February Mutiny. Kido's appointment meant that the Emperor would scarcely be in a position to adopt a firm stand against policies desired by the army; for it would be extremely difficult, if not virtually impossible, for him to ignore the counsel of his daily political adviser, the Lord Keeper of the Privy Seal. The appointment was not engineered by the army; but it was none the less profitable to the army on that account.

With Kido in his new and vital post the time was now ripe, in the view of military nationalists, for the overthrow of the Yonai government. There is no reason to suppose that officers of the

[1] Memoirs, Part XXIII, Ch. 364 (4th June, 1940). The Emperor's only doubt was whether Kido might not be too young for the position.

[2] *Ibid.*, Part XXII, Ch. 358 (29th March, 1940).

[3] Harada noted that the problem discussed by Yonai and Ikeda was "very serious" and that they talked about it "very secretly". *Ibid.*

General Staff and Ministry of War would have hesitated to consider the violent methods of a *coup d'état*, had the situation demanded it. However, by the beginning of July—by the time of the outbreak planned for 5th July—it was apparent that sufficient pressure could be exerted on General Hata, the Minister of War, to compel him to resign.

At the beginning of the month—July, 1940—the section chiefs of the General Staff—those medium-grade officers whom Kido described, at the time, as "forming the central core"[1]—informed their superiors that the Yonai government was unfitted to deal with the existing international situation;[2] in other words, its composition was too moderate and liberal. Such a government could not be trusted to move closer to the Axis.

On 8th July the Vice-Minister of War, Lieutenant-General Anami Korechika, called on Kido and said:

> Now, when a political change may be unavoidable within the next four or five days and the military have been perfecting preparations to meet the abrupt changes in the latest world situation, the character of the Yonai cabinet is not at all suitable for conducting negotiations with Germany and Italy, and it might even cause a fatal delay. The conclusion is that a cabinet change is inevitable in order to face this grave situation. The army will support unanimously the candidature of Prince Konoye.[3]

At the same time Prince Kanin, still Chief of the Army General Staff, spoke to the Minister of War and told him that it was the view of the General Staff that the cabinet was no longer fitted to carry on foreign affairs satisfactorily.[4]

The circumstances of the cabinet resignation—it took place on 16th July—were as follows. A memorandum containing the army's views, with particular reference to the desirability of an immediate alliance with the Axis, was handed to the Premier by the Minister of War. Yonai rejected the memorandum as being unacceptable to the cabinet as a whole; and he told Hata, bluntly,

---

[1] Kido's Diary, 8th July, 1940. I.M.T.F.E. Exhibit 532.
[2] *Ibid.*   [3] *Ibid.*
[4] *Ibid.* Anami and Muto Akira, Chief of the Military Affairs Bureau, visited the Chief Secretary of the Cabinet and told him the government would have to resign, otherwise they would force the resignation of Gen. Hata. Memoirs, *op. cit.*, Part XXIV, Ch. 370 (20th July, 1940).

to resign if he was not satisfied with this reply.[1] Whereupon Hata resigned. Yonai asked him to recommend a successor, although he was probably well aware that nobody would be recommended.

The "Big Three" met in conference, but, in Kido's words: "It was said that, although the selection of a successor was not being refused, it was difficult to choose one and no forecast was possible."[2]

Accordingly the cabinet resigned.

The choice of the new Premier was made at a meeting, in the Palace, of the Lord Keeper of the Privy Seal, the President of the Privy Council, and the former Premiers. Opinion in favour of Konoye was unanimous. The choice was then reported, as a matter of form, to the *genro* for his approval; but he begged to be excused from offering any advice to the Throne.[3]

The Emperor, with good reason, felt sad at the departure of Yonai. He told Kido that he still had faith in the Yonai government, and in spite of the inevitable change he wanted his feelings conveyed to Yonai.[4] The Emperor must have had a sense of foreboding when this moderate administration was forced to give way to one committed to the hazards of a full alliance with the European fascist powers. At his final audience to Hata the Emperor declared: "This business is very regrettable, but I feel it is one consolation that we can see where the responsibility lies."[5]

There is little doubt that here the Emperor was referring to the pressure exerted by such officers as Anami and Muto Akira and their juniors, as well as by nationalists in the Foreign Ministry. For it was these groups—assisted by funds from the German Embassy—that had pushed the issue of an Axis alliance to the forefront, for the second time in eighteen months.

[1] Kido's Diary, 16th July, 1940. I.M.T.F.E. Exhibit 532. Transcript, p. 6247.
[2] *Ibid.*
[3] Memoirs, *op. cit.*, Part XXIV, Ch. 370 (20th July, 1940).
[4] Kido's Diary, 14th July, 1940. I.M.T.F.E. Exhibit 534.
[5] *Ibid.*, 17th July, 1940.

12

STEPS TO PEARL HARBOUR

i

IT may be recalled that shortly before the resignation of the Yonai cabinet General Anami, the Vice-Minister of War, informed Marquis Kido that the army was "perfecting preparations to meet the abrupt changes in the world situation".[1] These preparations were of a political, rather than military, nature.[2] They related to the matter of the Axis alliance.

Arrangements for concluding an alliance were probably completed by the beginning of July, 1940; but certain final points were not settled until 16th July, the date on which the Yonai cabinet resigned. This at least is suggested by the minutes of a joint conference of the Foreign, War, and Navy Ministries, held on the 12th and 16th July.[3]

The purpose of the conference was to discuss questions relating to the proposed alliance. The members of the conference were comparatively junior officers and officials. At their first gathering, on 12th July, they were five in number—namely, two section chiefs from the Foreign Ministry, a lieutenant-colonel from the Ministry of War, a captain from the Naval General Staff, and a commander from the Navy Ministry.[4]

As the meetings were held at the Foreign Ministry they were presided over by one of the Ministry's staff. Indeed the main

[1] p. 264 (*supra*).

[2] There was, however, at this time a plan for an attack on Hong Kong. Heavy artillery was mobilised for this purpose (Telegram, Ott to Berlin for German General Staff, 17th July, 1940. I.M.T.F.E. Transcript, p. 6257). This particular measure of mobilisation appears to have been approved by a Five Ministers' Conference on 12th July (Kido's Diary, 14th July, 1940). Presumably this plan was drawn up to meet any eventuality that might arise from a successful German invasion of England.

[3] I.M.T.F.E. Exhibit 527. Transcript, pp. 6191–202.

[4] They were Ando (Foreign Ministry), Ishizawa (possibly Ishizawa Yutaka, who was to become director of the Southern Regions Bureau, Greater East Asia Ministry, in 1944), Lt.-Col. Takayama, Capt. Ono, and Comd. Shiba.

topic of discussion related to proposals drawn up by the Foreign Ministry. These were based—as the presiding Foreign Ministry representative (Ando) pointed out—on the hypothesis that Germany would defeat Great Britain, and their purpose, in Ando's words, was to have Japan "join hands with the Reich to the fullest extent short of being driven into war".[1]

Lieutenant-Colonel Takayama (Ministry of War) asked if it was proposed merely to seek some agreement at the conference and then to submit the consensus of opinion to higher authorities for consideration. Ando replied that prompt action was necessary. He wanted the agreed decisions of the conference submitted to higher authorities and then put into practice as the national policy as soon as possible.[2]

This gathering, then, of middle-grade officials was more than an inter-departmental committee of an advisory nature. It was a policy-making body.

It is unnecessary to summarise all the points discussed—interesting as they are. But some of the views expressed should be recorded.

Ando, of the Foreign Ministry, stated that one of the most important offers Japan had to make to Berlin was her readiness to embarrass Great Britain in the Far East. He referred to secret Japanese help to the independence movements in India and Burma, and he asked the army and navy representatives to think of other practical ways of annoying Great Britain.[3]

When the conference reassembled, on 16th July, the Foreign Ministry representatives numbered three, and Takayama, of the Ministry of War, was supported by an officer from the Army General Staff. Shiba again represented the Navy Ministry; there was no representative from the Naval General Staff.[4]

Takayama made reference to an important phrase (in the proposals to be sent to Berlin)—"the construction of a new order in the Far East, including the South Seas".

I would like to have it mean [said Takayama] that it is Japan's intention to include the territory extending from Burma and Eastern

[1] I.M.T.F.E. Exhibit 527. Transcript, p. 6194.
[2] *Ibid.* [3] *Ibid.*, p. 6196.
[4] *Ibid.* Ando and Ishizawa were now joined by Tajiri (no doubt Tajiri Akiyoshi, formerly Consul-General in Hong-Kong). The Army General Staff representative was Major Tanemura.

India on the west to Australia and New Zealand on the east; but since there should be a South Seas of the first sense and also of the second sense, the South Seas to be expressed in Japan's attitude for the present should be a narrower South Seas excluding Australia, New Zealand and Burma. Nevertheless I think we should consider . . . the South Seas of the wider sense.

Ando: "I agree with Takayama—for the time being the South Seas of the first sense must be adopted; although of course Japan's ideal includes Australia, New Zealand and Burma."

Shiba (Navy Ministry): "I agree to that." [1]

It was agreed that Japan must resist any claim by Germany, at the end of the war, to the possession of French Indo-China and the Dutch East Indies. Ando gave a warning that if there was a German-Japanese dispute over these colonies Germany might try to use Russia "to check Japan from the north". However, Major Tanemura (Army General Staff) argued that Russia was unlikely to allow herself to be Germany's tool and would not "carelessly meddle in this with the hope of securing Northern Manchuria". Russia would be more interested in India and the Near East.[2]

There was some discussion on methods of embarrassing Great Britain. It was decided that an anti-British press campaign must be launched; and there was a suggestion, supported by Commander Shiba, that "vessels of unknown nationality" might be used to harass British interests—presumably as commerce raiders. But the conference agreed that for the time being Japan's anti-British policy should not envisage a resort to war.[3]

Little anxiety was expressed on the subject of Japanese-American relations. "There is no real difference," said Shiba, "between Japan and the United States, and the existing antagonism between the two countries is economic and for the most part emotional." [4]

There might be trouble between the United States and Germany—after the latter had defeated Great Britain—over German economic penetration in South America; on this issue Japan, as Germany's ally, might have to consider joint action with Germany against the United States in the future. But, as Ando

---

[1] I.M.T.F.E. Transcript, p. 6215.   [2] Ibid., p. 6219.
[3] Ibid., p. 6224.   [4] Ibid., p. 6231.

emphasised, German-American relations were satisfactory; indeed Schacht expected to obtain an American loan after the war.[1]

The general conclusion, then, was that Japan should ally herself with the Axis and seize every chance of doing harm, short of war, to British interests in the Far East. Russia must be "guided" towards India and the Near East. Friendly relations should be maintained with the United States. "Now opinion among us, the officials concerned, has been unified," said Ando, "it is essential that no time be lost in its execution." [2]

The others agreed, Takayama adding that he thought he "could settle with the army along the line discussed". Shiba, on behalf of the navy, gave a similar undertaking.[3]

The general policy, and many of the particular measures, decided upon at this conference found expression in decisions of such bodies as the Five Ministers' Conference and the Privy Council within the next three months. And it is significant that the arrests of Reuters' Correspondent and fourteen other British subjects, on charges of espionage, followed within a fortnight of the conference that has just been described. Furthermore, the press launched its anti-British campaign—one newspaper, the *Kokumin*, beginning a series of personal attacks on the British Ambassador.[4]

High policy was often, though not invariably, thus decided by a group of lieutenant-colonels and other officials of similar rank; for they occupied an important middle position between the higher commanders and officials and such adventurers as Okawa, Maeda Torao and other nationalist "ronin".

ii

On 19th September, 1940, a Liaison Conference of great importance was held.[5] This Conference decided that Japan, Germany and Italy would co-operate in a joint military alliance; and

---

[1] *Ibid.*, p. 6226.   [2] *Ibid.*, p. 6231.   [3] *Ibid.*

[4] Craigie, *op. cit.*, p. 113. The *Kokumin* had close relations with the Ministry of War. The arrests of Mr. Cox (of Reuters) and the others were made on 27th July. On 27th July Cox "fell" to his death from a third-story window at *Kempei* headquarters in Tokyo.

[5] The Liaison Conferences were instituted during the China hostilities. At

it was agreed that unless Japan was prepared to use armed force, if necessary, it would be impossible for her to carry on effective talks with Germany. There were to be none of the reservations and marks of hesitation that characterised the Japanese side in the negotiations of 1939.

Regarding Russia it was agreed that an understanding was to "be reached with respect to consultation, or to the action to be taken, in the event of a danger of either Japan or Germany or Italy entering upon a state of war with the Soviet Union, if, in the course of negotiations with Germany and Italy, it turns out that such desire is entertained by the two countries".[1] The fundamental policy towards Russia was expressed thus:

> Being destined to be the leader of East Asia in the post-war new order of things, wherein it is anticipated that the world will be divided into the four large fields of East Asia, the Soviet Union, Europe and the American Continent, Japan—acting in close collaboration with Germany and Italy who will constitute the guiding force of Europe—will restrain the Soviet Union on the east, west and south . . . and will endeavour to cause the advance of the Soviet sphere of influence to be orientated towards a direction where the advance has little effect on the interests of Japan, Germany and Italy —a direction such as the Persian Gulf; it being also possible that, in case of need, Soviet advance towards India may have to be recognised.[2]

The three Axis powers would co-operate to prevent the United States from interfering in areas outside "the Western Hemisphere and the United States' possessions".[3] At the same

meetings of the cabinet and of the Five Ministers' Conference the views of the Supreme Command were conveyed by the War and Navy Ministers. But the General Staffs of the two services regarded the method of working through the War and Navy Ministers as inadequate. Therefore the larger Liaison Conferences came into being. They met at frequent intervals. (For example, during the first six months of 1941 there were thirty Liaison Conferences.) The regular members were the Prime Minister, the War, Navy, Foreign and Finance Ministers, the Chiefs of the General Staff, the Vice-Chiefs of Staff and the directors of the Military Affairs and Naval Affairs Bureaux.

There is no record of the attendance at the Liaison Conference, on 19th September, discussed here.

[1] I.M.T.F.E. Exhibit 541. Transcript, p. 6311.
[2] *Ibid.*, p. 6316.   [3] *Ibid.*, p. 6311.

time Japan would intensify her pressure on British interests in East Asia.

It was decided that armed action would be taken against Great Britain and the United States, provided a favourable opportunity presented itself, and provided the China Incident had "nearly been settled". Resort to war against these countries would not be envisaged if the China Incident was still in progress, with its end not in sight. But even under these circumstances Japan would resort to armed force if the international situation appeared to be favourable.[1]

The Liaison Conference agreed that in her dealings with the Axis Japan's sphere—her "new order" in Asia—was to comprise:

> The former German Islands under Mandate, French Indo-China and Pacific Islands, Thailand, British Malaya, British Borneo, Dutch East Indies, Burma, Australia, New Zealand, India, etc., with Japan, Manchukuo and China as the backbone.

> It is understood, however, that the South Seas Region to be indicated by Japan, in conducting the negotiations with Germany and Italy, will be the region from Burma eastward, including the Dutch East Indies, and New Caledonia northward. It is further understood that India may be recognised, for immediate purposes, as being included in the Living Sphere of the Soviet Union.[2]

The decisions of the Conference are of great interest—the extent of Japan's ambitions should be remarked—but of principal concern to us is the fact that this Liaison Conference merely endorsed, and enlarged upon, conclusions already reached at the inter-departmental conference of relatively junior army and navy officers and Foreign Ministry officials two months earlier.[3] At that meeting in July, it will be remembered, the national policy with regard to Russia had been agreed upon—as well as the question of policy towards England and the United States—and Japan's sphere in Asia and the South Seas had been defined.

The second Konoye cabinet, which came into power in July, was well fitted to execute these policies; for it had a decidedly nationalist complexion. The new War Minister was Tojo. Oikawa, the Navy Minister, was prepared, though with little enthusiasm,

---

[1] *Ibid.*, p. 6319.   [2] *Ibid.*, p. 6315.   [3] pp. 266–9 (*supra*).

to fight the United States.[1] And Matsuoka, who succeeded Arita at the Foreign Ministry, was a talkative chauvinist whose first important act on taking office was to conduct a "purge" of the diplomatic service, with the aim of rooting out those who were known or suspected to have English or American sympathies, or to be otherwise out of harmony with pro-Axis ideas.[2]

As for Konoye himself, he appears to have consented to the Tripartite Pact as a means of dissuading the United States from entering the European War, and as a bargaining counter in Japanese-American negotiations. In the final discussions of the Privy Council, on 26th September (the day previous to the official conclusion of the Alliance), Konoye said:

> I think it is necessary for us to show a firm attitude, because if we act humbly it will only make the United States presumptuous. If the worst should come to the worst I think that the government must adopt policies with firm resolution in both diplomatic and domestic affairs. The other day when I presented myself at the Imperial Palace to report on this matter, I found His Majesty the Emperor also to have possessed a very firm resolution, which was very impressive. I hope that this treaty will be satisfactorily executed, even at the risk of my very life.[3]

Konoye's remark here about the Emperor's "firm resolution" —implying support for the Tripartite Alliance—is not easily reconciled with what Harada has to say on the subject of the Emperor's attitude. This is described as being very much opposed to the Pact. Harada notes that Saionji was at a loss to know how

[1] Record of Privy Council Session, 26th September, 1940. I.M.T.F.E. Exhibit 1030, p. 9757; which shows that Oikawa was moderately confident of the outcome of a naval struggle with America. Nevertheless, it is only fair to emphasise that Oikawa was more cautious in 1941, during the months before the attack on Pearl Harbour, and was replaced, in October of that year, by the less pessimistic Admiral Shimada.

[2] Apart from changes made within the Ministry in Tokyo, no fewer than thirty-nine diplomats were recalled from posts abroad. Matsuoka also agreed to the appointment of Shiratori as the representative for foreign affairs on the Preparatory Commission for the New Political Structure.

[3] Konoye prefaced this statement by saying that the basic idea of the Pact was the avoidance of a Japanese-U.S. clash. In the first sentence quoted, the dependent clause can also read: "because if we make a blunder the United States will become presumptuous". (As noted by the translator.) I.M.T.F.E. Exhibit 1030. Transcript, p. 9762.

Konoye and Kido had managed to obtain the Emperor's approval.[1] Furthermore, Matsudaira, the Minister of the Imperial Household, is reported as having said: "The Emperor invariably intimated his feelings of regret on this matter." [2]

These no doubt represented the Emperor's true sentiments regarding the Pact. But perhaps they were mollified to some extent by the argument that its terms would act as a deterrent on the United States, that in any case the European War would soon end in a German victory and that therefore the possibility of Japan having to redeem any promises made to Germany was remote.[3]

Kido, by reason of his position, was able to exercise a paramount influence on the Emperor in favour of the Pact; and at the same time he was able to prevent the Emperor from receiving advice from quarters hostile to the Axis. For instance, he failed to inform the *genro* of the negotiations leading up to the signing of the Alliance, and in fact kept the whole matter completely secret from him. Kido had, it is true, the good excuse that Saionji was now failing rapidly in health. But Harada was extremely indignant at Kido's behaviour. In protesting to Kido he pointed out that although the *genro's* physical condition was now very weak, his mental powers were still robust, and he ought to have been consulted, or at least informed, regarding the Tripartite Pact.[4]

But thanks to the rise of nationalist thought in Japan during the previous nine years, and to the dazzling military and diplomatic successes of Germany, the attitude of mind represented by the *genro* was now regarded, at best, as dangerously ineffective. Mercifully the aged Prince—the Cassandra of the nineteen-thirties—died before the close of the year.[5]

[1] Memoirs, *op. cit.*, Part XXIV, Ch. 378 (23rd October, 1940).   [2] *Ibid.*

[3] It is interesting to note that one of Saionji's last political utterances related to the course of the European War. Forecasting its future, he said (to Harada): "It may appear as if Germany will become the victor, but in the end I believe that Great Britain will be victorious." *Ibid.*, Part XXIV, Ch. 375(a) (22nd September, 1940).

[4] *Ibid.*, Part XXIV, Ch. 378 (23rd October, 1940).

[5] Prince Saionji died on 24th November, 1940. In his last illness he was glad to hear that the temperate Admiral Nomura was going to Washington as Ambassador. "Is Nomura really going?" he asked Harada. When assured that this was so, he asked Harada to give Nomura his best wishes. *Ibid.*, Part XXIV, Ch. 381 (21st November, 1940).

Only Ishii, the veteran diplomat, uttered a warning, with regard to German intentions, when the Privy Council discussed the Pact.[1] He said:

It is a conspicuous fact that there is not a single country that has gained any benefit from allying itself with Germany and with her predecessor, Prussia. Not only this—but there are countries which because of this alliance have suffered unforeseen disasters and have finally lost their national entity. Bismarck once said that in international alliances one horseman and one donkey are required, and that Germany must always be the horseman.[2]

Yet he concluded by declaring himself to be in favour of the Pact.

The exuberance of nationalist feeling was well expressed by Shiratori in an article, written at the end of the year, for the edification of foreign readers.[3] Having stated that the basis of Western civilisation, from the time of ancient Greece to the present day, was the individualist view of the world, Shiratori declared that the movement for *kultur* associated with the rise of Prussia represented the first revolt against the individualist concept. He went on to describe the totalitarian movement as "spreading like a prairie fire". There was a similar movement in Japan—"for going back to intrinsically Japanese ways of ancient times". The evils of liberal civilisation had poisoned Japanese tradition for the past fifty years; but "at last the nation revolted", a revolt expressed in the Manchurian Incident. This was "a bursting out of the suppressed racial instinct of the nation". Shiratori continued:

Centuries' old mental habits controlling mankind must be broken. Everything requires reappraisal, including the essential qualities of God. Such things as freedom and equality of individuals, the inherent rights of man, the absolute sovereignty of a state, the right of self-determination of the people—all must be viewed from a completely different angle from that of the past.[4]

[1] Viscount Ishii Kikujiro, Foreign Minister 1915–16.
[2] I.M.T.F.E. Exhibit 553. Transcript, p. 6386. Ishii went on to say that Germany's attitude towards Austria and Turkey in the First World War "was like that of a horseman, shouting at and whipping a donkey".
[3] "The 3-Power Pact and the World of Tomorrow", *Contemporary Japan*, Vol. IX, December, 1940.   [4] *Ibid.*

The relevance of these words for the prospective beneficiaries of the Japanese New Order—including the inhabitants of Australia and New Zealand—is apparent. A reappraisal of "the essential qualities of God" would certainly be desirable among any population newly incorporated in the Japanese Empire; the theocratic nature of the Imperial Throne demanded it. Similarly, in such circumstances a regard for hierarchy and the Confucian concept of reciprocal obligations would be of more importance than ideas of the equality of individuals and their inherent rights. And the nations within the proposed New Order—even those permitted to be "independent"—would have to abandon such outworn aspirations as the sovereignty of the state and popular self-determination. Manchukuo, perhaps, could be regarded as the model to be followed.

While Article III—providing for full assistance in case of attack by a power not at present engaged in the European War[1] —was the core of the Tripartite Pact, Article II had great importance for Japanese nationalists. This read: "Germany and Italy shall recognise and respect the leadership of Japan in the establishment of a new order in Greater Asia." [2]

For the first time two foreign nations—great powers of the Western world—accorded official recognition to that deeply cherished Japanese nationalist ideal, *Hakko Ichi-u* in Asia and the South Seas.[3]

[1] The operative words were: "If and when any one of the signatories be attacked by any third power not presently engaged in the European War or the China Incident, the other two shall aid her in any way, political, economic or military." I.M.T.F.E. Exhibit 43 (Text of the Tripartite Pact). Transcript, p. 6392.   [2] *Ibid.*

[3] *Hakko Ichi-u*—lit. "eight cords under one roof"—an expression dating, by tradition, from the time of the first Emperor, Jimmu *Tenno*. The relevant passage from the *Nihongi* and its modern interpretations are discussed by Dr. Holtom in *Modern Japan and Shinto Nationalism* (cited), pp. 21–3. It is possible that in its earliest form the phrase referred—in a limited, architectural sense—to the completion of Jimmu *Tenno's* Palace.

Very broad interpretations are suggested in modern times. In the most extreme nationalist sense the phrase was taken to mean the unity of the eight corners of the world under the supervision of Japan. The mildest interpretation suggested that it represented merely an ideal of world brotherhood and peace.

The Konoye cabinet, on 26th July, 1940, had issued a statement declaring that the basic national policy was the "establishment of world peace in accordance with the lofty ideal of *Hakko Ichi-u* on which the Empire is founded".

The truth is that this celebrated phrase was a pious and vague aspiration, perverted by nationalists to justify their fanatical ambitions.

The scope of the proposed New Order—or "Co-Prosperity Sphere" as it came to be called—has already been suggested, in earlier paragraphs dealing with the proceedings of the inter-departmental and Liaison Conferences. But it is not perhaps generally realised how ambitious were the plans for the future expansion of Japanese power.

Certain countries in Asia—such as Burma and the Malay States—were to be organised as independent monarchies. Australia, New Zealand and Ceylon were to be incorporated in the Japanese Empire under Governors-General. There were, also, to be Governments-General of Alaska (including the Yukon district of Canada, Alberta, British Columbia and the State of Washington), and of Central America (not including Mexico, but embracing the other Latin American republics in that area as well as the British, French and Dutch West Indies).[1] It was appreciated that such spoils could hardly be gathered in one war. Therefore it was anticipated that having gained the British, French and Dutch Asiatic colonies by taking part in the European War—and these colonies, together with the Phillippines, constituted the "smaller" Co-Prosperity Sphere, or "the South Seas of the first sense"[2]—Japan must prepare for a further great war some twenty years later. These plans were prepared by the Research Section of the Ministry of War, in collaboration with the Army and Navy General Staffs and the Overseas Ministry. They were completed in December, 1941.[3]

The Research Section of the Ministry of War worked in intimate association with a body known as the *Kokusaku Kenkyukai* ("The National Policy Investigation Society"). Indeed the chief of the General Affairs Bureau of this society—Yatsugi Kazuo—was also, from 1938 to 1944, on the non-official staff of the Research Section of the Ministry of War.[4]

The *Kokusaku Kenkyukai* was established at the beginning of 1937, largely on the initiative of the wealthy industrialist, Baron Okura Kimmochi. Its declared purpose was "to investigate the

---

[1] For details of the planned New Order, in its most ambitious form, *Vide* Appendix II (*infra*).

[2] Cf. p. 268 (*supra*).

[3] "Land Disposal Plan in the Gt. Asia Co-Prosperity Sphere." I.M.T.F.E. Exhibit 1334. Transcript, pp. 11969–73.

[4] Affidavit by Yatsugi. I.M.T.F.E. Transcript, pp. 7359–74.

graver political problems of immediate attention to our country and to submit the resulting reports to the Japanese government". Official interest in the society was very considerable.[1] It received yearly subscriptions from the Premier's Secretariat and from the Ministries of War, Navy and Foreign Affairs. Mitsui, Mitsubishi, the South Manchurian Railway and other large business concerns were collective members of the society, and provided regular financial support. In addition, both government departments and business firms contributed occasional capital sums to the society.[2] And government departments supplied it with data and information, including those in the most secret category.[3]

In respectability and standing, though hardly in any other way, the *Kokusaku Kenkyukai* might almost be described as a Japanese "Chatham House". The army, as one would expect, exercised a dominant influence on the policy of the society.[4]

This semi-official and, from the Japanese standpoint, entirely reputable organisation must share much of the credit for the preparation of the grandiose plans, that have been outlined, for the future New Order in Asia.

For the Japanese nationalist movement as a whole the late

---

[1] *Ibid.* There were approximately two thousand individual members—mostly political leaders, senior bureaucrats, retired officers and influential businessmen.

[2] The Home Ministry, Overseas Ministry and Ministry of Railways also gave annual contributions. The annual subscriptions from government departments and big business houses averaged 3,000 *yen*. Mitsubishi and the Aikawa concern gave the largest yearly subscription—5,000 *yen* (rather more than £250 at the then existing rate of exchange). The capital sums for special projects involving long-term investigations—for example the plan for the construction of the Co-Prosperity Sphere—were very large. The Ministry of War, for instance, contributed 20,000 *yen*; and the Navy and Foreign Ministries and the Mitsui concern—to mention only three of several other collective backers—gave like sums. I.M.T.F.E. Transcript, pp. 11969–73.

[3] *Ibid.*

[4] For example, in May, 1940, Col. Iwakuro, of the Military Affairs Bureau at the Ministry of War, hoped to make use of the *Kokusaku Kenkyukai* as one means of overthrowing the Yonai government. Konoye informed Harada that he had learned that the society had invited Aoki Kazuo (Finance Minister in the Abe cabinet) to assist them in compiling a plan for future policy in finance and economics. Konoye said that in fact the Military Affairs Bureau was behind the society in making this request, that when the plan was completed the army would use it "to shake the cabinet". When questioned by Harada, Aoki confirmed that he was drafting such a plan and he admitted his intimacy with Iwakuro, though he denied the imputation suggested by Konoye. Memoirs, *op. cit.*, Part XXIII, Ch. 362(a) (11th May, 1940).

nineteen-thirties constituted a period of study and preparation, for the future Pacific War, rather than a time of domestic agitation —although this was not neglected. Thus, in the years between the outbreak of the China Incident and the attack on Pearl Harbour Okawa Shumei concentrated most of his energies on the work of the Showa Foreign Language Institute and of the East Asia Economic Research Institute. The latter, founded and sponsored by the South Manchurian Railway Company, had long been subjected to Okawa's influence. Indeed he had become its chief director in 1931. The Showa Foreign Language Institute, on the other hand, was founded by Okawa after his release from prison and was sponsored by the Foreign Ministry. Nominally it was a school for teaching English, French, Urdu, Malay, Siamese and other languages. In reality it was primarily an intelligence training centre. Students were admitted for a two-year course, which included instruction in the history and economic geography of South East Asia and the South Pacific. Many graduates were to be found in consular and commercial posts abroad.

Okawa, by reason of his past connection with the S.M.R. East Asia Research Institute, was well equipped for these duties. With the *Tosei-ha* in power and with the expansion of the China Incident he could look forward hopefully to the coming struggle to establish Japanese control of Asia and the South Seas. For him, as for many other civilian nationalists, the days of violent conspiracy and agitation had largely given way to a period of constructive work under the shadow of powerful official support.

iii

It was in 1940 that the political parties in the Diet—so long the target of nationalist abuse—confirmed their own impotence by going into voluntary liquidation. The process began during the summer, when Prince Konoye gave up the Presidency of the Privy Council in order to organise and lead a mass party, to be devoted to the establishment of a new political structure. This was an aim long desired by the army. It will be recalled that in the spring of 1937 General Hayashi, as Premier, hoped that a new party would be formed under the leadership of Konoye.

There is little doubt that it was Konoye's intention to launch the New Structure movement as a private individual, and not to form a government until the venture was satisfactorily developed. His high prestige gave the idea, from the start, an appeal to members of the political parties; and when, on 17th July, he was called upon to form a cabinet the importance of his new position lent added weight to his standing as leader of the New Structure movement.

The last party to disband itself was the Minseito, which voted for its own demise on 15th August. Two months later—on 12th October—the new party, the "Imperial Rule Assistance Association" (*Taisei Yokusankai*), was inaugurated.

According to Konoye, the aims of the *Yokusankai* were the achievement of harmony between the Supreme Command and the civil administration, at all levels, and the promotion of better mutual understanding between government and people. Konoye declared that the *Yokusankai* was not a political party—it represented all the people rather than any particular interests or points of view—and that, nevertheless, it should not become a totalitarian organisation.

But from the beginning there were many signs that the New Structure movement—of which the *Yokusankai* was the centre—tended to promote a totalitarian outlook.[1] During the last months of 1940 Konoye lost control of the *Yokusankai*, and the organisation appeared to be dominated by the influence of such persons as Hashimoto, Nakano Seigo and Kamei Kanichiro. There was much talk of a "New Economic Structure", of the extermination of "commercialism and the system of individual profit".[2] Such economic ideas, derived from the doctrines of Takabatake and Kita Ikki, were much stimulated by those practised in Nazi Germany. However, they soon provoked a strong reaction from conservative politicians and businessmen; and the

---

[1] Fleisher (*op. cit.*, pp. 86–7) gives some interesting examples of this trend. There was, for instance, the recommendation that civilians should wear a national uniform "to conserve material and promote increasing interest in national defence projects". *Ibid.*

[2] The phrase was Hashimoto's. *Vide* Otto Tolischus, *Tokyo Record* (London, Hamish Hamilton, 1943), p. 65.

Yokusankai became the object of criticism in the Diet. The division of opinion, between conservative and radical nationalists, was, fundamentally, the same as that which had split many associations—and indeed the army itself—into two broad factions.

Nevertheless, early in 1941 Konoye, by a series of astute manœuvres, succeeded in reasserting control of the *Yokusankai*. The appointment of Hiranuma as Home Minister in December, 1940, was of some help to Konoye in these moves. For Hiranuma, who enjoyed great prestige among nationalists as a whole, was of course decidedly conservative, and he was a resolute opponent of any political and economic ideas not strictly in accordance with his own insular concept of *Nihon Shugi*.

In February and March, 1941, Konoye secured the resignations of Count Arima, Director-General of the *Yokusankai*, and of all officials holding positions of authority in the governing body of the organisation. In the new appointments that were made Hashimoto and other noted extreme nationalists were excluded—with the important exception of Admiral Suetsugu. The Policy, Planning and Diet Bureaux—through them the national socialists of the *Yokusankai* had hoped to bring pressure to bear on the cabinet—were abolished. On the other hand, the East Asia Section was made an independent bureau, under Nagai Ryutaro. This department of the *Yokusankai* was less concerned with matters of internal economic and political reform than with propaganda and research regarding Japanese expansion in Asia. Hence it could be enlarged with safety; indeed its purpose was to effect a merger of all societies in Japan interested in Asiatic affairs, and to maintain contact with similar bodies in China and Manchukuo (such as the Concordia Society). A further reform carried out by the government was to place the provincial branches of the *Yokusankai* under the prefectural governors. This, in fact, put the organisation as a whole under the supervision of Hiranuma and the Home Ministry.

The effect of these changes was to reassure conservatives that no threat to the Constitution was implied by the *Yokusankai*, and to satisfy the business world that there was to be no undermining of the fundamental rights of private property.

At the same time changes were made in the composition of the cabinet; and these underlined the action that Konoye had taken with regard to the *Yokusankai*. Hoshino, President of the Planning Board and known to be an advocate of the "New Economic Structure", was replaced by Lieutenant-General Suzuki Teiichi. To save Hoshino's face his chief opponent in the cabinet—Kobayashi Ichizo, the Minister of Commerce and Industry—gave way to Vice-Admiral Toyoda. Ogura Masatsune, a leading figure in the Sumitomo concern and a close friend of Hiranuma, was made Minister without Portfolio. Ogura was a pronounced nationalist, of the conservative school. His appointment was popular with big business, and was regarded as a further indication that the capitalist system was not to be attacked by the *Yokusankai*.

In an address to a conference of prefectural governors, at the beginning of April, 1941, Konoye said:

> The underlying spirit of the New Structure must always be the Japanese spirit. Indiscriminate acceptance of foreign ideologies in adopting forms of economic control from abroad must be rigidly guarded against.

Having failed to gain a permanent influence over the *Yokusankai* the radical nationalists lost the chance of controlling the single mass party that might have been transformed into something resembling the totalitarian organisations of Germany and Italy. The New Structure movement, it has been said, "was finally swallowed completely in the hegemony of the officials".[1]

This indeed was the grave of the nationalist associations. Although they continued, in many cases, their independent existence, their influence, as separate bodies, was lost.

During the Pacific War ultra-nationalist condemnation of the *Yokusankai* was summed up by Akao Bin, the veteran leader of the *Kenkokukai*, in a speech in the Diet. He declared:

> When I look at the present ideological composition of the *Yokusankai* I find liberals who want to uphold the "status quo", and many national socialists. There are *Nihon Shugi* men; there are revolutionary *Nihon Shugi* men—and there are a good many opportunists. Where will we get with such a confused guiding spirit? You

---

[1] Maruyama, *Nippon Fasshiʒmu, op. cit.,* p. 170.

have got a great band together, but the real body of *Nihon Shugi*, such as we had in the past, is gone, and you are trying to run a spiritual movement by gathering a lot of opportunists and bureaucrats together, trying to run it all with government money, and that is why the spirit has gone out of it.[1]

This was the voice of radicalism protesting against the authoritarianism of Tojo, the apotheosis of the *Tosei-ha*. The protest was made in 1943. It could hardly have been made publicly earlier in the war, when Japanese military and naval successes were undimmed. The change in the fortunes of the Pacific War, however, spelled the doom of the *Tosei-ha* and, indeed, opened the way for a revival of the *Kodo-ha*.[2] These developments are outside the scope of this study. But there is a certain ironic interest in the fact that popular opposition to the Tojo dictatorship came largely from the civilian nationalist groups that had played such a considerable part in spreading those ideas which had enabled the army, and ultimately General Tojo and his supporters, to gain power.[3]

iv

The reorganisation of the *Yokusankai* in March, 1941, was almost certainly related to the sudden Anglo-Japanese crisis that occurred during February. In January, so the German Ambassador in Tokyo reported to Berlin, Japanese ultra-nationalists—of whom Admiral Suetsugu and Shiratori were the most active— were pressing for an attack on Singapore.[4] At the end of January the Japanese dictated an armistice between the French and Siamese forces, who had been engaged in hostilities since the previous November following the Siamese assault on Cambodia. It may be noted that the head of the Siam-French Indo-China border commission, which was to rectify the frontier in favour of Siam, was that stormy petrel of the October Incident (1931) and Chang-

---

[1] Maruyama, *Nippon Fasshizmu, op. cit.*, p. 172.

[2] *Ibid.* "We come to find the resurgence of the *Kodo-ha* and the fact that the Right wing appear as democrats just because they say they opposed Tojo."

[3] Commenting on this development, Prof. Maruyama remarks: "History has turned full circle". *Ibid.*

[4] Telegram, Ott to Ribbentrop, 31st January, 1941. I.M.T.F.E. Exhibit 562.

kufeng, Cho Isamu—now a major-general and Chief of Staff of
the Japanese army in French Indo-China. The Siamese attack on
French Indo-China had been carried out with the connivance of
the Japanese; indeed it had been apparent during the fighting that
Siamese military activities synchronised with the fluctuations of
Japanese-French Indo-China economic negotiations in Tokyo.[1]

On 7th February the Japanese Ambassador in London,
Shigemitsu, was called to the Foreign Office. The Foreign
Secretary told him that reports from Tokyo suggested that a
crisis was imminent in the Far East. Shigemitsu was asked if
British Far Eastern territories were in danger of being attacked by
Japan.[2] Accordingly Matsuoka sent a series of reassuring tele-
grams to Shigemitsu. "Ambassador Craigie's report of the ap-
proach of a critical point in Far Eastern affairs", said Matsuoka,
"is really a ridiculous fantasy." [3] Again, on the following day,
Matsuoka cabled to the London Embassy:

> Eden seems to be disturbed by reports from Craigie and appar-
> ently presumes that Japanese activity regarding Siam and French
> Indo-China presages military action against England at the same
> time as a German invasion of the United Kingdom. It is difficult to
> know on what grounds Ambassador Craigie based the above alarm-
> ing report to his home government.[4]

Four days later, reporting a conversation with the British
Ambassador, Matsuoka cabled Shigemitsu: "I pointed out to
Craigie that there seemed to be an over-anxiety on the part of
Britain about the orientation of Japan's policy." [5]

At the same time the official spokesman for the Foreign
Ministry, Ishii Ko, stated in a press conference that there were
no grounds for entertaining alarming views on the situation in
East Asia, and he went on to say that Japan was ready to act as
mediator not only in East Asia but anywhere in the world.[6]

[1] A. Roth, *Japan Strikes South* (New York, I.P.R., 1941, p. 91).
[2] I.M.T.F.E. Exhibit 1039. Transcript, pp. 9784–5.
[3] Telegram, Matsuoka to Shigemitsu, 13th February, 1941. I.M.T.F.E. Exhibit 1041. Transcript, p. 9794.
[4] *Ibid.*, 14th February, 1941. Transcript, p. 9801.
[5] *Ibid.*, 18th February, 1941. Transcript, p. 9811.
[6] Ishii's reference to mediation was an indiscretion, being in fact a revelation
of part of a memorandum sent to the British Foreign Secretary through Shigemitsu. Ishii was privately reprimanded by Matsuoka. Grew, *op. cit.*, p. 322.

These disclaimers should be viewed in the light of various developments in progress during this period. For example, on 10th February naval air service ground staff were landed from a cruiser at Saigon in order to set up headquarters at the aerodrome; and on the same day Matsuoka, when informing the German Ambassador of his acceptance of Ribbentrop's invitation to visit Berlin, declared that among the topics he wished to discuss with the German government was the matter of a "preventive attack on Singapore".[1] And it was later in the same month, of February, that Oshima—once again Ambassador in Berlin—told Ribbentrop that preparations for an attack on Singapore would be ready by the end of May, and that Konoye and Matsuoka were both in favour of this project.[2] There was indeed considerable German pressure for early Japanese armed action against Great Britain.[3]

Nevertheless the Japanese government as a whole was clearly not in agreement on the matter. It may well be doubted whether Oshima had real grounds for telling Ribbentrop that Konoye favoured the proposed attack. On the contrary, there is every indication that Konoye, in preparation for talks with the United States, was taking steps to moderate the agitation for a further southward advance. The reorganisation of the *Yokusankai* was a measure towards this end.

When Matsuoka saw Hitler in Berlin at the end of March he stated that in general he agreed fully that the moment had come for Japan to enter the war against England.

> But [said Matsuoka] there are in Japan, as in other countries, certain intellectual circles which can be kept in check only by a strong man. This is the type which, though it would like to have the cubs of the tigress, is not prepared to go into the cave and snatch them from their mother.[4]

[1] Telegram, Ott to Ribbentrop, 10th February, 1941. I.M.T.F.E. Exhibit 569. Transcript, p. 6453.

[2] Memorandum by Ribbentrop, 27th February, 1941. I.M.T.F.E. Exhibit 571. Transcript, p. 6463.

[3] For example, on 27th February Ribbentrop cabled Ott: "I ask you to work with all the means at your command for Japan to seize Singapore by surprise as soon as possible." I.M.T.F.E. Exhibit 572. Transcript, p. 6468.

[4] Minutes of a conference between Hitler and Matsuoka (in the presence of Ribbentrop, Ott and Oshima), 27th March, 1941. I.M.T.F.E. Exhibit 577. Transcript, pp. 6486–96.

He remarked that it was regrettable that Japan could not yet suppress these "intellectual circles", for "some of these people indeed are in influential positions".[1] But he told Hitler that, none the less, Japan would act decisively, otherwise she would lose a chance that might not recur for a thousand years. It was only a matter of time before Japan attacked Singapore. Matsuoka said that he thought the assault should be made as soon as possible, but he pointed out that he did not govern Japan; he had to convert the rulers of the country to his opinion. Therefore he could promise nothing, except that on his return to Tokyo he would press for the course of action he desired. Matsuoka asked Hitler, as a matter of the utmost importance, to keep his statements secret. Otherwise members of the cabinet in Tokyo who differed from him would "turn pale" and try to force him out of office. He also informed Hitler that he had frequently and purposely created an impression of adopting a pro-British or pro-American attitude. But this was done, of course, to deceive his enemies.[2]

It is apparent, then, that Matsuoka's disclaimers to the British Ambassador, and to the British government through Shigemitsu, were insincere.[3] Yet they represented the views of at least some members of the cabinet—those who feared to "enter the cave and

[1] *Ibid.*

[2] *Ibid.* For a fuller discussion of Matsuoka's position in the Berlin conversations *vide* F. C. Jones, *Japan's New Orders, op. cit.,* pp. 252–5.

[3] Matsuoka told Ribbentrop that he was doing everything possible to reassure England on the question of Singapore, and that he was behaving as though Japan had no intentions at all regarding Singapore. But Germany—so Matsuoka emphasised—must not be deceived by his apparent friendship with the British. He assumed this attitude not only to lull the British into a false sense of security, but also in order to fool pro-British and pro-American elements in Japan. A sudden attack on Singapore would unite the entire Japanese nation immediately. Matsuoka told Ribbentrop that he proposed to raise the question of a Japanese-Russian Non-Aggression Pact when in Moscow on his way home. (This would be a protection for Japan's northern flank during operations against British possessions in S.E. Asia. Earlier in the conversation Ribbentrop promised Matsuoka that Germany would strike at Russia immediately if the latter were to attack Japan when she was engaged against Singapore.) Report of Conversation, Ribbentrop-Matsuoka, Berlin, 29th March, 1941. I.M.T.F.E. Exhibit 580. Transcript, pp. 6522–8. It may be noted that in January, 1941, the Japanese took aerial photographs of the Kota Bahru area (the scene of the first Japanese landings in Malaya, December, 1941) and that Japanese occupation currency for the Philippines, Malaya and Dutch East Indies was authorised at the end of January, 1941 by the Ministry of Finance (Transcript, pp. 9257 and 9287).

snatch the cubs from their mother". Among them was Konoye.

The remaining six months of Konoye's Premiership were devoted to the vain task of seeking some settlement with the United States—and so with England—while simultaneously reassuring the *Tosei-ha* that the army's gains on the Asiatic continent since 1937 would not be jeopardised. Even the occupation of bases in Southern Indo-China in July may be interpreted as part of Konoye's policy to divert and appease the restless army, which was eager for action following the initial successes of the German Army in Russia. Indeed the German attack on Russia—which Matsuoka, despite a fortnight's advance warning from Oshima, had regarded as an improbable contingency—was almost certain to cause some action by the Japanese Army.[1] There were some who wanted to attack both Russia and the European colonies in South-East Asia. Matsuoka himself seems to have shared this view.[2] And Germany, of course, was very eager to have Japan engage Russia from the rear.[3]

However, Konoye and a majority of the cabinet were opposed to any measures, at this stage, beyond the occupation of bases in Southern Indo-China.[4]

[1] Kido's Diary, 6th June, 1941; "Konoye telephoned to say that Ambassador Oshima had an interview with Hitler at Berchtesgaden and that Germany had at last decided to attack Russia." I.M.T.F.E. Exhibit 1084. Transcript, p. 9979. But Matsuoka told Kido that he thought there was "a 60% possibility of agreement" between Germany and Russia. *Ibid.*, p. 9980.

Kato Masuo, a press correspondent in Washington in 1941, relates that Col. Iwakuro, who was temporarily attached to Nomura's staff, told him that the German-Russian war was "certain to cause some action" by the army. Kato, *The Lost War*, *op cit.*, p. 30. It will be recalled that Iwakuro was one of the most influential younger officers of the General Staff and that he was particularly active, with Kagesa, in working for a full alliance with Germany in 1939. Iwakuro was called back to Japan at the end of July; soon afterwards he was posted to French Indo-China.

[2] This caused a clash of opinion between himself and Konoye. Matsuoka must have urged his point of view on the Emperor also. For after granting Matsuoka an audience on 22nd June, the Emperor informed Kido that "the Foreign Minister's policy would mean Japan's positive advance in both the northern and southern regions", and that it was very doubtful whether this policy was appropriate to Japan's national strength. Kido's Diary, 22nd June, 1941. I.M.T.F.E. Exhibit 1093. Transcript, p. 10022.

[3] Ribbentrop cabled Ott on 28th June, urging an immediate Japanese attack on Russia. I.M.T.F.E. Exhibit 1096. Transcript, pp. 10031–4.

[4] Furthermore, nationalist opinion was on the whole chary of the idea of Japanese action against Russia. "Noted nationalists, who always work closely together with the Embassy, have held various confidential conversations, in

V

The decision to move into Southern Indo-China was agreed upon at a Liaison Conference on 25th June.[1] It was officially ratified at an Imperial Conference, on 2nd July, of the Prime Minister and thirteen military and civilian leaders in the presence of the Emperor.[2] At this Conference it was further agreed that there would be no intervention in the German-Russian war, unless Russia was clearly in the process of suffering defeat.[3] It was also decided that Japan should be ready to fight England and the United States.[4]

However, Konoye was hopeful that he would be able to reach a settlement with the United States. To this end the removal of Matsuoka from the Foreign Ministry was obviously desirable. Kido advised Konoye to insist on Matsuoka's resignation; but Konoye thought this would be unwise, for in such an event Matsuoka and his friends would say that the resignation had been caused by American pressure on the government.[5] Konoye, therefore, resorted to the device of having the whole cabinet

which caution towards Russia and determined action in the south have been advocated." Telegram, Ott to Ribbentrop, 28th June, 1941. I.M.T.F.E. Exhibit 1097. Transcript, p. 10035.

[1] I.M.T.F.E. Exhibit 1306. Transcript, p. 11753. The Premier and nine others were present at this Conference. They were Tojo, Oikawa (Navy Minister), Matsuoka, Hiranuma, Gen. Sugiyama (who had succeeded Kanin as Chief of the Army General Staff), Admiral Nagano (successor to Fushimi as Chief of the Naval General Staff), Maj.-Gen. Muto (Chief of the Military Affairs Bureau), Rear-Admiral Oka (Chief of the Naval Affairs Bureau) and Tomita (Chief Cabinet Secretary).

[2] Imperial Conferences (*gozen kaigi*) were only held on rare occasions, of grave national importance. All those present at the Liaison Conference of 25th June, except Muto, attended the Imperial Conference on 2nd July. In addition the Finance Minister (Kawada), the President of the Planning Board (Lt.-Gen. Suzuki Teiichi), the President of the Privy Council (Hara) and the Vice-Chiefs of Staff (Lt.-Gen. Tsukada and Vice-Admiral Kondo) were present at this Conference.

[3] But it was resolved, in any case, that Japan should "secretly prepare arms against the Soviet Union". I.M.T.F.E. Exhibit 588. Transcript, p. 10147.

[4] "For the sake of self-preservation and self-defence Japan will continue the necessary diplomatic negotiations with relevant nations in the Southern regions. . . . For this purpose we shall make preparations for a war with Britain and the United States." *Ibid.*

[5] Kido's Diary, 15th July, 1941. I.M.T.F.E. Exhibit 1115. Transcript, p. 10163.

resign. He was then formally recommended as the new Prime Minister at a meeting of the Lord Keeper of the Privy Seal, the President of the Privy Council, and the ex-Premiers on 17th July.

Matsuoka, of course, had no office in the third Konoye Cabinet, his successor as Foreign Minister being Admiral Toyoda Teijiro. But any benefit that Konoye might have obtained from the disappearance of Matsuoka was offset by the sharp effect produced on American opinion by the Japanese occupation of the bases in Southern Indo-China towards the end of July. This was followed immediately by President Roosevelt's executive order freezing Japanese assets in the United States.[1]

Yet it must be admitted that the fundamental obstacle to a Japanese-American accord was the intransigence of the *Tosei-ha*, epitomised by Tojo, the Minister of War. The army was not prepared to make any real concessions to the United States, except the promise of withdrawal from Indo-China once the China Incident had been settled.

The navy, however, viewed the prospect of a struggle with the United States with realistic caution. At the end of July, in response to a request from the Emperor, Admiral Nagano, Chief of the Naval General Staff, submitted a report to the Throne on the question of Japanese-American relations. The report occasioned the Emperor a good deal of anxiety; for it showed that Nagano was extremely pessimistic regarding any settlement with America so long as Japan adhered to the Tripartite Pact, that in the event of war against America Japan's supplies of oil would last for only eighteen months, and that—so far from winning a sweeping victory as in the Russo-Japanese War—it was doubtful whether Japan could win a war fought against the United States.[2]

Much disturbed, the Emperor asked Kido for his views. Kido replied that Nagano's opinions were perhaps over simplified. He declared that it was questionable whether American confidence in Japan would be deepened by a Japanese abrogation of the

---

[1] Grew (*op. cit.*, p. 355) expresses the opinion that the Japanese never anticipated such a reaction on America's part. "In my personal opinion Admiral Toyoda shared the apparent belief of most Japanese officials that the U.S. would not resort to measures of retaliation; hence the action of the United States in freezing Japanese assets in retaliation for the Japanese move into Indo-China caught them unawares." *Ibid.*

[2] Kido's Diary, 31st July, 1941. I.M.T.F.E. Exhibit 1125.

Tripartite Pact, since the United States showed great respect for international treaties.[1]

Nevertheless, Kido perceived the wisdom of postponing Japan's southward advance, perhaps for a decade, until the balance of power *vis-à-vis* the United States had been adjusted more in Japan's favour. At the beginning of August he had an important conversation with Konoye. In a full and candid expression of his views, Kido declared that if the estimates of the oil supply situation were correct a Japanese war against the United States was hopeless. He continued:

> Despite external differences in the situation, we might be compelled to exercise the same self-restraint as we did after our victory in the Sino-Japanese War in 1895.
> We should be resolved to toil through ten years of hard struggle. Meanwhile we should do everything to restore friendly relations between the United States and Japan; and we must try to secure the materials we need.[2]

It must be stressed that Kido's policy was to postpone, not to halt permanently, Japan's expansion to the south. He told Konoye that the "ultimate objective" was Japan's "advance to the southern regions", and in order to further this aim he recommended a ten-year plan for the establishment of heavy industries and adequate machine tool production, the development of a synthetic oil industry and the expansion of shipping lines.[3]

August and September were months of mounting tension. Those eight weeks saw attempts on the lives of Konoye and Hiranuma,[4] Konoye's secret offer to meet the American President at Honolulu or Alaska, the Imperial Conference setting a time limit to the talks with America, and the final staff exercises at the

---

[1] *Ibid.*, Transcript, p. 10186.

[2] *Ibid.*, 7th August, 1941. I.M.T.F.E. Exhibit 1130. Transcript, pp. 10199–201. Kido repeated his advice—that Japan should build up her strength for ten years, "reculer pour mieux sauter"—to Konoye, at the Palace, on 9th October, Kido's Diary, 9th October, 1941. I.M.T.F.E. Exhibit 1146. Transcript, p. 10241.

[3] *Ibid.*, 7th August (cited).

[4] A gunman fired at Hiranuma, injuring his face on 14th August. An attempt to stab Konoye in his car was made on 18th September.

Naval War College, Tokyo, in preparation for the naval air action against Pearl Harbour.[1]

It must always remain a matter of speculation whether or not the suggested Konoye-Roosevelt meeting would have achieved a genuine settlement, thus saving peace in the Pacific. Yet despite assurances by Konoye, that he could guarantee to ensure the army's compliance with the terms of a settlement reached between himself and the President, it may be regarded, on the whole, as questionable whether the *Tosei-ha* would have submitted to any decision limiting further military activities in Asia.[2] It is certainly difficult to imagine the *Tosei-ha* agreeing to a substantial and permanent withdrawal from China. Furthermore, in spite of the American Ambassador's faith in Konoye's sincerity, the Japanese were prepared, naturally enough, to deceive the Americans in the execution of the terms—such as an evacuation of China—which might have been agreed upon at a Konoye-Roosevelt meeting. This will be illustrated in succeeding paragraphs, describing the circumstances leading up to Konoye's resignation. Nevertheless the venture was, perhaps, worth at least a trial.[3]

[1] A.T.I.S. Research Report No. 131, "Japan's Decision to Fight". I.M.T.F.E. Exhibit 809. Transcript, p. 9255. The Report refers to the exercises as "war games", and we may assume that they were manœuvres on paper and with models. They lasted from the 2nd to 13th September and were attended by the heads of the service. Operations against Malaya, Burma, the Philippines, Dutch East Indies, Solomons and Central Pacific Islands (including Hawaii) were studied in addition to problems relating to the proposed action against Pearl Harbour. Practical exercises, with torpedo-carrying aircraft flying in to attack ships in an enclosed anchorage, had been started in July, at Kagoshima.

[2] Mr. Grew's opinion at the time—as conveyed in a dispatch to Washington on 29th September—was that the proposed meeting between Konoye and the President stood some chance of success. He warned the State Department that it would be unsound to insist on clear-cut, specific commitments from Japan during the preliminary talks. He reported that Konoye had promised that in direct talks with Roosevelt he would be able to offer assurances satisfactory to the United States. Grew, *op. cit.*, p. 381.

In a private talk with Grew on the evening of 6th September, Konoye declared that he had the full support of the responsible chiefs of the armed services for his proposed mission to meet Roosevelt. *Ibid.*, p. 369.

[3] This is the view of M. Guillain, the well-informed Havas correspondent in Tokyo at the time. "One thing is certain; if there was a political flaw in the perfectly right attitude of the President it was here. Of course Washington could cite ten years of Japanese history to support the American view. They had been deceived before by the Japanese army." Guillain, *Le Peuple Japonais et La Guerre* (cited), p. 31. *Vide*, also, F. C. Jones, *Japan's New Order*, (*op. cit.*), pp. 457–60.

The Imperial Conference of 6th September decided that if the negotiations with the United States showed no signs of reaching a satisfactory conclusion by the beginning of October, Japan would "immediately determine to wage war against the United States and Britain and the Netherlands".[1]

When October came, with prospects of an understanding with America no nearer, an inevitable crisis developed in the relations between those, headed by Konoye, who wanted to continue the search for a Japanese-American settlement and the army—in particular the *Tosei-ha*, represented by Tojo and Sugiyama—which now felt that no further results could be obtained by the methods of diplomacy and that the time had come for the use of armed action.

Konoye's own account of the factors leading to his resignation on 16th October casts some light on this crisis.[2] At the beginning of October the army made it clear to Konoye that 15th October must be regarded as the latest time limit for negotiations with the United States. Accordingly Konoye asked the War, Navy, and Foreign Ministers, together with Lieutenant-General Suzuki Teiichi (President of the Planning Board) to come to his house on 12th October for what he called "a final conference". On the day before the conference Rear-Admiral Oka, Chief of the Naval Affairs Bureau, visited Konoye and told him that, with the exception of the Naval General Staff, "the brains of the navy" did not want a Japanese-American war. But the navy was not prepared to say so openly. The Navy Minister intended to leave the decision in the hands of the Premier.

At the conference on 12th October Konoye opened the proceedings by saying: "At last we have come to the stage where we must decide whether it is to be war or peace. Let us first study whether there is any hope for a successful conclusion of the diplomatic negotiations."[3]

[1] Those who were present at the Imperial Conference of 2nd July (with the exception of Hiranuma, Matsuoka, Kawada and Vice-Admiral Kondo) attended this Conference. New members, in addition to Toyoda (Foreign Minister), were Tanabe (Home Minister), Ogura (Finance Minister), Vice-Admiral Ito (Vice-Chief of the Naval General Staff) and Muto Akira (Director of the Military Affairs Bureau). I.M.T.F.E. Exhibit 588 (Resolutions adopted at the Imperial Conference, 6th September, 1941—a Foreign Ministry document). Transcript, pp. 10217–18.

[2] I.M.T.F.E. Exhibit 1148. Transcript, pp. 10251–72.   [3] *Ibid.*, p. 10253.

Tojo declared that there was absolutely no hope of the negotiations reaching a successful conclusion; but Oikawa countered by saying that this question should be decided by the Premier and the Foreign Minister. The navy, he said, would abide by that decision. The navy's view was that if there was any hope of success the negotiations in Washington should be continued. Tojo retorted that the matter could not be left solely in the Premier's hands. He then asked Toyoda, the Foreign Minister, if he felt confident of success in the diplomatic negotiations. Toyoda replied that the question of Japanese troops in China was the outstanding obstacle in the way of reaching an agreement with the United States. Tojo thereupon emphatically declared that Japan could not yield on the question of a withdrawal of troops. To which Konoye made the following rejoinder:

> If the Minister of War insists, as he does, it is not a question of whether there is any hope for the successful conclusion of diplomatic negotiations. There definitely is no hope. As for the Foreign Minister, he could consider it from the standpoint of the general situation and yield more. Only then can it be said that there is hope of a successful outcome of the negotiations. The Navy Minister is clamouring for a decision by the Premier, but I cannot decide on war at this time. Since I believe there is still hope of success I cannot help but adopt the Foreign Minister's opinion, if I must decide on one or the other.[1]

Tojo remarked that it was too early for the Premier to give a decision; and he asked Konoye to reconsider the matter. On this indecisive note the conference ended.

Next day, 13th October, Konoye asked Toyoda to visit him. The latter made it evident that the only possibility of reaching an agreement with America was by a Japanese readiness to evacuate the troops from China. So on 14th October Konoye called Tojo for a private conference. In the course of a long argument, designed to persuade Tojo to give way, Konoye said:

> I wonder if we should not make up our minds to readjust Japanese-U.S. relations, the future of which is very risky. . . . With the China Incident still unsettled I wonder if we should extend our

[1] I.M.T.F.E. Exhibit 1148. Transcript, p. 10256.

hands further towards the south. . . . The consensus of opinion, practically, is that if the arrow should leave the bow it may take five or ten years.[1]

Tojo, nevertheless, was adamant. He asserted that a withdrawal of troops from China was out of the question.

I cannot yield to this [he said]. America's real intention is to control the Far East. Therefore one concession by Japan would lead to another, and so on. . . . I must say that the Premier's view is too pessimistic.[2]

Later that day there was a meeting of the cabinet, at which Tojo—in Konoye's words—"was the absolute master of the situation, with no-one among the cabinet members voicing approval or disapproval".[3]

Throughout these critical discussions Konoye, in his efforts to induce Tojo to change his mind, stressed that it would be quite possible to pretend to give way to America on the question of the military evacuation of China, and yet at the same time to retain the reality of control. In other words, he seems to have had in mind a token withdrawal, which would allow a number of Japanese troops to be retained in China—perhaps by agreement between the Chinese government and the Japanese.[4] A certain deception, at the expense of the United States, is implied by this policy. In refusing to entertain the idea Tojo showed himself to be stupid as well as obstinate.

If at this juncture the navy had stated positively that it was not in favour of a war with the United States, the army might have agreed to some compromise on the question of the evacuation of China.[5] But the navy continued to shift the responsibility onto the shoulders of Konoye.[6]

On the night of 14th October Lieutenant-General Suzuki

---

[1] I.M.T.F.E. Transcript, pp. 10258-9.
[2] *Ibid.*, p. 10262.　　　　[3] *Ibid.*
[4] For example, Konoye said to Tojo at their talk on 14th October: "Regarding the question of the occupation [of China]—if we were to yield on our pretence [i.e. pretend to give way] and take the reality, I believe there is still hope in the negotiations." I.M.T.F.E. Exhibit 1148. Transcript, p. 10258.
[5] Konoye's account states that the army was prepared to enforce discipline within its own ranks if the navy firmly declared that a war with America could not be envisaged. *Ibid.*, p. 10263.　　　　[6] *Ibid.*

visited Konoye, bringing with him a message from Tojo. The latter stated that he had come to the conclusion that the only way to break the deadlock of opinion was to rescind the decision reached at the Imperial Conference of 6th September; namely the time limit set to the negotiations in Washington. In order to make a fresh start the cabinet ought to resign. "Then," said Tojo, "if the new men should decide we are not to fight, that may appear to be the end of it; but the army is straining at the leash..."[1]

He ended his message by saying that he favoured Prince Higashi-Kuni as the new Prime Minister.

On the following day, 15th October, Konoye went to the Palace. He told the Emperor:

> The navy does not want war, but cannot say so in view of the decision of the Imperial Conference. . . . I, as Prime Minister, am thus all the more in disagreement with the idea of war. I do think General Tojo's plan, to ask Prince Higashi-Kuni to take over, is a means of breaking the deadlock.[2]

To which the Emperor replied:

> I would like to maintain peace to the very end. Since the appearance of an Imperial prince would make him appear to be my personal representative it would be bad for an Imperial prince to take over and decide on war. If peace should be decided upon will the army submit to regulations?[3]

This, of course, was the supreme question, at the heart of the problem facing Japan's rulers—Emperor, civilian ministers, and *Tosei-ha* alike. Konoye, accordingly, at once asked Tojo, through Suzuki, if the army would submit to regulations, "in the event that peace were to be decided upon—a matter of concern to the Emperor".[4]

Tojo's reply was that he was unable to guarantee that the army would submit; he added that in such circumstances nobody else but an Imperial prince "would be able to suppress the army".[5]

That night Konoye visited Prince Higashi-Kuni and asked him to accept the responsibility of becoming Prime Minister. Higashi-

[1] I.M.T.F.E. Transcript, p. 10265.　　　　　　[2] *Ibid.*, p. 10266.
[3] *Ibid.*, p. 10267.　　　　[4] *Ibid.*　　　[5] *Ibid.*, p. 10269.

Kuni declined to give a positive answer, but he expressed doubts about his ability to keep the army under control.[1]

On the next day, 16th October, Konoye handed in the resignation of his cabinet to the Emperor. He learned from Kido that the Emperor had decided to summon both Tojo and Oikawa to the Palace at the same time and to offer the Premiership to one of them, telling the other to co-operate. Kido himself favoured Oikawa. But Konoye said that he felt the appointment should be given to "the strongest side"—the army. If the Tojo cabinet carried on the negotiations in Washington the American government would be both surprised and relieved, and thus a more favourable atmosphere would be created.[2]

The idea of a Higashi-Kuni cabinet had been strongly resisted by Kido, on the general principle that it was unwise to have a member of the Imperial Family participating in politics. On 16th October he told both Suzuki Teiichi and Tojo that the proposal could not be adopted.[3]

On 17th October the senior statesmen—the ex-Premiers—met at the Palace to decide formally on the question of Konoye's successor. Among the ex-Premiers was the ninety-two-year-old Count Kiyoura.[4] Kido and Hara, President of the Privy Council, were also present. Kido presided. In his account of this gathering he wrote:

> Except for a recommendation of Ugaki by Wakatsuki, and the suggestion of a cabinet under a member of the Imperial Family, by General Hayashi, nobody had a definite opinion. I stressed the importance of the revision of the decisions taken at the Imperial Conference of 6th September and the importance of army-navy unity. I suggested a Tojo cabinet, with Tojo as Prime Minister and War Minister, even though he is on active duty. There was no objection to my proposal—Hirota, Abe and Hara giving me positive approval.[5]

[1] I.M.T.F.E. Transcript, p. 10269.   [2] *Ibid.*, p. 10271.
[3] Kido's Diary, 16th October, 1941. I.M.T.F.E. Exhibit 1151. Transcript, pp. 10282–3.   [4] Prime Minister, January–June, 1924.
[5] Kido's Diary, 17th October, 1941. I.M.T.F.E. Exhibit 1154. Transcript, pp. 10291–2. The initiative taken by Kido at this meeting is apparent. Evidently it was recognised by the Emperor. For three days later Kido noted: "I received gracious words from His Majesty for my efforts in connection with the cabinet change." *Ibid.*, 20th October, 1941. Exhibit 1156. Transcript, p. 10295.

That afternoon Tojo was received in audience at the Palace and was appointed Premier.

Within a few days Nomura, in Washington, cabled Togo Shigenori, the new Foreign Minister, saying that he felt he ought to resign.

> I am sure that I too should go out with the former cabinet [cabled Nomura]. I know that for some time the Secretary of State has known how sincere I was, yet knew how little influence I have in Tokyo. I hear the President also holds the same opinion. . . . I do not want to continue this hypocritical existence, deceiving other people. Please do not think I am trying to flee from the field of battle, but as a man of honour this is the only way that is open for me to tread.[1]

However, this plea was disregarded. But it was decided that Nomura should be fortified by the assistance of Kurusu Saburo —former Ambassador in Berlin—as special envoy.

Events now moved with gathering momentum to the climax of war. At the beginning of November the American Ambassador noted in his diary that Japan, to render herself invulnerable to foreign economic pressure, might take drastic action which would amount to national *hara-kiri*.[2] And it was on 3rd November that Admiral Nagano, Chief of the Naval General Staff, officially approved the decision to attack Pearl Harbour.[3]

On 5th November a further Imperial Conference was held.[4] At this Conference the time limit to the American negotiations was advanced to 25th November; and it was decided that hostilities must be started as soon as possible after that date, provided no settlement with the United States had been reached in the meantime. At the end of the month there was a meeting of the ex-Premiers in the presence of the Emperor. Like a ghost of liberalism from the past, the voice of Wakatsuki was raised in cautious protest against nationalist ambitions.

---

[1] Telegram, Nomura to Togo, 22nd October, 1941. I.M.T.F.E. Exhibit 1161.
[2] Grew, *op. cit.*, p. 406.
[3] A.T.I.S. Research Report No. 131 (cited). I.M.T.F.E. Exhibit 809. Transcript, p. 10317.
[4] I.M.T.F.E. Exhibit 1169. Transcript, pp. 10333–47. The attendance was almost the same as that on 6th September (with the exceptions caused by the change of cabinet).

If it is necessary for the preservation and self-defence of the Empire [said Wakatsuki], we must rise to arms, even though the country be reduced to ashes and though we can foresee defeat. But it is dangerous indeed to execute state policy or to make use of the national strength to achieve such ideals as the "Establishment of the Greater East Asia Co-Prosperity Sphere" or the "Stabilising of power in East Asia". I pray that Your Majesty will give careful consideration to this point.[1]

Almost at the last moment, being disturbed by a report from his brother, Prince Takamatsu (a naval officer), that the navy wanted to avoid war, the Emperor summoned the Navy Minister and the Chief of the Naval General Staff and asked them if they were really confident of success. They assured the Emperor that they were.[2] This was on 30th November. The die had been cast. The naval task force was already on its way from the Kuriles to its appointed objective at Hawaii.[3]

Thus the nationalist movement ran its course to the end. This, indeed, might have been war with Russia—as desired by the leaders of the *Kodo-ha*, when they were in power. The eventual outcome, however, would have been the same—namely war with either Russia or the United States, or with both; in each event a consummation fatal to Japan.

[1] Kido's Diary, 29th November, 1941. I.M.T.F.E. Exhibit 1196. Transcript, p. 10455.

[2] *Ibid.*, 30th November, 1941. I.M.T.F.E. Exhibit 1198. Transcript, p. 10468.

[3] The task force sailed from the Kuriles on the morning of 26th November. It would have been possible, of course, to recall the ships to Japanese waters at any time before the attack on Pearl Harbour.

An Imperial Conference on 1st December decided upon war with the United States, Great Britain and the Netherlands. Immediately after this Conference Tojo visited Kido to discuss the phrasing of the Imperial Rescript declaring war. Kido's Diary, 1st December, 1941. I.M.T.F.E. Exhibit 1210. Transcript, p. 10523.

13

SOME CONCLUSIONS

HITLER, in *Mein Kampf*, laid down, for all to see, the broad outline of his plans for achieving the conquest of Europe. About Japanese intentions in the same period we have no such brazenly frank and comprehensive document. For it must be remembered that the extremely important and interesting plans for the establishment of the "Co-Prosperity Sphere" were not drafted until after the opening of the war with China in 1937, and possibly not before the summer of 1940.[1] It is true that the Chinese published in 1927 the details of the so-called "Tanaka Memorial", a Japanese "master plan" for Asiatic conquest said to have been laid before the Emperor by Premier Tanaka Giichi in July of that year. This document forecast the order of priorities favoured by the *Tosei-ha*—namely Manchuria first, China second. However, accepting for the sake of the argument the authenticity of the Tanaka Memorial, it proves little beyond the fact that well before 1931 there were Japanese in high places who wanted to gain political and economic control of China as a prelude to further expansion in Asia. This was widely suspected several years earlier, in 1915, for example, when Japan presented China with the Twenty-One Demands. Before 1914 it was not uncommon, so it is said, to find Prussian officers drinking to "Der Tag". Similarly, those who knew Japan before the Pacific War can recall occasions when conviviality loosened tongues to release all manner of extravagant but vaguely phrased predictions of Japan's march to her destiny as the mistress of Asia. But this was part of the climate of the day. If the Tanaka Memorial existed and if it was in fact a blueprint, rather than a general statement of national aspirations, then it came near to being drastically modified, if not discarded, by the *Kodo-ha* during Araki's period of power in 1932 and 1933.

Thus it would be a distortion of the facts to interpret the

[1] *Vide* pp. 276–7 (*supra*) and Appendix II.

political history of Japan, in the decade between the Manchurian Incident and Pearl Harbour, as the product of a single grand conspiracy. Nevertheless, the plots and "Incidents" that have been discussed in this book conformed very broadly—with the possible exception of the *Ketsumeidan* affair—to the same general design.

Japan, after all, was governed in the inter-War years by a fairly narrow but disunited collective leadership. The disunity of this leadership made it peculiarly susceptible to various pressures from outside. Among these must be included what Japanese authority recognised as the force of public opinion. But to the Japanese bureaucracy "public opinion" meant, of necessity, "patriotic opinion". The force of a religious tradition, revived and greatly invigorated during the nineteenth century, made it extremely difficult for any Japanese, let alone a Japanese holding a high official position in the state, to think in terms beyond those of nationality or of national interests. It was particularly embarrassing, then, for Japanese leaders to be openly hostile to their ultra-nationalist compatriots; for the latter invariably had something to say about the conduct of Japan's external relations. If they had confined themselves to purely internal issues—to programmes of radical economic reform, for example—they might have been ignored or suppressed with some assurance. But in that event they would not have been true nationalists, as the Japanese understand the term. Of course their more ferocious activities sometimes encountered rebuff, suppression or punishment. Tachibana and Inouye Nissho went to gaol; Okawa, too, for a time. Hashimoto was ejected from the army. Kita Ikki and Nishida Zei were shot. But what must be considered significant is the way in which violent nationalism, like some deep-sea cuttle fish, was able to emit a fluid that would stain and darken and, finally, blacken the surrounding waters. The pervasiveness of ultra-nationalist thought during the nineteen-thirties was, perhaps, its most arresting feature.

For this there were several reasons, most of them suggested already in the text of this book—the political immaturity of the Japanese people as a whole, the tradition of a matchless *kokutai*, the acute economic consequences for Japan of the World Depression. But the decisive factor, undoubtedly, was the readiness of the collective leadership to accept as public opinion, and therefore actively to promote, the general ultra-nationalist thesis of an urgently expanding Japan.

Accordingly the most consistently active extreme nationalists could influence, and indeed shape, high policy without holding any position of governmental responsibility. In the furtherance of this influence threats of assassination played their part. But of greater importance was the curious moral pressure that could be exercised, almost unfailingly, by the agitators of the Right wing. The mildest accusation of disloyalty to the *kokutai* seems to have been enough to disturb the self-confidence of a Japanese official or politician at any date between, let us say, the close of 1931 and the beginning of the Pacific War. Moral courage was displayed, it is true, by a few men in public life; and from this honourable category the Emperor himself is not excluded. But devotion to principle, to a rationally thought-out and accepted personal point of view, was a very rare phenomenon. All the more, then, is respect owed to the memory of those, such as Prince Saionji, who remained firm when so many bowed before the storm.

It is worth noting that the emphasis throughout the nationalist movement, with *Nohon Shugi* as a probable exception,[1] was on foreign rather than domestic affairs; although the latter sometimes provided the initial impetus behind particular manifestations of the movement. This was no new development in recent Japanese history. Indeed from the time of Perry's arrival in Yedo Bay in 1853 to the Bikini hydrogen bomb "incident" of 1954 it has been the impact of external events that, time and again, has fascinated the Japanese, sometimes to the exclusion of internal issues. It should not be forgotten that the Japanese started their modern history, and endured its first decades, as the victims of external pressure. This may have produced, in a race of such marked gusto, a neurosis demanding the response of continual assertive counteraction.

Looking back over the ruin and ashes of the Pacific War the majority of the Japanese people are inclined to dismiss the old ultra-nationalists, in or out of uniform, as crazy fools. Which, in a sense, they were. Certainly the public activities since the

[1] pp. 96–100 (*supra*).

Peace Treaty of such perennials as Tachibana and Inouye Nissho have done little to modify this particular interpretation.

Nobody can dare to predict that such insanity will not again infect the body politic of Japan. But if it does, the resistance that can be offered will be more robust and lasting than it was before the Pacific War. There will be at least an even chance of fighting off the disease. More than this cannot be said.

SELECTED BIBLIOGRAPHY

[Works mentioned here but not referred to in the body of the book are marked by an asterisk (*)]

TWO prime sources should be mentioned first, the Transcript and Exhibits of the International Military Tribunal for the Far East (I.M.T.F.E.) and the Saionji-Harada Memoirs. The massive I.M.T.F.E. material is a goldmine for the student of recent Japanese political history. Quite apart from the verbatim record of the Trial itself, the Transcript, there is a vast amount of information contained in the telegrams, letters, affidavits, extracts from unpublished state papers and diaries, that comprise the Exhibits gathered together by the Prosecution and Defence for the purposes of the Trial. This material, of course, has to be handled with some caution. Translations were at times challenged in Court, and several affidavits, reflecting the bias that arises from the need for special pleading, must be treated with reserve. But it is worth noting that the Japanese documents in question were available for examination by three separate teams of translators (Prosecution, Defence, and a third team attached to the Court). When every allowance is made, the I.M.T.F.E. material remains an invaluable source of historical information.

The same can be said of the Harada record, commonly known as the Saionji-Harada Memoirs. Translation here presented serious problems at times, as anyone will agree who has seen the Japanese version, *Saionji Ko to Seikyoku* ("Prince Saionji and the Political Situation"; Tokyo, 1950–2). Nevertheless the work was undertaken with great care. The only cautionary remark to be made on the Memoirs is that their compiler, Baron Harada, from about the year 1938 onwards, began to be less closely in touch than formerly with all the movements of inner politics in Tokyo.

The standard work in Japanese on the modern nationalist movement is possibly Kinoshita Hanji, *Nippon Kokka Shugi Undo Shi* ("A History of the Japanese Nationalist Movement"; Tokyo, 1940). A revised and enlarged edition of this work has appeared since the Pacific War. But perhaps the most interesting Japanese writer on the subject is Maruyama Masao. Of particular value, as a very perceptive analysis, is his contribution, *Nippon Fasshizmu no Shiso to Undo* ("The Movement and Thought of Japanese Fascism"), to a collection of four substantial articles entitled *Sonjo Shiso to Zettai Shugi* (" 'Sonno Joi' Thought and Absolutism"; Tokyo, 1948). Professor Maruyama's essay, "A Study of the Minds of the Rulers of a Militarist Nation", in the magazine *Choryu* (May, 1949), is also of outstanding merit. Of rather less value are the works of Tsukui Tatsui, for example his *Nippon Kokka Shugi Undo Shiron* ("Historical Essays on the Japanese Nationalist Movement"; Tokyo, 1942). An important source, from the ideological point of view, is of course Kita Ikki's famous book, *Nihon Kaizo Hoan Taiko* ("An Outline for the Reconstruction of Japan"; Tokyo, 1924).

For the purposes of this study attention was paid to a Japanese Foreign Ministry paper, *Uyoku Undo no Gensei* ("The Present Situation of the Right-wing Movement"; Tokyo, 1935), and to a War Ministry copy, now in the possession of the National Diet Library, of Muranaka and Isobe, *Shukugun ni kansuru Ikensho* ("Views on the Housecleaning of the Army"). Much use was made of a printed manual (in the Library of Congress) entitled *Shiso Keisatsu Tsuron* ("Introduction to Thought Police"; Tokyo, 1936) by Shigematsu Koei. Some instructive points were also found in Baba Tsunego, *Konoye Naikaku Shiron* ("Historical Essays on the Konoye Cabinets"; Tokyo, 1946); although here it should be remembered that the leading Japanese authority on Prince Konoye is probably Professor Yabe Sadaji, author of *Konoye Fumimaro Den** ("Biography of Konoye Fumimaro"; Tokyo, 1952). However, for a more exhaustive bibliography of Japanese works on the subject of nationalism the specialist is recommended to see Delmer M. Brown, *Nationalism in Japan** (Berkeley and Los Angeles, 1955).

For those who do not read Japanese there are few books, or special articles, dealing specifically with modern Japanese nationalism as such. Tanin and Yohan, *Militarism and Fascism in Japan* (London, 1934) is now a rare book. It abounds in errors of a relatively unimportant kind, in the spelling, for example, of Japanese surnames. There are, also, one or two more serious shortcomings, such as mistakes in interpreting events or in the use of dates. Nevertheless, this work, despite its defects, cannot be neglected; provided that full allowance is made for the fact that its authors were Marxists. This poisons much of their comment, and indeed so affects their style as to make the book difficult to read. A very readable work, on the other hand, is Hugh Byas, *Government by Assassination* (London, 1943). The author, an experienced and extremely well-informed *Times* correspondent in Tokyo before the Pacific War, writes with great verve and understanding of his subject. Mention has already been made, in the previous paragraph, of Delmer Brown's *Nationalism in Japan*. This deals, in a broad but scholarly manner, with the huge subject of nationalism from the earliest historical times up to the days of the Occupation. For the religious elements inherent in the subject the reader is recommended to see D. C. Holtom, *Modern Japan and Shinto Nationalism* (Chicago, 1947), an authoritative work of the highest order. In a related field is J. O. Gauntlett and R. K. Hall, *Kokutai no Hongi* ("Cardinal Principles of the National Entity"; Cambridge, Mass., 1949).

Those who wish to study in greater detail the activities of some of the earlier Japanese nationalist adventurers are advised to read Marius B. Jansen, *The Japanese and Sun Yat-sen* (Cambridge, Mass., 1954). This scholarly account of one little-known aspect of Sino-Japanese relations has much of interest to reveal about such personalities as Toyama Mitsuru and Uchida Ryohei. With this book the author joined the select company of those who can claim to be authorities on various aspects of Meiji Japan. Among these an important place must be given to E. H. Norman, whose standard work, *Japan's Emergence as a Modern State* (New York, 1940), is not likely to be superseded. On the subject of Meiji Japanese nationalism, in its extreme manifestations, Dr. Norman made a substantial contribution with his article, "The Genyosha", in *Pacific Affairs* (Vol. XVII, No. 3) for September, 1944.

Two excellent histories of Japan during the three reigns of the modern period are C. Yanaga, *Japan Since Perry* (New York, 1949) and Hugh Borton, *Japan's Modern Century* (New York, 1955). Both these books, the first in some detail, cover various aspects of the modern nationalist movement, particularly during the decade before Pearl Harbour. For a study of the interplay of

foreign and domestic issues in Japanese political life before the
Pacific War, more especially during the nineteen-twenties, an
indispensable guide is T. Takeuchi, *War and Diplomacy in the
Japanese Empire* (London, 1936). Two books by A. Morgan
Young—*Japan under Taisho "Tenno"* (London, 1928) and *Imperial Japan* (London, 1938)—are worth reading, although they
remain controversial; for the author is by no means a detached
and calm observer of what he describes. His irony gives a bite
to his work, but its total effect may be one of unfairness to his
subject. Morgan Young's books are not documented. But he
knew what he was writing about.

Useful works on the army and its political activities before the
War are K. W. Colegrove, *Militarism in Japan** (Boston, World
Peace Foundation, 1936) and Hillis Lory, *Japan's Military
Masters* (London, 1947).

Among many memoirs relating to the period, 1931–41, the
following are of particular interest; Joseph C. Grew, *Ten Years in
Japan* (London, 1944); Sir Robert Craigie, *Behind the Japanese
Mask* (London, 1946); Wilfred Fleisher, *Volcanic Isle* (London,
1942); F. S. G. Piggott, *Broken Thread* (Aldershot, 1950); and
Otto Tolischus, *Tokyo Record* (London, 1943).

For the political background, especially among the parties in
the Diet, the period is conscientiously dealt with by Robert A.
Scalapino, *Democracy and the Party Movement in Prewar Japan**
(Berkeley and Los Angeles; University of California Press, 1953).
For political manœuvres between 1937 and 1941, notably with
regard to Japanese-German relations, the reader should see
F. C. Jones, *Japan's New Order in East Asia* (Oxford, 1954).
Robert Guillain, *Le Peuple Japonais et La Guerre* (Paris, 1947),
has some penetrating early chapters on the period shortly before
Pearl Harbour. Another book to be recommended, for its first-
hand account of Japanese aggression in North China, is John
Goette's *Japan Fights for Asia* (London, n.d.).

Japanese works, translated into English, dealing with modern
nationalism are regrettably rare. Two works in particular are
available in the English language. These are Y. Hibino, *"Nippon
Shindo Ron"*, or the *National Ideals of the Japanese People* (Cambridge, 1928) and C. Fujisawa, *Japanese and Oriental Political
Philosophy* (Tokyo, 1935). The files of the *Japan Advertiser* and

Japan Times for the years between the two World Wars provide a number of articles dealing, in an uncritical manner, with nationalist ideology. The periodical, *Contemporary Japan*, also contains a certain number of articles on this question.

APPENDIX I

SOME SOCIETIES WITH THEIR LEADING PERSONALITIES

Aikoku Kinroto ("The Patriotic Labour Party")

Amano Tatsuo (Chairman)

Okawa Shumei, Kita Reikichi, Kanokogi Kazunobu (Advisers)

Akagami Ryojo	Mizumori Kamenosuke
Ayakawa Takeharu	Nagano Akira
Fukuda Masataro	Nakatani Takeo
Kaminaga Bunzo	Oguri Keitaro
Kuchida Yasunobu	Tsukui Tatsuo
Maeda Torao	Yabe Shu

Aikoku Seiji Domei ("Patriotic Government League")

Koike Shiro (Chairman)

Igarashi Harutaka, Nakazato Yoshiharu (Advisers)

Fujioka Bunroku	Okawa Kenichi
Fukuhara Jinei	Otsuki Masaaki
Hagiwara Katsujiro	Sasaki Takeo
Imamura Hitoshi	Suyama Atsutaro
Ishibashi Wataru	Yamamoto Kamejiro
Matsushita Hikoichi	Yochi Yutaka
Mori Naoji	

Dai Nippon Seisanto ("The Japan Production Party")

Uchida Ryohei (President)

Toyama Mitsuru (Adviser)

Akamatsu Katsumaro	Inouye Shiro
Domae Sonzaburo	Iwase Kozaburo
Ikeda Hiroshi	Kuzuo Yoshihisa

Matsuda Teisuke
Obata Torataro
Ogata Eizo
Shibayama Mitsuru
Suzuki Zenichi

Tachibana Ryosuke
Tsukui Tatsuo
Yamamoto Senichi
Yawata Hakudo
Yoshida Ekizo

The *Seisanto* organised the *Dai Nippon Seisanto Shokugyo Kumiai Rengokai* ("The Japan Production Party Amalgamation of Trade Unions"). This included:

Osaka Kinzoku Rodosha Kumiai ("Osaka Metalworkers' Union")

Osaka Kagaku Sangyo Rodo Kumiai ("Osaka Chemical Industries' Union")

Osaka Boshoku Sangyo Rodo Kumiai ("Osaka Spinning and Weaving Industries' Union")

Osaka Seizai Jugyoin Kojokai ("Osaka Lumber Workers' Friendly Society")

Jimmukai ("The Jimmu Society")

Okawa Shumei (President)

Hinozuki Suehiro
Imamaki Yoshio
Ishihara Koichiro
Kaneuchi Yoshisuke
Karino Toshi
Kataoka Kisuke
Kawamata Kogi
Kawamoto Daisuke

Baron Kikuchi Takeo
Matsunobu Shigeji
Oishi Shigeru
Sakakibara Bunshiro
Suzuki Kan
Utsunomiya Yoshihisa
Yukitake Sakae

Ketsumeidan ("The League of Blood")

Inouye Akira (Nissho)

Furuuchi Eiji
Hisanuma Goro
Hoshiko Tsuyoshi
Ikebukuro Seihachiro
Kawasaki Nagamitsu

Konuma Tadashi
Kukida Sukehiro
Kurosawa Kanekichi
Kurosawa Taiji
Mori Kenji

Suda Taro
Tagura Toshiyuki
Tanaka Kunio

Terunuma Hatsutaro
Yotsumoto Yoshitaka

Gyochisha ("The Society of Action")

Okawa Shumei (President)

Ayakawa Takeharu
Kaneuchi Yoshisuke
Karino Toshi
Kasagi Yoshiaki
Baron Kikuchi Takeo
Kita Reikichi
Matsunobu Shigeji
Mitsukawa Kametaro

Nakatani Takeo
Nishida Zei
Shimano Saburo
Shimizu Gionosuke
Sugita Seigo
Takamura Takaji
Tsuda Kozo
Yasuoka Masaatsu

Kokuhonsha ("The National Foundations Society")

Baron Hiranuma Kiichiro (President)

Admiral Togo, Marshal Uehara, Admiral Saito Makoto (Advisers)

Gen. Araki Sadao
Araki Torasaburo
Adm. Arima Ryokitsu
Goto Fumio
Hara Yoshimichi
Gen. Hata Shinji
Hiramatsu Ichizo
Honda Kumataro
Ikeda Seishin
Count Kabayama Sukehide
Adm. Kato Kanji
Kato Keizaburo
Kawada Retsu
Kawamura Teishiro
Baron Kikuchi Takeo
Gen. Koiso Kuniaki
Koyama Matsukichi
Gen. Matsui Iwane

Gen. Mazaki Jinsaburo
Maj.-Gen. Nagata Tetsuzan
Obara Tadashi
Visct. Ogasawara Chosei
Ogura Masatsune
Adm. Osumi Mineo
Baron Sato Shosuke
Sawada Ushomaro
Shiono Suehiko
Shirakami Yukichi
Adm. Suetsugu Nobumasa
Sukuri Eiji
Suzuki Kisaburo
Takeuchi Yakiji
Tanabe Harumichi
Gen. Ugaki Issei
Wani Naokichi
Yuki Toyotaro

Kokuryukai ("The Amur River Society"—lit. "The Black Dragon Society")

Uchida Ryohei (Founder and first President)
Kuzuo Yoshihisa (succeeded Uchida as President, 1937)

Akiyama Teisuke
Ebara Motoroku
Fukuda Wagoro
Gondo Shinji
Hayashi Itsuro
Hirayama Shu
Homma Kyusuke
Honjo Kenko
Ikeda Hiroshi
Iogi Ryozo
Ishihara Sekido
Ito Tomoya
Kaji Nagakazu
Kamiizumi Tokuya
Kawabara Shinichiro
Kawashima Naniwa
Kita Reikichi
Kita Terujiro
Kito Koshichiro
Kobata Torataro
Kobayashi Ushisaburo
Koizumi Sakutaro
Komai Kijiro
Kowatari Shin
Kuzuo Tosuke
Masuda Ryozo
Matsuda Yusuke
Minoura Katsundo
Miyazaki Kurushiro
Morikawa Keizaburo
Nagashima Ryuji
Nakanishi Masaki
Nakano Jiro
Nakano Kumataro

Nakata Shinsaburo
Nonaka Katsuaki
Ogawa Heikichi
Okawa Shumei
Oki Teisuke
Omiya Eiji
Osei Yoshikura
Oshikawa Katayoshi
Otake Kanichi
Otani Masao
Otsu Junichiro
Ozaki Kosho
Saichi Iwao
Sakai Rokusuke
Sakatani Yoshiro
Sano Kenkichi
Sasaki Yasujiro
Sato Hajime
Seki Naohiko
Shimomura Umataro
Shirai Jiro
Shirai Shintaro
Soejima Giichi
Suenaga Ichizo
Suenaga Masao
Sugita Teiichi
Suzuki Ichiro
Tachibana Ryosuke
Taga Muneyuki
Takahashi Hidetomi
Takata Sanroku
Takayama Kimimichi
Tanabe Yasunosuke
Tanaka Hiroyuki

Tanaka Sutemi
Tano Katsuji
Terao Tei
Toyama Daihachiro
Tsuchikata Yasushi
Tsuji Akira
Tsukuda Nobuo
Uesugi Shinkichi

Uetsuka Tsukasa
Yamagata Yasushi
Yamaji Kazuyoshi
Yamaza Enjiro
Yokogawa Seigo
Yoneda Minoru
Yoshida Ekizo

The following were affiliated members of the *Kokuryukai*:

Adachi Kenzo
Arakawa Goro
'Asa Tanekazu
Visct. Enomoto Takeo
Hachisuka Mochiaki
Higashi Koji
Honda Kumataro
Horiuchi Bunjiro
Visct. Itakura Katsunori
Kata Masanosuke
Kawasaki Takukichi
Baron Kikuchi Takeo
Matsumura Sukeishi
Miyake Kakutaro

Miyake Yuji
Nagaoka Keizaburo
Nagata Chuichi
Nakanishi Rokusaburo
Nakata Noriyoshi
Oishi Masami
Oshima Kosei
Oyama Kunitaro
Ozaki Yukio
Shima Ryuji
Lt.-Gen. Shioden Nobutake
Suzuki Otohei
Tsurumi Yusuke

Kokka Shakai Shugi Gakumei ("The National Socialist League")

Ishikawa Junjuro (President)

Shimonaka Yasaburo, Okawa Shumei (Advisers)

Akamatsu Katsumaro
Beppu Shunsuke
Hayashi Kimio
Hirano Rikizo
Igarashi Takashi
Iiishi Toyoichi
Imasato Katsuo
Karino Toshi
Koike Shiro

Kondo Eizo
Matsunobu Shigeji
Ota Takashi
Sasai Icho
Tashiro Kozo
Tsukui Tatsuo
Yabe Shu
Yabumoto Masayoshi
Yamana Gihaku

APPENDIX I

Nomin Kesshitai ("The Death-defying Farmers' Band")

Goto Kunihiko (Leader)

Horikawa Hideo
Kawasaki Nagamitsu
Komuro Rikiya
Kurosawa Kanekichi
Nukumizu Hidenori
Okuda Hideo

Onuki Meikan
Sugiura Takashi
Takanezawa Yoichi
Terunuma Misao
Yabuki Seigo
Yokosuka Kikuo

Sakurakai ("The Society of the Cherry")

Lt.-Col. Adachi Futomi (Toyama Army School)
Capt. Akafuji Shoji (*Kempei* H.Q.)
Capt. Aki Sashun (Gen. Staff)
Lt. Amano Isamu (Toyama Army School)
Capt. Aoki Isshi (Gen. Staff)
Capt. Aotsu Kikutaro (Toyama Army School)
Capt. Cho Isamu (Toyama Army School)
Capt. Cho Kosho (Imp. Guards, 3rd Inf. Regt.)
Maj. Endo Saburo (Gen. Staff)
Maj. Fujizuka (Toyama Army School)
Capt. Fukuchi Haruo (Imp. Guards, Field Arty. Regt.)
Capt. Fukuyama Niro-o (Gen. Staff)
Capt. Futami Shusaburo (Gen. Staff)
Capt. Hamada Taira (Gen. Staff)
Maj. Haraguchi Toshinosuke (Army Automobile School)
Lt.-Col. Hashimoto Kingoro (Gen. Staff)
Lt.-Col. Hata Yusaburo (War College)
Capt. Hayashi Mureomi (Ministry of War)
Lt.-Col. Higuchi Kiichiro (Imp. Guards Div. H.Q.)
Maj. Hinoki Masao (Imp. Guards, Field Arty. Regt.)
Maj. Hirata Masanori (Gen. Staff)
Capt. Hongo Tadao (Gen. Staff)
Lt.-Col. Hori Matayuki (War College)
Capt. Ihara Junjiro (Gen. Staff)
Maj. Iida Yasujiro (Toyama Army School)
Lt. Ikeda Sanae (War College)
Lt. Ikudame Tsuneo (Scientific Research Institute)

314

Maj. Ikuta Torao (1st Inf. Regt.)
Capt. Imai Takeo (Toyama Army School)
Maj. Isayama Haruki (Toyama Army School)
Lt. Ishikawa Kanichi (War College)
Lt.-Col. Ishimoto Torazo (Toyama Army School)
Lt. Ito Tomoshiro (War College)
Capt. Iwakuro Takeo (Ministry of War)
Maj. Iwasa Shun (Imp. Guards, 1st Inf. Regt.)
Maj. Kagesa Sadaaki (Toyama Army School)
Capt. Karakawa Yasuo (Toyama Army School)
Maj. Kataoka Kin (Gen. Staff)
Maj. Kawabe Torashiro (Gen. Staff)
Lt. Kawahara Sadao (Toyama Army School)
Capt. Kawamura Aizo (*Kempei* H.Q.)
Maj. Kitajima Takumi (Inspectorate-General of Military Training)
Maj. Kohama Daizen (Imp. Guards, 2nd Inf. Regt.)
Lt. Kondo Denpachi (Imp. Guards, 2nd Inf. Regt.)
Lt.-Col. Ko-on Ryo (H.Q. Azabu Regtl. District)
Maj. Maeda Masami (Ministry of War)
Capt. Matsumura Shuitsu (Gen. Staff)
Capt. Matsumura Tomokatsu (Gen. Staff)
Maj. Matsuzaki Naotsu (Imp. Guards, 2nd Inf. Regt.)
Maj. Megata Shunosuke (1st Inf. Regt.)
Capt. Mihara Toshio (Toyama Army School)
Capt. Mishima Yoshisada (Gen. Staff)
Maj. Miura Saburo (*Kempei* H.Q.)
Capt. Morimoto Gunzo (Gen. Staff)
Lt.-Col. Mutaguchi Renya (Gen. Staff)
Maj. Muto Akira (Toyama Army School)
Capt. Nagai Yatsuji (Gen. Staff)
Maj. Nakano Hidemitsu (Toyama Army School)
Capt. Nakayama Neijin (Gen. Staff)
Lt.-Col. Nemoto Hiroshi (Toyama Army School)
Maj. Noda Kengo (Gen. Staff)
Capt. Obara Shigetaka (Toyama Army School)
Capt. Ohashi Kumao (Toyama Army School)
Maj. Okazaki Seizaburo (Ministry of War)
Maj. Oki Shigeru (Kojimachi *Kempei* Detachment)
Maj. Okuda Chisato (Toyama Army School)

Capt. Ono Takeshiro (Gen. Staff)
Capt. Ono Uchihiro (Toyama Army School)
Maj. Ouchi Susumu (Gen. Staff)
Capt. Sakai Yoshio (Gen. Staff)
Lt.-Col. Sakanishi Kazunaga (Inspectorate-General of Military Training)
Lt.-Col. Sakata Yoshiro (Ministry of War)
Capt. Sanada Joichiro (Ministry of War)
Maj. Sano Tadayoshi (War College)
Capt. Sasaji Taro (Gen. Staff)
Maj. Sato Yukinori (Toyama Army School)
Capt. Shikata Ryoji (*Kempei* H.Q.)
Capt. Tanaka Kiyoshi (Ministry of War)
Maj. Tanaka Nobuo (Imp. Guards, 2nd Inf. Regt.)
Capt. Tanaka Wataru (Toyama Army School)
Maj. Tasaka Yasohachi (3rd. Inf. Regt.)
Capt. Terada Saiichi (Gen. Staff)
Maj. Tominaga Kyoji (Ministry of War)
Maj. Tsuchihashi Yuitsu (1st Inf. Regt.)
Lt. Tsuji Masanobu (Gen. Staff)
Capt. Tsuruta Kunie (War College)
Lt. Ueda Minoru (War College)
Maj. Ueki Shizuo (*Kempei* H.Q.)
Lt.-Col. Ueno Kanichiro (Toyama Army School)
Maj. Wachi Takazo (Toyama Army School)
Capt. Watanabe Fujio (Gen. Staff)
Capt. Watanabe Hideto (Ministry of War)
Capt. Yamamoto Seiei (Military Academy)
Capt. Yokoyama Kenzo (*Kempei* H.Q.)
Maj. Yonefuji Tomobumi (Infantry School)
Capt. Yoshikura Tokinari (*Kempei* H.Q.)

San Roku Kurabu ("The '36 Club")

Arima Seisuke	Baron Kikuchi Takeo
Horiguchi Kumaichi	Matsumoto Yuhei
Baron Ida Bannan	Miyashita Zenkichi
Inouye Kiyozumi	Ryokaku Saburo
Kobayashi Junichiro	Lt.-Gen. Shioden Nobutaka

APPENDIX II

PLANS FOR THE NEW ORDER
IN EAST ASIA AND THE SOUTH SEAS

(*Vide* Ch. 11, pp. 276–7, *supra*)

"Land Disposal Plan in the Greater East Asia Co-Prosperity Sphere" (I.M.T.F.E. Exhibit 1334. Transcript, pp. 11969–73), December, 1941. Ministry of War, Research Section

1. Regions to be under the jurisdiction of the Government-General of Formosa:
   Hong Kong
   Macao (to be purchased)
   The Philippine Islands
   Paracel Islands
   Hainan Island (to be purchased from China)
2. To be administered by the South Seas Government Office:
   Guam
   Nauru
   Ocean Island
   Gilbert Islands
   Wake
3. The Melanesia Region Government-General or South Pacific Government-General (provisional titles):
   New Guinea (the British and Australian mandated territories east of Long. 141° E.)
   The Admiralty Archipelago
   New Britain, New Ireland and the islands in the vicinity
   The Solomons
   Santa Cruz Archipelago
   Ellice Islands
   Fiji Islands
   New Hebrides
   New Caledonia

Loyalty Island
Chesterfield Island
4. Eastern Pacific Government-General:
   Hawaii
   Howland, Baker and Phoenix Islands. Rain Islands
   Marquesas and Tuamotu Islands. Society Islands
   Cook and Austral Islands
   Samoa
   Tonga
5. The Australian Government-General:
   The whole of Australia, and Tasmania
6. The New Zealand Government-General (provisional title):
   The North and South Islands of New Zealand
   Macquarie Island
   The sea, south of the Tropic of Capricorn and east of
   Long. 160° E., as far as the S. Pole region
7. The Ceylon Government-General:
   Ceylon; and India lying south of the following boundary:
   from the west coast on the northern frontier of Portu-
   guese Goa, thence to the north of Dharwar and Bellary
   and to the River Penner, and along the north bank of the
   Penner to the east coast at Nellore
   Laccadive Islands
   Maldive Islands
   Chagos Islands
   Seychelles
   Mauritius
8. Alaska Government-General:
   Alaska
   The Yukon Province, and the land between that Province
   and the Mackenzie River
   Alberta
   British Columbia
   The State of Washington
9. The Government-General of Central America:
   Guatemala
   San Salvador
   Honduras
   British Honduras

Nicaragua
Costa Rica
Panama
Colombia, and the Maracaibo district of Venezuela
Ecuador
Cuba
Haiti
Dominica
Jamaica
Bahamas
The future of Trinidad, British and Dutch Guiana and British and French possessions in the Leeward Islands to be decided by agreement between Japan and Germany after the war

10. In the event of her declaring war on Japan, Mexico to cede territory east of Long. 95° 30′. Should Peru join in the war against Japan it must cede territory north of Lat. 10°; and if Chile enters the war it shall cede the nitre zone north of Lat. 24°

Independent States

1. The East Indies Kingdom:
    All Dutch possessions in the E. Indies
    British Borneo, Labuan, Sarawak, Brunei
    Cocos
    Christmas Island
    Andamans
    Nicobars
    Portuguese Timor (to be purchased)
2. The Kingdom of Burma:
    British Burma and Assam, together with part of Bengal between the Ganges and Brahmaputra
3. The Malay Kingdom
4. The Kingdom of Thailand
5. The Kingdom of Cambodia:
    Cambodia and French Cochin China
6. The Kingdom of Annam
    Annam, Laos and Tongking

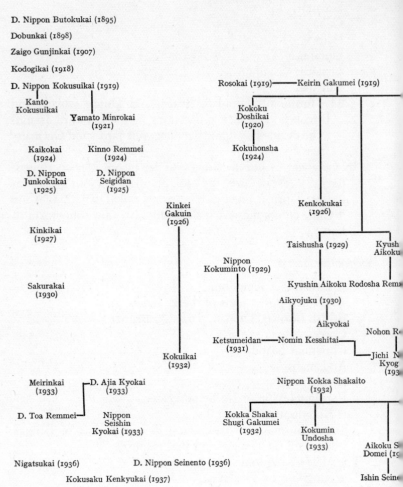

D. Nippon Butokukai (1895)

Dobunkai (1898)

Zaigo Gunjinkai (1907)

Kodogikai (1918)

D. Nippon Kokusuikai (1919)
  Kanto
  Kokusuikai
    Yamato Minrokai
    (1921)

Kaikokai   Kinno Remmei
(1924)   (1924)
D. Nippon   D. Nippon
Junkokukai Seigidan
(1925)   (1925)

Kinkikai
(1927)

Sakurakai
(1930)

Meirinkai   D. Ajia Kyokai
(1933)   (1933)

D. Toa Remmei Nippon
           Seishin
           Kyokai (1933)

Nigatsukai (1936)   D. Nippon Seinento (1936)

    Kokusaku Kenkyukai (1937)

Rosokai (1919)————Keirin Gakumei (1919)

Kokoku
Doshikai
(1920)

Kokuhonsha
(1924)

Kinkei
Gakuin
(1926)

Kenkokukai
(1926)

Taishusha (1929)   Kyush
               Aikoku

Nippon
Kokuminto (1929)

Kyushin Aikoku Rodosha Rem

Aikyojuku (1930)

        Aikyokai

               Nohon R

Ketsumeidan————Nomin Kesshitai
(1931)
                     Jichi N
Kokuikai   Kyog
(1932)   (193

Nippon Kokka Shakaito
(1932)

Kokka Shakai
Shugi Gakumei
(1932)   Kokumin
        Undosha
        (1933)   Aikoku S
                 Domei (19

                    Ishin Seine

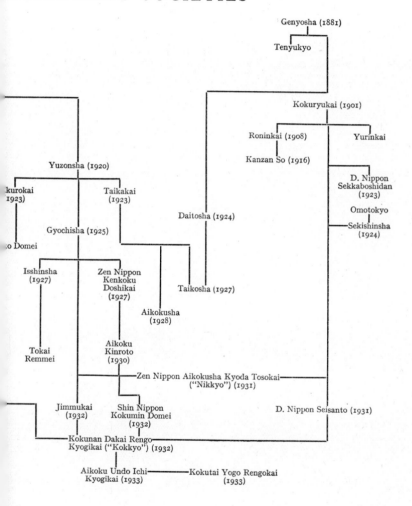

Genyosha (1881)

Tenyukyo

Kokuryukai (1901)

Roninkai (1908)   Yurinkai

Kanzan So (1916)

D. Nippon
Sekkaboshidan
(1923)

Omotokyo

Yuzonsha (1920)

kurokai
1923)   Taikakai
(1923)

Daitosha (1924)

Sekishinsha
(1924)

Gyochisha (1925)

o Domei

Isshinsha   Zen Nippon
(1927)   Kenkoku
Doshikai
(1927)   Taikosha (1927)

Aikokusha
(1928)

Tokai   Aikoku
Remmei   Kinroto
(1930)   Zen Nippon Aikokusha Kyoda Tosokai
("Nikkyo") (1931)

Jimmukai   Shin Nippon   D. Nippon Seisanto (1931)
(1932)   Kokumin Domei
(1932)
Kokunan Dakai Rengo
Kyogikai ("Kokkyo") (1932)

Aikoku Undo Ichi   Kokutai Yogo Rengokai
Kyogikai (1933)   (1933)

INDEX

INDEX

Printed in Great Britain by
Butler & Tanner Ltd.,
Frome and London